The French Revolution
and Social Democracy

D1519382

Historical Materialism Book Series

The Historical Materialism Book Series is a major publishing initiative of the radical left. The capitalist crisis of the twenty-first century has been met by a resurgence of interest in critical Marxist theory. At the same time, the publishing institutions committed to Marxism have contracted markedly since the high point of the 1970s. The Historical Materialism Book Series is dedicated to addressing this situation by making available important works of Marxist theory. The aim of the series is to publish important theoretical contributions as the basis for vigorous intellectual debate and exchange on the left.

The peer-reviewed series publishes original monographs, translated texts, and reprints of classics across the bounds of academic disciplinary agendas and across the divisions of the left. The series is particularly concerned to encourage the internationalization of Marxist debate and aims to translate significant studies from beyond the English-speaking world.

For a full list of titles in the Historical Materialism Book Series available in paperback from Haymarket Books, visit:
https://www.haymarketbooks.org/series_collections/1-historical-materialism

The French Revolution and Social Democracy

The Transmission of History and Its Political Uses in Germany and Austria, 1889–1934

Jean-Numa Ducange

Translated by
David Broder

Haymarket Books
Chicago, IL

First published in 2018 by Brill Academic Publishers, The Netherlands
© 2018 Koninklijke Brill NV, Leiden, The Netherlands

Published in paperback in 2019 by
Haymarket Books
P.O. Box 180165
Chicago, IL 60618
773-583-7884
www.haymarketbooks.org

ISBN: 978-1-64259-053-1

Distributed to the trade in the US through Consortium Book Sales and
Distribution (www.cbsd.com) and internationally through Ingram
Publisher Services International (www.ingramcontent.com).

This book was published with the generous support of Lannan
Foundation and Wallace Action Fund.

Special discounts are available for bulk purchases by organizations and
institutions. Please call 773-583-7884 or email info@haymarketbooks.org
for more information.

Cover design by Jamie Kerry and Ragina Johnson.

Printed in the United States.

10 9 8 7 6 5 4 3 2 1

Library of Congress Cataloging-in-Publication data is available.

Contents

PART 3

Reinterpretations and New Approaches, 1917–34

Preface to the English Edition

When the original version of this book was published in 2012, it had been a long time since any history of pre-Nazi-era German social democracy had come out in French. The exception was the general history by Jacques-Pierre Gougeon, a work whose rather debatable approach above all emphasised the SPD's turn toward a reformist, managerialist politics. This dearth of publications is symptomatic of the near-disappearance of academic studies of the history of the workers' movement and Marxism in the French-speaking countries. The decline has been just as manifest in Germany, after the spectacular output in such histories in both East and West Germany from the 1960s to the 1980s – a period in which the origins of 'state socialism' in the East, and the SPD's compatibility with the market in the West, were both hot topics. In Italy, in the Netherlands with the publications linked to the IISG, and indeed in the Soviet Union, 'Second International Marxism' was long a central focus. But after 1990, the crisis of the various forms of organised socialist politics and the end of the 'Soviet century' brought a striking collapse in research connected to this subject. English-speaking academia is a more varied terrain and one also less directly affected by the crisis of Marxism (for want of mass political forces that identified with it), and in this context the publication of such works has developed in a different direction. More recently, especially thanks to the Historical Materialism Book Series, we have seen the appearance of numerous important works on this period in Marxism's history.

The 'Kautskyan Moment'

The first thing to underline this small renewal is the historiographical importance of the 'Kautskyan moment', for instance in Lars Lih's work on the history of Russian social democracy. Here is not the right place to examine in detail the works of the 'pope of German social-democracy': the book that you are about to read gives sufficient account of those. But what is worth underlining in advance is the limits of the critique of 'Kautskyism'. A whole Marxist tradition from Karl Korsch to Michel Löwy has cast Kautsky as the emblem of a cold and dogmatic orthodoxy, a scientist positivism more akin to Darwinism than to Marxism. For these authors, 'Kautskyism' opened the way to the worst kind of regression in the workers' movement, legitimising both the reformist social democracy that maintained a formal relationship with Marxism and the worst kind of statist tendencies, ultimately culminating in Stalin. There are thus countless texts which compare the pre-1914 vulgate of the Second International, forged by Kautsky, and the vulgate of the Stalinised Third International.

This critique doubtless has certain merits and a certain coherence, especially if we remain at the level of theoretical considerations. But it has also had the effect of repressing major historical realities. First among these is the fact that, even simply at the level of theoretical debates, the incontestably dogmatic aspects of so-called 'Second International Marxism' are rooted only in Kautsky's very most mechanical texts. Yet any attentive reader of reviews like *Die Neue Zeit* or *Der Kampf* will see what a high level some of the contributions reached, far less dogmatic than in the 1920s when the Comintern set up barriers to most debate.

From historians' point of view, the radical critique of 'Kautskyism' also delegitimised research into the impressive mass movement embodied by the various expressions of German and Austrian social democracy. Two reviews of the French edition of the present work underlined this consideration. In the pages of *Actuel Marx* the Marxist historian of the French Revolution Claude Mazauric remarked that: 'As an admiring reader of this strong dissertation, I can only repeat the powerful conclusion reached by the late Henri Lefebvre: the worst historical tragedy of the twentieth century was the collapse of the German workers' movement and the destruction of its social organisations in the German-speaking countries, where they were deliberately uprooted. To that we can compare the weight of the unrelenting counter-revolution which is still on our heels'. Similarly, in a piece on this book appearing in the *American Historical Review*, the historian of Germany and Eastern Europe William W. Hagen concluded that: 'It is another reminder of what was lost to Adolf Hitler's national socialism'. To delve into this universe is to return to the origins of the first great emancipation project in Western Europe before it was finally destroyed by Nazism.

Questions of Method

This is not to say that our approach is some sort of exercise in rehabilitation, which would not make much sense. Rather, this study seeks to pursue a certain tradition in writing the history of Marxism, as embodied by various figures from Georges Haupt to Eric Hobsbawm, and illustrated in the English-speaking world by contributions like those by Robert Stuart or Andrew Bonnell which do not only concern themselves with intellectual history. From this point of view, *The French Revolution and Social Democracy* seeks to get to grips with a number of methodological problems in order to set out an approach attentive to the full historical density of Marxism and the workers' movement.

In reaction against an overly ideological history – the history of the Internationals, or what we might call the 'history of conference resolutions' – numerous historians have instead focused on a working-class history 'from below'. This has incontestable merits. But in its conviction that all theoretical reflection begins and ends with 'theorists' it also tends to reject any remotely serious study of the content of the texts, which are reduced to debates among intellectuals cut off from the mass of their respective political organisations' militants and sympathisers. We instead consider it essential to combine a sustained interest in the content of the texts with a history more centred on grassroots actors. That, at least, was one of the ambitions that inspired us as we wrote this book.

As we mounted our study of the 'popularisation' of Marxism, we did not find a dogmatic and fossilised universe. It is by no means certain that Kautsky's cold, rigid, vulgarised Marxism was as grey and dismal as his later interpreters would make out. Pamphlets, leaflets, propaganda, historical myths – especially the ambiguous myth around the cult of the French Revolution – fed an 'alternative culture', full of elements that could mobilise hundreds of thousands of militants and leave an enduring mark on their class mentality. Yet this popularisation – sometimes limited to the mention of a few historical dates in a workers' calendar, a bibliographical reference or even a few short citations from Kautsky – can never be entirely separated from doctrinal debate and the political developments of the moment. The Russian Revolutions of 1905 and 1917 are a striking example of this, for the theoretical debates surrounding these revolutionary processes were in part linked to the propaganda and the idea of revolution that coloured the party at all levels.

Our other methodological concern was to write an 'entangled history' [*histoire croisée*] set in relation with 'cultural transfers' – concepts elaborated by Michel Espagne and Michel Werner that are relatively influential in writing on Franco-German history. Particularly important in this regard, when we look at the historiography of the French Revolution specifically, was a focus on the reception of the great classics of our period, from Jean Jaurès's *Histoire socialiste de la Révolution française* to Albert Mathiez's works.

Karl Kautsky and Franz Mehring in fact did little to get to grips with the tradition of French Marxist studies of the Revolution. They often mentioned the existence of such a tradition but never studied it in detail. The interpretation that the liberal historian François Furet terms a 'Jacobin-Marxist reading' – a term he uses pejoratively, but which can also be used in a descriptive sense – deeply influenced the whole Left's reading of 1789, mixing republicanism and socialism. And it is interesting to note that one of the key problems for Kautsky and other Marxists in this period was precisely this connection between Marxism and republicanism, which they considered rather suspect. For a whole left-wing tradition in nineteenth-century France, Robespierre was to be admired, but in Germany and Austria he was the object of a great deal of suspicion.

Knocking down the walls that surround a tradition strongly rooted in French national heritage allows us to show what Jaurès owed to his engagement with Germany and the SPD. What might, reading these pages, seem rather obvious, was not in fact evident in any historiographical summary at the time. Many saw Jaurès as such a genius that he could be considered self-sufficient, or almost that. In reality, Jaurès's whole complex relationship with revolution and Marxism passed precisely by way of this engagement. The study of transnational networks has become widespread in recent years and could doubtless shed light on other aspects not sufficiently addressed in the present volume, especially by means of a history of mobility, migration and points of contact between different nationalities.

Historical Time and Historical Narration

On many points, our work is only a first approach, which could well be developed further. The first such point concerns the 'grand narratives' that entered into crisis in the 1980s. Our concern was to understand how a coherent narrative of the past was first constructed in a left-wing political organisation. We did this by basing ourselves on an example that everyone at the time considered an undeniable moment of rupture: 1789. While in 1880s France the history of the Revolution was known through the transmission of memory and the mediation of the school classroom – which meant that the socialists' task was more a matter of making the republican reading more left-wing, rather than defining a new one – in Germany and Austria, it was an opposition party that defined an interpretation of the French Revolution through thinkers like Kautsky. In fact, in this period the German social-democrats' interpretation counted for far more than the French socialists' did, including with regard to events of universal significance like the 'Great French Revolution'. For instance, the narrative advanced by Kautsky was translated and read across much of *Mitteleuropa*, unlike Jaurès's. Any synthesis on the history of the French Revolution must integrate this fact, even if it above all focuses on French authors.

The second point concerns other political camps. The narrative on revolutions elaborated by the social-democrats cannot be reduced to questions internal to the history of socialism, or indeed ones linked to the historiography of the French Revolution. At the end of the nineteenth century, even the spec-tacular progress German social democracy had made was unable to mask the rising strength of anti-Semitism and pan-Germanism, which violently attacked the internationalism of the workers' movement. As we know, behind its façade of internationalism a 'negative integration' led social democracy to become increasingly assimilated to Wilhemine Germany, ultimately explaining its turn to support for the war effort in 1914. It would be naïve to imagine that the Ger-man social-democrats had no attachment to Germany, even in their narratives on the French Revolution. Even in the 1880s, one of the works that was most read by SPD militants, Wilhelm Blos's study, admired the popular action of the Revolution but was sharply critical of the brutality of revolutionary change. One of the best-informed readers of the Revolution, Heinrich Cunow – author of a remarkable, pioneering study on the press during the Revolution – placed his knowledge in service of the 'ideas of 1914' and German imperialism.

Nonetheless, the social-democratic milieu can hardly be totally identified with the other political camps ('*lager*') on this point, for its internationalist outlook remained one of its constant specificities, even after it had temporar-ily been overwhelmed by the war. The SPD's lasting attachment to the French revolutionary tradition – sometimes challenged but never rejected – was abso-lutely exceptional in the Germany of the time, and thus in itself constituted an exceptional historical reality. In this lay the seeds of a great clash between different conceptions of the world and of history, which would end tragically with the triumph of Nazism. There was, indeed, another modernity, 'another Germany', whose bearings and points of reference included the French Revolu-tion – not because it was French, but because it had opened up a new period in human history. Significantly, traces of this outlook remained up till 1933: the experience of 1914–18 did not totally break the pre-1914 Marxist narrative on the French Revolution. The 'Kautskyist' narrative did not disappear from SPD ranks, and it would also inspire the vulgate defined in the USSR, which in turn coloured the young KPD. It was here that Kautskyism doubtless had something of a family relationship with the Third International, contributing to the development of its dogmas, but also spreading an internationalist culture that championed the French revolutionary moment in opposition to a narrow and aggressive chauvinism.

We still need further reflection on temporalities in Marxism, a theme only timidly outlined in this book. Julian Wright has provided us with brilliant elab-orations on this point. The socialists' timeframe was that of history with a capital H. History occupied a decisive place. In our own time, when what Fran-çois Hartog calls 'presentism' – the obsession with immediacy and imminent action, at the expense of an analysis of past experience – has taken over wide layers of activist politics, it is difficult to understand what this sense of History might have represented in a different era. From this point of view, the Marxism of the 1880s–1930s was a transitional phase that made up part of a regime of temporality in which the past conditioned action or was even its precondition. This shows the limits of the 'Second International Marxism' that assumed a rigid approach toward the relationship between past, present, and future, and which denied legitimacy to non-linear narratives. At the same time, it also shows the incontestable pedagogical force of this Marxism, a confident and powerful Marxism that contributed to the best elements of the history of the workers' movement and the 'workers' dream' that it once represented.

Some will ask if this debate, however interesting it may be, is perhaps a little dated. From the perspective of contemporary French politics, that is certainly not the case. Understanding the Marxist reading of the French Revolution allows us to grasp the specific political culture of the workers' movement and the Left in France even in our own time, in which references to republicanism remain a hot topic. Even in the 2017 election we saw the former Socialist Party left-winger Jean-Luc Mélenchon draw inspiration from Ernesto Laclau and Chantal Mouffe at the same time as he remained viscerally attached to Robespierre and Jaurès. Much has changed, but it is striking that even in July 2017, the same Robespierre and Jaurès so disdained by a certain Marxist tradition elaborated in the Germany of the 1880s–1930s were being cited by new France Insoumise MPs in the Assemblée Nationale ... A few days later, the hard-right French weekly *Le Point* ran the title 'From Robespierre to Mélenchon, a History of Political Violence', in order to attack the bloodshed that must come with any attempt to challenge the social and political order.

Political conditions have developed and changed considerably. But the fact remains that these figures so connected to the memory of the Revolution, and so passionately debated in the late nineteenth century, are still evoked in contemporary political debate. This gives us yet further reason to plunge into this history and these debates on the foundational moment that was the Revolution of 1789–93.

Abbreviations

ADAV   *Allgemeiner Deutscher Arbeiterverein*: General German Workers' Association

BRD   *Bundesrepublik Deutschland*: Federal Republic of Germany

DDR   *Deutsche Demokratische Republik*: German Democratic Republic

SDAP   (Germany) *Sozialdemokratische Arbeiterpartei*: Social-Democratic Workers' Party

SPD   *Sozialdemokratische Partei Deutschlands*: Social-Democratic Party of Germany

USPD   *Unabhängige Sozialdemokratische Partei Deutschlands*: Independent Social-Democratic Party of Germany

KPD   Kommunistische Partei Deutschlands: Communist Party of Germany

KAPD   Kommunistische Arbeiterpartei Deutschlands: Communist Workers' Party of Germany

SDAP   (Austria) *Sozialdemokratische Arbeiterpartei in Österreich*: Social-Democratic Workers' Party in Austria

SPÖ   *Sozialdemokratische Partei Österreichs*: Social-Democratic Party of Austria

KPÖ   *Kommunistische Partei Österreichs*: Communist Party of Austria

POF   *Parti Ouvrier Français*: French Workers' Party

PCF   *Parti communiste français*: French Communist Party

SFIO   *Section française de l'Internationale ouvrière*: French Section of the Workers' International

Illustrations

ILL. 1   *Class Contradictions in 1789. For the Centenary of the Great Revolution*
(Karl Kautsky, 1889)

ILL. 2   *Maifeier* (May Day paper, Vienna, 1907)

ILL. 3   'What belongs to "dream" and "reality"', *Glühlicher*, 8 August 1891

ILL. 4   'And you'll accept our whole programme!' *Glühlichter*, 10 January 1891

ILL. 5   'The citizen, yesterday and today', *Glühlichter*, 21 December 1899

Wovon man in Zarskoje Selo träumt

ILL. 6   'A dream for Tsarskoye Selo' (i.e. the Tsar's residence), *Der Wahre Jacob*, 23 January 1906

Olimpe de Gouges.

Olimpe de Gouges.

Olimpe de Gouges war 38 oder, wie die böse Welt behauptete, 40 Jahre alt, als ihr Haupt unter dem Beil der Guillotine fiel. Am 2. November 1793 unterlag diese Feindin der Schreckensherrschaft dem Hass Robespierres, und ihr heldenhafter Kampf für die Rechte der Frauen war grausam unterbrochen.

Ihr Dasein hatte etwas Seltsames, Ueberspanntes, Trotzdem sie weder lesen noch schreiben konnte, hat sie zahlreiche Bücher veröffentlicht! Sie, die schwache Frau, verstand es, manchem Manne Schrecken einzujagen, und selbst Robespierre machte sie zurückweichen. Sie genoss das Leben in vollen Zügen, aber jeder Augenblick fand sie bereit, es freudig zu opfern. Ihre Gedanken waren nicht immer sehr klar, oft sogar verworren, trotzdem findet man in ihren Werken geistsprühende Stellen, voll von Genialität, aber das meiste in sehr nachlässigem Stil geschrieben.

Sie war in allem, was sie tat, leidenschaftlich, alle ihre Handlungen zeugten von einem heftigen Temperament und glichen wahren Ausbrüchen der Leidenschaft, aber sie waren immer von Aufopferung und Begeisterung erfüllt Sie bildete ein Gemisch von Grösse und von Lächerlichkeit, von Tugenden und von Fehlern. In jeder Beziehung exzentrisch, brach sie auch die Fesseln, die die Frauen hemmten, und von einem unbändigen Wunsch nach Freiheit getrieben, verstand sie es, die Rechte der Frauen in energischen Broschüren, oder auf der Tribüne des Jakobinerklubs in leidenschaftlichen Reden zu verteidigen. Olimpe de Gouges ist die erste politische Red-

ILL. 8   Workers' calendar, Vienna, 1914

Name des Bestellers:

Wohnung:

Zentralbildungsausschuß der Sozialdemokratischen Partei Deutschlands

Disposition und Schriftenverzeichnis

zu dem Kursus des Genossen Bernhard Rausch über:

Das Zeitalter der großen Französischen Revolution und die Befreiungskriege (1789—1815). (6 Vorträge).

1. Disposition.

1. Vortrag. Die Klassenkampftheorie und die Französische Revolution. Der Absolutismus in Frankreich. Die soziale Struktur des französischen Ständestaates vor der Revolution. Die Finanzen und Reformversuche (Turgot, Calonne). Der Todeskampf des ancien régime. Berufung der Generalstände. Der Schwur im Ballsaal. Das Volk von Paris. Die Aufklärung.

2. Vortrag. Der Sturm auf die Bastille. Die Bauernerhebungen in den Provinzen. Der 4. August. Die Hungersnot in Paris. Die beginnende Reaktion im Pariser Gemeinderat. Der 5./6. Oktober. Der Bourgeoischarakter der konstituierenden Nationalversammlung. Verfassungsbeschlüsse. Mirabeau. Anschläge des Hofes. Die Flucht des Königs. Die gesetzgebende Nationalversammlung. Feuillants, Girondisten, Jakobiner. Die Kriegserklärung 20. April 1792. Der 20. Juni. Das Vaterland in Gefahr. Der 10. August. Die Septembermorde.

3. Vortrag. Der Nationalkonvent. Die Abschaffung des Königtums. Der Prozeß gegen Ludwig Capet. Der Kampf zwischen Gironde und Bergpartei. Wachsende Gefahren. Das Ende der Gironde. Marat. Die „Schreckensherrschaft". Die soziale Gesetzgebung des Konvents. Danton, Robespierre, Hébert. Kommunistische und anarchistische Tendenzen. Zusammenbruch der kleinbürgerlichen Demokratie. Die Reaktion der Thermidorianer. Babeuf. Das Direktorium. Die ökonomische Bedeutung der Revolutionskriege für Frankreich. Der 18. Brumaire. Napoleons Konsulat und Kaisertum. Die geschichtliche Bedeutung der Französischen Revolution.

4. Vortrag. Das Heilige Römische Reich Deutscher Nation. Die Aufklärung in Deutschland. Die Wurzeln der Revolutionskriege. Die feudalen Gegner Frankreichs. Der erste Koalitionskrieg. Der Friede von Basel. Der altpreußische Staat. Der Friede von Campo Formio. Der Reichsdeputationshauptschluß 1803. Die Allianz der süddeutschen Staaten mit Frankreich. Reformversuche in Preußen. Das Ende des Reiches.

ILL. 10   Section of the 1919 *Almanach of the German Revolution*, pp. 66–7

ILL. 11   Heinrich Cunow's *Political Cafés* (1924)

ARBEITER-BILDUNGSSCHULE BERLIN

ARBEITSPLAN FÜR DAS 38. LEHRJAHR 1928–1929

BEZIRKSAUSSCHUSS FÜR SOZIALISTISCHE BILDUNGSARBEIT, BERLIN / SW, LINDENSTR. 3

ILL. 12   Berlin Workers' Education School. Workplan for the 38th year

Introduction

My friends! We can summarise our programme in just a few words. These words – *Liberté, Égalité, Fraternité* – are for us not only a sacred memory of the glorious Revolution of 1789, but also the basic thinking, the fundamental idea of our programme

WILHELM LIEBKNECHT, 1872[1]

• • •

Those who support the eight-hour day, are told 'You are of good faith, but beware; all these ideas are coming here from the other side of the Rhine; your socialism wears a spiked helmet; you are deserting the tradition of the French Revolution' ... in Germany, they tell Bebel and Liebknecht that they are traitors to the German fatherland, first because they are socialists, and then because they love France.

JEAN JAURÈS, 1891[2]

• •
•

The different interpretations of the French Revolution have sparked a wide variety of debates. But despite the breadth of this discussion – or perhaps for this very reason – it is over four decades since the last historiographical synthesis of this subject, in the very country in which the Revolution was born. The last French-language attempt to capture this phenomenon as a whole, at least at the European level, was the short but richly-textured work by Alice Gérard.[3] In the wake of the 1989 bicentenary, some of the many conferences that were held internationally provided an opportunity to revisit the past decades of disputes, which had still far from died out.[4] This made it possible to measure the long-term importance of the questions raised by the French Revolution, across a great variety of national contexts. In the months immediately prior

---

1 *Protokoll über den 3. Congress der sozial-demokratischen Arbeiter-Partei, abgehalten zu Mainz am 7., 8., 9., 10. und 11. September 1872*, Mainz, 1872, p. 16.
2 Jaures, J. 'Français et étrangers', *La Dépêche*, 8 April 1891.
3 Gérard 1970.
4 Vovelle 1990.

to the fall of the Berlin Wall, there were numerous events in the two Germanies to mark the bicentenary of the French Revolution, which themselves built on a great tradition. If the French Revolution had long been negatively perceived in the context of Germany's own national construction process, from the 1950s onward the study of the Revolution moved toward new perspectives. A similar shift could be observed in Austria, where there were few pre-World War II studies on the Revolution.[5] Yet while these new publications heralded important changes, it is also true that the France of 1789 had already previously had at least *some* favourable echoes in the German-speaking countries, ever since the very outset of the revolutionary process. Countering the conservative historiography that long predominated in these countries, over the nineteenth century a tradition developed that saw the French Revolution in positive terms. The early working-class organisations in fact embraced the legacy of the Revolution. Understanding this is fundamental to understanding social democracy's complex relationship with reference points connected to the French Revolution.

The Historiography of the French Revolution

While publications on this subject doubtless slowed in the period following the bicentenary, the historiography of interpretations of the Revolution seems to be enjoying a certain resurgence. Multiple recent publications are testament to this. The French translation of Eric Hobsbawm's essay *Echoes of the Marseillaise: Two Centuries Look Back on the French Revolution*,[6] and soon after this the republication of François Furet's writings upon the tenth anniversary of his death, attest to the renewed interest in the great divides that have persisted throughout decades of historiography on the Revolution.[7] Equally, numerous representatives of the 'classical' school of historiography have revisited earlier debates in which they were themselves protagonists. In his *1789. L'héritage et la mémoire*, Michel Vovelle spoke of his own role in the historiography and in the debates that surrounded the bicentenary;[8] more recently, Claude Mazauric has published a study that built on his series of research projects regarding the complex relationship between Marxism and the Marxist-derived interpreta-

---

5   Reinalter 1990, vol. 1, p. 60.
6   In French, *Aux armes, historiens: deux siècles d'histoire de la Révolution française*. Published by La Découverte, Paris, 2007.
7   Furet 2007.
8   Vovelle 2007.

tions of the revolutionary sequence of 1789–99.[9] In 2008, the journal widely known as the point of reference for studies of the 1770–1820 period devoted an issue to the centenary of the Société des Études Robespierristes founded by Albert Mathiez. Resulting from a conference, this issue of *Annales historiques de la Révolution française* provided an opportunity to look back on a century of scholarly activity and its controversies.[10]

Two centuries on, studies of the Revolution have largely reoriented their focus toward other themes.[11] Yet some of the problematics that emerged from the classical tradition continue to be interrogated. The synthesis of a certain Jacobin legacy blended with Marxist influences, this current long made particular reference to Jean Jaurès. It considered his *Histoire socialiste de la Révolution française* a pioneering work in driving a new socio-economic reading of the Revolution.[12] The staging of major recent conferences shows the continued interest in two among these themes in particular. The first is the origins of the French Revolution, the question of the bourgeoisie's place within it, and the way in which a 'bourgeois order' constituted itself in the wake of the Revolution. The very concept of a 'bourgeois revolution' continues to be interrogated, albeit according to different approaches. Recently, the position that this question assumed at the heart of the discussions in numerous nineteenth- and twentieth-century historiographical debates has itself been the subject of research.[13] The second theme concerns the so-called Terror of 1793–4, probably the most controversial episode of the Revolution's history. Rich works explaining the Terror's institutional, social and cultural mechanisms are today seeking to revisit the previously-established interpretations. These latter had long depended on a historiographical conjuncture in which debates corresponded to the critique or championing of the political models that emerged from the revolutionary process.[14]

These two themes have been debated ever since the Revolution itself. Karl Marx and Friedrich Engels interrogated them repeatedly throughout their work, as they laid the bases of a new interpretation of history in the 1840s. In their era, almost every political current or sensibility had written its own his-

---

9   Mazauric 2009.
10   'Un siècle d'études révolutionnaires (1907–2007)', *Annales historiques de la Révolution française*, 3/2008.
11   Including a greater attention to political sociabilities and particularly the Directory period, which was little-studied until recently. For example, Gainot 2001.
12   Vovelle and Peyrard 2002.
13   Middell 2007. For a recent English-language summary working with the concept of bourgeois revolution, see Heller 2006.
14   Biard (ed.) 2008.

tory of what was termed the 'Great Revolution'. Marx never had time to write his
planned history of the Revolution. Yet inspired by some of his comments, the
German and Austrian social-democrats would from the 1880s onward embark
on writing their own histories. This took multiple forms, and it was also connected to their attempts to disseminate the new materialist conception of history
as widely as possible through the different structures that they created. This
was an important moment for both Marxism and the traditions of the interpretation of the French Revolution. Yet it has not previously been the object
of any overall study. The most critical works on this tradition, like those by
François Furet, instead limited themselves to a valorisation of the young Marx
as against his later evolution.[15] They 'jumped' directly from Marx to so-called
'Leninist' interpretations; and in so doing, they overlooked several decades of
historiography.

Indeed, social-democratic writing on the French Revolution remains relatively overlooked. Even the one work that does address this topic[16] does not
investigate the particularities of the 'Great Revolution' of 1789–99, and the process through which it unfolded. Yet more decisively, it stops in 1905, at the
beginning of the most important period of social-democratic books and articles on the Revolution; it moreover does very little to analyse the exchanges
that took place, and especially the debates with the French. A collective work
that appeared in the DDR upon the bicentenary also contained numerous contributions on this subject, but they were often limited to examining the content
of intellectual debates, and rarely interrogated the relationship between these
discussions and the rest of the party's production.[17] The specificity of social-
democratic writings – meaning not only the interpretations that they advanced
over several decades, but also the accompanying mechanisms for transmitting
a reading of history at all levels of the party – has not thus far been brought into
frame. But new studies on European social democracy and socialism do today
allow us to gain such a perspective.

The Historiography of the Social-Democratic Parties

Social democracy was long an important historiographical battleground, contested by the historians of the two German states. Their rivalry was symbolised
by the existence of two publishers called Dietz, with both the West and East

---

15   Furet 1986.
16   Bouvier 1982.
17   Schmidt (ed.) 1989.

German versions claiming the inheritance of their pre-1933 social-democratic forebear. The countless debates on questions that ranged from the SPD's level of integration into Wilhelmian society to the place that Marxist reference points occupied in its ranks, contributed to a better understanding of the SPD's history, particularly with regard to the pre-1914 period. In Austria, the SPÖ's history was much less of a Cold War battleground,[18] but it was also the focus of major studies, in particular those revolving around the question of 'Austro-Marxism' and the specificities of the 'third way' advanced by Austrian social democracy. Over the last two decades, the interest in these subjects has dried up, even though some reviews and institutes in the German-speaking countries continue to publish on these themes.[19]

We can see a similar shift in France, albeit in different conditions. The generation of Germanists and historians of the workers' movement that paid such attention to the German and Austrian social-democratic parties was part of a historiographical context in which the Second International, and the European space it encompassed, constituted an important object of study. This context revolved around a heritage that was discussed and contested by different political sensibilities, and first of all the socialists and communists.[20] With the collapse of the Soviet bloc and the opening of the archives on what was called 'the international communist movement', there was a sharp turn toward the study of communism and its various national ramifications.[21] In a different context, albeit one with certain historiographical similarities, part of the historical writing on contemporary Germany has turned toward the history of the DDR – itself an exceptional case of 'the opening of the archives'.[22] Telling in this regard is the fact that the last overall study of the history of German social democracy was published some fifteen years ago.[23]

Nonetheless, research on communism in Europe has sometimes crossed paths with research on socialism,[24] and on closer inspection we see that the pre-1914 history of the parties of the Second International continues to drive research. Such studies are certainly lesser in extent than they were thirty years

---

18   For our period, the Austrian party up till 1934 was called SDAP (*Sozialdemokratische Arbeit-erpartei in Österreich*). 'SPD' designates the German party from 1890 onward.

19   See in particular the works in the orbit of the SPD's party foundation (Friedrich Ebert Stiftung) and their ambitious programme for digitalising party sources (www.fes.de).

20   These historians included, among others, Gilbert Badia, Georges Haupt, Jacques Droz, Yvon Bourdet, Claudie Weill, and Felix Kreissler.

21   Wolikow (ed.) 1996.

22   Kott 2001.

23   Gougeon 1996.

24   Wolikow and Vigreux (eds.) 2007.

ago, and they are are also different in orientation; as the title of *L'histoire des gauches en France* suggests, they largely focus on the national context.[25] If the history of internationalism was still investigated from time to time in the 1990s,[26] this nonetheless marked a striking contrast with the *Histoire générale du socialisme* of 1972–8, which spanned every continent.[27]

Over time, political-theoretical history has gradually taken on board the lessons of social history. Historians moved away from research too narrowly focused on political debates, and which lacked an analysis of the lived experience of organisations and their members. We will add that the end of the passions that had once surrounded the history of the Second International, compounded by the considerable weakening of left-wing parties' references to the past, today encourages a rather calmer re-exploration of the content of these debates. This allows a greater emphasis on contextualisation, without setting up any particular anathemas. Pursuing a historiographical dynamic that looks beyond the 'party's organisational and ideological representations, and particularly its leading bodies',[28] and moreover criticising the history conveyed by parties themselves, numerous historians have instead turned their attentions to political and militant practices. This attests to a renewed interest in studying social-democratic and socialist organisations.

What we need, then, is to grasp – insofar as the sources allow – the diversity of party structures and their modes of functioning, the way in which militants participated in them, and the ideas that these latter assimilated through the vulgate that was preached at the various different levels of the organisation.[29] Here, we consider the mass of documentation that social democracy itself produced, and especially the short pamphlets and transcriptions of lectures, which are also the object of research by other historians.[30] We moreover seek to understand how the reference to Marxism – however rudimentary it may have been – was constructed in a political organisation, and how militants themselves adopted and referred to this reference. In this context, divergences over immediate political and strategic questions also encompassed fields that were less directly affected by conjunctural fluctuations, such as culture.[31] History, too, is affected by these imperatives, especially when it comes to a major

---

25   Candar and Becker 2004.
26   Wolikow and Cordillot 1993.
27   Droz 1972–8.
28   Haupt 1980, p. 12.
29   Pasteur 2003, Stuart 1992. See also Stuart 2006.
30   Bonnell 2002.
31   Bonnell 2005.

event like the French Revolution: indeed, historical reference points and their teaching occupied an important place in the 'alternative culture' that the social-democrats sought to project.[32] From this point of view, works regarding other organisations, at the hinge between sociology and history, can also help us to understand how a militant memory of the French Revolution was constituted, and provide elements for understanding how a historical reference point is transmitted and spread through a political organisation across different eras.[33]

The *histoire croisée* of Socialisms

In parallel to those works which seek a better understanding of the concrete reality of the social-democratic parties, other research has studied the transfer of ideas from one country to another, throughout the history of socialism.[34] The history of the French Revolution – an event of global or at least European significance, and one which the different currents of the nineteenth-century workers' movement characterised as the 'Great Revolution' – offers a unique example of transnational history in the context of party-political organisations which had a long-standing internationalist identity.[35]

Recent developments in *histoire croisée* allow us to think through the complex interactions that traversed European socialism's debates over the course of several decades.[36] They have built on earlier works on 'cultural transfers', which had already given orientation to several studies that allowed a break with past histories framed only in terms of the national context.[37] Reviewing the use of such transfers, Werner and Zimmermann note that 'the original situations and those which result from the transfer are grasped by way of stable and supposedly known national reference points, for example "German" or "French" historiography'.[38] The pair instead suggest that we should go beyond the limits that some such research has encountered, and imagine 'theoretical frameworks and methodological tools that allow us to address phenomena of interaction, implying a plurality of directions and a multiplicity of effects. We think

---

32   Lidtke 1985, pp. 159–60. See also Florath 1999.
33   Hincker 1988–9; Lavabre.
34   Charle 2001. See also Prochasson 1993.
35   Schumacher 2001. A pioneering study of the perception of French politics, it limits itself to the perspective of a review which was only very little-read as compared to other sources.
36   Werner and Zimmermann 2003.
37   Werner and Espagne 1987. For an example of studies on the Austrian context, see Weinmann 2006.
38   Werner and Zimmermann 2003, p. 14.

that "entanglement" [*croisement*] affords us the possibility of thinking through these configurations'.[39] If our interests concern the history of socialisms and social-democracy, such a framework allows us to grasp the complex confront-ation between the different histories of the 'Great Revolution' in Germany and France. *Histoire croisée* allows us to grasp why a work is or is not discussed, or brought into a debate or not;[40] it opens up routes to understanding the decision to translate a book at a given moment, or else the refusal to do so, given the interactions between these two situations when many works appeared simul-taneously. This 'means analysing the resistances, the inertias, the changes – of trajectories, of forms, of contents'.[41] *Histoire croisée* thus enjoins us to expand the historiography of the French Revolution into other national and linguistic spaces; not only in terms of how these events were received abroad, but also in terms of understanding the way in which the Revolution was gradually defined by way of debates and exchanges that took place at the international level.

So here we will take a dual perspective, which seeks to integrate new break-throughs in approaches to the history of social democracy, and also to give account of these organisations' own intellectual production. The relationship between the two has rarely been examined, and yet it is at the heart of the social-democratic conception of history. Rarely is anything published by chance: theoretical production is closely connected to political activity, and the concern to get to grips with the history of the French Revolution is often the reflection of wider preoccupations. It is in this sense that it is worth relat-ing the great debates that cut through political parties and events, shaking up the organisation's everyday existence. Writing cannot simply be reduced to the publication of scholarly tomes: history based on research, together with the consultation or even translation of sources, cannot be put on the same plane as occasional rhetorical references to 1789 in political articles or speeches, which were much more dependent on the immediate conjuncture. Hence the import-ance of referring to different types of document, if we are to understand this writing and its intended audience. Such documents range from a short pop-ularising pamphlet to a detailed article, a book review in a newspaper or a theoretical journal, or an erudite, scholarly work mainly designed for intellec-tual discussion ... up to the transcription of talks given at meetings.

The fact that the party combined such different types of writing also poses the question of how they were circulated. When we look at an organisation like

39   Werner and Zimmermann 2003, p. 15.
40   Emmanuel Jousse's book allows us to see how useful this kind of approach is: Jousse 2007.
41   Jousse 2007, p. 16.

the SPD, which was very hierarchically organised and had multiple ramifications,[42] we have to mount a specific study of the different kinds of document through which it constructed a vulgate of the history of the French Revolution. We should measure the reception and the influence of a given work not only in terms of its initial readership, which was sometimes rather low, but also in terms of the different ways in which it was reproduced and summarised. A book could serve as the basis for a pamphlet that popularised its arguments, which could in turn be a starting point for the detailed curriculums published by party training schools where thousands of intermediate cadres would acquire a basic understanding, and then themselves be tasked with transmitting these points of reference. In this volume, we will accord a special place to something that is often left aside in studies on social democracy: namely the 'second-fiddle' figures, often read en masse, who wrote for a thousands-strong readership in papers, workers' almanacs and historical calendars.[43] There is also a constant attention toward the tensions between a transmission of history that was necessarily affected by the twists and turns of political life, and the parallel attempts to lay down an interpretative tradition that sought to 'establish a continuity with a suitable historic past',[44] which necessarily implied 'norms of behaviour by repetition'.[45] One of the central focuses of our study will be the developments in history-writing that evolved in consequence of the social-democratic parties' changing imperatives.

Taking this perspective, we will study in some detail the works of certain prominent social-democrats such as Karl Kautsky, but also, to a lesser extent, Heinrich Cunow and Hermann Wendel. All of these wrote about the French Revolution, to varying degrees, across almost this whole period. For Kautsky, this meant devoting considerable attention to the history of the Revolution in specific connection with the political events of his own time. For others, this was a matter of asserting themselves as 'specialists' on the revolutionary period by way of their published writings. Learning his trade in Austria before he became the leading theorist of the SPD, Kautsky embodies the links between Germany and Austria in the history of social democracy. So even if the original link between Austria and the French Revolution was weaker, the relations that the German party entertained with Austrian social democracy nonetheless imply a common study of this history. Austrian publications offer an interest-

---

42   Michels 2009.
43   See bibliography for the specific locations at which the different sources are held. The richest archival centre is the International Institute of Social History (IISG) in Amsterdam.
44   Hobsbawm and Ranger 2012, p. 1.
45   Hobsbawm and Ranger 2012, p. 2.

ing example of the reception of publications from Germany, at the same time as they exhibit some of their own differences and particularities with regard to the history of the Revolution.[46]

What Revolution?

In social-democratic works and educational documents, the Revolution was most often framed in terms of the years from 1789 to 1799, or 1789 to 1794. Before 1914, at least, they also displayed a specific interest for Babeuf. In Germany, there was an obvious line of continuity with Napoleon, who in a certain sense pursued the work of the Revolution and spread it to German territories, introducing major reforms across part of the country. The Napoleonic occupation of Germany – which could itself be the object of a specific study – will here be addressed insofar as it occasionally made up part of the history of the 'Great Revolution', especially upon the centenary of the Wars of Liberation of 1813.

The history of the French Revolution had its own specific characteristics. This was not, *a priori*, a history that directly challenged the party, in the manner of the history of the First International, whose instrumental use has been well-documented.[47] Referring to this French past did not imply the same strategic consequences as did a national revolution like 1848, many of whose actors remained alive even into the early twentieth century. Indeed, what interests us here is the specificity of the French Revolution. At the same time, we will not completely overlook the other revolutionary processes of the nineteenth century, insofar as they themselves had a certain resonance with 1789–99. The revolutions of 1830 and 1848, and even more so the 1871 Paris Commune, posed questions that often cross paths with the heritage of the French Revolution of 1789. But the specific debates that they raised would be the object of a different study.

From Legalisation to Suppression, 1889–1934

The chronological span of this work begins with the writings that appeared on the centenary of 1789. This anniversary came a few months after the lifting of the proscriptions which had previously weighed down on the German party,

---

46 It would take a further study to examine the relations between the other peoples of the Austro-Hungarian empire, and especially the Hungarians, and the French Revolution.

47 Haupt 1980, p. 26.

and 1889 was also the year of the creation of the Second International, within which the SPD would henceforth occupy a central position.

In our preamble, we will note how a particular reading gradually developed-from the 1840s to the 1880s, which would lay the foundations of the contributions that appeared from the 1889 centenary onward. How did the social-democrats see the French Revolution upon its hundredth anniversary? After studying the centenary itself, we will direct particular attention to the debates that drove discussions of revolutionary history, and especially Eduard Bernstein's 'revision' and his confrontation with Jaurès's conceptions. Then we will turn to the period of the 1905 Russian Revolution, which put more immediately contemporary analogies back on the agenda.

The period running from the 1906 Congress to the Russian Revolution of 1917 constituted an important moment for the social-democracies. It was in these years that they became powerful and structured parties. In this perspective, we will seek to understand the place that the French Revolution occupied in their existing frameworks, and the conditions in which new works on this subject were published, in an era where local and national party education bodies became widespread and defined detailed programmes. How, then, was the historical reference to the French Revolution inscribed in the militant's everyday environment? Who were the readers, the teachers, who 'ferried across' this revolutionary history?

Profound changes took place between the Russian Revolution and the suppression of the social-democratic parties in 1933–4. The Russian and German revolutions of 1917–23, the test of power, as well as the competition on the Left from the communists, multiplied analogies with the Terror, as did the political polarisation of the late 1920s. Having passed from being a counter-society to a party that managed the affairs of state, social democracy saw important upheavals. How could the history of the French Revolution now be written, within such a changed context? Given this complex mix of new elements and continuities, it is quite proper that our analysis should extend across more than four decades of history.

Social Democracy and the French Revolution before 1889

There has been a tradition of reference to the French Revolution in the German-speaking countries ever since 1789. Here, we will focus on the social-democrats, or more accurately the social and political forces that allowed the birth of the social-democratic parties. To this end, we should briefly recall just how important this tradition was from the beginning of the nineteenth century up till the 1880s. Marx and Engels's writings obviously occupied a significant place within this tradition, and numerous studies have been dedicated to the content of their texts. For an overall view, we can look to Matthias Middell's piece in the *Historisch-Kritisches Wörterbuch des Marxismus*[1] as well as Claude Mazauric's recent book on *Marxist Thought and the History of the French Revolution*,[2] and the rich bibliographies of each of these works. Our concern here is not to present Marx and Engels's various interpretations of the French Revolution, but rather to understand what the social democrats knew and read on the eve of the 1889 centenary, and what texts influenced them.

Born in 1818 in Rhenish Prussia – a region heavily marked by the imprint left by Napoleon – Karl Marx studied the French Revolution right from his first stay in Paris in 1843. His notebooks from 1843–6 attest to a variety of reading, from Buchez and Roux's study[3] to the Laponneraye edition of the works of Robespierre.[4] During these years, Marx and Engels wrote several important contributions, laying the bases of the materialist conception of history. One of their most significant works – *The German Ideology*, which the pair wrote together – was not published until 1932, and thus remained unknown to the social-democrats.[5] Marx particularly attentively read the works of the liberal historians Mignet, Guizot and Thiers, from which he drew 'the predominance of the social over the political; individualism as a characteristic of bourgeois modernity ...; the French Revolution as a manifestation of the class struggle between the nobility and bourgeoisie, which, consistent with its laws, intensi-

---

1   Middell 1999.
2   Mazauric 2009.
3   Buchez and Roux, 1834–8.
4   Laponneraye 1840.
5   In *MECW*, Vol. 5.

fied and led to a new stage of societal development'.[6] Elements of a materialist reading of the history of the Revolution were put forward, while in *The Holy Family* Babeuf and some of the radical currents were mentioned as precursors of the communist idea.[7] Thus the French Revolution was seen as a class struggle in which the bourgeoisie had emerged triumphant, and the revolutionary process was also seen in terms of the first manifestations of the communist idea. These were two of the essential ideas that were passed on to the social-democrats.

This tradition of reference to the 'Great Revolution' was not limited to Marx alone. It came out of significant exchanges between France and Germany, a *histoire croisée*[8] consisting of encounters between German émigrés and the first socialist currents in France. In the Paris of the early 1840s, it was the circles of artisans and workers, inheritors to the *sans-culottes* of the late nineteenth century, that nurtured the memory of the Revolution. In this period, the French capital became home to numerous émigrés, and the first associations of the German workers' movement emerged in this same city.[9] One of the most famous émigrés was Heinrich Heine.[10] In the 1840s Heine like many German intellectuals had a complex and sometimes contradictory relationship with the French Revolution, divided as he was between an admiration of the revolutionary act and a repudiation of its more radical forms. Lucien Calvié notes that for Heine as for Marx, the reference to 1789 was, 'in a certain phase of their intellectual development, a first rejection of the unbearable realities of the *ancien régime* and above all of the German misery, i.e. the political immobilism which had prevailed in Germany since 1815'.[11] The idea of a 'complementarity between a Germany devoted to thought and a France with rather more of a propensity toward social life'[12] developed around a few intellectuals in the Left-Hegelian milieu. Moses Hess, who played an important role in social democracy's very first steps,[13] gradually laid the terms of a tripartite division between Britain, Germany and France. His 'European Triarchy' of Berlin, Paris and London picked up on one of the young Hegelians' central ideas,[14] already

---

6   Middell 1999, pp. 807–8.
7   *MECW*, Vol. 4, p. 119.
8   Werner and Zimmermann, 2003.
9   The League of the Banned (*Bund der Geächteten*) was founded in 1834. On the Germans in France see Grandjonc and Werner 1983.
10   Calvié 2006.
11   Calvié 2006, p. 214.
12   Espagne 1999, p. 23.
13   Droz 1990, pp. 233–7.
14   Hess 1841.

popularised by Heine in his 1835 work *On the History of Religion and Philosophy in Germany*. Even if we should avoid projecting this any further – for in the 1830s matters were not yet as canonical and as well-defined as they were among the social-democrats at the end of the nineteenth century – the tripartite division between French politics (originating in the 'Great Revolution' of 1789), German philosophy and British economics, the *doxa* of social democracy up till 1914, did originate in the debates of this earlier era.

Ferdinand Lassalle and the Idea of *Bildung*

The birth of the organised workers' movement in the German-speaking countries is owing to Ferdinand Lassalle in particular. In 1863 he founded the ADAV (*Allgemeiner deutscher Arbeiterverein*), the first party of the German workers' movement and one of the ancestors of the SPD of 1889. For Lassalle, the greatest necessity for the workers' movement was that it should be independent and separate from the bourgeois world; and *Bildung* would play a major role in realising this division. *Bildung* simultaneously means instruction, training, education and culture; it is an ancient concept[15] essential to an understanding of Germanic culture. It evokes the instruction that had been reserved to an élite, but which social democracy now adopted anew, for the benefit of the world of labour. 'To freedom, through education'; for social democracy, socialism was inextricably linked to access to culture, which would itself be achieved through the training of militants. The workers' movement had a foundational link with *Bildung*: the first workers' education circle – the *Arbeiterbildungsverein*, ancestor of the Social-Democratic Party – was created in 1867, linking professional and intellectual education.[16] Hence from the outset social democracy was a political and social movement, wider than the party organisation in the narrow sense: 'the education, press, literature, theatre and fêtes put on by the Party's associations must not be left without purpose, but must contribute to the politicisation of defined, targeted groups'.[17] Social democracy attached significant importance to education, especially through literature and talks. The social-democratic parties and the movement they embodied sought to make their supporters and militants read, in the interests of developing a workers' culture (*Arbeiterkultur*) that was itself considered a means of attain-

---

15   Assmann 1994.
16   Assmann 1994, p. 21.
17   Von Rüden (ed.) 1979, p. 21.

ing autonomy from the bourgeois world. We find this idea throughout their propaganda pamphlets, and it was expressed through the creation of numerous organisations in the party's orbit, as well as the social-democratic attachment to newspapers.[18] The famous account given by Heinrich Georg Dikreiter, which has been reproduced on numerous occasions, attests to the place that books and pamphlets had in militants' training: 'That era saw the appearance of illustrated history books, published by Dietz in Stuttgart, on the French and German revolutions, the peasants' war, the history of the Earth, of animals and plants, etc'.[19] For one Austrian militant, party pamphlets and booklets were 'genuine textbooks and catechisms'.[20]

In *Knowledge is Power, Power is Knowledge* [*Wissen ist Macht, Macht ist Wissen*] – a famous formula which was also the title of a talk Wilhelm Liebknecht gave in 1872 – this latter presented the social-democrats as the 'defenders of culture'; the party considered itself a 'cultural institution' [*Bildungsinstitution*].[21] Liebknecht defined *Bildung* as the Greeks' classical idea of the development of the individual faculties; an ideal which the bourgeoisie, in his view, reserved to a tiny minority. For Liebknecht, these limits could be overcome by way of an uprising comparable to that of 1789, which it was social democracy's task to realise.

Interpreting the French Revolution

If there was to be any possibility of a fresh 1789, the German working class would have to know its history. In the late 1840s Lassalle gave lectures in Düsseldorf which specifically concerned the early years of the French Revolution. The few written traces of these talks, known under the title *Geschichte der sozialen Entwicklung*[22] ['History of Social Development'] are important to understanding the transmission of the reference to the Revolution between 1848 and the 1860s.[23] In his notes, Lassalle took less of an interest in the events themselves than in the philosophy of history. He foregrounded the great struggles

---

18   On the Austrian party, see the picture of these different organisations as portrayed in Pasteur 1994, p. 117.

19   Dikreiter 1988, p. 136. This work was first published as a series in the social-democratic newspaper *Leipziger Volkszeitung* in 1913–14.

20   Cited by Pasteur 1994, p. 263.

21   Liebknecht 1968, p. 88.

22   Lassalle 1926, pp. 92–155.

23   Dayan-Herzbrun 1990, pp. 121–5.

and their historical succession: the absolutist monarchy's fight against feudalism, the bourgeoisie's fight against the nobility, and, finally, the contemporary clash between bourgeoisie and proletariat. Beyond these generalities, one
thing worth noting is Lassalle's peculiar reading of the revolutionary sequence:
one of the great ruptures was identified in the Champ-de-Mars massacre of
17 July 1791.[24] Robespierre came under criticism while Babeuf's endeavours
were presented as unrealisable in the conditions of the time, though neither
of these points was really elaborated. Beyond these lectures, it is worth noting
that Lassalle regularly evoked the 'Fourth Estate' – the workers' *Stand* – including in his famous *Arbeiterprogramm*.[25] What Lassalle taught about the French
Revolution was no original creation of his, and still less a history. But it began a
long tradition of teaching [*Bildung*] on the French Revolution. Continuing on
from Lassalle's work, the social-democratic parties would organise numerous
courses and talks on this topic across several decades.

Lassalle's writings expressed the desire to pass on what was, indeed, a singular history. By no means was this specific to the workers' movement. A nation
state-in-construction, just like a social group-in-becoming, seeks to equip itself
with a historical consciousness that will allow it to justify the struggles of the
present. As Reinhart Koselleck notes, 'what went for bourgeois national consciousness, Marx and Engels also sought to establish for the workers' class consciousness' – a consciousness that would have to be developed by means of
historical reflection.[26]

As we have mentioned, Marx long planned to write a history of the Convention, though he never managed to produce such a work. He did, however, write
numerous contributions on the 1848 Revolution, works of 'immediate history'.
The Class Struggles in France 1848 to 1850, the *Eighteenth Brumaire of Louis Napoleon* and articles he published in the *Neue Rheinische Zeitung*[27] all reflected the
importance of the echo of the 1848 revolutions in the German-speaking countries, where they represented the first revolutions of the contemporary era.[28]
Their multiple political, economic, national and social dimensions (notably the
question of labour) were specific to this experience, and only partly crossed
paths with the questions posed by the 'Great French Revolutions'. As the first
revolution in Germany and the Habsburg lands, their memory would be nur-

---

24 Cited in Dayan-Herzbrun 1990, p. 123.
25 Lassalle 1970, pp. 22–61.
26 Koselleck 1997, p. 72.
27 *Class Struggles in France 1848 to 1850* (MECW, Vol. 10); *The Eighteenth Brumaire of Louis
    Bonaparte* (MECW, Vol. 21).
28 See the historiographical balance sheet drawn up in Haupt Heinz-Gerhard 2002.

tured by the social democrats. This was particularly true in Austria, where from 1898 onward an annual publication was issued in order to commemorate the revolution.[29] Nonetheless, over the years 1848–50, reflection on the history of the French Revolution was itself governed by the questions raised by the revolutions of 1848.[30] The problem of alliances, and in particular the alliance between the bourgeoisie and the popular masses, had been posed anew. The means necessary to achieving a victorious revolution were constantly debated in the German workers' movement, as in the works of Marx and Engels. Indeed, from the aftermath of 1848 up till Engels's last texts in 1895, the social democrats would discuss the suitability of the revolutionary road in light of the defeat that 1848 represented, especially in Germany. But beyond the different social and national content, the great difference from 1789 was that this defeat set 1848 within a narrative of 'German misery' whereas the 'Great Revolution' was the model of a revolution that had succeeded, however bourgeois in character. Numerous social-democratic texts held that the proletariat's coming revolution would necessarily be at least as significant in character as 1789, and thus of the same historical import. However, from Marx onward there were also criticisms of a certain legacy of the French Revolution: *Eighteenth Brumaire* featured a sharp characterisation of the Montagnards of 1848–9, and more particularly their sterile imitation of 1793. This was an important inheritance from Marx, for this text was republished by Engels and very widely read among SPD leaders.[31] Indeed, it also bore a certain influence on the German social-democrats' severe judgements on French politics a few decades later, especially as concerned the French socialist currents that made reference to the examples of the 1789–94 period.[32]

Against Robespierre?

References to the French Revolution remained just as numerous in the wake of the 1871 Paris Commune and the onset of the Third Republic, even as Marx also turned his attentions to the *mir* and the historiography of Russia.[33] The

---

29   The *März-Zeitung* was published each year from 1898 to 1914 by the party publishing house, the Wiener Volksbuchhandlung.

30   There were references to the French Revolution during the German Revolution of 1848. See Middell 1994, p. 97.

31   Wilhelm Liebknecht spoke of this work in reverential terms in his memoirs (see text at https://www.marxists.org/archive/liebknecht-w/1896/karl-marx.htm).

32   See Chapter Three on the divide between Kautsky and Jaurès.

33   See the texts collected in Marx 1964.

Paris Commune was an experience which had rather less effect on the social-democracies in the German-speaking countries, notwithstanding the importance of Marx's text on *The Civil War in France*. Certainly, there were expressions of solidarity in Germany, and in the 1870s the commemorations [*Gedenktage*] of 18 March, 1848 and 1871 were of some significance, without there being any equivalent for the French Revolution.[34] Up till the end of the 1880s these two revolutions were, *a priori*, adopted by the workers' movement as its own.[35] Nonetheless, across most theoretical and political texts the Commune was often referenced in negative terms. If its martyrs provided a powerful and oft-commemorated symbol, the political model that the Commune might offer was often criticised on account of the violence to which it had led – and especially its ultimate repression.[36]

Yet 1871 like 1848 contributed to reviving interest in the French Revolution, and in particular the first Paris Commune. When Bernhard Becker – the former ADAV leader, successor to Lassalle and member of the party of Eisenach – published a *History of the Revolutionary Paris Commune* in 1875,[37] his interest for the Commune of 1793 was a direct echo of the 1871 Commune and the problems that it posed. Right from the introduction to this work, Becker clearly expressed a point of view hostile to Robespierre.[38] To celebrate the Paris Commune of 1793 in counterposition to the Convention, and to assimilate Robespierre to the beginning of the period of reaction, was hardly an isolated view in this era. Such hostility was also found in Wilhelm Liebknecht's writings in the social-democratic paper *Volksstaat* ['People's State'] in 1873, as he reviewed Gustav Tridon's book rehabilitating the Hébertists.[39] A discussion in *Volksstaat* addressed the respective roles of Robespierre and the Hébertists; these latter were clearly favoured. As Béatrix Bouvier put it, 'whoever chose the party of Robespierre thus found himself on the side of the bourgeoisie against the proletariat'.[40] We find similar references in certain texts by August Bebel, including in an 1878 pamphlet in which he emphasised that 'the fight for the Commune in Paris in 1793 and again in 1871 was the natural reaction to a senseless and exaggerated centralisation which bound all autonomous life to bureaucratic forms and con-

---

34   After the death of Marx on 14 March 1883 a link was established beween these three events, all taking place in the same month.
35   Schmidt 1990, pp. 317–18.
36   Haupt 1980, pp. 45–77.
37   Becker 1875.
38   Becker 1875, p. 5.
39   This polemic is mentioned in Bouvier 1988, pp. 95–100.
40   Ibid.

stituted an obstacle to progress'.[41] It is notable that in Bebel's *Woman and Socialism* – which was widely read across several decades, and indeed one of the most popular works among the German social-democrats – the author repeatedly pointed to the French Revolution as a great turning point in Germany's own history.[42] The German workers' movement made all the more reference to the French Revolution when it had resonances with the national context in which social democracy was itself developing. For example, the Mainz Jacobins soon grasped the social-democrats' attention, and in 1875 the social-democrat Wilhelm Blos edited a collection of annotated texts on the history of the Revolution in Mainz in 1792–3.[43]

Upon Marx's death in 1883 there was no unitary and definitive conception of the revolutionary model, nor a precise reading of the sequence that had begun in 1789. In an introduction to a selection of Marx and Engels's texts on the French Revolution, Claude Mainfroy makes the difficult-to-challenge argument that even if their writings were not necessarily contradictory, and were based on a reading of a 'bourgeois revolution' with popular excrescences, they did not make up a homogenous whole such as would have allowed the definition of a 'Marxist' vision of the French Revolution.[44] We would struggle to find a coherent *doxa* even on such a fundamental episode as the Terror, for readings of the French Revolution have long closely depended on the context in which they were written. Claude Mazauric remarks that Marx captures the Revolution 'according to rhythms and temporalities that differ in function of the objects being observed'.[45] Nor do the few recurrences of references to the French Revolution in texts like *Woman and Socialism* or essays like Bernhard Becker's text on the Paris Commune offer a unitary vision of the French Revolution. Mattias Middell concludes, from this, that Marx was 'very far from drawing out a unitary vision of the Revolution of 1789; this latter thus appeared in very disparate senses to the Marxism created under his authority'.[46]

---

41   Bebel 1878, p. 44.
42   Bebel 1950, p. 150.
43   Blos 1875.
44   Foreword to Marx and Engels 1985.
45   Mazauric 2009, p. 16.
46   Middell 1999, p. 814.

Toward 'Marxism'

If we want to understand the significance of the writings published in 1889, we should devote a few words to the social-democrats' situation on the eve of the centenary of the 'Great Revolution'. The German party's programme was still that which had emerged from the Gotha Congress of 1875, a programme which remained famous because it marked the unity of the two currents of the German workers' movement, and also thanks to – or rather, because of – Karl Marx's critique of this same programme.[47] For their part, at the Neudörfl Congress in 1874 the Austrian social democrats adopted a programme inspired by the Eisenach Programme of 1869.

In 1878 Bismarck promulgated the first of the anti-socialist laws [*Sozialistengesetze*], which would until 1890 proscribe a large proportion of all social-democratic political activities in Germany.[48] The social-democrats were forced to adapt their militant practices in order to meet these difficult conditions. Since directly political modes of action were now restricted, education and literature – which were less directly subject to censorship – would now assume a predominant role. This was the context in which a more systematic vision of the French Revolution took form in the 1880s, at the very moment that 'Marxism' became a term with a systematic use that began to give it a defined historical meaning. 'Marxism' spread through the German party in the 1880s even before Engels had published some of his important texts on the interpretation of revolutions, and in particular his 1895 introduction to Marx's *Class Struggles in France 1848 to 1850*.[49] The historian Georges Haupt has shown how 'Marxism' gradually assumed an established definition, beyond merely polemical uses of this term.[50] More recently, adopting a similar perspective to Haupt, Robert Stuart has reviewed the parallel development of this term in France.[51] The party established various means of transmission that allowed the emergence of a 'Marxist' vulgate among militants, both for the purposes of spreading the main terms of the party's programme and for understanding how historical events ought to be interpreted. This 'Marxism' was in fact inextricably linked to the particular contributions that gradually filled it with content. Numerous

---

47   The Gotha Congress saw the fusion between the 'Marxists' of the party of Eisenach (SDAP) of 1869 (around August Bebel and Wilhelm Liebknecht) and the Lassalleans of the ADAV.
48   Even under the ban, the social-democrats retained their right to have a parliamentary group.
49   See Engels's 1895 introduction to Marx's *Class Struggles in France 1848 to 1850*, in MECW, Vol. 27.
50   'De Marx au marxisme' in Haupt 1980, pp. 77–109.
51   Stuart 1992.

pamphlets contributed to the formation of this 'Marxism'. But Engels's *Anti-Dühring*, which was published in 1878 and widely distributed in the 1880s after Marx's death, was the most characteristic example of a militant handbook that served as the basis for an overall interpretation of the world.[52] *Anti-Dühring* did not really contain new elaborations regarding the history of the French Revolution, but is nonetheless of interest, for our purposes, insofar as it contributed to the formation of 'Marxism' and the establishment of a certain doctrine, in light of which a series of historical tomes would now be written. This militant handbook had a particularly decisive effect on the militants of this era; Kautsky would speak of the 'upheaval' that this work prompted.[53]

Karl Kautsky has to be understood in terms of his particular connection with this social democracy, of which he would become one of the most visible theorists. His writings had a decisive impact across several decades.[54] Born in Prague in 1854, he was first involved in the ranks of the Austrian party. Even if in the 1880s he was not yet at the height of his prestige – as he would be after Engels's death in 1895 – he had already emerged as one of German social democracy's most reputed theorists.[55] What was particular about Kautsky was that he remained a party intellectual, and only occupied what his biographer Ingrid Gilcher-Holtey aptly called an 'intellectual's mandate'. He was never a member of the party leadership, did not become an elected representative, and was at most Under-Secretary of State for Foreign Affairs in 1918–19. His role as a theorist extended beyond the German-speaking countries alone: he was a highly influential figure in the pre-1914 Second International, and his writings were translated all across Europe.[56] He was central to writing the social-democratic parties' programmes on a series of occasions, from the Erfurt Congress in 1891 to the Heidelberg Congress of 1925. He devoted much of his time to writing, and up till 1917[57] with editing the theoretical review *Die Neue Zeit*. Reading this

---

52   *Anti-Dühring*, in MECW, Vol. 25.
53   'Darwinismus und Marxismus', *Die Neue Zeit*, 1894–1895, p. 403, cited by Haupt 1980, p. 93.
54   The fullest work on this subject is Waldenberg 1980, a work by a Polish historian which also exists in Italian translation. A German work worth noting is Gilcher-Holtey 1986, and in French the pieces in the *Maitron Allemagne* (Droz 1990, pp. 271–4) and *Maitron Autriche* (Haupt and Maitron 1971, pp. 161–3).
55   Having started out in the Austrian context he soon established himself in Germany. While remaining in frequent contact with the Austrian social-democrats he was above all a theorist and militant of the SPD. There has been no particular study of the special role he played in the exchange between Germany and Austria, though this fact is often mentioned. Indeed, we will see its importance as we look at his writings on the French Revolution.
56   For his multi-lingual bibliography see Blumenberg 1960.
57   When Kautsky was removed from his editorial post and replaced by Heinrich Cunow.

review founded in 1883, the same year as Marx's death, allows us to better grasp the Marxism of the 1880s.[58] Over several decades the main orientations of not only the German but also the international workers' movement were debated in its pages. Through *Die Neue Zeit* we can see how 'Marxism' remained a subject of debate, at the historical as well as the theoretical and strategic levels. The review was published by J HW Dietz (named after its founder), which was created at the end of 1881 and originally located in Stuttgart.[59] At first its print run stood at 5,000 copies, and the review was legally on sale throughout the Reich, unlike the weekly *Der Sozialdemokrat*, which was published first in Zurich and then in London. Studies on *Die Neue Zeit* have often focused on its more political articles, but little addressed the historical contributions in its pages or, indeed, its book reviews, despite the fact that these texts occupied an important place in this review until 1923.

Its very first issue in 1883 featured a historical-economic article devoted to the role of the *assignats* in the French Revolution.[60] While this piece was unsigned, Karl Kautsky's memoirs tell us that he was, in fact, the author.[61] This article was a panorama of the economic situation in the 1780s, up till the period of the Directory. It thus addressed the budgetary situation at the end of Louis XVI's reign, and then the circumstances in which the *assignats* were issued, the nationalisation of clerical property, and finally the difficult economic conditions of year II. If this text was not particularly original, its importance above all owed to the fact that it demonstrated the desire to understand the revolutionary phenomenon from a particular perspective.[62] Even in its first issue, *Die Neue Zeit* showed its interest in history and more specifically the history of the French Revolution, seen from a social and economic point of view. This review would be one of the two major sites of elaborations and writing on the history of the 'Great Revolution'.

Eric Hobsbawm reminds us that in this period 'plenty of political institutions, ideological movements and groups ... were so unprecedented that even historical continuity had to be invented, for example by creating an ancient past beyond effective historical continuity'.[63] This remark could well apply to German social democracy, which sought to attach itself to a revolutionary past

---

58   The Friedrich Ebert Stiftung has produced an electronic version of almost all the pre-1914 articles. See the introduction to this review at: http://library.fes.de/nz/nz-intro.html. In French, see Schumacher 2001.

59   Emig 1981.

60   Kautsky, K., 'Die Assignaten der französischen Revolution', *Die Neue Zeit*, 1883, pp. 181–6.

61   Kautsky 1960, p. 523.

62   Kautsky, K., 'Die Assignaten der französischen Revolution', *Die Neue Zeit*, 1883, p. 186.

63   Hobsbawm and Ranger 2012, p. 7.

that was not limited to domestic reference points alone. Without doubt, certain elements of continuity with the French Revolution dated back to the 1840s, or even to the Revolution itself. But if a particular reading of the French Revolution was to be popularised and communicated more widely, then books and pamphlets were required in order to establish the content of this interpretation. The 1889 centenary would provide the opportunity for this.

PART 1

The Development, Crisis and Renewal of the Reference to the French Revolution and Its History (1889–1905)

∴

1889: the Social-Democrats' Centenary

1889, the year that France commemorated the hundredth anniversary of the Revolution, coincided with the birth of the Second International. With great symbolism, the International held its first congress in Paris on 14 July 1889. For the German and Austrian parties, 1889 also provided an appropriate moment to publish books and articles on the 'Great Revolution'. While the two books by Wilhelm Blos and Karl Kautsky are often remembered as the works that were published in order to mark the centenary,[1] this year was also the first time that the history of the Revolution was spread by various different means of communication. The French Revolution now became a major point of reference, from the theoretical articles in *Die Neue Zeit* to the public talks given by the Berlin workers' instruction school [*Arbeiterbildungsschule*].

At the political level, 1889 was the final year of the ban on the SPD. Counter to what had been expected, the German party had gained influence over the course of the 1880s, and at the beginning of the 1890s it would become a highly prominent force. As for Austria, at the Hainfeld Congress of 31 December 1888– 1 January 1889 the party decided to adopt the name *Sozialdemokratische Arbeiterpartei in Österreich* (SDAP). The unification of the different currents owed to the efforts of Victor Adler, the main inspirer of a programme whose central axis – beyond the long-term perspective of socialism – was a set of reforms that sought to democratise Austria, including universal suffrage as its most essential demand. Reacting against the wave of terrorist attacks that the anarchists had committed at the beginning of the 1880s, the programme rejected any recourse to terror and illegal methods.[2] This relationship to legality is worth bearing in mind, for it would influence these parties' references to revolution, in the past as in the present.

On the Eve of the Centenary

In Germany, the social-democrats faced the particular challenge of responding to the counter-commemorations that were organised by Bismarck. Indeed,

---

1   Kautsky 1889; Blos 1888.
2   Kreissler 1971, p. 59.

since 1870 he had made the confrontation with France one of the pillars of his authority. Moreover, in early 1889 the party still had to endure several more months of illegality. This was a time in which the German state was promoting its own conceptions of the nation, which it portrayed in ethnic terms, as opposed to the French universalism of the Enlightenment and, more generally, any tradition of revolutionary rupture.[3] Where it did emphasise 1789, it did so for the sake of contrasting French history to Germany's own special course of development, the so-called *Sonderweg*;[4] this date was mobilised 'in an essentially negative sense, ... first and foremost as a pretext to highlight and celebrate a particularly German experience, and to oppose two irreconcilable philosophies of history, with one – Germany's – based on continuity and the other – France's – based on rupture'.[5] 1871, the foundation of the Reich, was Germany's response to 1789.

The History of the Revolution in Germany

Before delving into the social-democratic output on this question, it is worth highlighting the existence of a number of German-language histories of the French Revolution. Nineteenth-century German historiography long remained hostile to the Revolution: historian Walter Grab notes that 'the dominant tendency in the historiography over five generations was a unanimous condemnation of the overthrow of the French state, both in theory and in practice, and an expression of disgust at the violent realisation of Enlightenment ideals'.[6] Among the most important references we could cite Leopold von Ranke. Given his significant contribution to distinguishing historical sources from historical myths, and his application of rigorous rules of historical critique, Von Ranke became known as the founder of scientific historiography in Germany.[7] He wrote no overall study of the French Revolution *per se*, but he did 'emphasise that the danger of the French Revolution resided in the propagation of "morals of apparently universal character", and that everything important that Germany had achieved since the Enlightenment sprung not from imitation of the French way of thinking, but, on the contrary, from opposition to it'.[8]

---

3 Espagne 1999, p. 243.
4 See Smith 2008 for a recent summary of the state of the debate on the *Sonderweg*.
5 Von Bueltzingsloewen 1992, p. 39.
6 Grab 1983. On the German historiography see also Dippel 1990.
7 Grab 1983, p. 303.
8 Grab 1983, p. 304. See his work Von Ranke 1875.

While numerous histories of the French Revolution were published already before 1848,[9] the first historian who truly worked with the sources was Von Ranke's pupil Heinrich von Sybel, founder of the *Historische Zeitschrift* review.[10] His *History of the Revolutionary Epoch from 1789 to 1800*, which appeared in multiple volumes between 1853 and 1858, was greatly hostile to the French Revolution.[11] Written under the influence of the 1848 revolution and the failed attempts at unification that followed, this work would dominate the second half of the nineteenth century. It had great influence in Germany, and Von Sybel was long considered the historian of reference.[12] He was the first historian to consult international sources, and in this sense he wrote one of the first European histories of this period, even if his hatred of the French Revolution 'took away most of the advantage that he could have gained from the "European" viewpoint that he had tried to adopt'.[13] He moreover contributed to eclipsing other less well-known histories.[14] Von Sybel was particularly opposed to the ideas of democracy and popular sovereignty, and presented Robespierre as a forerunner of 'communism'.[15] He gave full-throated support to Prussian state policy, especially the *Kulturkampf*, and in 1876 he was appointed director of the State Archives in Berlin.

Apart from works by German historians, some French historians were also translated. Mignet's history published in 1825[16] was considered a work of reference, including among the social-democrats, even though its author stood very far from them politically. Adolphe Thiers was also immediately translated in 1826–30,[17] as was Hippolyte Taine. This latter was very hostile to the French Revolution and especially the popular movement, but in Germany his study was considered a standard work.[18]

In this era 'history [*Geschichte*] was not, then, in any sense a special science limited to the past and its memory; it maintained its political actuality, and the characteristic social challenge which it addressed to contemporaries. These were two qualities that it had gained around the end of the Enlighten-

---

9   Werner 1987, p. 127.
10   For a history, see Gall 2009.
11   Von Sybel 1853–79.
12   Grab 1983, p. 308.
13   Godechot 1974, p. 204.
14   Dippel 1990, p. 1253.
15   Cited in Grab 1983, pp. 307–8.
16   Mignet 1825.
17   Thiers 1826–30.
18   Taine 1877–93.

ment era'.[19] It was all the more markedly political in character when it came to the history of the French Revolution. Reinhart Koselleck remarks that in 1889 the historian Heinrich von Sybel 'openly referred to his Prussian and national-liberal convictions'.[20]

These dominant ideas were also found in teaching. Republican demands were banned and in the classroom students were enjoined to 'shut their ears to revolutionary discourse' and to 'do their duty in time of war'.[21] As the *Volksschule* expanded over the 1870s, the authorities saw falling levels of illiteracy as something of a risk, and insisted on the celebration of the monarch, the state and the church.[22] In this context, anything with any resemblance to France – and even more so its revolutionary heritage – was to be repudiated. The ideas communicated at all levels focused on German unification and the construction of a new state without any revolutionary tradition.

Translating Gabriel Deville

In 1887 Eduard Bernstein, director of the weekly *Sozialdemokrat*, remained in exile in Switzerland. His translation of a text on Babeuf by Gabriel Deville[23] expressed the social-democrats' 1880s interest in writing another kind of history of the French Revolution. The French socialist's arguments built on the few positive evaluations of the Revolution put forward by Karl Marx. This was the first case where a French socialist's work on this subject was transferred across to Germany. This text ought not to be confused with the part on the Directory in the *Histoire socialiste de la France contemporaine*, which Deville would write only much later, and in a very different context.[24] Like *Der Sozialdemokrat* newspaper, this short pamphlet was published in exile, in Zurich. To our knowledge, it was never published in French in this form. It would occupy quite a unique place in social-democratic historiography, because at least up till the First World War it featured in certain party libraries. Originally it had appeared as a series of installments in Jules Guesde and Paul Lafargue's newspaper *Le Socialiste*, from 27 August to 10 November 1887.[25] Gabriel Deville was at that time one of the most prominent figures in the *Parti Ouvrier Français* (POF), a 'Guesdist' force on the left of the socialist movement.

---

19   Koselleck 1997, p. 71.
20   Ibid.
21   Mély 2004, p. 447.
22   Bonnell 2005, p. 21.
23   Deville 1887.
24   Deville 1901.
25   Citations are from this original French edition.

In this text Deville elaborated a general vision of the Revolution. For him, this was above all a bourgeois revolution, led by a social class which had captured the popular movement in order to satisfy its own interests.[26] Having offered this overview, the text emphasised that while Babeuf represented a 'rising class', his initiative was 'condemned to ultimate economic failure'.[27] Babeuf thus appeared as the forerunner of an idea that would later be developed by the workers' movement, and not as a man who could have realised communism in his own time. Providing a rather one-dimensional biography of the revolutionary and the development of his Conspiracy's organisation, Deville's work was unique for offering long extracts from Babeuf's writings (for example from the *Manifeste des Égaux*) and various documents taken from Buonarroti's book,[28] at that time unavailable to German readers.[29]

Bernstein's goal was not simply to shed light on the history of Babeuf and Babouvism. In a long appendix Bernstein revisited the history of the French Revolution. If the German readership was liable to misunderstand certain aspects of Deville's argument, which had originally been addressed to French socialists more familiar with the context, Bernstein provided them with a presentation of the different currents in the Revolution.[30] In seeking to explain the revolutionary process, Bernstein emphasised its economic factors: he spoke of the transmission of land ownership from the nobility to the bourgeoisie and part of the peasantry, the question of *assignats* and the specific context of the Directory, which explained the *raison d'être* of the Babouvist Conspiracy. Extending Deville's argument, he argued that if the Conspiracy had no chance of succeeding in the context of the time, the ideas it had proclaimed were the right ones, and 'the proletariat ha[d] every reason to hold in high esteem the memory of the pioneers of its emancipation'.[31]

Bernstein ended his argument by citing Babeuf's 25 July 1789 letter to his wife. This text lamented the violent deaths of Foulon and Berthier;[32] the German social democrat foregrounded the critique of revolutionary violence which this entailed.[33] It seems logical enough to detect, here, the premises of

---

26   *Le Socialiste*, 27 August 1887.
27   Ibid.
28   Buonarroti 1957.
29   It would, however, be published by the SPD in 1909. See Chapter Five.
30   A translation (probably by Laura Lafargue) appeared in installments in *Le Socialiste* from 26 November 1887 to 24 December 1887. We here base ourselves on this version.
31   Ibid.
32   Foulon and Berthier were killed by the people of Paris at the end of July 1789. This event had a particular impact on contemporary observers.
33   This letter has often been cited in order to show Babeuf's disdain for violence. See Mazauric 1989, p. 63.

a doctrine that prefigured Bernstein's turn-of-the-century revisionism.[34] But even beyond the fact that such a condemnation of violence must be seen in terms of the party's own present conditions – having to deal with a degree of clandestinity – Bernstein was not the only social-democrat to express himself in these terms. As the texts published during the centenary would make clear, numerous social-democrats distanced themselves from revolutionary violence. And whatever importance we place on this critique of violence, it should not make us forget the essential thing, here: namely, that Bernstein wanted to transfer a history of the French Revolution that had been written by one of his French socialist comrades.

In this same spirit, from the start of 1889 the French Revolution occupied a unique place in the social-democratic imaginary. On 1 January, upon the birth of the Austrian party, August Bebel wrote an article for the Austrian newspaper *Die Gleichheit*,[35] entitled 'For the 100th Anniversary of the French Revolution'.[36] This offered no specific explanation of the history of the French Revolution; it was rather more a way of celebrating the emergence of the workers' movement, which could – and should – realise for the proletariat what the bourgeoisie had achieved for itself a century before.[37] The workers' movement would have to be up to the standard of history, and prepare a historic rupture comparable to 1789: 'Following the example of the Great Revolution, it will establish a new order of things in which there will no longer be either oppressed or masters; a new order which will realise in the domain of facts and reality what the men of '89 and '93 could only experiment'.[38]

Wilhelm Blos and Karl Kautsky's Books

Two books from the social-democratic centenary of the Revolution would have a lasting importance, namely the works by Wilhelm Blos and Karl Kautsky. They were written in order to mark the hundredth anniversary of 1789. They feature among the best-known works that social democracy produced, even if they are often little-mentioned or appreciated by the historiography of the Revolution.

---

34   Such is the hypothesis advanced in Angel 1961, p. 122.
35   The ancestor of the *Arbeiter-Zeitung*, this publication is not to be confused with Clara Zetkin's paper *Die Gleichheit* in Germany.
36   Bebel 1970, vol. 1, p. 519.
37   Bebel 1970, vol. 1, p. 509.
38   Bebel 1970, vol. 1, p. 520.

A History of Class Struggle

Before delving into the content of Karl Kautsky's book, we should say something about how it came to be published, the better to understand the conditions in which it was produced. Like Blos's work, Kautsky's study was published by Dietz. This publishing house had existed since 1881, and as two leading social democrats joined its personnel it became *de facto* party property,[39] even though it would take until 1906 before this was formalised. Kautsky's book *Die Klassengegensätze von 1789* (literally, 'The Class Contradictions in 1789')[40] appeared in the *Internationale Bibliothek* collection, which among other things published theoretical and historical texts. As its subtitle indicated, this volume was published upon the centenary.[41] Given its author's great influence, this was the best-known social-democratic history of the Revolution. Kautsky's exchanges with Engels on this work – a correspondence which was published in the 1930s – and its multiple foreign translations explain why this work had such a continuous echo.[42] Even in the 1980s, those who referred to Marx or Jaurès's writings on the French Revolution would often also highlight this work,[43] while some studies in Germany also set it in a wider landscape.[44] But only very rarely was it set in its proper context. This was a short 'Marxist' history book: it was intended to be a sort of *Anti-Dühring* of the French Revolution, meaning, a short textbook that presented the main lines of development of the revolutionary period, with the aid of the historical materialism elaborated in the 1880s. It is worth noting that Kautsky's text had at first been a series of articles appearing in instalments in *Die Neue Zeit*, which itself sought to be the organ for the elaboration of this Marxism. The decision to publish it as a pamphlet resulted from an exchange with Dietz. We should also highlight the fact that there were certain changes between these articles and the published book, following Kautsky's exchange of letters with Friedrich Engels.[45] Formulations were altered and the argument was enriched by long notes presenting some of

---

39   Emig 1981.
40   It was translated into French in 1901 under the title *La lutte des classes en France en 1789*. See Ducange 2008, as well as the 2010 edition of Kautsky's work published by Demopolis (*Socialisme et Révolution française*).
41   '*Zum 100jährigen Gedenktag der grossen Revolution*'; 'On the Hundredth Anniversary of the Great Revolution'.
42   On the 1933–5 publication of Engels's letter, see Chapter Twelve.
43   For example, in the anthology of Marx and Engels's writings on the French Revolution: Marx and Engels 1985, p. 285.
44   Bouvier 1992. See also Müller 1989.
45   On the changes between the two versions see Engels 2002, pp. 1262–70.

the sources that Engels had sent him; indeed, this latter was also named in the acknowledgements at the beginning of the book.

As for the author's own motivations, while the centenary was the immediate factor explaining the publication of this work, Kautsky had in fact long been interested in the subject. It is no surprise that a social-democrat would be attached to the history of the 'Great Revolution'; Kautsky's memoirs moreover tell us that he had previously planned to write a dissertation on Jefferson's time in Paris in 1789. Kautsky had long taken an interest in history and he lamented the fact that his historical works had not achieved as wide an interest as his economic writings;[46] indeed, the most successful of his works had been his synopsis of Marx's *Capital*.[47] Just before the publication of *Die Klassengegensätze von 1789*, the man known as the 'Pope of Marxism' had already published a book on a famous 'forerunner', *Thomas More und seine Utopie*.[48] His intellectual formation led him to take a close look into the literature on the French Revolution, especially seeing as he had so mastered French that he was able to write in it. The lack of any Marxist study on this subject – unlike other revolutions essential to the social-democrats' tradition, like the Peasant War in Germany or the Paris Commune – probably also motivated the writing of this book. His concern was to write a unique work that would distinguish itself from the histories that had been written up till that point: 'In most accounts of the Revolution, the class struggle [*Klassenkampf*] did not appear, and even in those cases where it does, it appears not as the wellspring of the whole social upheaval, but as an episode inserted among the struggles between philosophers, orators and statesmen, as if these latter were not the necessary consequence of the class struggle itself!'[49]

What exactly had Kautsky read, in order to write this study? Not a lot: and this is what Engels, as well as part of the historiography, criticised him for. He had not consulted the sources, which – as Engels granted – would have been difficult from where he was working, in Vienna. Nor do Karl Kautsky's personal archives (or indeed, Wilhelm Blos's) shed any more light on this question.[50] The works Kautsky had read were considered classics, at the time: Hippolyte Taine's *Les origines de la France contemporaine* and Alexis de Tocqueville's *L'Ancien Régime et la Révolution* were used to shed light on certain facts; as for socialist

46   Kautsky 1960, p. 522.
47   Kautsky 1887.
48   Kautsky 1888.
49   Kautsky 1901, p. 8. Here we draw on Edouard Berth's French translation, making small edits as necessary.
50   *Karl Kautsky archiv* (IISG, Amsterdam); *Wilhelm Blos archiv* (Bundesarchiv Koblenz).

texts, Kautsky referred to Louis Blanc's *Histoire de la Révolution française*. This was a work which Lassalle held in high esteem, but Marx and Engels criticised it very severely in their correspondence, this being a mostly Robespierrian work which was only very weakly based on a study of social forces.[51] He also made use of the 'classic' German reference works by Leopold von Ranke and Heinrich von Sybel, whose importance we have already highlighted. The few sources he cited from the Russian historian of the peasantry Karéiew,[52] for instance, owed to Engels's contributions. So from his base in Vienna, Kautsky used only very broad overviews of the French Revolution in order to write his study, and it was on this basis that he expounded his own perspective.

Far from a chronological history, this was an overview covering a vast period, and which extended from the contradictions of the absolute monarchy to the consequences of the Napoleonic era. The few events that were mentioned played an only secondary role. For example, 9 Thermidor was not taken for a rupture in itself; rather, it was important to grasp the whole revolutionary process, without any particular sympathy. Here Kautsky was a historian of the long term; while the domestic conflicts during the revolutionary process were foregrounded, he also considered the Napoleonic era very much part of the revolutionary period, seeing the effect that the Napoleonic occupation of Germany had in eliminating certain vestiges of feudalism.[53] The rule of the popular forces, the peasants and *sans-culottes*, and the alliance they made with the bourgeoisie, constituted the most original themes addressed in this work.[54] The chapter on the peasants – the longest in the whole work – presented the differences within the peasantry, and especially across the various regions; Kautsky sought to understand the socio-economic reasons behind the Vendée revolt.[55] For him, the structuring of the clergy and the nobility in these regions corresponded to a different 'mode of production'; what had elsewhere become unbearable chains instead served in the Vendée as a protective buckle.

The *sans-culottes*, whose social heterogeneity Kautsky emphasised, constituted the other social force that particularly captured his attention. As the predominant 'revolutionary mass', they played a decisive role in this process,

---

51   See Blanc 1847–67. Marx and Engels' correspondence, MECW 38.

52   Karéiew 1879.

53   'The Jacobins saved the Revolution in France; Napoleon revolutionised Europe': Kautsky 1901, p. 109.

54   Kautsky 1901, p. 82.

55   This was a point of debate with Engels. Claude Mainfroy emphasises that this was one of the first discussions of the Vendée to explain the uprising in terms of social factors, as against the ideological characterisations promoted by certain republican approaches from the time. Mainfroy 1985, p. 21.

and allowed the Republic to be saved from both domestic and foreign attacks.[56]
The *sans-culottes'* 'tax demands', and their illusory character in this era, were
the object of particular attention:

> Suppressing or at the very least limiting the different sorts of capitalist
> exploitation, and in particular commerce, speculation and agiotage, soon
> appeared to the *sans-culottes* to be just as important as combatting the
> counter-revolution. But overthrowing capitalism from below was some-
> thing impossible: the conditions for the transition to a new, higher form
> of production were not yet there.[57]

Kautsky also elaborated some remarks on the 'new mode of production' and
characterised the 'bourgeois' or 'capitalist revolution' and its consequences:

> The Jacobins and the *faubourgs* of Paris were thwarted, because the cir-
> cumstances did not allow for a petty-bourgeois or proletarian revolution,
> and their efforts were incompatible with the capitalist revolution. Yet
> their activity was not in vain. It was they who prepared and laid the way
> on which a new form of production, a new society would now mount such
> a rapid, marvellous rise, within the space of just a few years under the Dir-
> ectory and then the Empire.[58]

This was an echo of polemics with Lassalle and the prelude to the programmatic clarifications that would mark the Erfurt Congress of 1891, as Kautsky
sought to make a clear distinction between the popular categories of the French
Revolution and the contemporary proletariat. In response to the formula in the
Gotha Programme for which 'The emancipation of labor must be the work of
the working class, relative to which all other classes are only one reactionary
mass', Kautsky criticised those who saw 'two classes in struggle, two compact,
homogenous masses, the revolutionary and reactionary masses, one below
and one above'.[59] As against Lassalle's vision, which assimilated the proletariat to the Fourth Estate [*Stand*],[60] Kautsky asserted its class [*Klasse*] charac-

---

56   Kautsky 1901, p. 83.
57   Kautsky 1901, p. 84.
58   Ibid.
59   Kautsky 1901, p. 9.
60   For Lassalle, the state [*Staat*] of the future would be dominated by the worker-'estate'
     [*State*], here defined in the sense of the 'Fourth Estate'.

ter.[61] Finally, it is worth emphasising the final sentence of his chapter on the *sans-culottes*, according to which 'The truth is that today the Jacobin traditions are among the most serious obstacles impeding the formation in France of a great, united and independent workers' party'.[62] Building on some of the critiques that Marx had advanced in his *Eighteenth Brumaire*, 'Jacobin traditions' here appeared as something harmful, indeed the source of the dispersion of the French socialist currents – a situation which contrasted, in this period, with the strength of a united party in Germany. In these years, the question of analysing the 'Jacobin traditions' of 1789–94 and their effect on contemporary politics was at the heart of the social-democrats' reflection, and would remain so at least up till 1905 as they examined the orientations of the French socialist currents.

If the content of *Die Klassengegensätze von 1789* can easily be criticised for its schematism, we should once again insist on the context in which it was published. As the first essay of this kind, Kautsky's work effectively constituted the textbook to which the social-democrats would turn, indeed over a long period. The desire to analyse such a complex period as part of a general framework, in such a short volume, inevitably produced a certain schematism – not least considering the author's lack of concern for sources.[63] There was nonetheless something rather audacious in Kautsky's approach, and it also responded to a real need, related to the objectives of *Bildung*. Following in the spirit of the Marxism that had developed over the 1880s, this work sought to offer social democrats a short manual that could provide some general characterisations which the party's cadres would be able to take on board. From this point of view, the book's historic role was, indeed, an important one, and we can trace its influence over several decades – perhaps less in terms of it being directly read, as in terms of the model of popularisation it proposed. Before the manuals written within the Communist Parties, up till the 1920s this work had no equivalent in the European socialist movement.

A People's History

Our presentation of the Revolution is based on the materialist conception of history, which explains historical events in terms of their economic cir-

---

61   Kautsky 1901, p. 55.
62   Ibid.
63   Since Matthias 1957, Kautsky's thinking has often been presented as schematic. A certain form of fatalism and mechanicism also owed to his reading of Darwin, whose heritage he claimed alongside Marx.

cumstances. For us, therefore, the different phases of the French Revolution constitute a series of class struggles ...[64]

These lines at the beginning of Wilhelm Blos's work suggest that his argument little differed from Kautsky's. Published at the end of 1888 and then re-issued from 1889 onward, this 'people's history' of the French Revolution nonetheless greatly differed from *Die Klassengegensätze von 1789*.

According to library statistics and several other accounts, this was one of the history books that was most read among the social-democrats up till 1914, and it was issued in tens of thousands of copies into the 1920s. It was more addressed to a wider audience of activists than to party cadres as such. Including numerous illustrations, this book's writing style had nothing to do with Kautsky's conceptually-grounded Marxism. The subtitle set the tone of the work: this was a *Popular History of the Events in France from 1789 to 1804. With Numerous Portraits and Historical Images*.

The author's statements regarding historical materialism and the class struggle at the beginning of this work contrasted with the reality of how it was written. This itself had to do with the author's particular concerns. Having received a university education and then quickly been elected to the Reichstag in 1877 – where he would sit until 1918 – Blos played an important local role in Wurtemberg. Though he was not of any particular interest for theory and discussions on Marxism, for the historiography of social democracy he remained one of the 1880s figures who most favoured reformism.[65] His involvement in the satirical paper *Der Wahre Jacob* and in the workers' almanacs [*Arbeiter-Kalender*] demonstrated Blos's will to address himself to the wider social-democratic audience. He was more a populariser than a theorist, for instance making very few interventions in the pages of *Die Neue Zeit*. While he was known among the party base thanks to his multiple articles, his influence was not, however, comparable with the prestige of Karl Kautsky – especially at the international level.[66]

As for the book's content, despite the author's manifest sympathies for the popular mobilisation and in particular the actions of the people of Paris, this work offered a more traditional political history, revolving around the 'great men' of the era. This history set down a very classic periodisation, from the National Assembly to the Consulate; each revolutionary assembly took up the

64   Blos 1888, p. 1.
65   Krause 1980. See also the biography in Droz 1990, pp. 108–9.
66   For instance, this work was not translated into French.

space of a chapter. Hostile to Robespierre, Blos presented the Hébertists and Danton in a favourable light, while emphasising that 9 Thermidor represented the halting of the revolutionary movement. Also notable was Blos's specific interest in Babeuf, probably echoing the translation of the Deville texts published in 1887. This also distinguished him from Kautsky. As in this latter's case, this was a work based on broad overviews and not individual archives. It also featured significant annexes which did show more of a concern for documentation, for instance the translation of the 1793 Constitution. This was the beginning of a long publishing tradition, for in the following years the social-democrats would regularly translate documents from the revolutionary period.

In the final pages of the work, Blos very clearly asserted his political pragmatism and his belief in gradual progress. This in fact contrasted with some other passages in which he clearly showed sympathy with the work of the Revolution. Blos concluded that if the French Revolution was rich in lessons, it could not be a model for contemporary Germany. He expressed his own sharp rejection of revolutionary violence, and opposed the idea of adopting the French model, which had led to 'bloody catastrophes'.[67] If in both cases there was a certain attention to the popular layers, alongside the stated intention of writing a history that differed from the dominant historiography, these two works were not the same, either in terms of their content or the readership they addressed. This divide corresponded to the different types of party intellectuals,[68] and to the difference between a 'people's' history like Blos's and a more scientific and theoretical history in the case of Kautsky. Such a difference of intellectuals and writing styles matched with the divisions that would be set in stone a few years later in the party libraries, whose catalogues separated 'educational' from 'recreational' reading.[69] So the social-democrats did not produce just one genre of history-writing.

Apart from these works, it is also worth mentioning Wilhelm Liebknecht's initiative to write an essay on this same theme. This is mentioned in the *Maitron: Allemagne* following the biography of the social-democratic leader. Béatrix Bouvier does not, however, refer to it, while Götz Langkau – a researcher at the IISG who edited Liebknecht's correspondence with exacting detail[70] – has told us that he has 'never seen' any such text. However, what look like drafts

---

67   Blos 1888, p. 613.
68   For an introduction to these different types of intellectual, based on the early twentieth-century example of the social-democrat Heinrich Cunow, see Florath 2005. We will look more closely at Cunov in Chapter Five.
69   See Chapter Seven.
70   Liebknecht, Wilhelm 1988.

of this work are preserved in Liebknecht's personal archive in Berlin.[71] This was an unfinished work; a few sparse notes held in the other part of his archives, in Amsterdam, give some idea of the research he had conducted.[72]

For his part, Friedrich Engels did not write any articles for the centenary. Yet it is worth mentioning two important letters of his, which were not published at the time. The first is the one he sent to Kautsky about his study on the Revolution; here, Engels particularly addressed the nature of the monarchy and the question of the Terror. The other, less well-known letter is the one that he sent to Victor Adler on 4 December 1889, concerning an unfinished project for a book dedicated to Anacharsis Cloots. As well as displaying his considerable interest for the role of the popular masses, here Engels mentioned that it was not Marx or he himself who had explained the mechanisms of the Terror, but rather a certain Karl Friedrich Köppen, Marx's best friend while he was researching in Berlin. According to Engels, Köppen shed light on the relationship between the domestic Terror and the war with foreign powers: after the military victory at Fleurus at the end of June 1794, the means of coercion were no longer useful, because they were no longer justifiable.[73]

From Workers' Almanacs to Lectures

Like Blos and Kautsky's books, Engels's letters evidenced the main themes that the social-democrats addressed upon the centenary of the French Revolution. But they do not alone suffice to grasp the full array of social-democratic publications. Few studies have addressed the articles that appeared in newspapers or other widely distributed organs. Yet only by looking at these can we understand how the reference to the French Revolution took on a wider importance.

From the Sozialdemokrat to the Arbeiter-Zeitung

In July 1889 social-democratic newspaper *Berliner Volksblatt*, ancestor of *Vorwärts* ['Forward'] was cautious about making references to the Revolution: it was published in Berlin, but under the censor. Only one short 14 July 1889 article, at the bottom of the final page, reconstructed the first events of the French

---

71   *Wilhelm Liebknecht Archiv*, Bundesarchiv, Berlin. L13.
72   Liebknecht's project dated back to the 1870s. See Schröder 1989.
73   Schmidt, Walter 1989, 'Karl Friedrich Köppen, Friedrich Engels und die Erklärung der historischen Funktion des Terrorismus in der Grossen Französiche Revolution', *Studien zur Geschichte*, 12: 166–87.

Revolution and celebrated the popular action. In July–August 1889 an insert mentioned the recent publication of Karl Kautsky and Wilhelm Blos's works.[74]

The articles in *Der Sozialdemokrat*, a weekly published in Zurich and then in London up till 1890 on account of the ban measures, were rather more significant. Over the course of 1889 numerous articles were dedicated to the French situation; these pieces dealt with the state of the contemporary French socialist movement, the *Boulangiste* crisis and, of course, the centenary of the Revolution. The catalogue in the 3 February 1889 issue advertised numerous books, just one of which was on the French Revolution, namely the work by Gabriel Deville translated by Bernstein. From May onward, just like in the *Berliner Volksblatt*, inserts promoted the books by Blos and Kautsky.[75] Most importantly, on 5 January 1889, the first page carried an article on the first page entitled '1889', evoking the commemoration of the centenary and the official dates chosen by the French government (17 June, 14 July, 4 August) and then attacked the 'bourgeois' Republic.[76] An 11 May 1889 article criticised the failings of 1848 and held up 1789 as a model on which Germans ought to reflect, for 'no people owes as much to the Great French Revolution, or indeed the other French revolutions, as the German people'.[77]

The same article described the first events held to mark the centenary. *Der Sozialdemokrat* regularly gave news of the commemorations in Paris. From June onward the heritage of 1789 was set in relation with the tasks incumbent on social democracy. The week of the commemoration of the storming of the Bastille, a long article was dedicated to this event:

> When the French bourgeoisie celebrates the national day on 14 July it enters into a strange contradiction. This day glorifies everything that it today condemns: the revolutionary arming of the people, fraternisation between the people and troops, and revolutionary people's justice.[78]

Various formulas emphasised how many Bastilles still remained to be destroyed: the struggles waged by the workers' movement were just as historically important as the bourgeoisie's struggles against feudalism had once been.[79]

---

74 *Berliner Volksblatt*, 14 July 1889.
75 *Sozialdemokrat*, 18 May 1889, pp. 2–3. The final page advertises several books, and the first one listed is Wilhelm Blos's work on the French Revolution.
76 '1889', *Der Sozialdemokrat*, 5 January 1889. As was most often the case in the social-democratic press of this period, the articles were unsigned.
77 '1789 und 1848', *Der Sozialdemokrat*, 11 May 1889.
78 'Sozialpolitische Rundschau', *Der Sozialdemokrat*, 11 May 1889.
79 Ibid.

Like *Der Sozialdemokrat*, the Austrian *Arbeiter-Zeitung* ['Workers' Newspaper'] carried a front page headline on 14 July. The famous Austrian party newspaper *Arbeiter-Zeitung* was born on 12 July 1889, two days before the foundation of the Second International. It adopted the title of a workers' paper from the revolution of 1848. At first it only came out twice a month, before rapidly becoming a weekly.[80] The first article in the first issue in this paper's long history was thus a piece whose title referred to the 'Great Revolution'. This unsigned article immediately established a link with the creation of the Second International, and expressed great confidence in the future of socialism, for 'the liberation of humanity is no longer but a question of a few more years'.[81] The conclusion had similar themes to those expounded in *Der Sozialdemokrat*: 'If the International Congress in Paris has the same influence for the whole proletarian movement in all lands, it will constitute a worthy introduction to the twentieth century, in the image of the Great Revolution. This is no longer a matter of storming a few Bastilles, but of making them all impossible'.[82]

However, emphasis was also placed on the differences between the two eras: indeed, the article's whole concern was to distinguish the methods of the eighteenth century,

> Today a congress of workers has the same importance for the evolution of politics and society as a street battle did a century ago ... In fact, secret societies played a certain role in the French Revolution and its extensions, just as they still do in Russia. But the capitalist revolution which has since come into effect has changed everything, including the methods of political struggle.[83]

Organisation and education had replaced the methods that revolutionaries had classically used. After all, political struggle was 'no longer a matter of plotting, of arming a few determined elements at some specific moment, but of organising and enlightening the great masses across the whole country'.[84] At the heart of this article was the critique of the old methods that had been developed during the French Revolution: 1789 had its place in history, and, indeed, had been

---

80   It would not become a daily until 1 January 1895. See Pelinka and Scheuch 1989.
81   'Der 14. Juli', *Arbeiter-Zeitung*, 12 July 1889.
82   Ibid.
83   Ibid.
84   Ibid.

decisive for humanity's fate, but the necessary means of action had changed utterly. Bebel's text here converged with the critical remarks that Eduard Bernstein had formulated in 1887, and in some measure also those Wilhelm Blos had made in his 'people's history'.

Karl Kautsky published two articles on the French Revolution in the Austrian monthly *Sozialdemokratische Monatsschrift*. These pieces have remained unknown and have rarely been referenced, probably due to the ephemeral appearance of this publication.[85] As their titles indicated, '28 April 1789' and 'On 4 August 1789' dealt with two major events in the Revolution. Both appeared on the front page.[86] Like his book *Die Klassengegensätze von 1789*, they emphasised the role of popular action during the French Revolution, and indeed made use of very similar formulas.[87] The piece devoted to 28 April sought to counter the 'bourgeois and legalistic conception' of history[88] which saw the Revolution as having begun 'from above' with the opening of the Estates General on 5 May, or with the constitution of the Third Estate as the National Assembly on 17 June. For Kautsky, the popular action had come before the parliamentary acts: 'all the great decisions came from the people and the Parliament only confirmed its acts'.[89] Reviewing the people's miserable situation on the eve of the Revolution, as well as the state's various different attempts at reform, Kautsky analysed the popular uprisings of early 1789 and in particular the 28 April revolt by the workers of the Réveillon factory, which he described in some detail. His overview of the Paris situation noted that the traders had formed the 'revolutionary mass' – and not the 'proletariat', which was not yet sufficiently developed. He focused at some length on the factors that separated the French artisan of 1789 from his counterpart in the Austria of 1889. So just like in his book, Kautsky emphasised the decisive role that the common people of Paris had played in the unfolding of the Revolution. His other article, on the events of 4 August, largely drew on the same themes.[90] It is worth noting that like Bebel, Kautsky here distanced himself from anything that might resemble a violent upheaval in 1889. He stated that 'in referring to 4 August 1789, we simply want

---

85   There is no trace of it except in 1889–90.

86   Kautsky, K., 'Der 28. April 1789', *Sozialdemokratische Monatsschrift*, 3, 31 March 1889, pp. 1–8; 'Zum 4. August 1789', *Sozialdemokratische Monatsschrift*, 7, 31 July, pp. 1–6.

87   The article was published in March 1889. Kautsky must have written it at the same time as he made fresh use of his articles for *Die Neue Zeit*, for the letter from Engels advising changes dates from February of that same year.

88   Kautsky, K., 'Der 28. April 1789', *Sozialdemokratische Monatsschrift*, 3, 31 March 1889.

89   Ibid.

90   Kautsky, K., 'Zum 4. August 1789', *Sozialdemokratische Monatsschrift*, 7, 31 July 1889, p. 1.

to prove that achieving our objectives does not necessarily demand that we aim for or stage a violent revolution'.[91]

The Workers' Almanacs (Arbeiter-Kalender)

In this era the circulation of papers like *Der Sozialdemokrat* or the *Arbeiter-Zeitung* remained rather modest, and in 1889 the propaganda machine was still relatively limited. But there already existed *Arbeiter-Kalender*, workers' almanacs that were very widely distributed.[92] These developed over the 1870s, as the party itself grew, but they made up part of the longer tradition of the *Volkskalender* and *Bauernkalender* of the eighteenth century, which aimed to spread German Enlightenment thinking among the people. Their direct ancestors were *Der arme Conrad* (organ of the then-recently united German party) from 1875, and the *Volkskalender* launched at the initiative of Wilhelm Bracke. Already in this period, tens of thousands of copies were distributed (for *Der arme Conrad*, between 41,000 and 60,000 copies between 1876 and 1878). Their content was very varied: art and literature occupied an important place, but (often brief) biographical, historical and political contributions were also to be found therein, not to forget the numerous articles on the natural sciences. Featuring an abundance of illustrations, these almanacs were aimed at a wide audience, and so their articles cannot be compared to the ones in *Die Neue Zeit* or books of several hundred pages. Nonetheless, thanks to the brief contributions included in their pages they did at least help 'smuggle across' a certain vision of history. The texts published therein were very much representative of the social-democratic vulgate, and they followed in the educational spirit of Lassallean *Bildung*. In this era some influential social-democrats, including Wilhelm Blos, wrote numerous articles in this type of publication. The popularity of great social-democratic figures like Karl Kautsky, whose name and writings were referenced ever more frequently, is evident in this type of publication. The advertisements [*Anzeige*] included therein would often highlight the works of the 'Pope of Marxism'. Forbidden after the introduction of the anti-socialist laws, the *Arbeiter-Kalender* were republished just like *Die Neue Zeit*, indeed with the same publisher. From 1883 onward the *Illustrierter Neue-Welt-Kalender*, until 1933 an SPD organ, came out each year with Dietz. As for Austria, there was in fact a remarkable continuity. We find one same title, the *Österreichischer Arbeiter-Kalender*, from 1875 to 1930. Short biographies of the great revolutionaries occupied a particularly important place, and from 1878 the *Volk-*

91   Kautsky, K., 'Zum 4. August 1789', *Sozialdemokratische Monatsschrift*, 7, 31 July 1889, p. 5.
92   Friedrich 1994.

skalender included very many portraits of this type: Karl Marx, of course, but also many citations from Danton, Marat, Mirabeau, Robespierre and others.

We can also see how deep-seated the reference to the French Revolution had become when we look, for example, at a short 1886 article highly characteristic of this organ: a brief, two-page history of calendars since ancient Greece and Rome.[93] The article ended with a republican calendar introduced by the Convention on 5 October 1793. But the importance of this point of reference was particularly telling on the centenary itself.

It does not seem that any *Arbeiter-Kalender* was published in Germany in 1889: this was, in fact, a frequent occurrence during the years of the antisocialist laws. Conversely, a copious edition came out in Austria. It contained short, unsigned biographies of the great figures of the Revolution, which – in the spirit of these almanacs – were also largely illustrated.[94] These biographies were brought together in an article entitled 'Vor hundert Jahren' ['A Hundred Years Ago']. This piece outlined the same themes as had appeared in Kautsky's book and the articles published in *Der Sozialdemokrat*, popularising their arguments in a more accessible language. This article was clear about its intention, and well-summarised the perspective of the *Arbeiter-Kalender*:

> This article is trying to write the history of the French Revolution, for a workers' calendar does not have enough space to do that. But we think that, all the same, it would interest our readers if we included the portraits – together with short biographies – of certain men who were very directly involved in the history of France, one hundred years ago.[95]

The figures it presented were Mirabeau, Desmoulins, Danton, Hébert and Robespierre. These short, descriptive biographies were not free of error (for instance, saying that Danton was sentenced to death in 1793 and not 1794), and remained very general in scope. The important thing is the text's relatively neutral sympathies toward these revolutionaries, albeit with two telling exceptions: Hébert, and Robespierre. If it recognised the importance of Robespierre – 'the history of Robespierre's life is, up to a certain point, the history of the French Revolution',[96] its sympathies clearly went with Hébert and his allies:

---

93   *Volkskalender*, 1886, pp. 19–20.
94   'Vor Hundert Jahren', *Österreichischer Arbeiter-Kalender*, 1889, pp. 51–60.
95   'Vor Hundert Jahren', *Österreichischer Arbeiter-Kalender*, 1889, p. 52.
96   'Vor Hundert Jahren', *Österreichischer Arbeiter-Kalender*, 1889, p. 60.

The Hébertist party took its name from him. This was the party of revolutionaries who recognised, together with Hébert, that if the Revolution had only changed society's political forms and not altered its social content, then its work was not yet finished. In short, the Hébertists embodied the social element of the French Revolution, insofar as this element could be developed at that time. Hébert was sent to the scaffold in spring 1794 by the petty-bourgeois fanatic Robespierre ... With this coup d'état against the Hébertists, [Robespierre] himself cut off the branch on which he had been sitting.[97]

We have already encountered repeated examples of this 'pro-Hébertism' and hostility to Robespierre, and it was also apparent in these very widely-circulated almanacs. In their pages we similarly find the idea that even though the French Revolution remained above all the fight of the bourgeoisie against the feudal nobility, already in this era the 'Fourth Estate' had emerged, and was now awaiting its liberation.[98] This reference to the 'Fourth Estate' adopted an expression of Lassalle's, whose importance we noted above. This was a good example of a discrepancy from Karl Kautsky's argument, for in his *Die Klassengegensätze von 1789* he criticised any assimilation of the proletariat to the 'Fourth Estate'; indeed, we can hypothesise that he wrote his contributions after already having read articles of this type, which attested to the continued importance of Lassallean vocabulary among the social-democrats.[99] While this probably had little effect on militants' vision of the 'Great Revolution', there certainly were differences between the articles addressed at a wide audience and 'Marxist' theoretical works which had little impact on the vulgate spread through the workers' almanacs.

Speeches and Songs

There was also mention of the French Revolution in more political speeches, in which references to history were essentially rhetorical in character. August Bebel, a popular social-democratic figure, offers two such examples of this. Firstly, in the text of a leaflet [*Flugblatt*] entitled 'A warning to the labouring classes', he began

---

97   Ibid.
98   'In the course of the Great French Revolution it was possible to see, within the liberated Third Estate, the germs of a Fourth Estate that remains enslaved, an Estate that still today awaits its both economic and political liberation'.
99   Perfahl 1982.

Workers, petit-bourgeois, peasants

In the year 1889, which has just now begun, our neighbour France cel-
ebrates the centenary of the Great Revolution, which cast off the feudal
state and its domination by lords and priests … and allowed the victory of
a class that had recently emerged, the bourgeoisie … History is a lesson for
peoples – or rather, it ought to be … The hundred years that we look upon
today, together with men all over the world, have done no less than revolu-
tionise everything … All of men's feeling and thought has changed, and
still today we cannot yet see where this revolution in minds and things
will ultimately finish.[100]

Another example came in a Reichstag speech of 20 May 1889, in response to
Chancellor Bismarck's accusation that he wanted to mount a Revolution like
in France in 1789. Bebel replied:

To generate a revolution, that is to say, a violent coup d'état, does not even
enter into our thinking … I am convinced – and I have already said – that
we will live to see the moment where wars in Europe are impossible, just
like an older style of revolution, on account of the formidable propagation of culture and the immense means of destruction. Gentlemen, today
it is no longer possible to mount revolutions with barricades and street-
fighting. (*Opposition*).[101]

Even where the inheritance of 1789 was embraced, the violence that had accompanied the Revolution was, once again, something from which the social-
democrats sought to distance themselves. While they also gave other speeches
and public talks upon the centenary, there is not always any remaining trace of
these texts. Also notable is that the liberals sometimes addressed this theme,
and the *Arbeiter-Zeitung* occasionally gave account of their interventions. For
example, on the last page of the 1 November 1889 *Arbeiter-Zeitung* we found
an advertisement for a print edition of a speech a Vienna liberal MP had given
on 1789.[102] Even if this text stood at some distance from social democracy, the
fact that the paper promoted it shows that talks on this theme were still being
given several months after July–August 1889. Social-democrats very frequently
gave talks on the most varied of themes; they 'occupied a significant place in
militants everyday lives, feeding both their understanding and their affective

---

100   Bebel 1970, Vol. 1, p. 537.
101   Bebel 1970, Vol. 1, pp. 590–591.
102   *Arbeiter-Zeitung*, 1 November 1889.

links with the workers' movement'.[103] Usually it is difficult to discern the content of these talks, but a few fragmentary notes in Eduard Bernstein's personal archive allow us to have some general idea.[104] His notes concern a talk on '14 July 1789 and 14 July 1889'. They are very partial, and we do not know what exactly the intended audience was. Nonetheless, in their general spirit they were similar to Kautsky's writings: he began from Louis XIV's absolutism,[105] before rapidly moving on to the eighteenth-century Enlightenment, the utopians (Mably, Morelly) and the reforms under Louis XVI. The rest essentially concerned the chronology of 1789, with a rapid run-through of the different social forces.

These talks were often accompanied by songs, which 'were written to serve the workers' movement and the organisations affiliated to it. These political songs' most important function was that they were symbols of identity and unity'.[106] During the period of the anti-socialist laws they could play an essential role in imparting social democracy's values; workers' song-books [*Arbeiterliederbücher*] were themselves subject to bans.[107] Between 1870 and 1914, German social democracy published some 250 pamphlets with such songs. The rewriting of tradition popular songs with words that echoed the values of the German workers' movement is highlighted by Eric Hobsbawm as a characteristic example of an 'invented tradition'.[108] Yet among all the great variety of songs that were published, circulated and sung, one was particularly famous: the *Workers' Marseillaise* [*Arbeiter-Marseillaise*], which militants often knew simply as 'the *Marseillaise*'.[109] Since the period of the Revolution the *Marseillaise* had been translated and promoted by the German Jacobins.[110] The *Arbeiter-Marseillaise*, 'the quasi-official anthem of the social-democratic movement in Imperial Germany',[111] was also 'one of the most popular songs of the international workers' movement'[112] in the pre-1914 Second International. The words of the most widespread version of the *Arbeiter-Marseillaise*, circulating from the 1870s onward, were written by Jakob Audorf. It paid particular tribute to Lassalle, sometimes earning it the nickname 'the *Lassalleaise*'. It was sung at

---

103   Pasteur 2003, p. 136.
104   Eduard Bernstein Archiv, IISG, E 87a.
105   Ibid.
106   Lidtke 1985, p. 103. See also Lidtke 1979.
107   Lidtke 1985, p. 104.
108   Hobsbawm and Ranger 2012.
109   As well as Lidtke's works, for a general approach to this question see Bouvier 1988.
110   Bouvier 1988, p. 142.
111   Bouvier 1988, p. 112.
112   Bouvier 1988, p. 137.

the end of each party congress: thus the most widespread and famous melody of the German workers' movement was the tune of the *Marseillaise*. When it became the anthem of the French Republic in 1879, in Germany this was one of the elements that contributed to shaping the social-democrats' political identity: 'when the social-democrats adopted the tune of the *Marseillaise*, they assumed control – in Germany, to be clear – of the musical symbol of the most powerful revolution in Europe'.[113] The *Internationale* did not become widely known in Germany before the beginning of the twentieth century. But given the strong presence of the *Marseillaise*, 'the link with the heritage of 1789 was continually invoked anew'.[114]

The First Historiographical Critiques

Neither Wilhelm Blos nor Karl Kautsky's arguments devoted any place to a developed criticism of the historians of the French Revolution. But in 1890, once the time for commemorating the events of 1789 had passed, a few critical contributions did appear in *Die Neue Zeit* which testified to an interest in historiography. This was the beginning of a long series of reviews of the different histories of the French Revolution, and especially those resulting from academic research. However, they often had a rather peculiar relationship with such research, for up till the First World War the social-democrats were excluded from the universities. The Arons affair of 1899–1900 demonstrated as much.[115] Born to a family of Berlin Jewish millionaires, Léo Arons qualified as a physics *Privatdozent* at Berlin University in 1889. His peers backed him to become an *Ausserordentlicher Professor*[116] in 1892, but this proposal was knocked back by the Prussian Minister of Religious and Educational Affairs. The reason for this was Arons's engagement alongside the SPD. Top officials attempted to exclude him from the university entirely, but this was not possible because, only being a *Privatdozent*, he did not count as a civil servant. However, in 1898 a law proposed by Wilhelm II personally, later known as the *Lex Arons*, put an end to the dispute by giving the Ministry authority to impose a sanction, over the heads of the university council. Since the Berlin professors rejected this procedure, Arons was sacked only in function of a law directed at him personally, in disregard for the freedom of education [*Lehrfreiheit*] that had tra-

---

113   Lidtke 1985, p. 127.
114   Bouvier 2003, p. 121.
115   Charle 1996, pp. 287–8.
116   On German university titles see Chapter Eleven, p. 275.

ditionally been supposed to ensure freedom of opinion within the university.[117]
In this context, the social-democrats' works had very little echo within German
academia.[118]

Karl Kautsky began the series of critical reviews by taking a look at a work
by Eugen Jäger,[119] an MP for the Catholic Centre who was fiercely hostile to the
Revolution. Jäger had already authored a history of the social movement and
socialism in France, and now produced a further work building on this.[120] Kautsky's judgement was unsparing: 'We will miss the time that reading this book
has cost us'.[121] There was nothing surprising about such a riposte: seeking to
go beyond just presenting Marxist contributions, the editor of *Die Neue Zeit*
also criticised the dominant historiography. Social-democratic history was to
be constructed in opposition to other, liberal and conservative histories. The
same logic was at work in an article drawing up an assessment of the centenary. The author was a certain Georgi Plekhanov, considered one of the main
founders of Russian Marxism.[122] Indeed, one of the vocations of *Die Neue Zeit*
was to publish foreign contributions on various different subjects, and a number of Marxists from across Europe found a place in its columns. Sometimes
texts were even published in German, and only much later reproduced in the
author's own language.[123] Plekhanov drew up a balance-sheet of the 'bourgeois
interpretation' of the Revolution on the occasion of the hundredth anniversary.
The article constituted a sort of summary of the application of the materialist
conception of history to the events of the Revolution, adopting the same broad
conclusions as Kautsky's book. Plekhanov clearly indicated the predominantly
bourgeois character of the Revolution, and he did so essentially on the basis of a
critique of *Centenaire de 1789, Histoire de la Révolution française* – a work by Paul
Janet, the 'official' philosopher of the centenary.[124] Janet admired the results

117   Fricke 1960.
118   Grab 1983, p. 310.
119   Kautsky, K., 'Eugen Jäger, Die französische Revolution und die soziale Bewegung, Berlin,
      1889', *Die Neue Zeit*, 1890, pp. 143–4.
120   *Die Neue Zeit*, 1890, p. 143.
121   *Die Neue Zeit*, 1890, p. 144.
122   Plekhanov, G., 'Wie die Bourgeoisie ihrer Revolution gedenkt', *Die Neue Zeit*, 1890–1, Vol. 1,
      pp. 97–102 and 135–40 (translated from the Russian by Kritchevsky). Published at the
      beginning of 1890, it must therefore have been written at the end of 1889 at the latest.
      This article appeared in Russian at the beginning of 1890 in the London edition of *Sozial-
      demokrat*.
123   We could think of the texts of the socialist Paul Lafargue – some of which his wife trans-
      lated directly – which had to be translated anew after his death in the absence of the
      original French-language texts.
124   Janet 1889.

of the 'Great Revolution', including civic equality and political freedom, even though he was hostile to the means employed by certain revolutionaries. It had, indeed, been necessary to eliminate the king, but the 'means were dreadful'. Janet managed to express his sympathy with each of the successive dominant groups, except the 'despotic' Montagnards who had led the way to a 'cruel Republic'. Plekhanov's response to this anathema against the Montagnards was to emphasise that the Terror of 1793 was nothing compared to the bloodshed among the Communards of 1871. The Russian social-democrat reconstructed both the domestic and international problems the Revolution faced, invoking circumstance as justification for the extraordinary measures that had been taken. Here he adopted formulas from Kautsky's work, emphasising that the measures of the Terror had been necessary for France's salvation. His analysis of the Montagne foregrounded its bourgeois character, while Babeuf was presented only as 'the last actor in the great tragedy'.[125] As for the infringements on property under pressure from the *sans-culottes*, Plekhanov emphasised that it would have been impossible for a still-embryonic proletariat to go any further in this era: and here again, we find the trace of Kautsky's interpretation.

Having explained the history of the French Revolution, Plekhanov interrogated its meaning in the contemporary context. He paid tribute to Sièyes's famous text *Qu'est-ce que le Tiers-Etat?*, which he presented as the manifesto most characteristic of the bourgeoisie of the 1789 Revolution.[126] Repeatedly cited, this text constituted a model that could be useful for the future revolution. Its division of society into two great camps was also to be adopted in the present, this time with the workers joining together in an autonomous party in opposition to the bourgeoisie.[127] As for the 'terrible' means that had been employed in 1793, and the possibility that they would be used again in a future revolution, Plekhanov adopted the social-democratic arguments which we have seen several times already. He insisted that 'if the proletariat has achieved a high level of development and the required economic conditions have come together, then it will not be necessary to use such terror measures'.[128]

As against Janet, Plekhanov thought it necessary to remain loyal to the spirit of the revolution, for this meant 'waging an implacable war against all that is old

---

125   Plekhanov, G., 'Wie die Bourgeoisie ihrer Revolution gedenkt', *Die Neue Zeit*, 1890–1, Vol. 1, p. 140.

126   This reference to Sièyes was rather telling, because this latter is often taken for one of the figures from which the concept 'bourgeois revolution' originates. See Heller 2006.

127   Plekhanov, G., 'Wie die Bourgeoisie ihrer Revolution gedenkt', *Die Neue Zeit*, 1890–1, Vol. 1, p. 139.

128   Plekhanov, G., 'Wie die Bourgeoisie ihrer Revolution gedenkt', *Die Neue Zeit*, 1890–1, Vol. 1, pp. 136–7.

and obsolete'.[129] But in 1890, a developed and organised proletariat had no need for terror. The article ended on the optimistic note typical of texts of this era, convinced as they were of the coming advent of socialism. The coming revolution would be 'glorious', indeed even more so than the 'great revolutions' that had gone before ... For want of a fresh revolution, the social-democrats' attention to past revolutionary history would continue until 1893, the date when they commemorated the events of 1793.

---

129   Plekhanov, G., 'Wie die Bourgeoisie ihrer Revolution gedenkt', *Die Neue Zeit*, 1890–1, Vol. 1, p. 139.

CHAPTER 2

The 'Long Centenary', 1890–5

If there have been some studies on the manner in which the social-democrats marked the centenary in 1889, much less known is their interest for the 'Great Revolution' over the years that followed. Nonetheless, it is important that we also understand the 'long centenary', which was not limited to the commemoration of the events of 1789 alone. The minutes from the Halle Congress of 1890 tell us that the motto *'Liberté, égalité, fraternité'* appeared on the rostrum.[1] It was written on the banner of social democracy, which officially adopted the name of the *Sozial-demokratische Partei Deutschlands* (SPD) at this congress. The fact that they branded themselves with such a motto represented a strong marker of the social-democrats' political identity. While in France the Revolution had been 'institutionalised' by the Third Republic,[2] in Germany even to mention 1789 – and even more so 1792–3 – was subversive. The imperial state attacked social democracy's foreign, and particularly French, reference points, and some commemorations were forbidden.

While the 1890s did not see the publication of any new book devoted to the 'Great Revolution' as such, there were numerous articles and contributions on this theme. Reading a variety of publications from articles in *Die Neue Zeit* to the *Maifestschrift* (special issues in honour of May Day),[3] shows that the French Revolution continued to spark the German and Austrian social-democrats' interest even after 1889. In the first educational structures that they created, the 'Great Revolution' was in the front rank of the great events whose history was taught.

We also ought to set the continuity of this reference point in the context of the qualitative changes taking place in these parties. As well as these initial educational structures, there was also a great expansion of their publishing apparatus. 1890 saw the foundation of the *Buchhandlung Vorwärts* publishing house, which published numerous low-cost pamphlets. This complemented the work of Dietz, which was more oriented to works of theory and history. Dailies were created across all of Germany; the most important was *Vorwärts*,

---

1 *Protokoll über die Verhandlungen des Parteitages der Sozialdemokratischen Partei Deutschlands: Halle, 12. bis 18. Oktober 1890*, Berlin, 1890, p. 11.
2 Gérard 1970, p. 71.
3 In Germany, their title varied, between different years and sites of publication (*Mai-Feier, Maizeitung* ...). In Austria they were called *Maifestschrift* across this entire period.

whose first issues came out at the beginning of 1891. In Austria, the *Wiener Volksbuchhandlung* was established in 1894, and on 1 January 1895 the *Arbeiter-Zeitung* became a daily. Powerful demonstrations and strikes between 1893 and 1895 advanced the demand for universal suffrage. This allowed a first electoral reform in 1895, ultimately leading to the election of 14 social-democratic MPs in 1897. For its part, the SPD's number of MPs rose from 35 in 1890 to 56 in 1898.

From *Die Neue Zeit* to the Party Congresses

There are numerous examples that show the variety of ways in which this historical reference point appeared in the writings of the social-democratic leaders. Here, we will note four in particular: the articles and book reviews that appeared in *Die Neue Zeit*; the link established between the history of social democracy and the Revolution in the opening address at a party congress; numerous contributions on women's history in the revolutionary period; and finally, Rosa Luxemburg's first text on the French Revolution, published in Paris in 1893.

Die Neue Zeit, *the Continuity of a Reference Point*

Friedrich Engels published an article in the *Parti ouvrier* almanac for 1892, on 'Socialism in Germany'. He had himself written this piece in French; it simultaneously appeared in German, in *Die Neue Zeit*.[4] Notable in this article was Engels's comparison of the pre-1789 absolute monarchy and present-day Russia: numerous examples served to demonstrate the social-democrats' hatred of Tsarist Russia, the 'bastion of reaction', by comparing it to France's own *ancien régime*. The Bastille often served as a hostile metaphor: one 1892 article in *Die Neue Zeit* referred to the Russian régime using the name of the Parisian prison.[5] France, conversely, was regularly mentioned in positive terms, in relation to the revolutionary inheritance of 1789–93.

Franz Mehring's book *The Lessing Legend* was a typical example of the new social-democratic history which established its importance through *Die Neue Zeit*.[6] Born in 1846 and initially hostile to social-democracy, Mehring then drew

---

4   Engels, F. 'Le socialisme en Allemagne', *Almanach du Parti Ouvrier*, 1892, pp. 3–10; 'Der Sozialismus in Deutschland', *Die Neue Zeit*, 1891–1892, Vol. 1, pp. 580–9. English text taken from *MECW*, Vol. 26, pp. 235–50.
5   Kennan, G.F., 'Die russische Bastille', *Die Neue Zeit*, 1891–1892, Vol. 1, pp. 292–8 and pp. 333–9.
6   Mehring 1893. On Mehring, see in particular Mirow 1981, p. 74, which refers to this work's role within the social-democratic historiography.

closer to it and joined the staff of *Die Neue Zeit* in 1891.[7] Originally published in Kautsky's review in instalments, his book sought to set out a materialist-inspired history of Prussia's specific development over the course of the eighteenth century and the flowering of the German Enlightenment. He wanted to understand what had prevented a revolution like France's from developing in Germany. In his time, Georges Haupt broke with orthodoxy by emphasising the uniqueness of Franz Mehring, 'whose stature, talent, theoretical competence and critical spirit were exceptional indeed for the pre-1914 era'.[8] Indeed, Mehring distinguished himself from a certain vulgate prevalent among the social-democrats; he was 'convinced that for the historian there can be no choice and no kind of compromise between the demands of the moment and historical truth. This latter must prevail over any other interests, even if they are claimed to be the interests of the party or of *raison d'état*'.[9] Mehring's book was repeatedly reissued, and had such an echo that ten years later Jean Jaurès would discuss some of its conclusions in his *Histoire socialiste de la France contemporaine*.[10]

Die Neue Zeit published critiques of books as well as substantial articles devoted to the history of socialism and revolutions. An article by Wilhelm Blos[11] took a critical note with regard to the dominant historiography in which, for example, Taine was considered the characteristic historian of the national-liberal historiography. For his part, Carl Hugo published a series of articles on socialism in France before and then during the French Revolution:[12] he made particular reference to François Boissel and his *Catéchisme du Genre humain*, whose ideas – he argued – were forerunners of the socialism and communism of the nineteenth century. It is also worth noting the two articles by Louis Héritier – better-known for his history of the 1848 revolution[13] – on the thought of Jean-Paul Marat in the years before 1789. This, too, expressed a concern to exhume little-known texts by the French revolutionaries and to present their fundamental arguments to the review's readership.[14] For his part – again in

7   Droz (ed.) 1990, pp. 390–1.
8   Haupt 1980, p. 27.
9   Ibid.
10   On the debate Jaurès, See Chapter Three, p. 86.
11   Blos, W., 'Professoren als Geschichtschreiber', *Die Neue Zeit*, 1892–3, Vol. 2, pp. 19–23.
12   Hugo, C., 'Der Sozialismus in Frankreich vor der grossen Revolution', *Die Neue Zeit*, 1892–3, Vol. 1, pp. 460–9.
13   Héritier 1897.
14   Héritier, L., 'Jean Paul Marat vor 1789: seine politischen und sozialen Ideen', *Die Neue Zeit*, 1894–5, Vol. 2, pp. 165–70, 205–11.

the pages of *Die Neue Zeit* – Karl Kautsky reviewed a work by Boris Minzes on the *biens nationaux*.[15] For the 'pope of Marxism', the confiscation of the *biens nationaux* was 'one of the most important, perhaps the most important process ... in the violent class struggle which we call the Great French Revolution'.[16] This book review provided Kautsky with a space in which he could present the various expropriations and property transfers that had taken place since the Reformation. Looking at the French Revolution more specifically, Kautsky highlighted that these changes had been made to the advantage of the bourgeoisie, for most of the peasants did not have sufficient resources to buy up this property; in support of his argument he drew on the figures from Minzes's study on the Seine-et-Oise *département*.[17] Kautsky paid tribute to the research that had gone into this work, while also underlining some of its limitations.[18] He was interested in understanding the revolutionary process as a whole: he built further on the remarks that he had made in 1889, for instance noting that 'the bourgeoisie kept the reins of the Revolution in its own hands [and it] almost entirely left out the rural proletariat'.[19] The interlude after the fall of the Girondins was characterised as the 'domination of the petty-bourgeoisie and the proletariat, contradicting the aspirations of the bourgeoisie';[20] a formula similar to those which he had employed in *Die Klassengegensätze von 1789*. Moreover, Kautsky adopted the revolutionaries' method with regard to his own contemporary political situation, and noted that 'if it were necessary to mount expropriations, the social-democrats would simply follow the example that bourgeois liberalism has already provided them'.[21] His argument concluded with an allusion to the Russian historiography, and in particular Karéiew – whose work he knew

---

15 Kautsky, K., 'Boris Minzes, Die Nationalgüterveräusserung während der französischen Revolution, Jena, 1892', *Die Neue Zeit*, 1892–3, Vol. 1, pp. 600–603. Boris Minzes was a professor at the University of Sofia and one of the first to conduct an in-depth study of the *biens nationaux*. See INRA (ed.) 1989, p. 235.

16 Kautsky, K., 'Boris Minzes, Die Nationalgüterveräusserung während der französischen Revolution, Jena, 1892', *Die Neue Zeit*, 1892–3, Vol. 1, p. 600. With all the necessary caveats that such a comparison demands, it is worth noting that one conference title described the sale of the *biens nationaux* as the most important event of the French Revolution. See Bodinier 2000.

17 One of the 83 *départements* created in 1790.

18 Kautsky, K., 'Boris Minzes, Die Nationalgüterveräusserung während der französischen Revolution, Jena, 1892', *Die Neue Zeit*, 1892–3, Vol. 1, p. 601.

19 Ibid.

20 Ibid.

21 Kautsky, K., 'Boris Minzes, Die Nationalgüterveräusserung während der französischen Revolution, Jena, 1892', *Die Neue Zeit*, 1892–3, Vol. 1, p. 600.

thanks to Engels – and emphasised that an understanding of the contemporary situation in Russia was dependent on a proper understanding of the French Revolution.

Celebrating 1793?

As we have already indicated, already in the year of the Gotha Congress (1875) Wilhelm Blos had published a collection of sources on the Republic of Mainz, with his own preface.[22] German history was repeatedly connected to France's revolutionary history. We see this when we look at the address with which Wilhelm Liebknecht opened the Frankfurt Congress of 1894:

> *Liebknecht*: Comrades! In the name of the party leadership, I declare the beginning of the party congress.
> This is not the first time that Frankfurt has played an important role in the history of social-democracy. Frankfurt, the city of the Franks and the Free, has long been a freedom-loving place, a den of freedom. Here the bourgeoisie fought ... It is here that the bourgeoisie's ideal of freedom, which had made its rise in France a hundred years earlier, was to be put into effect ... [The bourgeois-democratic movement] failed just as much as the French Revolution to create a free state community ... In the struggle for freedom, the bourgeoisie had been detached from the working class.[23]

Liebknecht then evoked the first steps that social democracy had taken in the 1860s, and its growth over the subsequent two decades. Here, the French Revolution appeared as a foundational moment, on which basis he elaborated the history of the bourgeoisie and then of the social-democratic party.

Several articles in the same spirit appeared in *Die Gleichheit*, the paper edited by Clara Zetkin and aimed at social-democratic women in Germany. These pieces celebrated the forerunners of the feminist struggles that the social-democratic movement was now waging in the present. In the second issue of 1893 a portrait of 'Madame Legros' provided an opportunity to recall the decisive role that women had played in the French Revolution.[24] An article devoted to women's role on 5 and 6 October 1789 reviewed these events and their causes

---

22   Blos 1875.

23   *Protokoll über die Verhandlungen des Parteitages der Sozialdemokratischen Partei Deutschlands, Frankfurt am Main, 21 bis 27 Oktober 1894*, Berlin, 1894, pp. 61–2.

24   'Madame Legros', *Die Gleichheit*, 1892, pp. 22–4, 159, 167. The articles were anonymous, but the author may have been Clara Zetkin herself.

in an essentially narrative style;[25] the social-democratic women's contemporary struggle continued the first movements of 1789, and the article invited them to follow the example of the heroic action of 'your sisters, from among the people of Paris'.[26] At the beginning of 1894 a long portrait of Madame Roland was published in a series of pieces.[27] *Die Gleichheit* hailed her as one of the most important women of the French Revolution, the 'typical representative of the French bourgeois woman of the eighteenth century'.[28] The Gironde and Madame Roland – who was one of its most eminent representatives – were presented as the 'bourgeois' elements *par excellence* in the Revolution, even though their struggles also made up part of women's history.

It is also worth mentioning a piece by Rosa Luxemburg on the centenary of 1793.[29] Published in Polish in 1893 in *Sprawa Robonicza*, the review of the Polish exiles in Paris (of which she would soon become editor, during her spell in the French capital), it was not, to our knowledge, published in German.[30] This rare text was very little read at the time, but deserves particular attention on account of its particular content, namely the commemoration of 1793. Born in 1871 and of Polish-Jewish origin, Rosa Luxemburg was politically active from 16 years of age. Before she came to Germany and joined the SPD in 1898, she was involved in a group of revolutionary socialists in Poland, and for this reason came under threat of expulsion. She emigrated first to Switzerland, where she continued her studies, and then in 1893 moved to Paris, soon after writing this text on the French Revolution. In this piece, she sought to commemorate the activity of the 'working people' in 1793: 'The working people in France and particularly in its capital, Paris, for the first time shook off the centuries-old yoke and undertook to try to put an end to exploitation and begin a new and free life'.[31]

---

25 'Die Pariser Frauen des 5. und 6. Oktober 1789', *Die Gleichheit*, 1893, pp. 159–60, pp. 167–8.

26 'Die Pariser Frauen des 5. und 6. Oktober 1789', *Die Gleichheit*, 1893, p. 168.

27 'Madame Roland', *Die Gleichheit*, 1894, pp. 3–5, 11–13, 19–20.

28 'Madame Roland', *Die Gleichheit*, 1894, p. 3.

29 Luxemburg, R., 'Heute und vor Hundert Jahren. Aus Anlass des 100. Jahrestages der Revolution von 1793', *Sprawa Robonicza*, Paris, no. 1, July 1893 (Archives Rosa Luxemburg, Friedrich Ebert Stiftung, original copy held at RGASPI, Moscow).

30 The text was originally in Polish. But once they were in Moscow, Rosa Luxemburg's texts may, for example, have been translated into German in the 1920s with a view to their publication. According to Felix Tych, a historian at Warsaw University and a specialist in Luxemburg's 'Polish period', both hypotheses are possibilities. I would like to thank him for the information he provided. Here, I make use of the archival numbering system.

31 Luxemburg, R., 'Heute und vor Hundert Jahren. Aus Anlass des 100. Jahrestages der Revolution von 1793', *Sprawa Robonicza*, Paris, no. 1, July 1893, p. 1.

After a summary of the events of the Revolution and a presentation of the role the popular classes had played during the Revolution – a portrayal seemingly inspired by Kautsky's *Die Klassengegensätze von 1789* – it was the conflicts between the different 'parties' after 10 August 1792 that captured her attention, and in particular the clash between the Gironde and the Paris Commune. The Montagne in power was presented as the 'people's party' [*Volkspartei*]. Luxemburg then referred to the people's rule [*Herrschaft*]. The Montagnards wanted not just 'formal' but also 'economic' equality. But they could only go a very little way along the path of social democracy;[32] the social conditions for an advance toward socialism had not yet come together. Some of the formulations resembled Kautsky's chapter on the *sans-culottes* almost word-for-word.[33] Luxemburg repeatedly emphasised the impossibility of socialism in that era, and its distance from 1893; even if the Montagnards' measures did temporarily assuage the popular aspirations, they remained 'superficial' [*oberflächlichei*]. If there were 'socialists' in this period, they were the radical groups to the left of Robespierre, the Enragés and the Hébertists;[34] Luxemburg here built on the 1889 texts in which Hébert was held up as a forerunner of socialism.

1793 in Mass-Circulation Publications

In parallel to these articles written by party members for low-circulation reviews, there was also a wider-scale reference to the French Revolution, conveyed by various different publications.

Pamphlets

Examining the contents of social-democratic propaganda in a spirit comparable to Georges Haupt's, many historians have recently drawn attention to texts that were circulated in hundreds of thousands of copies, for some rank-and-file militants constituting the first political materials they read. In his studies on 'militant practices', Paul Pasteur has worked to demonstrate the importance

---

32   Luxemburg, R., 'Heute und vor Hundert Jahren. Aus Anlass des 100. Jahrestages der Revolution von 1793', *Sprawa Robonicza*, Paris, no. 1, July 1893, p. 5.

33   'The Montagnards' brief rule was the dictatorship of the people of Paris over all of France': Luxemburg, R., 'Heute und vor Hundert Jahren. Aus Anlass des 100. Jahrestages der Revolution von 1793', *Sprawa Robonicza*, Paris, no. 1, July 1893, p. 11.

34   Luxemburg, R., 'Heute und vor Hundert Jahren. Aus Anlass des 100. Jahrestages der Revolution von 1793', *Sprawa Robonicza*, Paris, no. 1, July 1893, p. 9.

to Austrian social democracy of a 'vulgate' that was especially spread by way of the party's newspapers.[35]

The most widely-read pamphlet in party ranks in this era, Karl Kautsky and Bruno Schoenlank's commentary on the Erfurt Programme, had a print run of some 120,000 copies.[36] This text was highly characteristic of the 'Marxist' vulgate spread by the social-democratic party, and was principally renowned for its directly political aspects. There were at most indirect references to 1848, and there was nothing on the Paris Commune of 1871. The two great revolutions that it did cite were the Peasants' War in Germany and the 1789 revolution, by way of the historical details it provided on the 'uprising of the proletariat'.[37] Similarly, a reference to the 1793 Constitution appeared in a point of the programme devoted to 'direct legislation by the people:'

> The natural consequence of the representative constitution, which is to say the constitution through which the people participates in the legislative power by way of its representatives, is direct legislation by the people. This is simply the popular extension of this same measure. Already in 1793 the new French Constitution – which sadly never came into effect – provided for the people's direct legislative power. Even if this was still little-developed, thanks to the so-called veto a certain number of voters could oppose a new law, which would be subjected to popular approval (articles 53, 58, and 59 of the 1793 Constitution).[38]

These references to the 1793 Constitution were perhaps linked to the publication of Wilhelm Blos's book – as we have seen, it contained a translation of the Constitution's text in an annex. In any case, they spoke to the French Revolution's continued presence even within programmatic references. In this brief commentary on the social-democratic programme, read by hundreds of thousands of militants, the only constitutional text mentioned was a French constitution. Wilhelm Liebknecht's pamphlet on *What the Social Democrats Are and What They Want* was written in a similar vein.[39] This was a reworking of the speech he had given at the Erfurt Congress, now published in thousands

---

35   Pasteur 2003. The paper is all the more important as a source as it was long the element
      that determined party affiliation.
36   Bonnell 2002, p. 133.
37   Kautsky and Schoenlank 1897, p. 22.
38   Kautsky and Schoenlank 1897, p. 27.
39   Liebknecht 1891.

of copies as a pamphlet.[40] It made just one reference to the French Revolution, and similarly for the 1848 Revolution. Yet while Liebknecht did not refer to any direct actor in this latter revolution, he did refer to 'Lakanal's famous schooling reform almost a hundred years ago ... which was presented and accepted by the Convention soon after Louis XVI was beheaded.[41] This law asserted the principle that the state should compel parents to send their children to school, and moreover that the state was itself obliged to provide for children's bodily needs. The schooling question is thus also a social question ...'.[42] Indeed, the schooling question was very important for social democracy, within the perspective of democratising the state: and here as in the commentary on the Erfurt Programme, the model for contemporary political reform was explicitly inspired by the French revolutionary past.

Satirical and Commemorative Papers

The emergence and then the success of *Der Wahre Jacob* newspaper should be placed in the context of the considerable rise of the German satirical press in the final two decades of the nineteenth century. The social-democratic movement very quickly recognised the importance of this new means of propaganda. The German social-democrats published two satirical papers, the *Süddeutscher Postillon* and most significantly *Der Wahre Jacob*. Here we will concentrate on the latter publication.[43]

Der Wahre Jacob's first editor was Wilhelm Blos. We have already noted how important he considered illustrations, in his history of the French Revolution. A bi-monthly review, *Der Wahre Jacob*, appeared legally from 1884 onwards – albeit irregularly – in spite of the anti-socialist laws, and by 1890 it could count around 100,000 subscribers.[44] By 1914, this figure would reach 400,000, and its readership was estimated to be more than a million. In 1890 the social-democratic publisher Dietz himself became the editor. *Der Wahre Jacob* was sold for ten pfennigs a copy, the price of half a pint of beer.[45] In the period up to 1914 it was one of the most popular and widely-read papers among the German party's ranks; it sought to be, more than a satirical paper [*Witzblatt*], a genuine

---

40   40,000 copies, according to *Protokoll über die Verhandlungen des Parteitages der Sozialde-
      mokratischen Partei Deutschlands, Berlin, 14. bis 21. November 1892*, Berlin, 1892, p. 45.
41   Lakanal played a decisive role in the *Comité d'instruction publique* of 1793–4, of which he
      was one of the leading commissioners. See Julia 1989.
42   Liebknecht 1891, p. 47.
43   Gardes 1981. See also Gardes 1995.
44   Looking across various different collections, we have not been able to find any issue from
      1889.
45   Gardes 1981, p. 33.

organ of struggle [*Kampfblatt*]. The title was a reference to an expression, dating back to the Middle Ages, which meant 'getting to the heart of the problem'. As Jean-Claude Gardes notes, Russia was 'without doubt the foreign country that recurred most often in [*Der Wahre Jacob's*] caricatures and satire'.[46] As a bastion of Tsarism and reaction, Russia was logically enough foregrounded in this paper, which above all aimed at criticising social democrats' adversaries. Conversely, it showed far more goodwill toward France, which it even saw in fraternal, friendly terms.[47] It played down the negative aspects of France, which remained, above all, the land of the 'Great Revolution'. It was especially its illustrations that expressed this positive reference to revolutionary France – overall, there were few textual references.[48] *Der Wahre Jacob* imported the republican imagery whose role in France we well know. Maurice Agulhon has closely studied the evolving representation of the different Mariannes in France over the course of the nineteenth century.[49] The French workers' movement's complex relationship with the Republic can be measured by the 'Mariannophilia' or 'Mariannophobia' of its different currents.[50] Judging by *Der Wahre Jacob*, German social democracy was resolutely 'Mariannophile': in the early 1890s it offered numerous positive portrayals of Marianne. The Phrygian cap (*Jakobinermütze*) was the other symbol associated with the French Revolution with a significant presence in its pages. Following in a similar vein to Engels's arguments, one text offered this image of France, as counterposed to Russia: 'The France that allies with Russia is not, moreover, the French people; rather, it is the bourgeoisie. You may be little, French bourgeoisie, but it is just as right that we make fun of you! ... You have bound yourself to the old hereditary enemy of culture ... But that will never be enough to beat down the brave, alert people of Franks! The labouring people, stirred by a fraternal spirit, will extend a hand to the German'.[51]

We find this same type of representation in the *Glühlichter*, the Austrian equivalent of *Der Wahre Jacob*. The first page of the 26 July 1891 issue portrayed Marianne in connection with 'liberty'; numerous issues reproduced this same idea, albeit with certain differences.[52] The final page of the 8 August 1891 none-

---

46   Gardes 1981, p. 145.

47   Gardes 1981, pp. 149–50.

48   France was often represented positively in the guise of Marianne.

49   Agulhon 1989. See also François (et al.) 1998 and the catalogue of an exhibition on Marianne and Germania, Koch (ed.) 1999.

50   Agulhon 1989, pp. 295–316.

51   *Der Wahre Jacob*, 1892, p. 1664, cited by Gardes 1981, p. 324.

52   *Glühlichter*, 10 January 1891.

theless made clear which France was really in question, here: the France of the French Revolution. Two medallions showed how the country had evolved: one portrayed the French Republic with a worker, the France of 1789 (which was now a dream, a *Fantaisie*); the other, a soldier with a prison, the bourgeois France of the present day (the reality, *Wirklichkeit*).[53]

At its founding congress in Paris on 14 July 1889 the Second International decided to make 1 May a day of international demonstrations for the eight-hour day. This ritual henceforth constituted one of the 'invented traditions' of the workers' movement. This was especially true in the German-speaking countries, with the SPD at this time being the most powerful workers' party in Europe.[54] A special edition was published each May Day, devoted to the commemoration of the repression of the Chicago workers in 1886. In both Germany and Austria a *Maifestschrift* appeared from 1890 onward. These *Maifestschrift* were very high-circulation, and this paper was very widely read among social-democratic militants, indeed in numbers comparable to those for the *Arbeiter-Kalender*. Historical contributions occupied an important place in these *Maifestschrift*:[55] this often meant a comparison between the workers' May Day and other great anniversaries, in order to make it, too, an event of primary importance. If there were references to national histories – the revolution of 1848 – in the first years of May Day it was above all linked to the commemoration of 1789.

The 1891 *Maifestschrift*, dominated by the theme of the eight-hour day ('Long live the eight-hour day!'),[56] began with an article by Wilhelm Liebknecht on 'The Workers' Day in May'. It is worth citing the whole first part of this piece:

> The Bastille of feudalism had fallen on 14 July 1789. But already the bourgeoisie of the 'Third Estate' had erected a new Bastille on its ruins: the Bastille of capitalism, which established a new feudalism.
>
> Waging the struggle against the Bastille of capitalism, and organising this struggle at the international level – this would be the mission of the international workers' congress.
>
> And on 14 July 1889, as the government and the authorities of the French Republic fêted the centenary of the 'Great Revolution' with much pomp and circumstance – a revolution whose answer of 'freedom and

53   *Glühlichter*, 8 August 1891. Such a counterposition recurred frequently.
54   Hobsbawm and Ranger 2012, p. 284.
55   Seidel 1999. On Austria see Seiter 1990.
56   'Es lebe der Achtstundentag!', *Maifestschrift*, 1891, p. 1.

equality' had been transformed into a lie by the victorious bourgeoisie – the workers' delegates of all countries greeted each other in a small hall in Paris, which was not big enough to fit the crowd.[57]

The rest of the article was a profession of internationalist faith which distinguished social democracy from the other German parties: social-democratic internationalism was here conceived as the extension of the promise of 1789. As a universal, victorious revolution, 1789 was the ancestor of the workers' May Day, which sought finally to realise the demands of the end of the eighteenth century. The following year, in 1892, a large illustration bore the motto 'Liberté, Égalité, Fraternité'. As well as the *Maifestschrift* it is also worth mentioning the postcards and posters that appeared on May Day, which offered lyrical portraits of Marianne similar to those which appeared in *Der Wahre Jacob*. The 1892 *Maifestschrift* referred in the following terms to the Second International congress that had taken place on the centenary: '14 July 1889 was rightly one of the greatest if not the greatest day in world history'.[58]

Workers' Almanacs and Die Neue Welt
In 1893, upon the hundredth anniversary of the Terror, an anonymous article of several pages was published in the German workers' annual almanac. It expressed its wish to commemorate this date and then explained the international context and the reasons for the 'civil war' [*Bürgerkrieg*]. In its judgment, 'the French Revolution has become one of the most grandiose and profound events in world history, but also one of the bloodiest'.[59] The article recalled all the major events of the Revolution after 1789, continuing in the pedagogic vein of the vulgate spread through this type of organ. There was a sharply negative portrayal of *ancien régime* France, insofar as it was compared to contemporary Russia ... Very much a narrative and descriptive text, it insisted on who was really responsible for the violence, attributed to the revolutionaries' adversaries: for it was 'not the revolutionaries but the king and his courtiers who began the bloody acts of violence in 1789'.[60] After a year of 'peaceful reforms' it was, indeed, the nobility's intransigent attitude which had driven the radicalisation of the revolution. The rise of the 'republican party' was attributed to the king's errors alone. As for the Montagnards, 'they had neither the design nor still

57   Liebknecht, W., 'Das Maifest der Arbeit', *Maifestschrift*, 1891, p. 2.
58   *Maifestschrift*, 1892, p. 3.
59   '1793', *Neue-Welt Kalender*, 1893. p. 61.
60   Ibid.

less the possibility of replacing the existing mode of production with a social-ist mode of production ...'.[61] The article thus adopted Karl Kautsky's formulas, while also simplifying them.

Another example from the Austrian *Arbeiter-Kalender* shows us how the French Revolution was integrated into a wider issue we have already men-tioned above, namely the women's question. This was addressed in an article by Luise Kautsky.[62] Married to the famous social-democratic theorist, in this article she sought to demonstrate the differences between 'bourgeois' femin-ism and the SPD's own feminism. Although this article was essentially focused on the present day, she also returned at some length to the roots of the femin-ist movement across Europe and the United States. She highlighted the role of pioneer feminists, and notably that of Mary Wollstonecraft during the French Revolution.[63] Wollstonecraft had demonstrated the link between women's situ-ation and their economic situation, and thus shown the way to achieve the objectives set by the contemporary social-democratic movement.[64]

But the resonance of this reference point among the German social-democrats is most noticeable in the pages of *Die Neue Welt* ['The New World'].[65] This was the weekly Sunday supplement for twenty-nine German social-democratic dailies, and was published between 1876 and 1878 and then from 1892 to 1919. For these years (1892–3) its circulation was estimated at 112,000 copies, and before the start of World War I it reached 650,000. As its subtitle (*Illustriertes Unterhaltungsblatt für das Volk*; 'Diverting Illustrated Paper for the People') indicated, *Die Neue Welt* was very much focused on entertainment and literature. A reading of several years' worth of issues shows its particular atten-tion to history. Often the key articles were signed but sometimes they were anonymous, as were most of the various short pieces featured on the final page.

Numerous short contributions on the French Revolution appeared in *Die Neue Welt* between 1893 and 1895. It was less their – often rather summary – content that showed the importance of this reference point, as their regularity. We can cite the relevant pieces for 1893: firstly, a long series of articles, almost a set of instalments, on Louis XVI and his role during the first years of the Revolu-

---

61   Ibid.

62   Kautsky, L., 'Die bürgerliche Frauenrechtsbewegung', *Österreichischer Arbeiter-Kalender*, 1893, pp. 87–104.

63   Kautsky, L., 'Die bürgerliche Frauenrechtsbewegung', *Österreichischer Arbeiter-Kalender*, 1893, p. 98.

64   Kautsky, L., 'Die bürgerliche Frauenrechtsbewegung', *Österreichischer Arbeiter-Kalender*, 1893, p. 103.

65   Bürgel 1994.

tion. This was accompanied by a basic chronology.[66] This series of descriptive texts was written in a simple style and portrayed the errors of an ever-less popular monarch. Not long afterward it also published a poem by Robespierre,[67] an article on Marie Antoinette,[68] and a double-page spread covered by the reproduction of a 1793 painting which portrayed the 'cult of Reason', accompanied by a brief presentation of this work.[69] This latter piece of text briefly explained the motives of the Hébertist 'party', here presented as the forerunner of socialism, since 'this party also had social conceptions, which necessarily remained little-developed'.[70] After a summary of the anti-religious measures taken by the Paris Commune of 1793, it explained why it sought to replace religion with reason, rather than take a measure like the separation of Church and state.[71] Robespierre's fight against atheism drew a sharp rebuke from the author.[72]

The most developed contribution from 1893 deserves particular attention, because it was devoted to the revolutionary *fêtes*.[73] This piece reflected the tone of the other articles that appeared in the pages of *Die Neue Welt*. Far from taking any kind of theoretical approach, it instead sought to present the Revolution through the lens of its festive practices, within the context of wider themes. Linking the revolutionary history of the past to the social-democratic present, it placed the French Revolution at the origin of a long series of festive practices that the SPD was continuing in the present. The importance of workers' popular *fêtes* was considered in continuity with the *fêtes* to which the Revolution had itself given rise. 14 July 1889 was one of the expressions of this: 'the first *fête* of the freedom of the French people, which was thus consolidated by the alliance of the proletariat of all countries and sealed by the inauguration of May Day'.[74]

---

66 Our citations here follow the continuous pagination used by the IISG's bound instalments: 'Die Enthauptung Ludwig XVI.', 'Ludwig XVI. Vermählung', 'Ludwig XVI. Bei seinem Regierungsantritt', 'Ludwig XVI. Finanzminister', 'Der Geist Ludwigs XVI', 'Die Flucht Ludwig XVI', *Die Neue Welt*, 1893, pp. 31–2. 'Ludwig XVI. gegen die Konstitution', pp. 47–8. 'Die Verstörung der Bastille durch – Ludwig XVI.', p. 55. 'Die Willenschwäche Ludwigs XVI.', p. 63.
67 'Ein Gedicht Robespierres', *Die Neue Welt*, 1893, p. 95.
68 'Marie-Antoinette und die Hurrahkanaille', *Die Neue Welt*, 1893, pp. 143–4.
69 'Der Kultus der Vernunft in Paris 1793', *Die Neue Welt*, 1893, pp. 156–7 and pp. 159–60.
70 'Der Kultus der Vernunft in Paris 1793', *Die Neue Welt*, 1893, p. 160.
71 The Erfurt Programme and social-democratic propaganda both considered religion a private matter. The social-democrats did circulate numerous anti-clerical pamphlets in this era, but in practice those who took this too far were marginalised. See Kaiser 1981.
72 'Der Kultus der Vernunft in Paris 1793', *Die Neue Welt*, 1893, p. 160.
73 Pflüger, K., 'Die Festage der französischen Revolution', *Die Neue Welt*, 1893, pp. 228–31 and 236–239.
74 Pflüger, K., 'Die Festage der französischen Revolution', *Die Neue Welt*, 1893, p. 239.

Teaching and Representing the Revolution

In this era there were local educational schools around Germany, which sought to fulfil the objectives of *Bildung*, as defined by Lassalle. This educational work was not yet centralised, at this point: the schools for national-level cadres (in Germany as in Austria) only opened later, in 1906–7.

A few documents offer us some insight into their activities during the period of the centenary, and especially the activities of the Berlin educational school (*Arbeiter-Bildungsschule Berlin*).[75] Several works have studied its creation.[76] Its opening in January 1891 was accompanied by a series of public talks that attracted many hundreds of people. Thanks to the reports on these meetings in *Vorwärts*, we know the talks' content in some detail. Education schools offered both courses that resembled school education, which were gradually structured into real training schools, and public talks that were held in Party locals or even outdoors, during workers' free time.[77] In the first year of its life, on 12 January 1891 Wilhelm Blos gave a talk on 'Robespierre as a person and as a statement', and then on 4 August 1891 Wilhelm Liebknecht spoke on 'The French Revolution'. On 24 May this latter also gave a talk on 9 Thermidor; then on 14 October and 4 November 1894 another social-democrat, Albert Witz, addressed the theme 'Robespierre and Marat'.[78]

The 17 February 1891 issue of *Vorwärts* announced a fresh talk on Robespierre by Wilhelm Blos,[79] part of which was reproduced in print in its 22 February edition. The article indicated that 1,500 people had attended the talk by the Reichstag MP Blos, speaking on the same theme as a month previously. The transcription of the talk took up two columns; a brief conclusion indicated that there had been a debate including the audience. Blos explained the conditions in which Robespierre had conducted a policy of Terror, and retraced the revolutionary's biography in simple language. His talk was very critical of Robespierre, for it accused him of being a demagogue, and of having established a 'dictatorship' and broken the popular movement – in particular, the Paris Commune and the Hébertists. Here Blos picked up on the argument in his 1889 book, and advanced similar conclusions critical of the revolutionaries' political voluntarism.[80] He concluded the talk by insisting that it was necessary to study history

---

75 Detailed plans for the Berlin school are available, from 1898 onward: *Arbeiter-Bildungs-schule Berlin. Bericht über die Tätigkeit*, Berlin, 1898–1914.
76 Bagger 1983; see also Lidtke 1985, pp. 162–5.
77 Bagger 1983, p. 106.
78 According to the respective daily editions of *Vorwärts*.
79 'Maximilian Robespierre als Mensch und Staatsmann', Vorwärts, 17 February 1891, p. 8.
80 Ibid.

in order to be able to understand developments in the present – a claim that was often found in social-democratic publications.

On 12 March 1891, *Vorwärts* published an article on 'Thermidor in Berlin'.[81] Victorien Sardou's play on Thermidor had been staged in Berlin, to coincide with the international exhibition in Berlin. The social-democratic daily was indignant:

> But this is nothing ... compared to the immense shame that the old playwright Sardou has prepared for his people in the eyes of all 'good Europeans'. This shame is called Thermidor ... and in Berlin, in a theatre that bore Lessing's name above its door, the bourgeoisie applauded quite vehemently when its revolution, the only event in its family history, was sullied by a shiner of dramatic boots.[82]

Stigmatising both Robespierre as a figure and the Terror itself, Victorien Sardou's play on Thermidor sparked an important debate in France in the early 1890s.[83] Sardou was very hostile to not only Robespierre but also popular action, and adopted a vocabulary inherited from Taine ('populace', 'halfwits', 'bandits', 'rabble').[84] It is thus easy to understand why this play irritated the social-democrats, even though they themselves had little sympathy for Robespierre. The fact that they wrote their own plays showing a wholly different face of the revolutionary period was doubtless a reaction to the staging of Sardou's piece, though this was also part of a wider context: social democracy was expanding its theatrical initiatives through the Völksbühnen ['People's Theatres'], in order to make plays accessible to workers. 'The workers' movement very quickly equipped itself with a theatre at the edges of the established arts, a workers' theatre played by workers, sometimes written by anonymous authors and sometimes by intellectuals committed to social democracy, or more simply, trained in its ranks'.[85] Cultural questions gave rise to major debates in the SPD, particularly regarding the characterisation of naturalism and the position that art should occupy in politics. The social-democrats thus involved themselves in theatre, but there were also certain tensions over the policy they should adopt in this field: they intensely debated whether they should continue and extend bourgeois culture, or else try to elaborate a theatre

---

81   'Thermidor in Berlin', *Vorwärts*, 12 March 1891, p. 4.
82   Ibid.
83   Gérard 1970, p. 72.
84   Pouffary 2009, p. 93.
85   Ivernel 1987.

of a new type. Andrew Bonnell has detailed the different aspects of this debate: even if this discussion took place in the 'upper echelons' of the party, it non-etheless had concrete consequences.[86]

Historical themes were frequently present in this theatre: at the begin-ning of the new century, Büchner's famous play *The Death of Danton* was first staged by the *Freie Volksbühne*, an association close to the SPD.[87] Much less well-known are the plays that were written and performed within the dynamic opened up by the centenary of the French Revolution. These were 'epic-dramatic poems' accompanied by *tableaux vivants*,[88] pieces in which the actors remained motionless. The *tableaux* were presented for a certain period of time in order to allow the audience to contemplate the scene. A single reciter would read an accompanying text, and just one voice would read the poems. In these markedly didactic pieces, there was a clear element of commemorating the past. The *tableaux* made up part of a theatrical genre that was widespread within social-democratic ranks at the time, indeed the one which broke least from the traditional 'pompous' aesthetic vaunted by Wilhelm II.[89] What did distinguish them was their portrayal of revolutionary scenes – there was thus more a difference of content than of form.

The two pieces devoted to the French Revolution dated from 1893. This was an important year for the theatre, for this was the moment of the first staging of Gerhard Hauptmann's *The Weavers*, a play which was repeatedly banned before gaining authorisation.[90] Witz's *Images of the Great Revolution* was effectively in honour of the centenary of 1793. The episodes chosen showed that its pre-dominant themes were the popular insurrection of 10 August 1793 and even more so the events of 1793, with the two characters at the heart of the narrat-ive: Louis XVI (and his execution) and Marat. The piece resumed the tradition of paying tribute to the popular tribune:

> People, when you hear Marat, stand up straight!
> From your poverty, proudly look down at the rich! ...
> Think only of that man! You should indeed
> Hold him in high esteem. Only for you
> Did he live, search, defend himself
> And wound others. Never did he think of himself[91]

86   Bonnell 2005.
87   It was first performed in 1902. On the reception of Büchner see Ek, Sverker 1989.
88   Witz 1893; Scävola 1893, reproduced in Knilli and Münchow 1970, pp. 290–302.
89   Ivernel 1987, pp. 30–1.
90   Hauptmann 1894.
91   Witz 1893, p. 9.

For Witz the revolutionaries with whom one ought to identify after Marat's death were those whom Robespierre had sent to the guillotine, although it was not clearly indicated who they were.[92] A glorious inheritance, the French Revolution heralded the promise of the future:

> We reflect, after a hundred years, on our actions
> And faced with them, we feel so tiny, so weak and small.
> These were great times, during which the battle cry of
> The rumbling *Marseillaise* surged through every heart[93]

Scävola's second piece in 1893, *The French Revolution*, offered similar content, albeit with more marked historical explanations and a wider panorama of the French Revolution less centred on this or that figure. It is worth noting that this was a longer, more detailed poem accompanied by music (notably Rouget de l'Isle's *Marseillaise*). Scävola enjoyed a certain renown among the social-democrats in this era, and after the abrogation of the anti-socialist laws his many poems and plays were widely circulated.[94] The fall of the king and his execution, and the few stages leading up to this (the Flight to Varennes, the people at the Tuileries on 20 June 1792, and so on) played an important role in the *tableau*, which finished with 9 Thermidor. Like Witz's piece it showed no preference for any particular revolutionary, beyond portraying 9 Thermidor as the end of the revolutionary cycle.

The staging of these two *tableaux* and the authorities' reaction to them show the echo they enjoyed and, more broadly, the political aspect of the reference to 1793. On 21 January – anniversary of the execution of the king – the Berlin training school's *fête* paid tribute to the 'Great Revolution';[95] two years later a report in the social-democrat daily revealed the authorities' reaction to this commemoration of the execution of Louis XVI. *Vorwärts* even reproduced a letter that had been sent to the SPD by the police, issuing a prohibition against Scävola's *Images of the French Revolution*.[96] One month later, there was a further ban against this same *tableau*, which had been going to be performed by an association of Berlin metalworkers.[97]

---

92   Ibid.
93   Witz 1893, p. 10.
94   Klatt 1994.
95   *Vorwärts*, 20 January 1893, p. 6.
96   *Vorwärts*, 22 January 1893, p. 4.
97   'Berlin, 4 February 93. The Prefect of Police ... The performance planned for Saturday evening, the eleventh day of this current month, of the epic and dramatic play *Images of the*

There would be similar bans on individual pieces and performances throughout the pre-1914 period: the Prussian police produced a vast number of reports showing the extent to which the SPD was subject to surveillance, especially in Berlin. These police reports represent a valuable source not only for our knowledge of the variety of social-democratic activities, but also for understanding the authorities' own state of mind, in their great hostility to what they considered the party's subversive activities. In these reports we can even see the SPD's references to the French revolutionaries: we can cite, for example, an 1893 report that spoke of social-democrats 'who took particular pleasure, in these days in memory of the French Revolution, in honouring the terrorists of 1793-4 in their speeches and exhibitions ...'.[98]

Assessing the 1895 Centenary

'No social movement has ever known such attachment to its own history, or so much felt the need, even the imperative, to relate the present to the past, as has the workers' movement'.[99] Across all its tendencies, this movement for many decades continued to publish a type of history that sought to anchor contemporary socialism in a long-term perspective by way of major events or precursor figures.[100] As both a 'Great' bourgeois revolution and an event that saw the first emergence of socialist and communist ideas (Babeuf and even the *groupes populaires* of 1793), the French Revolution of 1789-99 occupied a prominent place in this overall picture.

However, the interest in the French Revolution should also be set in a wider context. 1895 saw the publication of a multi-volume history of the evolution of socialism. Published by the social-democratic publisher Dietz, it was initially intended to cover all revolutionary history; but only volumes I and III actually came out. The third volume, by Franz Mehring, concerned the history of German social democracy;[101] it was repeatedly reissued. The first volume was made up of two parts: Kautsky's *Forerunners of Modern Socialism*[102] and *From*

Great Revolution, is with this present [notice] forbidden. [Signed] the Prefect of Police, Von Richthofen': *Vorwärts*, 10 February 1893, p. 7.

98   Fricke (ed.) 1989, Vol. 2, p. 17.
99   Haupt 1980, p. 23.
100 A phenomenon that was especially propagated by the communist movement. See Wolikow and Vigreux (eds.), 2003.
101 Mehring 1897-8.
102 Kautsky 1895.

Thomas More to the Eve of the French Revolution. The following chapters were
published in this second part of the first volume:

IV. *The two first great utopians; Thomas More* by Karl Kautsky and *Thomas
Campanella* by Paul Lafargue.[103]

V. *Democratic-socialist and communist currents during the English Revolution,* by Eduard Bernstein.[104]

VI. *The Jesuit state in Paraguay,* by Paul Lafargue.[105]

According to the initial plan for this non-national or even non-European history, there was also meant to be a second volume on *The French Revolution, at
the Birth of Social-Democracy.*[106] The articles by Carl Hugo highlighted earlier in
this chapter would very likely have served as the basis for this volume. However,
the project would not materialise. The existence of the books on the French
Revolution by Karl Kautsky and Wilhelm Blos probably meant that it was unne-
cessary immediately to bring out such a volume, and in fact it would never be
published.[107]

Social-Democratic History

From the critique of the dominant historiography in *Die Neue Zeit* to the celebration of 1789 and 1793 in papers and almanacs, the German and Austrian
social-democrats promoted a specific history of the French Revolution. The
writing of this history took various forms, from Karl Kautsky's theoretical essay
seeking to overcome the absence of a Marxist history of these events, to Wilhelm Blos's 'people's' history. Nonetheless, we can indicate certain characteristics that these different publications had in common. The 'Great Revolution',
understood in light of historical materialism, was above all the bourgeoisie's
revolution, a global event and major rupture in human history – Germany's
included. At the same time, the Revolution heralded promises whose motto
Liberté, Égalité, Fraternité social democracy – organiser of the social class of the

---

103   Kautsky and Lafargue 1895.
104   Bernstein 1895.
105   Kautsky and Lafargue 1895.
106   We can also find some useful indications on this in Kautsky's correspondence with Bern-
       stein: see Schelz-Brandenburg (ed.) 2003, pp. 78–80.
107   Also worth noting in this same period is the publication of Blos's history of the German
       revolution of 1848–9 (Blos 1893) and the translation of Lissagaray's history of the Paris
       Commune (Lissagaray 1891).

future – had to bring to realisation. The multiple assertions, with the birth of the Second International, of the foundational link between 1789 and the workers' movement helped make the French Revolution a major historical reference point.

Beyond the broad terms of their analyses, these histories also foregrounded some rather more specific episodes. Like the dominant historiography of the time, the Revolution was seen much less in view of the Thermidorian Convention and the Directory than the years between 1789 and 1794. The variety between the different types of writing did not allow the definition of any precise vision. Yet there were some constants throughout this vulgate. From Liebknecht's review of Tridon's book to Rosa Luxemburg's 1893 text – and so, too, in the workers' almanacs – the Hébertist group was presented as the authentic representation of the *sans-culotte* common people; it was even sometimes seen as a first emergence of the proletariat or even of the 'Fourth Estate', a popular movement of which the social-democratic proletarians were supposedly the inheritors. Meanwhile, Robespierre was sharply criticised, for he was seen as the figure who had put an end to the popular dynamic of these years. Thermidor was rarely presented as a rupture, except, perhaps, in the case of theatrical representations of the Revolution; and even this has to be seen in the context of the social-democrats' reaction to Victorien Sardou's play.

We can also note a discrepancy between the texts published in *Die Neue Zeit* by Plekhanov and Kautsky, which explained the Terror and the context in which it took place, and the more widely-distributed texts (in newspapers and the *Arbeiter-Kalender*) which frequently criticised Robespierre, the revolutionary government – and, indeed, anything that could be associated with political violence – without similar nuance. This also meant that the social-democrats were rather reserved about Marat's calls to violence, preferring to highlight only certain aspects of his history. Indeed, apart from Hébert, Marat was the figure whom they most championed, a popular tribune that militants were enjoined to identify with. With his publication *l'Ami du peuple*, Marat had got a very early view of social antagonisms, and his connection with his newspaper moreover constituted an effective means of identification for social-democratic militants.

History and Tradition

At the heart of many historiographical works which seek to distinguish between the writing of history and the multiple references to the past carried forth by individuals and social groups is the opposition and articulation between history and memory. In a recent work, Pascal Blanchard and Nicolas Bancel revisited this distinction:

For historians, history is built on verified, objective sources, which are indispensable to constructing the 'historical fact'. For its part, memory is an – individual or collective – reconstruction of the past, which is not based on scientific methodologies. Rather, it encourages the formation of myths and legends, as part of the emotional relation with the past which individuals or groups entertain.[108]

Yet the social-democratic organisations also responded to specific logics. The typology that Georges Haupt established in a long article on the workers' movement's inheritance from the 1871 Paris Commune – a piece published on the centenary in 1971 – seems to offer a more appropriate way of understanding the different levels at which a historical phenomenon is interpreted within a political organisation. After all, we could hardly simply say that Kautsky's writings, for example, are 'history' while the inscription of this reference point within the various sources we have studied is 'memory'.[109] For Haupt, the Commune first of all constituted 'material for political and theoretical reflection'.[110] The French Revolution itself posed political problems: firstly, the use of revolutionary violence that using this period as a political model could imply (and Wilhelm Blos's book, for example, rejected this bloody tradition, even while being sympathetic to the Revolution), and secondly the contribution that the Revolution made to the social-democrats' reflection on the measures that they wanted to carry out in their own country (for example, Karl Kautsky's reference to expropriations in his review of Minske's book). Parallel to these uses of history, the Revolution of 1789–94 also corresponded to 'symbols anchored in collective mentalities'[111] and made up part of the workers' movement's 'invented traditions'. The revolutionary motto, *Liberté, Égalité, Fraternité* written on social-democratic banners; the Mariannes portrayed on numerous occasions; and the *Marseillaise* all made up part of the cultural environment that militants regularly encountered. From illustrated newspapers to public talks and plays, the 'Great Revolution' was, at least during this centenary period, at the heart of social-democratic identity.[112] Finally, Georges Haupt highlights that the Commune was an 'argument or reference point within the fight between tendencies, in the attempt to mobilise

---

108   Blanchard 2008, p. 140.
109   Haupt 1980, p. 62.
110   Ibid.
111   Ibid.
112   An exhaustive study of the German-speaking world would also demand a treatment of German Switzerland. On the centenary of 1795 in Switzerland, see Grenlich 1895.

an ideological system'.[113] However, while there were some differences of evaluation, on the eve of the 'revisionism crisis' the interpretation of the French Revolution was not truly a matter of dispute. Beyond all the various nuances, the Revolution was considered a reference point that was even less a matter of debate insofar as it was identified as a herald of both past and future struggles. From this point of view, this reference point seems to have been rather more inscribed in an already well-anchored tradition. The adjective 'Great', almost systematically associated with the noun 'Revolution', was itself testament to this.

Nonetheless, a demarcation between the different methods used in the 1789–94 period – and especially in 1793 – also exhibited a negative use of this reference point, particularly when it came to speaking of the Revolution's possible relevance in the present. 1893–4 saw the first revision of the orthodoxy defined by the Erfurt Congress. It came at the hands of Georg von Vollmar, a Bavarian social-democrat who took a very different position on the agrarian question. This was the first fulcrum of exchanges on the concrete possibilities of improving the existing order without there being any revolutionary rupture. Vollmar highlighted that the maintenance of peasants' small property units would oblige the party to revisit its unilateral vision of the socialisation of the land, and thus its doctrine of expropriating the property-owners. While Vollmar's arguments were rebuffed at the Breslau Congress in 1895,[114] he had now developed a set of arguments hostile to the most radical measures advanced by the party. Matthias Lembke has recently noted that Vollmar's critiques can be compared to the ones Edmund Burke made at the beginning of the French Revolution:

> With this evolutionist presentation of history and his rejection of the idea of *progressive violence*, Vollmar's critique recalled the one Edmund Burke had formulated in 1790 in his *Reflections on the Revolution*. This latter had criticised a French Revolution seen as unnatural and illegitimate, and thus implicitly anticipated the excesses of violence in the Jacobin Terror[115]

Such a comparison may seem anachronistic, especially given that the rejection of violence was far from limited to Vollmar alone. But the critiques which this latter had made would also now be extended on another terrain. In the

---

113   Haupt 1980, p. 62.
114   Droz 1974, pp. 40–1.
115   Lemke 2008, pp. 50–1.

mid-1890s, the revolutionary Terror, Jacobinism and, more generally, the tradition incarnated by the French Revolution, made up a set of themes which the father of revisionism, Eduard Bernstein, addressed with what was then an unprecedented critical approach. For to challenge the fundamentals of the social-democratic programme did, indeed, imply a revision of the historical reference points on which it was based.

Revising Orthodoxy, Re-exploring History

Until recently the revisionist dispute at the turn of the nineteenth and twentieth century was a subject regularly interrogated by the historiography on German social democracy.[1] The importance that this had for the history of the European Left – this being the first real challenge to the orthodoxy of a social-democratic party – explains this long-term interest. This debate also made up part of the political recomposition of the French and German Left in the period following the fall of the Berlin Wall.

The place that historical references occupied in these debates – and especially the reference to Blanquism – has often been highlighted. But except for one article published during the 1989 bicentenary,[2] to our knowledge no contribution has studied the place of the French Revolution specifically. When we set this debate within a wider context – especially by taking into account the reception of Jean Jaurès's *Socialist History* in Germany – we can measure how important the mobilisation of historical reference points was to a proper understanding of what was here in dispute.

The Weakening of a Reference Point

Before we get into the substance of this debate, it is worth recalling certain aspects of the changes that were taking place in the late 1890s. The evolution of the contents of the *Arbeiter-Kalender* was revealing, in this regard. Once the confrontation with the state during the years of the anti-socialist laws had passed, over the 1890s the *Arbeiter-Kalender* gradually lost their political and historical content in favour of contributions more oriented to leisure, technology, free time, and such like.[3] This balance was also apparent in the Sunday supplement, *Die Neue Zeit*. To take one further example, while in 1896 the *Maifestschrift* did devote a few pages to the French Revolution, this was a simple historical piece on *La Marseillaise*, without any political connotation.[4] Jean-Claude Gardes notes this same phenomenon taking place in the pages of *Der*

---

1   See in particular Jousse 2007; Traverso 2005; Lemke 2008.
2   Harald 1989.
3   Friedrich 1994, p. 235.
4   'La Marseillaise', *Maifesschrift*, 1896, pp. 5–6.

Wahre Jacob, as he highlights 'the gradual abandonment of long historical, literary or biographical treatises in favour of caricatures'.[5]

These changes did not mean that references to the 'Great Revolution' disappeared entirely. The 6 January 1902 *Vorwärts* reviewed Büchner's play on the death of Danton, which was being staged by the *Neue Freie Volksbühne*.[6] The 22 April 1902 *Der Wahre Jacob* carried a two-page centre-spread presenting Marianne, Louis XVI and ... the guillotine.[7] As part of its regular promotion of various books, in 1897 the Austrian social democrats' satirical paper *Die Glüh-lichter* regularly carried an advertisement for the translation of Victor Hugo's *Quatre-vingt-treize*.[8] The link that *Der Wahre Jacob* made between itself and the Jacobins indicated how anchored this reference point still was:

> 1900: with this date we enter into the twentieth century. All the world's Jacobins are preparing for a decisive battle: the arsenals are full ... [and] the mobilisation plan has been fixed, down to the last detail. But not all Jacobins are subscribers to *Der Wahre Jacob*, and so they are not accurately informed. In the twentieth century, that must change! We will first of all print one hundred thousand extra copies to satisfy the new subscribers flooding to us. The following hundred thousand copies can easily be provided.[9]

Yet taking the 1889 to 1914 period as a whole, the years between 1895 and 1905 undoubtedly marked a downturn in social-democratic studies of the French Revolution. If such publications had blossomed in the period of the centenary in *Die Neue Zeit*, only in the aftermath of 1905 would there again appear a specific concern for studies on the Revolution. The same is also true of book-length studies: nothing specifically concerning the French Revolution was published in this period; by way of example, Kautsky's short textbook from 1889 would not again be reprinted until 1908. This drop-off in publications also corresponded to its weakening place in party educational structures. To again take the example of the Berlin educational school, where history was taught without interruption from 1891 to 1914,[10] the detailed course plans indicate that from

---

5   Gardes 1981, p. 51.
6   'Danton', *Vorwärts*, 15 January 1902, p. 3.
7   *Der Wahre Jacob*, 22 April 1902, p. 3904.
8   *Glühlichter*, 11 November 1897. This advertisement would reappear across many issues in late 1897. In 1904 the German SPD published an edition of this same title through the *Buchhandlung Vorwärts*.
9   *Der Wahre Jacob*, 5 January 1900, p. 3.
10   *Arbeiter-Bildungsschule Berlin. Bericht über die Tätigkeit*, Berlin, 1899–1914.

1899 up to the first trimester of 1905 there was no course planned on the French Revolution.[11] Its reduced place also correlated with the predominance of another anniversary, namely the fifty-year anniversary of the 1848 revolutions in 1898. Indeed, in Austria numerous works on 1848 would appear in the years up to 1905.[12] The 18 March 1897 *Glühlichter* paid tribute to those who had died on 13 March 1848. From 1898 up till 1914 *Märzfestschriften* ['Papers in Honour of March'] were published in Austria.[13] This was an exaltation of 13 March 1848, a 'glorious day in Austria's history', and celebrated the main proclamations of the Revolution, and its dead. Of course, in the *Märzfestschriften* there was also reference to 1789, just as the actors of 1848 had situated themselves in continuity with this revolutionary past. Marianne and the motto *Liberté, Égalité, Fraternité* regularly featured in these publications. But these few references should not make us forget the essential fact, that even beyond evident national considerations, the foregrounding of 1848 and the specific questions with which it was associated made it easier to evade the problems that the 'Great Revolution' had posed. These latter problems notably included the exercise of power and the question of what means should be employed in order to remain in power. Paul Pasteur thus highlights that 'already having adopted a reformist path, the social-democrats were not committed to celebrating the Terror and actions which they judged "extreme". At the turn of the century they preferred to foreground the Revolution of 1848'.[14]

This hostility to revolutionary violence had already become clearly apparent in the years following 1889, and it would ultimately be at the heart of the revisionism debate. In this process, Engels's final texts, which Bernstein would use insupport of his argument, represented one important stage. Most significant of these was Engels's 1895 introduction to an edition of Karl Marx's writings on the revolutions of 1848–50.[15] Engels here distanced himself from the path of revolution, and outlined the possibility that contemporary social democracy would enjoy peaceful development and the triumph of socialism through elections and parliamentary action.

---

11   The last reference of this kind came in 1899. See *Arbeiter-Bildungsschule Berlin. Bericht über die Tätigkeit*, p. 3.

12   Especially Bach 1898.

13   Schroth (ed.) 1977, p. 50.

14   Pasteur 2003, p. 45.

15   Reproduced in *MECW*, Vol. 27.

80

Revisonism and History

History may at first glance seem like a rather marginal concern compared to the major points of revisionism, which related to the economic, political and philosophical postulates implied by the orthodoxy that had emerged from the Erfurt Congress. Yet it made up a far from negligible aspect of Bernstein's revision, as he mounted a critique of the historical and political traditions that had emerged from the French Revolution.

Eduard Bernstein and the 'Revisionists'

There were several reasons why Bernstein revised the doctrine that had resulted from the Erfurt Congress. He was not, as it happens, the first to mount such a revision,[16] but no one had previously theorised what already existed in practice. Bernstein emphasised the disparity between the revolutionary phraseology employed by the SPD and the reality of what it had become, as a party of reforms.[17] Eduard Bernstein noted that the workers' economic conditions were not in fact deteriorating, and moreover that the means of action had considerably changed – in this regard also invoking the late Engels's writings. He published a series of articles on these themes in *Die Neue Zeit* from 1896 onward. These texts would later be lightly edited and collected as a book, entitled *The Preconditions of Socialism*.[18] This work together with the rejoinder by Karl Kautsky (*Bernstein and the Social-Democratic Programme. A Counter-Critique*),[19] constituted the main contribution to the debate, though we also have to take other texts into account if we want to grasp the full measure of this dispute.[20]

Following his reading of Louis Héritier's book on 1848,[21] Bernstein like the late Engels did not believe that a struggle on the barricades was still possible in the social and economic conditions of Germany as it approached the turn of the twentieth century. The revisionism crisis thus put in question the historical categories to which the social-democrats referred. Logically enough,

---

16   Lemke 2008, pp. 48–53.
17   Until 1901 Bernstein remained in England, where he resided on account of proscriptions that dated back to the time of anti-socialist laws. On his time in England see Schelz-Brandenburg (ed.) 2003, p. xxxvii.
18   Bernstein 1899. For an English translation, see Bernstein 2004.
19   Kautsky 1899. On the revisionist debate, see Tudor (ed.) 1988.
20   Rosa Luxemburg's response *Reform or Revolution?* would mobilise only very few historical references (Luxemburg 1899).
21   Héritier 1897.

the Paris Commune was rejected as a negative example;[22] but the accusation went further still. Was revolution actually necessary? Should the social democrats identify with some useful revolutionary legacy? All these questions ran throughout Bernstein's work, and they implied a critical revisiting of the path France had taken since 1789.[23]

As we know, in his work Bernstein intended to revise the very foundations of the materialist conception of history.[24] For him, this theory did not allow a proper apprehension of social contradictions, and also sat at odds with the reality of society, which was more complex than the majority of the party understood. He used numerous different examples in support of his argument, and repeatedly invoked the history of the French Revolution. It was nonsensical to compare the present situation to the revolutionaries of 1789, for the contemporary proletariat was 'a mixture of extraordinarily varied elements, of social groups which are even more differentiated than was "the people" of 1789'.[25] One of the main negative models to which Bernstein referred was Blanquism, which, he asserted, had left important traces on Marx and Engels's theory.[26] He criticised Blanquism's minoritarian and secretive character, but also the violence that was implicit within it, given that its 'programme was the overthrow of the bourgeoisie by the proletariat by means of violent expropriation'.[27] In this presentation, the origins of Blanquism dated back to the French Revolution, and especially the political practices of the conspiracies. The Babouvists – whom Bernstein had studied soon before the centenary – figured particularly prominently among these latter. Bernstein thus tried to lay the foundations of a social-democratic tradition, from Proudhon to certain of Engels's arguments, that was not based on the French revolutionary model inherited from 1789.[28]

Also to be banished, should the social democracy make its way to power, was the idea of a 'dictatorship' such as Marx and Engels had sometimes invoked. For Bernstein, this had been outdated already in 1848. And 'in formulating their theory of the dictatorship of the proletariat, Marx and Engels had in mind

22   Haupt 1980, p. 71.
23   This was very much a Franco-German debate, but it also had a certain influence elsewhere: the new Austrian social-democratic programme adopted in 1901 is known to have been influenced by Bernstein's ideas.
24   Bernstein 2004, p. 20.
25   Bernstein 2004, p. 104.
26   Bernstein 2004, p. 37.
27   Ibid.
28   Ibid.

the Terror in the French Revolution as a typical example'.[29] He later noted
that a hypothetical imitation of 1793 was senseless, given that 'class dictatorship belongs to a lower civilisation'.[30] Bernstein also outlined the historical
link between liberalism and socialism, and tried to revise the idea according
to which they were irreconcilable: 'with respect to liberalism as a historical
movement, socialism is its legitimate heir, not only chronologically, but also
intellectually'.[31] Even episodes of the French Revolution usually presented in
the party *doxa* as forerunners of socialism were set in this historical continuity.
Bernstein took the example of the 1793 Constitution. He rejected the idea that it
contained elements of socialism and emphasised the aspects of this document
which consolidated private property.[32]

Those who identified with Bernstein's critique advanced similar views, albeit
sometimes on different subjects. Rarely did congress documents feature allusions to the French Revolution as such.[33] Such viewpoints critical of the revolutionary tradition were, however, expressed in the organ of the current close to
Bernstein, the *Sozialistische Monasthefte* ['Socialist Monthly'] founded in 1897
in order to compete with *Die Neue Zeit*.[34] These critical perspectives have often
been overlooked.

Among the authors featuring in the *Sozialistische Monasthefte* we can highlight the example of Therese Schlesinger. She joined the Austrian Social-
Democratic Party in 1897 and published numerous contributions on the wom-
en's question in the reviews of both the German and Austrian parties. We will
later return to these.[35] In the social-democratic women's discourse we often
come across the French revolutionary Olympe de Gouge's slogan that 'if women
have the right to go up on the scaffold, they should also have the right to take the
stand'.[36] Indeed, this slogan was constantly repeated by women's movements
in Austria. In one article for the *Sozialistische Monasthefte*, Therese Schlesinger
noted that 1789 had seen one of the first manifestations of an autonomous
women's movement. Its leading exponent was Mary Wollstonecraft, 'the brilliant forerunner of the women's movement ... She called on women to fight for
their independence, to widen their intellectual horizons, and to break with the

---

29   Bernstein 2004, p. 103.
30   Bernstein 2004, p. 146.
31   Bernstein 2004, p. 147.
32   Ibid.
33   Some of them are mentioned in Harald 1989.
34   Digital scans of the full set of this monthly are available on the website of the Friedrich
      Ebert Stiftung (www.fes.de).
35   'Therese Schlesinger' in Haupt and Maitron 1971.
36   Cited by Pasteur 1998, p. 458.

hypocritical morality of their century'.[37] Not long after this article she published a pamphlet on women in the nineteenth century, whose introduction itself included certain elaborations on the French Revolution: the women's march on Versailles in October 1789 was mentioned, as were the figures of Olympe de Gouges and Luise (sic) Lacombe.[38] Therese Schlesinger did draw from this experience the role of certain forerunners like Condorcet and Mary Wollestonecraft. But highlighting the systematic repression of the women's clubs, she was above all critical of a revolution which had allowed little place for women. She underlined that 'the Convention went so far in its hostility to women that it passed a law according to which women who met in groups of more than five would be threatened with imprisonment.[39] The publisher that issued this short essay brought out fifteen pamphlets addressing what was a general theme of the nineteenth century. The contributors to this series (Eduard Bernstein, Max Schippel, Eduard David, and Conrad Schmidt, among others), and the advertisements for the *Sozialistische Monatshefte* included in the pamphlets, clearly indicate that this was an editorial project taken at the initiative of the revisionists. It is interesting, in this context, to see such a radical critique of the French Revolution. For Therese Schlesinger, even if the Revolution saw the emergence of the first women's currents, it ultimately left them very little space for free expression.

As another example, in an article on feudal and bourgeois property Friedrich Ott criticised the *Communist Manifesto*'s sharp formulas on the French Revolution and the manner in which Karl Kautsky and Rosa Luxemburg had then adopted them.[40] Ott instead sought to relativise the historical rupture that the French Revolution had really represented, given that feudalism had begun to develop long before the rupture of 1789[41] ... Hence the aberration of what Luxemburg was demanding: it was mistaken to think that feudalism had disappeared in one night on 4 August, or indeed to deduce from this – as some did – that the same could be done with capitalism. For his part, Eduard David questioned whether 'violent overthrow' was 'the only possibility of achieving the end goal'.[42] His whole series of articles targeted the verbal 'revolutionism' of

---

37 Schlesinger-Eckstein, T., 'Bürgerliche und proletarische Frauen Bewegung', *Sozialistische Monatshefte*, 1898, p. 459.

38 Schlesinger-Eckstein 1902, pp. 5–7.

39 Schlesinger-Eckstein 1902, p. 6.

40 Ott, F., 'Feudales und bürgerliches Eigentum', *Sozialistische Monatshefte*, 1900, pp. 60–72.

41 Ott, F., 'Feudales und bürgerliches Eigentum', *Sozialistische Monatshefte*, 1900, pp. 66–7.

42 'The hope of obtaining power in this manner was rooted in the memory of the 1789 Revolution and its continuation into the early 1830s ...': David, E., 'Die Eroberung der politischen Macht', *Sozialistische Monatshefte*, 1904, pp. 9–18, 114–20, 199–207.

the social-democrats, an inheritance of the French Revolution. In David's view, this stood in contradiction with the party's concrete parliamentary activity.[43]

Exchanges and Disputes with Karl Kautsky

The most famous response to Bernstein's revisionism came from the 'Pope of Marxism', Karl Kautsky. Even before he published his *Bernstein and the Social-Democratic Programme. A Counter-Critique*, we can see from the two men's correspondence – almost day by day, over the course of several years – how the first great crisis of Marxism developed.[44] In these letters we see their divergences on historical questions. Kautsky defended past revolutionary leaders, where Bernstein only saw 'people of no value':

> It is not true that it was people of no value who managed to rise to the top during the Revolution. The likes of Cromwell, Mirabeau, Robespierre, etc. were not ideal figures, but they were certainly men of some importance – much more important than the statesmen of before the Revolution.[45]

In Bernstein's long reply on 20 February 1898, asserting that the possibilities of revolution in Germany now lay in the past, he repeatedly reduced Jacobinism to other negative terms. It was, for example, assimilated to 'dictatorship' and 'anarchy'.[46] He then went on to counterpose the development of the democratic idea with the history of Jacobinism, which essentially stood in contradiction with it:

> Jacobinism and democracy are opposites that we constantly find throughout all the modern history of socialism and popular movements, and even among individuals. I have, in fact, reflected on this subject a great deal in recent times. We can also conceive of this contradiction in terms of the 'liberal' and the 'radical'. There are liberal characteristics in all parties, just as there are radical ones.[47]

Robespierre was the figure in the Revolution whom Bernstein criticised most. He noted both his supposed opposition to democracy and his attacks on the left wing of the popular movement. In support of his argument, he invoked

---

43   Ibid.
44   Schelz-Brandenburg 2003.
45   Schelz-Brandenburg 2003, pp. 551–2 (letter from 18 February 1898).
46   Schelz-Brandenburg 2003, p. 558 (letter from 20 February 1898).
47   Schelz-Brandenburg 2003, p. 560.

Wilhelm Liebknecht's appraisal of Gustave Tridon's book: 'How Liebknecht fulminated against Robespierre, following the example of Tridon!'.[48]

In the book itself, Kautsky was essentially seeking to defend the party's political doctrine, and his response to Bernstein made only marginal reference to the history of the French Revolution. Nonetheless, he did revisit some of the elements of this history which Bernstein had addressed, and especially the 1793 Constitution. As we have seen, some of this document's articles were reproduced in the small pamphlet that popularised the Erfurt Programme. Recognising the 'principles of liberalism' that had been present in the 1793 Constitution, Kautsky explained that the Babouvists had nonetheless demanded the application of this document. This was not because it represented 'an excellent starting point for the realisation of their communist organisations'[49] but because the 1793 Constitution 'stipulated not only the recognition of private property and "laisser-faire" but also a democratic organisation of the state, which was again removed from the 1795 Constitution'.[50] As against Bernstein's claims regarding the differences between the proletariat and the 'people of 1789', Kautsky reaffirmed that while in *ancien régime* France the people had been highly fragmented, itself making a revolutionary process all the more necessary, the proletariat was gradually being united by wage labour.[51] But beyond this handful of considerations on the Revolution in response to Bernstein, Kautsky did not revisit the revolutionary tradition or the activity of the popular movements that had marked the years between 1789 and 1794. Nowhere, for example, did he contradict the rejection of revolutionary violence on which Bernstein had so repeatedly insisted.

Kautsky sought to pursue his struggle against Bernstein's ideas in a book published the following year, *Die soziale Revolution* ['The Social Revolution']. Here, he gave a more specific vision of the French revolutionary process.[52] He sought to define the coming revolution on the basis of prior models. Two fundamental aspects of the contemporary debate – the role of violence in history, and the importance of the reform/revolution divide – drove Kautsky's references to the history of the 1789 Revolution. Kautsky, in continuity with Engels,[53] did accord

48 Schelz-Brandenburg 2003, p. 563. On Wilhelm Liebknecht and Tridon, see the preamble, p. 18.
49 Kautsky 1899, p. 325.
50 Kautsky 1899, p. 324.
51 Kautsky 1899, pp. 346–7.
52 Kautsky 1902; English edition, Kautsky 1916.
53 An important section of the *Anti-Dühring*, later published separately, was devoted to the 'Role of Violence in History': see Engels 1964.

a place to violence in history. But he sought to demonstrate that a revolutionary process does not necessarily imply state violence, and that in some cases popular violence can even be at odds with the revolutionary movement:

> The constitution of the delegates of the Third Estate at the National Assembly of France, on June 17, 1789, was an eminently revolutionary act with no apparent use of force. This same France had, on the contrary, in 1774 and 1775, great insurrections for the single and in no way revolutionary purpose of changing the bread tax in order to stop the rise in the price of bread.[54]

Thus certain surges of popular emotion could have retrograde objectives, whereas a peaceful assembly could be revolutionary. In Kautsky's view, there was, indeed, going to be a future revolution. But while he did mention 1789 and recognise its historical importance, he also considered it necessary to steer clear of repeating the same methods in the present.

At the very moment that *The Social Revolution* was published, the social-democrats also had to get to grips with a new interpretation of the French Revolution, by Jean Jaurès. The reasons why this book garnered such attention owed to the status of its author and the intensity of the political conflicts which were taking place in France at the time, with important echoes throughout the International. Yet its reception was all the greater because of the lack of other social-democratic works on the French Revolution in this period.

The German Transfer of Jaurès's Arguments, and Its Importance

While several contributions have addressed Jean Jaurès's relationship with Germany,[55] no study has hitherto specifically brought into frame the reception of his writings. Yet at the beginning of the twentieth century, the publication of the *Histoire socialiste de la France contemporaine*, edited by Jean Jaurès, was an important moment in the historiography. Jaurès himself wrote the first volumes on the French Revolution.[56] For many decades, the whole 'classical' academic tradition from Albert Mathiez to Michel Vovelle has aligned itself with Jaurès's

---

54   Kautsky 1916, p. 7. Kautsky was alluding to the 1775 'Flour War', an important uprising against the liberalisation of trade and wheat prices.

55   Groh 1989. See also Guillet 2006.

56   Jaurès 1968–72. It was Albert Mathiez who later gave it the title 'Socialist History of the French Revolution', when it was republished in 1922–4.

analyses.[57] Under Jaurès's influence, in 1903 the Parliament created a 'historical commission on the French Revolution' to organise the collection of economic and social data. It would last in this form for almost a century, reflecting the enduring influence of Jaurès's work. Indeed, the impact of the *Histoire socialiste* should be understood in a long-term perspective: upon its publication this work had a rather more relative success, in both academic and socialist milieux.[58] The political context had an important role in this regard, and in particular the Guesdists' opposition to Jaurès. They looked unfavourably on this project carried forth by their main adversary. There can be no doubt as to the (sometimes-mentioned) international echo of this work: its numerous translations included Italian, Russian and (partial) Chinese editions. However, to our knowledge the *Histoire socialiste* was not translated into German in the form of a book, either in the era which we are addressing, or after the 1930s. This is all the more surprising given that part of Jaurès's work is devoted to the influence that the French Revolution had on Germany. It did have some notable historiographical echoes, for instance the attention devoted to it in the 1970s by the historian Irmgard Hartig. In a study focusing on this work in the *Annales Historiques de la Révolution française*, she reconstructed Mehring's perspective on Jaurès.[59] This publication should also be set in its particular context: for since the 1950s Mehring had become almost a national hero in the DDR; his works were considered fundamental, especially for historical scholarship.

It was, in fact, the nature of Jaurès's conceptions that led part of the SPD to refuse to introduce them into Germany.[60] This does not mean that his interpretation was totally hidden away: the discussions among German social-democrats, sparked by the publication of this work, attest to the major echo it encountered. The nature of these debates also poses the question of Franco-German transfers: what were the social-democrats reading? What did they choose to translate, and not to translate?

In this period of political rifts, we should be careful to separate the question of the German transfers of Jaurès's problematics from the question of their reception in France. The mediating role of the Second International – and thus, of the Germans – was important in these debates on the French Revolution, as for the debates on the constitution of socialist currents; after all, what was at

---

57   Vovelle and Peyrard 2002.
58   Candar 1991.
59   Hartig 1971.
60   Escudier 2004. The research presented here was inspired by reflections on what Escudier called 'the desire not to think through an utterly different theoretical choice that would explode one's own position' (p. 166).

play in these debates went far beyond a simple dispute on the interpretation of a historical period. Here, a detour via the French context is indispensable if we are to understand the conditions in which the *Histoire socialiste* was written. Whether they virulently attacked Jaurès's conceptions, discussed them or welcomed them positively, in any case the social-democrats directed particular attention to the issues that he had raised.

Jaurès, and the Writing of a New History of the French Revolution[61]

On 22 June 1899, Alexandre Millerand became Minister of Trade in Waldeck-Rousseau's government. This was the first time a socialist minister had participated in government. Despite the semblance of unity that had appeared among the French socialists earlier in 1899, this development fed their polarisation into two great tendencies. Here our concern is not to narrate in detail the debates sparked by this event. Coming at the same time as the revisionism debate in Germany, it should not, however, be totally reduced to this controversy, for the parameters of the different questions concerned were more complex than it may seem. Nonetheless, we can identify two key attitudes: one, around Jean Jaurès, which supported ministerial activity, and another around Jules Guesde which rejected a socialist minister taking a seat in cabinet alongside a hangman of the Commune like Gallifet.[62] Over in Germany, Karl Kautsky rejected Millerand's involvement in the cabinet, but did not absolutely condemn all participation in government if the situation demanded it. This position was expressed at the International's 1900 congress in what would later be characterised as the 'motion of rubber'.[63] A more radical amendment by Guesde was itself rebuffed. The tension between the socialist currents remained, and each sensibility would try to legitimise its historical activity by reference to the past. This was the context in which such a vast endeavour as the *Histoire socialiste* was published.

Following his electoral defeat, Jaurès took the initiative in producing a vast landscape of French history from the 'Great Revolution' up to the present, which he would write part of himself. There was to be a diverse range of contributors. At first Jules Guesde agreed to take part; we see as much on the first page

61   For the sake of getting a perspective based on the texts themselves, we will take the liberty of referring the reader to our edition of Jaurès and Kautsky texts on Socialism and the French Revolution: Ducange (ed.) 2010.

62   In a long letter to the social-democrat George von Vollmar, Jaures portrayed Gallifet as the main problem for a man like Vaillant who, he claimed, was in fact otherwise fundamentally in agreement with such participation. Letter from Jean Jaurès to Georg von Vollmar, IISG, Vollmar archives, 1027, 3 September 1902.

63   Lefranc 1977, p. 121.

of the first instalment, where his portrait appeared next to Jaurès's. Yet ultimately Guesde refused to contribute,[64] marking the sharp separation between
Jaurès and himself which would soon be formalised politically through the
existence in 1901–2 of two different French socialist parties, the *Parti socialiste de France* (mainly coming from Guesdism) and the *Parti socialiste français*
of which Jaurès was a particularly prominent leader. Nonetheless, this was not
the work of one man alone, for many socialists like Albert Thomas and Louis
Dubreuilh did contribute.[65]

Jaurès read German and remained marked by his 'university education ...
mastering not only classical German but also its philosophical vocation. It also
led him, like so many of his contemporaries, toward Germany ...: his generation ... took an interest not only in Kant, but in Fichte and Hegel'.[66] Guesde,
conversely, did not read German. Jaurès's complementary thesis in Latin concerned *The Origins of German Socialism* (1892), and studied the links between
socialism and German philosophy.[67] These prior approaches explained his
interest in the French Revolution's impact on Germany, to which he devoted
a considerable part of 'The Revolution in Europe', a long chapter of the *Histoire socialiste* dedicated to the influence the Revolution had on the rest of the
Continent and in England.[68] Even as he pursued this work Jaurès continued
to maintain a sizeable correspondence. His long letters to Georg von Vollmar
allow us to see the attention that he paid to sustaining his position in support
of Alexandre Millerand, and at the same time, his work on the French Revolution.[69]

Here we can certainly not hope to offer a summary of Jaures's work, which
stretches across thousands of pages – indeed, there were probably quite few
socialist militants who read it in full. But it is nonetheless necessary to highlight
its principal idea, for the sake of understanding the reactions that followed.

---

64   According to a letter from Jaurès to Bernstein he '... was prevented [from doing so] by his
      health condition, at least according to what he told me': IISG, 'France, various manuscripts
      Collection' Jaurès, 12, 19 January 1902. For the initial plan, see the general meeting that took
      place on 13 December 1898, which is known thanks to a letter from Jaurès to Fournière:
      Jaurès 2001, Vol. 7, p. 498. See our piece on this in *Annales historiques de la Révolution fran-
      çaise*, 2/2010, pp. 223–9.

65   This is an important consideration, given that since that time only the first part (Jaurès's
      section, extending up to the fall of Robespierre) has been republished.

66   Rebérioux 1977, p. 208.

67   Jaurès 1960.

68   Jaurès 1972.

69   Letter from Jean Jaurès to Georg von Vollmar, IISG, Vollmar archives, 1027, 3 September
      1902.

Looking beyond Jaurès's celebration of the Revolution's works and its main achievements – that is, within the framework of the 'bourgeois revolution' that was possible at the time – the important thing to grasp in this work is Jaurès's conception of contemporary socialism itself. Indeed, he saw it as a continuation of the republican idea that had emerged during the French Revolution, and which was then upheld by the workers' movement over the nineteenth century. Jaurès's writing was based on his own terminology, inspired by Plutarch, Michelet and Marx, and this set him at a distance from historical materialism such as the social-democrats saw it. This conception of the Revolution dated back to a much earlier point: already in 1890, at the moment when Jaurès was drawing closer to socialist beliefs, in numerous articles published in *La Dépêche* he closely linked socialism and the republican cause that had emerged from the French Revolution.[70] Already in these writings, he clearly expressed the political consequences of such an approach:

> For my part, I feel closer in my head and in my heart to a republican, however moderate, who sees the Republic as right and not just a reality, than supposed socialists who would not lay claim to the Republic or who would stand outside the great republican party. Our goal must be not to found socialist sects outside the republican majority, but rather to lead the party of the revolution boldly and explicitly to recognise itself for what it is, namely a socialist party.[71]

In the aftermath of the 1889 centenary, Jaurès was certain that any European socialist movement must necessarily draw its roots from the heritage of 1789. In support of his argument Jaurès cited the Austrian and German articles, making particular allusion to the reactions to Victorien Sardou's play:[72]

> A few months ago in Vienna, after a fiery speech the leader of the socialist democrats [sic.] read the *Declaration of the Rights of Man*, and all those in attendance avowed to remain faithful to it. In Berlin, when they wanted to perform *Thermidor*, they took care that no entry ticket was handed to any of the socialists, for their plan was to protest against the caricaturing of the French Revolution.[73]

---

70   Jaurès, J., 'Le socialisme de la Révolution française', *La Dépêche*, 22 October 1890.
71   Ibid.
72   See Chapter Two, p. 68.
73   Jaurès, J., 'Le socialisme de la Révolution française', *La Dépêche*, 22 October 1890.

The idea that the French Republic and the traditions of 1789 constituted the model *par excellence* for socialists – an idea that Jaurès very enthusiastically expressed in 1891 – was, however, far from unanimously shared. Even in France, there was a critical tradition that sought to oppose Jaurès by translating and circulating *Kautsky's Die Klassengegensätze von 1789*.

Opposing Jaurès, Publishing Kautsky

In strategic terms, many influential social-democrats – including Kautsky, but also Franz Mehring – were in effect much closer to the Guesdists than to Jaurès, and condemned the strategy of governmental participation which this latter supported. Nonetheless, relations were complex: Kautsky steered clear of adopting any overly trenchant stance, and during the Dreyfus affair he supported Jaurès's position.[74] Nonetheless, in their bid to oppose Jaurès's vision the Guesdists tried to promote Kautsky's short book *Die Klassengegensätze von 1789*. Up till that point this volume had not been introduced into France, though a first incomplete translation in *Le Socialiste du Midi* in 1894 did show the desire of this region's Guesdists to appropriate the 'Marxist' vulgate that had spread in Germany.[75] In 1901 the Guesdists' connections translated the book under the title *La lutte des classes en France en 1789*. This publication attracted attention even beyond the Guesdists' own ranks; Georges Sorel and Antonio Labriola, who could hardly be suspected of sympathy for the leading figure of German orthodoxy, held this work in high esteem.[76] This was also the moment in which Kautsky's short book began to be translated and circulated in several of the countries of central and Eastern Europe, starting with Russia. This reflected the geographical span of the German social-democrat's political and ideological influence.[77]

Guesde was himself associated with the publication of this book. As the correspondence between Kautsky and the publisher G. Jacques indicate, originally Guesde had been meant to write the preface. We find particular evidence of this in a letter in Guesde's own archives:

---

74   The first page of *La Petite République* of 24 July 1889 reproduced an extract from a letter to Jaurès in which Kautsky expressed his 'profound admiration for the incomparable fashion in which you have saved the honour of French socialism in the Dreyfus affair'.

75   *Le Socialiste du Midi*, 10 March 1894–16 June 1894.

76   See Ducange 2008.

77   Blumenberg 1960, pp. 43–4.

Dear comrade,

Citizen Jacques tells me that you will be so generous as to write a preface for the French edition of my 'Class Struggles in France'. I am very happy about this, and extend my many thanks for this great service you are doing me. To speak to the French, as a foreigner, about their great Revolution takes some temerity ...

If the French Marxists are in agreement with the Germans on this conception, then this will be of very great importance to our cause. I await your judgment on my little work with the greatest interest.

I shake your hand, and hope that I will soon be able to do so in person. *Au revoir*, dear comrade. I am at your disposal. Yours, Karl Kautsky.[78]

While this preface was not ultimately written,[79] Kautsky's thinking in this letter is clear, and points to the agreement between his and Guesde's respective conceptions of the revolution. At the same time, Guesde and those close to him were very severe in their comments on the *Histoire socialiste*. By way of example, it is worth noting a text by Lafargue and Guesde appearing in *Études socialistes*, a review published by G. Jacques, in 1903. First written in 1883, it was very critical of the legacy of the traditions of 1789. Upon its 1903 publication, it was preceded by an explicit foreword: Guesde and Lafargue's arguments 'still indicate well enough how socialism conceived and explained the events of the end of the eighteenth century twenty years ago, before its dilution into the most vulgar democracy'.[80] It ended with an explicit critique of Jaurès's *Histoire socialiste*.[81] Nonetheless, even this remained rather summary compared to the critiques that the Germans would now elaborate.

German Critiques of Jaurès

We ought to begin by noting that Jaurès's *Histoire socialiste* was never translated into German in the form of a book. For this reason, we cannot compare the *Histoire socialiste* with the French edition of Kautsky's work, even if we acknowledge that publishing a short volume of a hundred-odd pages was a rather easier endeavour – especially in this period – than publishing great

---

78   Letter from Karl Kautsky to Jules Guesde (in French), IISG, Archives Jules Guesde, 314/15,
      19 September 1900.

79   In Guesde's personal archives there is a copy of the proofs of *La lutte des classes en France
      en 1789*, subtitled 'Preface by Jules Guesde', IISG, Archives Jules Guesde, 577/2. However,
      we have found no trace of such a preface.

80   Guesde, J., Lafargue, P., 'Essai critique sur la Révolution française du xviiie siècle', *Études
      socialistes*, 2, March–April 1903, p. 65.

81   Ibid.

tomes that amounted to thousands of pages. Even so, it would have been possible for a selection from Jaurès's work to have been published, and yet even this did not happen. The only exception were the extracts that appeared in Bernstein's review *Dokumente des Sozialismus*, to which we shall return.

A reader of the social-democratic daily *Vorwärts* could, nonetheless, have got an idea of Jaures's main conceptions. Indeed, in the 12 January 1902 issue, Bernstein reviewed the first book of the *Histoire socialiste*, on the Constituent Assembly.[82] The beginning of his article, composed of long citations from the book translated into German, gave some idea of Jaurès's work with the sources. With comments from Bernstein appearing across several columns, this review was highly visible. It must have had an even greater readership given that it appeared in the Sunday edition of the daily, which was all the more popular because it was accompanied by the *Die Neue Welt* supplement. Having presented the plans for the *Histoire socialiste*, Bernstein emphasised the uniqueness of a far-reaching historical work that also described itself as socialist; he highlighted that 'the partisan character of Jaurès's work does not mean that it will not be a fully historical endeavour'.[83] Bernstein did make a few critical remarks, particularly regarding the birth of the republican idea; in this, he echoed his own past work on the Levellers.[84] But he highlighted the persuasiveness of Jaurès's demonstration, based on Barnave's view,[85] of the essentially bourgeois character of the evolution. He argued that this work was a turning point in the historiography:

> As legitimate heir of the Great French Revolution, social democracy has every reason to hold in esteem this essential movement, the creator of a new world, and to study it in depth. That is the spirit in which Jean Jaurès's work is written. From its wealth of documentation, to its profound and yet highly captivating description of the social bases of the Revolution and its political conflicts; from its unprejudiced evaluation of its actors, to its language rich in thought and expression – the works that went before can only offer a far paler impression of Jaurès's work.[86]

This very favourable review, which almost explicitly dismissed past historical studies on this same theme – and above all the one by Kautsky, who went

---

82   Bernstein, E., *Vorwärts*, 12 January 1902.
83   Ibid.
84   Bernstein 1895; English edition, Bernstein 1930.
85   Bernstein also translated and published extracts from Barnave. See p. 106.
86   Bernstein, E., *Vorwärts*, 12 January 1902.

unmentioned here – was nonetheless cautious in one regard: for no link was made with Jaurès's political activity in France.

In parallel to this, during a period in which two different socialist parties were being established in France, the SPD daily featured many reports on these parties' various congresses. For example, the *Vorwärts* of 6 March 1902 reproduced a discussion between Deville and Jaurès on the meaning of references to the French Revolution, and noted that Jaurès's conception was not shared by all members of the *Parti Socialiste Français*.[87] We could cite many such examples from *Vorwärts*, as the congress debates were reproduced over the course of several days. The essential fact, here, is that a press read in tens of thousands of copies in Germany offered an overview of the French socialists' debates on 1789.

Aside from this reproduction of French debates, which afforded a general understanding of Jaurès's vision, the socialist tribune was himself concerned to make his work known among his German comrades. A letter from Karl Kautsky conserved in his own archives,[88] as well as Jaurès's exchange with Bernstein (to which we will return), attest to the circulation of his work among the social-democratic leaders. There was no specific review of the *Histoire socialiste* in the SPD theoretical journal *Die Neue Zeit*. It is true that with a few exceptions,[89] *Die Neue Zeit* had almost never reviewed French-language works on the 1789 Revolution. Moreover, for the period between 1899 and 1905 there was but a single review of a book on the French Revolution, which was also very short and lacked any great significance.[90]

Conversely, in several of the articles appearing in *Die Neue Zeit*, Jaurès's *Histoire socialiste* was at the centre of the controversy. Germany took up most of the space in the *Histoire socialiste*'s book devoted to 'The Revolution and Europe'. For what were likely strategic reasons, Kautsky was spared criticism and his short 1889 book on the French Revolution went unmentioned; the only

---

87 'Der Kongress zu Tours, 3. März 1902', *Vorwärts*, 6 March 1902.
88 'My dear Jaurès!

     I have received your volume on the French Revolution and I very much thank you for it. I will read it with great interest. It is true that there are many questions on which we are not in agreement, and some, on which our disagreement is always growing. My regrets for that are without limit, but despite our differences I have always followed your writing with the profound esteem that one owes to a marvellous, independent mind. I salute you, my dear Jaures. Yours, Karl Kautsky'

     Letter from Karl Kautsky to Jean Jaurès (in French), IISG, Karl Kautsky archive, C 455, 19 December 1901. This is probably a copy of the letter sent to Jaurès.
89 For example (unsigned), 'Aulard, La société des Jacobins', *Die Neue Zeit*, 1898, Vol. 2, pp. 284–5.
90 Quessel, L., 'Dr. Adalbert Wahl, Studien zur Vorgeschichte der französischen Revolution', *Die Neue Zeit*, 1903, pp. 805–6.

occurrence of his name was a reference to the Erfurt Programme. However, Jaurès did not hesitate in mounting a virulent assault on certain conceptions of historical materialism which he considered too restricted, including the ones Franz Mehring had advanced in *Die Lessing-Legende*.[91] When he himself addressed Lessing and his relationship with Frederick II ['the Great'] – at the centre of Mehring's study – Jaurès repeatedly had sharp words for the German social-democrat:

> Where Mr. Mehring, with his meagrely economic and narrowly material- ist interpretation of human thought, sees only a reflection of what he calls 'German misery', I on the contrary see an admirable boldness of thought, directed at absolute freedom.[92]

Of course, the subject around which the disagreement was most manifest was the materialist conception of history, such as it was understood by part of Ger- man social-democracy. As we have seen, when Jaurès wrote his history of the French Revolution, he did not do so as a 'Marxist'; and indeed, this was what Mehring criticised him for in his long reply. This text amounted – by way of default – to the *Die Neue Zeit* 'review' of the *Histoire socialiste*, in a period in which he was part of this review's editorial board. Between 1900 and 1906 Mehring was one of its most productive contributors: he published 27 long articles, as against Kautsky's five.[93] Mehring's article 'For the King of Prus- sia' thus constituted a direct response to the passage in the *Histoire socialiste* which had taken him to task for his supposed dogmatism.[94] This was presen- ted as simply a piece in response to a specific point concerning his own book *Die Lessing Legende*. In fact, behind this apparent modesty, this text was a response to the *Histoire socialiste* with regard to method itself, namely the application of historical materialism. This long reply spread across some twelve pages, and it was almost immediately translated into French in Hubert Lagar- delle's *Le Mouvement socialiste*. This review particularly mobilised translations of German texts in opposition to what it considered Jaurès's ministerial 'oppor- tunism'.[95]

---

91 Mehring 1893.
92 Jaurès 1922–4.
93 Morel 1976, p. 10.
94 Mehring, F., 'Pour le roi de Prusse: eine Entgegnung', *Die Neue Zeit*, 1902–3, Vol. 1, pp. 517– 28. Mehring's article was almost immediately translated into French: Mehring, F., 'Jaurès historien', *Le Mouvement socialiste*, May 1901, pp. 46–62. Here we base ourselves on this translation by Léon Rémy.
95 Dachary de Flers 1982.

Considerations on method appeared throughout this text. Jaurès was not a serious figure: he 'settled for skim-reading' ... 'This is a fantasy of Jaurès's' and he criticised Jaurès's 'method for citations'. 'He reads books, scissors in hand. He cuts out what seems more or less plausible and throws the rest in the bin'. In short – and this formula caused quite a stir at the time – this was a 'chuff-chuff method'.[96] 'Indeed, for him it sufficed to run through his "sources" at the speed of a motor-car, and the scissors and the glue-pot kept providing more for the typesetting machine'. The central question at the heart of the polemic was 'why has no revolution like in France broken out in Germany?'[97] But quickly it was Jaurès's evaluation of 'Frederick II's heroic activity' for Germany that earned Mehring's revulsion – hence the ironic title, appearing in French in the original, 'Pour le roi de Prusse' ['For the King of Prussia']. His critique also made use of Jaurès's excesses, for instance where he portrayed Herder and Klopstock as supporters of Frederick II. This was all backed up by long citations:[98]

> We need demonstrate no further that Jaurès, who goes beyond even the Prussian historians in their work 'For the King of Prussia', again outdoes them when he applies himself to demolishing historical-materialist literature.[99]

Invoking the *Historische Zeitschrift*'s positive evaluation of his own work, Mehring concluded his argument in the following terms:

> Compare this critique with the insipid nonsense that Jaurès gives out over my book! It is not that I am complaining. I find this wholly as expected. As a revisionist, Jaurès takes the place due to him, as I do my own, as an 'orthodox Marxist'.[100]

This Mehring text is effectively the account that the majority of German social democracy would have given of Jaurès's book: and we should note that the debate did not revolve around the revolutionary traditions of 1789, which was the central question of Jaurès's own argument. Nonetheless, other articles from

---

96   Mehring, F., 'Jaurès historien', *Le Mouvement socialiste*, May 1901, p. 53.

97   Mehring, F., 'Jaurès historien', *Le Mouvement socialiste*, May 1901, p. 47.

98   The question of how to characterise Frederick II's endeavours recurred regularly among the social-democrats: note Karl Kautsky's comments on Eugen Jäger during the 1889 centenary in Chapter One, p. 50.

99   Mehring, F., 'Jaurès historien', *Le Mouvement socialiste*, May 1901, p. 62.

100   Ibid.

this same period did explicitly refer to the *Histoire socialiste* without subjecting it to a methodical critique. In this regard, it is worth reading the contributions by Karl Kautsky, and in particular those in which he sought to criticise Jaurès's call to integrate the 'revolutionary traditions' of 1789 into contemporary socialism. Indeed, an article by Kautsky published in *Die Neue Zeit* in early 1903 reviewed the debates in France concerning the socialist policy on religion.[101] He responded to a paper which Jaurès had published in *La Petite République* on 3 January, and explained why 'the traditions of the Revolution' were a danger to the French workers' movement.[102] While this article did not address the *Histoire socialiste* as such, the themes it addressed and the critiques that it advanced should without doubt be seen within the context of this work and its publication; indeed, one of Kautsky's allusions showed that he had read Jaurès's book and that his critique followed from his interpretation of this work. These two texts showed the two men's differences over the legacy of the Revolution for contemporary politics. Already in early 1892, Jaurès had written in *La Petite République* that 'despite their erudition and their efforts to be dialectical, Marx and Engels did not fully understand the French revolutionary tradition'.[103] Kautsky claimed that this polemic revolved around a single, badly translated line from Marx and Engels, and that as a polished Germanist Jaurès was here showing bad faith. But even beyond questions of philological rigour, the fundamental difference between Jaurès and Kautsky was real. We will pass over the immediate tactical questions posed in this debate, which related to religious congregations. For what was really at issue in this dispute was how to characterise, in the circumstances of 1903, the traditions that had resulted from the struggles of 1789. Jaurès invoked as self-evident 'the national conditions which determine the Socialist Party's immediate tactics in each country'.[104] He argued that 'the events in France show Kautsky that even when the proletariat has reached a very clear class consciousness, it can on some questions be driven to adopt the "bourgeois tactic" in order to give it greater vigour and greater impact'.[105] Jaurès championed the 'proletariat's revolutionary virtue' and accused his German counterpart of not having understood the French situation, 'standing at odds with the French revolutionary spirit [*génie*]' and

---

101   Kautsky Karl, 'Jaurès und die französische Kirchenpolitik', *Die Neue Zeit*, 1902–3, Vol. 1, pp. 504–510. For the French version, see Ducange (ed.) 2010, pp. 221–33.

102   Jaurès, J., 'Socialisme français', *La Petite République*, 3 January 1903, p. 1.

103   Jaurès, J., 'Les origines', *La Petite République*, 2 January 1902, p. 1.

104   Jaurès, J., 'Socialisme français', *La Petite République*, 3 January 1903, p. 1.

105   Ibid.

not understanding 'the revolutionary tradition of the French proletariat'.[106] In his reply, Kautsky emphasised that 'there are two types of policy for the proletariat: a dependent policy and an independent policy'.[107] Here we again find the major problem that he had posed in his work on the French Revolution in 1889, indeed in exactly the same terms,[108] building on Lassalle's idea. It is in this sense that we should understand the accusations that Kautsky levelled against Jaurès, charging him with wanting 'the enduring merger in one large organisation' of 'bourgeois democracy' and 'socialist democracy'. Again building on Lassalle, his insistence on the proletariat's 'intellectual life' echoed a concern for education and *Bildung*. The proletariat's objective had to be to achieve the intellectual development that would serve as the guarantee of its political independence; and it would access this education thanks to the social-democratic party. In these articles, Kautsky highlighted the dangers that would follow if the proletariat failed to distance itself from bourgeois traditions, before criticising Jaurès for trying 'to base Marxism ... on the Declaration of the Rights of Man from the eighteenth century. He thinks it a revolutionary act to inspire the French proletariat with the spirit of the revolutionary tradition'.[109] For Kautsky, the 1789 Declaration corresponded to a specific historical stage, characterised by bourgeois domination, while for Jaurès it found its natural extension in socialism – a view which he expressed both in the *Histoire socialiste* and at the congress of the *Parti socialiste français*. Kautsky ended his article with a biting evaluation of the *Histoire socialiste*: 'Jaurès is today full of memories of the French Revolution, whose history he has written. He assigns himself and his partisans the role that was previously played by Marat, Danton and Robespierre'.[110] The article allows us to understand the way in which Kautsky distanced himself from Jaurès's vision, which consisted of drawing the 'revolutionary virtue' of the proletariat from the 'Great Revolution'. In this period Kautsky laid claim to a strict materialist orthodoxy, and he countered any reading which saw the Revolution as a living heritage which should be appropriated for the sake of contemporary struggles. For Kautsky, the Revolution was an important stage of historical

---

106   Ibid.
107   Kautsky Karl, 'Jaurès und die französische Kirchenpolitik', reproduced in Ducange (ed.) 2010, p. 226.
108   In the 1889 book as in this 1903 text, Kautsky posed the question of the 'autonomy' [*selbstständigkeit*] or 'independence' of the proletariat from the bourgeois world. This had been a fundamental idea of the German-speaking workers' movement ever since Ferdinand Lassalle.
109   Ducange (ed.) 2010, p. 228.
110   Ducange (ed.) 2010, p. 230.

development, but socialist politics should reject any simple historical repetition. Otherwise, socialism would risk losing its uniqueness, and the political party would risk losing its independence.

Kautsky's article was no isolated case, but rather made up part of a lively political polemic against Jaurès. Indeed, we can compare this text to a series of pieces that he wrote a few months later on 'The Republic and Social Democracy', which also appeared in the pages of *Die Neue Zeit*.[111] Kautsky reviewed at some length the history of the French Republic and its relationship with socialism. Continuing in the same vein as his previous works, this series of pieces was based on a didactic narrative, illustrated with historical examples. Kautsky's argument sought to clarify the relations between the French socialists and the German social-democrats, with specific regard to this question. Kautsky noted that the 'bourgeois press' peddled the idea that Guesde and Bebel preferred the monarchy, an idea that had been picked up by 'Jaurès and his friends' ... and had even appeared in *Vorwärts*. Having reasserted that all concerned preferred the republic to the monarchy, he posed a series of questions, the last of which well summarised his perspective:

> Is social democracy's task to support the bourgeois republicans' current effort to mask class contradictions; is it its task to encourage, among the proletariat, the belief that the republican bourgeois would be better intentioned toward the workers than the monarchists? That is what is at issue.[112]

After a brief turn to the example of the United States, he emphasised that unlike in the French case, the republican 'superstition' [*Aberglaube*] in SPD ranks had dissipated. On this question he explicitly backed Guesde against a Jaurès who overestimated the virtues of the Republic.[113] At the heart of Kautsky's demonstration was the history of the profound change in the meaning of the republican reference point, from 1792 to the contemporary period. Unlike in the eighteenth century, the antagonisms between bourgeoisie and proletariat were now clear. Kautsky insisted that it was necessary to break with those traditions that stood in continuity with a certain Jacobinism. In this, he drew on arguments which could, on certain points, seem comparable to Bernstein's. But unlike this latter, he advanced this critique in order to demonstrate

111 Kautsky, K., 'Republik und Sozialdemokratie', *Die Neue Zeit*, 1904–5, Vol. 1, pp. 260–70; 300–9; 332–41; 363–71; 397–414; 436–49; 466–81.

112 Kautsky, K., 'Republik und Sozialdemokratie', *Die Neue Zeit*, 1904–5, Vol. 1, p. 263.

113 Kautsky, K., 'Republik und Sozialdemokratie', *Die Neue Zeit*, 1904–5, Vol. 1, p. 475.

the failings of a policy of integration into the republican state, which he identified with the state that had repressed the Commune.[114] The Republic could be defended only if it continued along the path of its very most democratic forms; for Kautsky 'only when the French state is reformed in the sense of the constitution of the First Republic and the Commune will it be able to become the form of Republic and the form of state for which the French proletariat has worked, struggled and spilled its blood across more than eleven decades'.[115]

The Reception of Jaurès by Bernstein and His Partisans

Given this vision of Jaurès's work and the authority which Kautsky enjoyed in the SPD at the time, it is easy to understand why there was very little prospect of the *Histoire socialiste* being translated into German. Nonetheless, in parallel to Kautsky's criticisms of Jaurès, Bernstein and his partisans did try to introduce Jaurès into Germany, following in the same vein as Bernstein's *Vorwärts* article. In fact, *Die Neue Zeit*'s critical approach was not hegemonic. Looking more closely at the various social-democratic reviews of the time, we see that Jaurès's argument was received in various different ways, corresponding to the party's own diverse sensibilities. As Mehring suggested in his aforementioned text, in what was probably an allusion to Bernstein's *Vorwärts* article, Jaurès's 'German friends represent these works as incomparable historical masterpieces'.[116] While it is often overlooked, the revisionists' publishing activity shows that some social-democrats held the *Histoire socialiste* in much greater esteem than did *Die Neue Zeit*.

As in the case of the presumed affiliation between Kautsky and the Guesdists, any attempt to identify Jaurès with the German revisionists requires some qualification. This first of all owes to the fact that Jaurès sharply distanced himself from Bernstein in his famous pamphlet *Bernstein et l'évolution de la méthode socialiste*.[117] Some today contend – not without certain solid arguments – that Jaurès was in fact fundamentally in agreement with the essentials of Bernstein's conceptions, but the strategic imperatives of the era, and first among them the concern to unify the various currents of French socialism, took priority over doctrinal questions.[118]

---

114   Kautsky, K., 'Republik und Sozialdemokratie', *Die Neue Zeit*, 1904–5, Vol. 1, p. 442.
115   Kautsky, K., 'Republik und Sozialdemokratie', *Die Neue Zeit*, 1904–5, Vol. 1, p. 481.
116   Mehring, F., 'Jaurès historien', *Le Mouvement socialiste*, May 1901, p. 46.
117   Jaurès, J., 'Bernstein et l'évolution de la méthode socialiste' (1900), reproduced in *Études socialistes* 1897–1901, Vol. 2, 1931, pp. 117–39.
118   Jousse 2009.

Some of Jaurès's articles were published in the *Sozialistische Monatshefte*.[119] Yet more significantly, to our knowledge the only collection of his articles translated into German was the work of the publisher that bore this journal's name.[120] This publisher was a rather short-lived enterprise: according to the Berlin Staatsbibliothek, it published just fifteen books between 1900 and 1902. Jaurès and Vandervelde were the only foreigners whose work was translated. The other books published by the Verlag der Sozialistischen Monatshefte were political texts defending the positions that Eduard Bernstein had elaborated on various different subjects. The Jaurès collection, published at the edges of the SPD by its revisionist wing, was prepared and translated by the Reichstag deputy Albert Südekum. He was one of the most active forces in *Kommunale Praxis*, the review dedicated to the municipal policy to be adopted in SPD-run local administrations. A partisan of local-level alliances with the 'bourgeois' parties, Südekum thus followed in the spirit of Bernstein's thinking. This collection is also worthy of our attention, for it provided a German militant audience with a series of extracts from Jaurès's works that would allow them to gain an understanding of his thought. This volume was the German translation of the *Études socialistes* that had originally been published in Charles Péguy's *Cahiers de la Quinzaine*. The subtitle that was added to the German version, 'on theory and practice', directly echoed the polemics around revisionism.[121] This collection was very well-known in France and repeatedly re-issued. It sought to expound Jaurès's method at the level of both immediate tactics – how to achieve unity among socialists – and the ultimate objective, the transition to socialism. Here Jaurès elaborated his method of 'revolutionary evolution'. Apart from a very small number of notes, references, and sub-titles added in the table of contents, this volume lacked either a critical apparatus or an introduction. The collection did not feature any extracts from the *Histoire socialiste*, but the history of the French Revolution did sometimes appear in its pages, for example in 'Republic and Socialism'. The greater part of this volume consisted of a set of political considerations that were largely illustrated by Marx, Engels and Liebknecht, and which sought to demonstrate the legitimacy of his strategy of sup-

---

119   Notably 'Die Einigung der französischen Sozialisten', and 'Auf der Warte des Brüssler Volkshauses' in 1899, and 'Republik und Sozialismus' and 'Einbildung oder Wirklichkeit?' in 1902. Jaurès published very little in *Die Neue Zeit*. It is, however, worth noting his famous dispute with Lafargue ('Die idealistische Geschichtsauffassung: Diskussion zwischen Jean Jaurès und Paul Lafargue', *Die Neue Zeit*, 1894–5, Vol. 2, pp. 545–57) and a translation of a text explaining his position in support of Millerand: Jaurès, J., 'Der Eintritt Millerands ins Ministerium', *Die Neue Zeit*, 1900–1, Vol. 2, pp. 109–15.

120   Jaurès 1902.

121   Jaurès 1901.

port for cabinet participation. But more than that, it also allowed the German reader to get an overview of Jaurès's idea of socialism as the extension of republican democracy. Basing himself on a few lines in a letter from Engels to Kautsky on the democratic republic – a text that would later be known as the 'Critique of the Erfurt Programme'[122] – Jaurès criticised those who saw the revolutionary period of 1789–94 as 'exclusively bourgeois'. In this text he closely linked his writings on the French Revolution to his political activity. The other texts translated in this collection included similar arguments on 1789 and its aftermath, and highlighted the indissoluble link that bound socialism to the works of the French Revolution; for Jaurès 'communism has roots even in revolutionary bourgeois right, in the Declaration of the Rights of Man and in the rights of life'.[123] For want of a volume with translations from the *Histoire socialiste*, these texts offered the German reader a clearer idea of Jaurès's arguments. This collection was thus a significant translation initiative, both on account of the texts it included and the channels through which it was circulated.

This was, in fact, no isolated example. The reception of the *Histoire socialiste* in *Dokumente des Sozialismus*, a review founded by Bernstein, made up part of this same initiative to introduce Jaurès's arguments to a German readership. While *Dokumente des Sozialismus* was certainly a short-lived publication, the ambitions which it expressed seem to respond to our interests in this study. Published between 1901 and 1905, it did not officially have any distinctly political character, and it was not a party review. Its subtitle gives us a sense of its priorities: these were 'Notebooks for the history, documents and bibliography of socialism'. Without doubt, the history of the workers' movement took up an important part of its pages, but the history of older revolutions was also very well-represented, continuing in the same vein as Bernstein's interest for the English Revolution. One of its aims was to publish previously unpublished texts: the most famous example was its publication of the first fragments of a text by Marx and Engels which would several decades later become known as *The German Ideology*.[124]

Dokumente des Sozialismus should be situated among the wider array of publications that Bernstein and his partisans created in order to compete with the party's official organs. The timeline of this review's existence between 1901 and 1905 in fact matches that of the publication of Jaurès's vast historical epic. Eduard Bernstein was, moreover, briefly mentioned in the *Histoire socialiste* in

---

122   Published for the first time in 1901. See *MECW*, Vol. 27, pp. 217–32.
123   Jaurès 1901, pp. 355–6.
124   Published in full for the first time in 1932. Appears in *MECW*, Vol. 5.

acknowledgement of the assistance he had given to Jaurès. The French socialist tribune had sought a rare text by a 'German communist' from the revolutionary period; taking an interest in the critiques of property among Germans during the French Revolution, Jaurès had found a reference in Forster to a 1792 book *On Man and His Condition*: 'I signalled this passage to Eduard Bernstein, who sought and found this book at the Royal Library in Berlin. He published the communist section in the third issue of his *Documents of Socialism*'.[125]

Indeed, a 1902 edition of *Dokumente des Sozialismus* published this text, which was in turn used by Jaurès in his *Histoire socialiste*.[126] We now know that this 'German communist' was Carl Wilhelm Fröhlich.[127]

In a letter conserved in Bernstein's archives, Jaurès requested a 'very great service' from his German correspondent as he 'studied the immediate effect of the French Revolution on the political and social ideas of Germany'. He proposed to Bernstein that 'if, in return, I can carry out some useful research for you in Paris, at the National Library or elsewhere, I am wholly at your disposal'.[128]

Beyond their shared interest in the history of revolutionary movements, the two men were also in agreement with regard to the conception of history itself. At the beginning of 1902 Jaurès wrote a second, twelve-page letter, again addressed to Bernstein,[129] to thank him for his review in *Vorwärts*; he also asked the German social-democrat to publish 'in the *Dokumente* or the *Monatshefte* anything from my book that might interest [their] readers', moreover declaring himself 'very grateful for [his] willingness to have it translated into German'. Explaining the work that he had done with the sources, he noted that 'the historical-materialist method is an excellent guide, so long as it is not understood in such truly infantile fashion as it is by Lafargue here and Mehring in your country'.[130] Having indicated the circumstances in which the *Histoire socialiste* had been composed (Guesde's refusal to write the preface for health reasons, and so on) he noted that the volumes devoted to the Legislative Assembly and the Convention would soon be delivered. He then repeatedly emphasised the links between democracy and socialism:

---

125   Jaurès 1972, Vol. IV, p. 274.

126   'Aus einer deutschen Kommunistischen Schrift von 1792. Der Mensch und seine Verhältnisse', *Dokumente des Sozialismus*, 1902, pp. 114–31.

127   Steiner 1961.

128   Letter from Jean Jaurès to Eduard Bernstein, IISG, Bernstein Archive, D 307, October 1901.

129   Letter from Jean Jaurès to Eduard Bernstein, IISG, 'France, various manuscripts', Jean Jaurès, no. 12, 19 January 1902. Note our piece focusing on this letter in *Annales historiques de la Révolution française*, 2/2010: 223–9.

130   Ibid.

As I have delved deeper into the history, and indeed as the events of the Revolution themselves develop, I have recognised a livelier awakening and a more precise formation of proletarian consciousness, under the effect of democracy ... I have tried to grasp the first points attaching the extreme democracy of the Revolution and socialism ... I take the liberty of telling you all this not in order to load you with my own labours (you have enough of your own) but to tell you the extent to which I am, together with you, a *democratic* socialist.[131]

I am pleased by the activity that you are conducting in Germany and I eagerly look forward to seeing you in the Reichstag.[132]

Once we are aware of this exchange, it is no longer so surprising that the *Dokumente des Sozialismus* was the only social-democratic review to devote such attention to the various volumes of Jaurès's work. Part of the third volume of the *Histoire socialiste* devoted to François-Joseph L'Ange, covering around twenty pages, was even translated into German.[133] This choice owed to a recommendation that Jaurès had himself made to Bernstein; in the letter cited above he argued that it was L'Ange 'who in Lyon in 1790, 1792 and 1795 [sic] formulated all of Fourier's doctrine with such extraordinary sharpness'.[134] Several contemporary reviews of the various volumes of the *Histoire socialiste* expressed this real interest in Jaurès. Mainly composed of book reviews, *Dokumente des Sozialismus* regularly reviewed Jaurès's publications. The *Histoire socialiste* was presented by way of three reviews, corresponding to the order in which the volumes were published: firstly the volume regarding the Constituent Assembly, and then the ones focusing on the Legislative Assembly and the Convention. All three pieces were unsigned, but we can imagine that Eduard Bernstein was their author. The first of these reviews – by far the most detailed of the three – was devoted to Jaurès's volume on the Constituent Assembly, and presented his work in positive terms. It featured a brief synopsis of Jaurès's portrayal of the bourgeoisie's conquest of power, based on a study that was attentive to France's social economic structures in 1789. The review praised the French socialist's diligent use of his sources.[135] It also consistently set Jaurès in comparison with Lassalle: 'Yet one very important point is not discussed, which offers very pre-

---

131   Underlined by Jaurès.
132   Ibid.
133   *Dokumente des Sozialismus*, 1902, pp. 158–216; 1903, pp. 316–25.
134   Letter from Jean Jaurès to Eduard Bernstein, IISG, 'France, various manuscripts', Jean Jaurès, no. 12, 19 January 1902.
135   *Dokumente des Sozialismus*, 1902, p. 196.

cious materials for a question to which Lassalle paid very particular attention in his workers' programme: namely, the question of the right to vote during the Revolution'.[136]

This was, indeed, a difference of evaluation: for Jaurès the property-based suffrage that prevailed at the beginning of the Revolution was not the expression of a class consciousness directed against the working people, for the real number of voters was in fact extended (to some four million people); Lassalle was thus wrong to range this system side-to-side with the Restoration and the July Monarchy. Indeed, given his focus on universal suffrage – a major demand of his 1863 programme – Lassalle saw the property-based suffrage of 1789 as nothing more than an instrument of bourgeois domination.[137]

Despite these differences, Bernstein emphasised that Jaurès did to some extent stand in continuity with Lassalle. This latter was an important point of reference, and by no means an inherently revisionist one: all the currents of German social democracy considered Lassalle a major figure. For example, when Mehring was planning to publish a selection of the works of Marx and Engels, he was sure also to include Lassalle.[138] It was nonetheless telling that Bernstein chose to set Jaurès in relation with Lassalle: in 1904 he would publish a major study of the ADAV founder, which he was already preparing as he wrote these lines.[139]

The author of the second review highlighted Jaurès's sympathy for the 'democrats' around Robespierre in 1791–2, as against the Girondins, and moreover emphasised the robustness of the French socialist's social and economic analysis. Nonetheless, the review also foregrounded themes that stood close to the 'revisionist' concerns expressed by Bernstein and the *Sozialistische Monatshefte*, for example the role of morality in history. This, in turn, provided a basis for closer relations with Jaurès.[140] While the article concluded with praise for the author, paying tribute to the quality of his writing style, it also emphasised that Jaurès's argument would have benefitted from being put in the most accessible possible terms, in line with the social-democratic idea of *Bildung*.[141]

---

136 *Dokumente des Sozialismus*, 1902, p. 194.
137 For Jaurès (1968–72, Vol. 1, p. 591), the property-based system was 'unstable', 'false', an 'intellectual artifice'. But he also emphasised that this was much more advanced than the monarchy, and moreover that no one – including even Robespierre and the far Left – had truly posed the question of universal suffrage at the time.
138 Engels, Lassalle and Marx 1902.
139 Bernstein 1904.
140 The *Histoire socialiste* emphasised the role of 'moral forces' and not only socio-economic considerations.
141 *Dokumente des Sozialismus*, 1902, p. 194.

The third review regarding the volume on the Convention,[142] was a very short piece, as had been the previous one concerning the Legislative Assembly. This third piece paid tribute to the new materials which the author had contributed, the parts of his study regarding the precursors of socialism (including the *Ange*; indeed, one note referred to the future publication of translated extracts on this subject, as we mentioned above),[143] and the importance of the European dimension of the Revolution. However, while the review referred to the point of polemic between Mehring and Jaurès on the Prussian question, it did not add any further insight on this debate.

One final part of this reception of Jaurès was the publication in *Dokumente des Sozialismus* of certain documents concerning the French Revolution, which are thus also of interest to our study. First among these was a long extract from Barnave's famous text from 1791–2, published posthumously in 1845.[144] Jaurès considered Barnave's text an *avant la lettre* handbook of historical materialism, and it was published in *Dokumente des Sozialismus* together with a presentation of the context in which it had been written.[145] We should also note the publication of a series of articles by the socialist Albert Thomas. He like the other authors contributing to the *Histoire socialiste* has long been overlooked. However, his role in the transfer of German revisionism's positions into France at the beginning of the twentieth century has been the focus of recent research.[146] Thomas had spent a year in Germany in 1902–3 during which he produced a study on the specificities of German trade unionism, in turn explaining his relations with the SPD.[147] It was his articles on Babeuf that were translated into German in the pages of *Dokumente des Sozialismus*.[148] The historiography of Babouvism remained limited in this period, though as we have already noted, Bernstein had been interested in this subject since the 1880s. Indeed, in his preface to Deville's book in 1887, he had highlighted Babeuf's 1789

---

142 *Dokumente des Sozialismus*, 1903, pp. 201–2.
143 *Dokumente des Sozialismus*, 1902, pp. 158–216 and 1903, pp. 316–25.
144 Barnave 1971.
145 *Dokumente des Sozialismus*, 1903, pp. 59–65. See also Bernstein, E., 'Der Marx-Cultus und das Recht der Revision, Ein Epilog', *Sozialistische Monatshefte*, p. 257. Bernstein cited Barnave in order to highlight the diverse origins of historical materialism.
146 Jousse 2007.
147 Thomas 1903.
148 Originally published in *La Revue socialiste*: Thomas, A., 'La pensée socialiste de Babeuf avant la conspiration des Egaux', *La Revue socialiste*, August 1904, pp. 226–36; November 1904, pp. 513–28; December 1904, pp. 696–712; January 1905, pp. 58–77; February 1905, pp. 179–202. Published in German in *Dokumente des Sozialismus*, 1904, pp. 505–17; 1905, pp. 422–34, 469–78, 514–32.

critique of violence. Finally, it is also worth mentioning that *Dokumente des Sozialismus* published a 24 July 1830 letter from Buonarroti to Felix Delhasse,[149] which itself bore witness to Bernstein's interest in the history of conspiracies. All these reasons help explain why *Dokumente des Sozialismus* translated texts by Albert Thomas which could offer a fresh understanding of Babeuf's pre-1789 history.

Thomas's text sought to offer a summary of Babeuf's biography, which had been little-explored in other recent works. Probably the most innovative aspect of this biography was that it explained how the communist idea had emerged in Babeuf's thinking before 1789. Thomas did this by making use of documents that had hitherto been overlooked, and in particular Babeuf's correspondence with Dubois de Fosseux as well as his *Le Cadastre Perpétuel*. He emphasised the revolutionary's pragmatism, which he termed Babeuf's 'admirable opportunism'.[150] Such formulas could be understood as the echo of Thomas's own reformism: indeed, he played the leading role in introducing Bernstein's ideas into France. A piece of Thomas's argument concerning the agrarian reform invoked Jaurès's *Histoire socialiste*, and provided the opportunity for the author to define his own positions:

> This was the most curious argument in the letter to Coupé (de l'Oise); and Jaurès, amidst the political struggle that he was himself fighting, perfectly grasped its significance. He excellently identified, in the letter to Coupé (de l'Oise), the first formulation of that opportunist tradition of French socialism, carried along in a wider democratic effort that it directs or revives, without relent, depending on the time. What is particularly important for us is to demonstrate how these profound ideas of Babeuf's connect to previous demonstrations.[151]

The French and the Germans

Thus on the eve of 1905, the *Histoire socialiste* was known only to a small section of the SPD élite, consisting of the party's French-speaking leaders and those who had read the extracts published in *Dokumente des Sozialismus*. German

149   *Dokumente des Sozialismus*, 1902, pp. 36–7.
150   Thomas, A., 'La pensée socialiste de Babeuf avant la conspiration des Egaux', *La Revue socialiste*, November 1904, pp. 515–21.
151   Thomas, A., 'La pensée socialiste de Babeuf avant la conspiration des Egaux', *La Revue socialiste*, December 1904, p. 707.

translations of the French socialists' writings on the Revolution remained limited. We have already noted the translation of Gabriel Deville's work on Babeuf, which though not reissued did continue to be recommended in party education programmes up till 1914. Thus in Germany it was easier to read the works of Gabriel Deville than the works of Jean Jaurès … Deville was, indeed, the writer of the section of the *Histoire socialiste* on the Directory; but given the oblivion into which he has fallen in France since then, this was rather a historical irony.

The most widely-circulated history was still that inspired by 'Marxism', in the sense that some sought to give this term as they built on Engels's efforts to codify a doctrine. This historiography continued in the same vein as the works of the 1880s–90s (*Die Klassengegensätze von 1789, Die Lessing-Legende*) and constructed itself in reaction against Jaurès's vision, in a context where the alliance policy advocated by the 'ministerialists' seemed like an abjuration of the history of socialism. What continued to be circulated and read – at a far from negligible scale – was a certain vulgate of the French Revolution that had emerged from the centenary. However, both Kautsky's distrust for 'revolutionary traditions' and Bernstein's critique, for quite different reasons, of the legacy of 1789 did in a certain sense cross paths. The writings of each figure reflected a weakening of references to the French Revolution, as compared to the centenary period – a decline that was visible at every level.

The Marxists in the SPD – or those who identified as such – were attached to a party that was socially independent of the bourgeoisie, and they saw the arguments that Jaurès advanced in the *Histoire socialiste* as a backward step. Jaurès's effort to delve into the archives and his attention to the *groupe populaires* do not seem to have had an effect on most of their number. In a tense political context, what they most took from Jaurès's work was the idea of a republican socialism. This was incomprehensible for German social-democrats who not only questioned Jaurès's challenge to the fundamentals of historical materialism, but also saw that the Third Republic was far from socially advanced. Of course, each country had its own very different context, and there was obviously a certain lack of understanding of the French situation. It is notable that despite its great openness to the international arena *Die Neue Zeit* remained 'a fundamentally German review, which reflected the preoccupations of the SPD'.[152] And we could also contrast the situation of figures like Karl Kautsky and other German militants who had been subject to state repression just fifteen years previously, with that of a republican like Jaurès who had gradually passed over to socialism and had never suffered the established régime in a sim-

---

152   Schumacher 2001, p. 65.

ilar way. The refusal 'to think through an utterly different theoretical choice'[153] –
the choice of a Marxism that did not conform to orthodoxy – probably contributed to the lack of any real circulation of the *Histoire socialiste* in Germany,
even if we look beyond the material problems that the translation of such a
work could have posed.

Was this the consequence of the social-democrats' integration into their
own national framework? Was it a misunderstanding, linked to the great difference between these two countries' cultural and historic situations? Michel
Espagne notes that 'the relationship between Jaurès's thesis on *The Origins of
German Socialism* and his *Histoire* (*sic!*) *de la Révolution française* demonstrates
the attempt to apply imported interpretative schemas to one's own national
history'.[154] But this was a partial 'import', for Jaurès – inspired by Marx – never
stuck to the principles of German orthodoxy. Rather, his conception of socialism and the reading of history that flowed from this were in part the result
of his engagement with the historical materialism advanced by the Germans,
as embodied by Kautsky and Mehring. Madeleine Rebérioux has argued that
Jaurès's 'language and philosophy made him incomprehensible to the Marxists
of his time, of whatever tendency. He was neither orthodox, nor revisionist, nor
radical, but unclassifiable'.[155] She highlights that in his reaction to the debate
with the Germans, Jaurès had 'strengthened the "French" element of his socialism'.[156]

For the Germans, the engagement with Jaurès had allowed a wider discussion around the nature of the French Revolution and the manner in which
its inheritance could be appropriated for the present. Rightly or wrongly, the
social-democrats thus looked critically on Jaurès's endeavours; indeed, theirs
was not just a purely 'German' reading, for the socialists in France who were in
dispute with Jaurès also made use of a similar interpretation. However, Jaurès's
approach did encounter a favourable reception in Germany among the partisans of Eduard Bernstein. This latter's record as a historian, after his long studies
of the English Revolution, certainly played a role, in this regard. Reading the
reviews of the *Histoire socialiste* in *Vorwärts* and *Dokumente des Sozialismus*,
we are struck by the fact that only the revisionists recognised the originality of its method and the quality of the research that underpinned it. *Dokumente des Sozialismus*'s publication policy moreover demonstrated an obvious
interest in the history of the French Revolution and its historiography (Barnave,

---

153   Escudier 2004, p. 166.
154   Espagne 1999, p. 226.
155   Rebérioux 1977, p. 237.
156   Rebérioux 1977, p. 238.

Albert Thomas) – indeed, the greatest such interest since the centenary years. The set of texts which it published highlighted points of similarity between Bernstein and Jaurès with regard to the conception of history, though this was less because they agreed on the interpretation of the revolutionary process, as because they each rejected the rigid materialism of a Kautsky or a Mehring as applied to the events of 1789–99.[157]

Even so, the lack of any translation of the *Histoire socialiste* – and even more so, its very weak circulation – was linked to the implicit and sometimes explicit veto that was exercised by the social-democratic leaders, who saw it as a historical justification for a politics that they were themselves fighting against. This consideration helps us better to understand the problems posed by the transfer of a reading of the 'Great Revolution'. Difficult to accept on the political terrain, Jaurès's history posed a real challenge to a social-democratic party that had not itself produced a history of this extent. In the years that followed it would take on the task of filling this gap, after events in Eastern Europe drove it to re-evaluate the path of revolution.

---

157   To get a measure of the separation between them (at least as concerns their reading of 1793), we need only compare their divergent evaluations of Robespierre. While Bernstein criticised 1793 and Robespierre, Jaurès praised the Convention's work and declared himself 'with Robespierre' in June 1793 (Jaurès 1968–72, Vol. VI, pp. 193–4).

CHAPTER 4

The Russian Revolution of 1905 and the Analogies with 1789

When the German and Austrian social-democrats imagined revolution in the years before 1905, they were largely contemplating revolutions in Western countries.[1] This was true no matter whether they were referring to the past, present or future. Without doubt, the dispute over revisionism had raised doubts over the revolutionary path to socialism. Yet both the SPD's Dresden Congress in 1903 and the International's Amsterdam Congress in 1904 officially condemned Bernstein's ideas. Despite this, the conception of a gradual transition to socialism was in fact increasingly confirmed in practice.[2] The Russian Revolution of 1905 would thus serve to disrupt certain established assumptions, if not undermine these conceptions entirely. Tsarism was a political régime which the social-democrats despised, and the possibility of its immediate collapse – through a revolutionary process, and not through the peaceful road – raised immense hopes.

The Russian Revolution of 1905 remains relatively little-known except in the guise of a 'dress rehearsal' for 1917, and its history has long been overshadowed by this 'big sister'.[3] We often forget what a great shock it was at the time, at least at the European level. Historian Christophe Charle emphasises that the Russian Revolution of 1905 represented a major event even far beyond the ranks of organised socialism. For example, for a time it helped prolong the great cause of the *dreyfusard* intellectuals in France.[4] The upheavals of 1905 spurred numerous social democrats to mount detailed analyses of events in Russia. Indeed, the aftermath of the Revolution saw major debates on such questions as the 'mass strike',[5] or even the reasons for the Japanese victory over Russia and the diplomatic realignments which this provoked. In Austria, the 1905 Revolution had the effect of reviving the campaign for the right to vote, in the run-up to the

---

1 Worth noting, in this regard, is the title of a collection of texts by Luxemburg, Kautsky and Anton Pannekoek edited by Henri Weber: *Socialisme, la voie occidentale* ['Socialism, the Western Road']. See Weber 1983.
2 Groh 1999.
3 Note the recent overview by Jean-Jacques Marie (Marie 2008). See also Weill 1986. On the French socialists, see Candar 2007.
4 Charle 1996, p. 265.
5 Among the many contributions regarding this question, see in particular Weill 1986.

elections due to be held that November; in February 1906 the law on universal male suffrage was finally promulgated. As the social-democrats sought to get to grips with the ongoing revolutionary process, they also deployed familiar categories: they revisited the revolutions of the past, the better to understand the revolution that was now playing out in the East. The immediate history of the Russian Revolution was thus considered in light of the 'great revolutions', first among them the French revolutionary process of 1789–99.[6]

The Play of Analogies[7]

Articles and memoirs by social-democratic leaders repeatedly expressed the great influence that the 1905 Revolution had exerted upon them, as they compared the sweep of this revolutionary process to 1789 itself. Analysing the Balkan Wars of 1912 even as they were still raging, Otto Bauer looked back to the Russian Revolution of 1905. Situating the Russian events in a historical perspective, Bauer concluded that 'just as the French Revolution sowed trouble across all central Europe, the great Russian Revolution of 1905 has shaken up the peoples of the whole East'.[8] Much later, in 1930 – in a period in which his prestige had considerably weakened – Karl Kautsky also revisited the importance of this period, as he produced a first autobiographical essay.[9] Even in the very moment of the 1905 Revolution, observers frequently had the impression that they were witnessing a revolutionary process of comparable importance to what had happened in France in 1789. 1905 almost immediately appeared as a ... revolution. In these conditions, party theorists necessarily had to be attentive to writing the history of the Revolution. While no German produced a book with an overview of these events, the array of articles published formed a far from negligible contribution. Karl Kautsky and Eduard Bernstein, among others, immediately conducted analyses of the Russian Revolution in order to compare it with what they considered their own models of the transition to socialism.

---

6   This chapter's discussion of 'immediate history' is loosely inspired by the contributions in Bourdin (ed.) 2008.
7   The anthologies Stern 1954–6 and Stern 1961 are fundamentally important sources on the German responses to the 1905 Revolution and its aftermath.
8   Bauer 1980b, p. 849.
9   Kautsky 1930, p. 137.

Understanding Russia

In Marx's later years, his attention had been captured by the specificities of Russia's economic structures. We see as much in his efforts to learn Russian and his letters to Vera Zasulich.[10] Marx's texts well illustrate the attention that some Western European socialists and social-democrats paid to developments in Russia in the second half of the nineteenth century.

The German social-democrats detested the Tsarist régime. To get a measure of their hatred for Tsarist-tyrannised Russia – in stark contrast to their perception of the French Republic – we need only look at Engels's 1892 comments on the diplomatic rapprochement between these two countries.[11] Russia, land 'of slavery', was seen as both very politically backward and as a country dominated by the social relations that had emerged from feudalism. A caricature in the 16 September 1897 issue of the *Glühlichter* – the Austrian social-democrats' satirical weekly – attacked the Tsar's alliance with France: in the background stood revolutionary France, and in the foreground the Tsar, listening to the *Marseillaise* ... This was portrayed as a betrayal of the heritage of the revolutionary anthem widely known among the pre-1914 social-democrats. When Karl Kautsky reviewed a series of books during the 1889 centenary and its aftermath, he had tried to shed light on Russia's situation in light of the history of the 'Great Revolution'. In his aforementioned review of Boris Minze's book on the *biens nationaux*, he concluded his argument by noting that it was in Russia that the Great Revolution could best be understood by analogy with the present situation.[12] In other terms, Russia stood at a certain stage – feudalism – which it could one day overcome. This could certainly be considered a mechanistic vision, which did not concern itself with the real specificities of Russia's political and economic development. This image of a 'pre-1789' Russia was not, however, limited to theoretical texts alone, for it was also perpetuated in the mass-circulation press. The *Arbeiter-Kalender* published upon the centenary of 1793 compared the situation of *ancien régime* France with that of contemporary Russia. This shows how Russia was represented to militants who probably knew little about that country: as a backward state, with archaic feudal structures.[13]

In this regard, the German social-democrats' schematism – which is often presented in terms of their inability to envisage a revolution outside of their

---

10 Marx 1964.

11 See Chapter Two, p. 62.

12 Kautsky, K., 'Boris Minzes, Die Nationalgüterver.usserung während der französischen Revolution, Jena, 1892', *Die Neue Zeit*, 1893, p. 603.

13 *Arbeiter-Kalender*, 1893, p. 61.

own national framework and their own preconceived model – ought to be relativised. Indeed, their hatred of the established régime was accompanied by a belief in Russia's potential for revolution: Karl Kautsky published an article in Austria in 1902 devoted to the Slavic peoples and revolution.[14] These analogies and prognoses for Russia, which we find from time to time even before 1905, would develop considerably in the wake of Red Sunday in St. Petersburg.

A Major Event

On 21 January 1905, a peaceful demonstration reverentially petitioned the Tsar. Led by Father Gapon, it came to the Winter Palace with a series of pleas. The troops opened fire on the crowd, leaving countless dead. This day would enter history as 'Red Sunday', and it marked the beginning of a revolutionary wave that would spread across the whole country. This movement was distinguished by very major strikes as well as the emergence of *soviets* [workers' councils], including the one in the capital chaired by Leon Trotsky.[15]

Karl Kautsky immediately underlined the importance of this event, in a *Leipziger Volkszeitung* article on 'The Revolution in Russia'. He emphasised its mass character, in contrast with the traditional modes of organisation in Russia. This was 'no longer simply the rebellion of students and workers, but of the totality of its subjects'.[16] For Kautsky, this was a major turning point; he could even remark that 'the twentieth century will begin in Eastern Europe, just as the nineteenth finished in the West ... 22 January of this year opened up a new historical epoch, not only in Russia but around the world'.[17] Had Nicholas II noticed the coincidence? As Kautsky noted, 21 January was also the day that Louis XVI had met his infamous fate. As we see from Leo Stern's anthology, such a comparison was far from particular to the social-democrats alone: certain liberal organs used the same analogy, even while taking a different interpretative approach. For her part, in a piece for *Die Neue Zeit* that appeared a few days after Red Sunday, Rosa Luxemburg emphasised the movement's pronounced 'class character', as compared to previous revolutions. She saluted the initiative of the masses 'and also that heroic and modest idealism, without the posing and the theatrics of the bourgeoise's great historic moments, which is a sure and typical symptom of all the class movements of the enlightened modern

---

14 The piece first appeared in the *März-Festschrift* (Vienna, 1902). For a scholarly presentation of this article see Day and Gaido (eds.) 2009, pp. 59–67.
15 It is worth noting that the *soviets* in fact had a very weak echo in the German debates of the time.
16 Kautsky, K., 'Die Revolution in Russland', *Leipziger Volkszeitung*, 22 January 1905, p. 1.
17 Ibid.

proletariat'.[18] Thus while she set these events in a historical continuity, Luxemburg also endeavoured to understand the originality of the revolutionary process that was now underway.[19]

A November 1905 article by Franz Mehring well illustrated the significance of the reference to 1789.[20] Mehring wrote that 1905 would be written in the history books just like 1789. 1848 was not comparable to 1789 in this regard, for the proletariat had not yet laid hands on the means of political action that would be necessary for its emancipation. And the power of the Russian Revolution, like that of 1789, was that it transcended national boundaries: 'In the long term, the Russian Revolution cannot be confined within Russia's borders alone, any more than the French Revolution could have been within French borders – and no one knows that better than the German ruling classes'.[21] Another article by Mehring published in *Die Neue Zeit* later that same year well translated the sentiments that had inspired the incredible strike wave of October 1905. As the commemoration of the first anniversary of the Russian Revolution approached, Mehring portrayed it as a global event, comparable to 1789.[22]

However, Karl Kautsky, Franz Mehring and Rosa Luxemburg did not represent the whole of social democratic opinion. In an article on the revolutions in Russia, Eduard Bernstein distanced himself from any kind of enthusiasm for the ongoing revolutionary process.[23] Even as he noted some of Russia's inherent differences – and in particular the weight of the urban and industrial centres where 'modern' ideas were more developed – Bernstein identified 1905 with the cycle of classically bourgeois revolutions that had stretched from the seventeenth century to 1848. For Bernstein, 'the class hierarchy in today's Russia and the nature of its production make it apparent that it is a vain utopia [to consider] its imminent revolution to be socialist in character ... Fundamentally, the revolution can only be bourgeois, liberal and democratic'.[24]

Behind these differences of appreciation, the key focus of the debate was the characterisation of the revolutionary process that was now underway. Was this the last of the bourgeois revolutions, and thus still part of the same cycle that had begun in 1789, or was it the first proletarian revolution? The debate revolved around how the revolution should be 'classed': if 1905 had important

---

18   Luxemburg, R., 'Die russische Revolution', *Die Neue Zeit*, 1905, Vol. 1, p. 575.

19   Luxemburg, R., 'Die russische Revolution', *Die Neue Zeit*, 1905, Vol. 1, p. 574.

20   Mehring, F., 'Die Revolution in Permanenz', *Die Neue Zeit*, 1905–6, Vol. 2, pp. 169–72.

21   Mehring, F., 'Die Revolution in Permanenz', *Die Neue Zeit*, 1905–6, Vol. 2, p. 172.

22   Mehring, F., 'Ein Jahr der Revolution', *Die Neue Zeit*, 1905–6, Vol. 2, p. 441.

23   Bernstein, E., 'Revolutionen und Russland', *Sozialistische Monatshefte*, 1905, pp. 289–95.

24   Bernstein, E., 'Revolutionen und Russland', *Sozialistische Monatshefte*, 1905, p. 292.

particularities – and in particular the emergence of the proletariat in a revolution – even these could only be understood by way of analogy with 1789. The differences and points in common with the French example made it possible to define the present situation in clearer terms. In this sense, the French Revolution was a central point of reference.

If we want to understand how certain conceptions entered into discussion at the moment of the Russian Revolution, it is worth noting Kautsky's remarks at the beginning of 1906, in an article published in *Vorwärts* where he argued that social democracy would have to revise Engels's 1895 judgment as to the inevitability of the peaceful road.[25] To pose the problem like this was to question a legalist strategy that had hitherto been largely shared among the social-democrats. It moreover implied revisiting the history of past revolutions whose characteristics no longer seemed so outdated as some had expected.

A Re-exploration of the History of the French Revolution

Our concern in this section is to investigate whether these analogies, which were present in some of the articles written by party theorists, were also recognised outside of these leadership circles. This means that we need to study the mass-circulation party organs that could have been read by large numbers of social-democratic militants. Here we will focus on three particularly telling examples (even if we could also choose others). These three examples are daily newspapers; the satirical organ *Der Wahre Jacob*; and most of all the papers for May Day. Finally, we will reserve particular attention for a pamphlet that the German social democracy published to mark the first anniversary of the 1905 Revolution, entitled *1649–1789–1905*.[26]

The Russian Revolution in Daily Newspapers

This analogy with 1789 was apparent in the Austrian social democrats' daily *Arbeiter-Zeitung* from the beginning of 1905. From January onward it published numerous articles on the Russian Revolution, including one front-page piece which concluded by drawing the analogy between Nicholas II and Louis XVI. This was the same article by Karl Kautsky that had appeared in the *Leipziger Volkszeitung* one week previously, which we already mentioned above.[27] On

---

25   Kautsky, K., 'Die Aussichten der russischen Revolution', *Vorwärts*, 28 January 1906, p. 1.

26   *1649–1789–1905*, Berlin: Vorwärts, 1905, 16 pp.

27   Kautsky, K., 'Die Revolution in Russland', *Arbeiter-Zeitung*, 29 January 1905, p. 1.

5 February 1905, it published a humorous imaginary letter from Louis XVI giving advice to Nicholas II. According to *Arbeiter-Zeitung*, this was the translation of a leaflet that was circulating in Russia.[28] Three days later, in a historical calendar – one of this daily's regular sections – there were several references to dates from the French Revolution, and again on 22 February – '1787. Beginning of the French Revolution. The Assembly of Notables' – and on 24 February – '1789. Calling of the Estates-General'. It continued this series of dates into March 1905. Such regular mentions of the French Revolution helped anchor this reference point, even if the historical dates mentioned were mostly either Austrian or German. They indicate how, even beyond the publication of theoretical articles, the reference to the French Revolution mounted an important 'comeback' in the wake of the Russian events of 1905. The 12 February edition highlighted a talk on the Russian Revolution, and offered a partial reproduction of what had been said; the speaker described the Russian events as a 'Great Revolution', an expression that typically referred to the French Revolution.[29]

The coverage of the Russian Revolution was comparable with that for another major event for international socialism in 1905, namely the creation of the *Section Française de l'Internationale Ouvrière* (SFIO; 'French Section of the Workers' International') that May. Both *Vorwärts* and *Arbeiter-Zeitung* reported on this development. Paradoxically, it was not the French context that most contributed to the resurgence in references to 1789. This despite the fact that 1905 was, indeed, marked by a series of events which led to the unification of the currents of French socialism. The Rouen Congress of the *Parti socialiste français*, the prelude to the unification itself, was covered with the reproduction of interventions by such figures as Jean Jaurès. The Globe Congress, which founded the SFIO, was the focus of several articles in both *Vorwärts* and *Arbeiter-Zeitung*. But just one such article made the front page of *Vorwärts*, on 3 May 1905.[30] This unification had been expected, having already been decided by the International in 1904; its relatively weak echo should moreover be understood in terms of the viewpoint of German-speaking countries whose social-democratic movements had already been united for decades. Conversely, the Russian Revolution was, by definition, an unexpected event, and it had a much more powerful impact on Germany and Austria. There is no doubt that the most important event in 1905 was in Eastern Europe. Moreover, the French unification congress took place at the end of April – that is, at a moment when

---

28   *Arbeiter-Zeitung*, 5 February 1905, p. 2.
29   'Russische Revolution', *Arbeiter-Zeitung*, 12 February 1905, p. 3.
30   'Die Einigung des französischen Sozialismus', *Vorwärts*, 3 May 1905, p. 1.

preparations for 1 May were already in full flow. May Day 1905 took on particular depth, with the call for solidarity with Russia. On 29 April 1905 a box in
Vorwärts announced the publication of that year's *Maizeitung*,[31] and in particular drew readers' attention to an article by Kautsky entitled '1789–1889–1905'.

As for visual representations of 1905, *Der Wahre Jacob* – whose great popularity among militants we have already mentioned – published numerous
illustrations of the Russian Revolution. Through the analogies that it made
between Russian and French events, *Der Wahre Jacob* reactivated the French
revolutionary symbolism which had been so present in its pages during the
1889 centenary. Nicholas II was depicted with the same features as Louis XVI,
while members of the Russian élite were shown being hung from the lamp-
posts in front of the applauding masses.[32] The introduction to the German
Maifeier (according to the minutes of the 1906 SPD Congress, it had a print-
run of 372,000 copies)[33] set the Russian events on the same level as the past
'great revolutions' of 1789 and 1848, even as it signalled that the revolution of
1848 had been less able to complete its work. However, the most important
comparison came in the article in the *Maifeier*'s centre pages, where 1905 was
above all compared to 1789. This piece, signed by Kautsky, was entitled '1789–
1889–1905'.[34] 1 May 1905 'came closer to the original character of this day than
any of those that went before'.[35] Kautsky thus began by setting 1905 in historical perspective. At the height of the revolutionary period in Russia, he echoed
the appeal that the European socialists and social-democrats had made at the
Second International's founding congress in 1889, when they decided to make
1 May a day of struggle. This Congress, Kautsky noted, was itself a historical
event at the same level as 1789, whose centenary the social-democrats had celebrated. Beyond this tie between these three events, there was also an analogy
between the French and Russian revolutions: for Tsarism's situation in 1905 was
comparable to that of the absolute monarchy in France at the end of the eighteenth century. Kautsky here once again expressed the profound conviction that

---

31   While *Vorwärts* gave this name, it was in fact called the *Maifeier*.
32   *Der Wahre Jacob*, 23 January 1906.
33   *Protokoll über die Verhandlungen des Parteitages der Sozialdemokratischen Partei Deutsch-
     lands. Mannheim, 23. bis 29. September 1906*, Berlin, 1906, p. 51.
34   Kautsky, K., '1789–1889–1905', *Maifeier*, 1905, p. 2. It is worth noting that this text also had
     an international resonance: *Le Socialiste* published it as the main article on the front page
     of its 1 May 1905 special edition. This was a historic issue if ever there was one: it was the
     last edition of *Le Socialiste* in its guise as the Guesdists' organ, before it became the central
     organ of the SFIO.
35   Ibid.

the Russian Revolution would be just as important as 1789.[36] Dominated by a heartfelt optimism, this text may in several regards appear rather caricatural. Yet it well expressed, 'in the heat of the moment', the profound impact of the Russian Revolution on 1 May 1905. For Kautsky, the hopes born of the foundation of the International in 1889, expecting 'the last revolution', were now being realised: 'a great revolution, the last revolution, the end of the cycles of political and thus economic crises'.[37]

1649–1789–1905: Its Content and Circulation[38]

When we take a close look at the social-democratic press, we find not only numerous articles devoted to the Russian Revolution and the analogies that they made with the French Revolution, but also, in late 1905, regular references to a pamphlet that sought to draw a balance-sheet of the past year of revolution in Russia. It was entitled *1649–1789–1905*,[39] and made up part of the preparations for the commemoration of the first anniversary of the Russian Revolution. The SPD's two influential party dailies repeatedly made great efforts to publicise this pamphlet. Thus in the 23 December 1905 edition of the *Leipziger Volkszeitung* (and then almost every day up till the end of the month) we read the following announcement:

> Leipzig Printing Company.
>
> For the end of the year Vorwärts Editions has published a richly illustrated magazine entitled *1649–1789–1905*. It deals with the great revolutions that the world has seen in the past – the English Revolution of 1649 and the French Revolution of 1789 – in their connection with the upheavals in Russia. The magazine consists of 16 large-format pages, and consists of the following contributions:
>
> Kautsky: Revolution, Old and New
> Schulz: The English Revolution
> Mehring: The French Revolution
> Luxemburg: The Russian Revolution
> This issue will cost twenty pfennig ...
>
> Comrade, act to ensure that this revolutionary issue is widely circulated![40]

---

36   Ibid.
37   Ibid.
38   Here we build on the remarks that we made in Ducange 2007.
39   See Karl Kautsky archives, IISG, H1/107.
40   *Leipziger Volkszeitung*, 23 December 1905.

Vorwärts also advertised the publication of *1649–1789–1905*, at around the same time. The pamphlet sought to emphasise the significance of 1905 and to establish it as part of 'world history', comparable to the great revolutions of the past. As these advertisements indicated, this was not theoretical literature: to some extent, the inclusion of illustrations set it in continuity with a paper like *Der Wahre Jacob*, whose great popularity among party members was well-known to SPD leaders. Indeed, the representation on each of its pages of the people in movement or great revolutionary figures distinguished this pamphlet from a narrowly theoretical review, or even the feature articles that were published in the dailies. Beyond the front page – which reproduced a famous portrayal of 1 May by Steinlen, followed by a poem by Preczgang[41] – the illustrations that appeared therein can be subdivided into three categories: depictions of the Tsarist authorities (which were all negative); a few small portraits of key figures in the 'great revolutions'; and finally larger pictures which portrayed major revolutionary episodes. In this third group, the one that took up most space (almost two whole pages – thus more than the Russian Revolution) was a depiction of the storming of the Bastille, reproducing a copper etching from this period.[42] It is worth adding that this was a short work, whose format and size favoured its mass distribution. Indeed, according to the minutes of the 1906 Mannheim Congress, some 100,000 copies were printed.[43] This was three times less than the print-run of the 1 May paper (372,000 copies), but it was still considerably higher than an organ like *Die Neue Zeit*, whose print-run never rose above a few thousand copies. It is thus worth dwelling on the content of the articles that were included in this pamphlet.

Featuring no specific contribution on the revolutions of 1848 or the Paris Commune of 1871, it framed 1905 in comparison with the two great bourgeois revolutions in England and France. Up till this point, the English Revolution had been known most of all by way of Eduard Bernstein's book.[44] Even if it could not be compared with the French Revolution, the English Revolution was nonetheless considered one of the great bourgeois revolutions, following in the same vein as what Marx had written in 1848:

> The revolutions of 1648 and 1789 were not English and French revolutions, they were revolutions of a European type. They did not represent

---

41 A poet and SPD fellow traveller.
42 *1649–1789–1905*, pp. 5–6.
43 *Protokoll über die Verhandlungen des Parteitages der Sozialdemokratischen Partei Deutschlands. Mannheim, 23. bis 29. September 1906*, Berlin, 1906, p. 51.
44 Bernstein 1895, 1930.

the victory of a particular class of society over the old political order; they proclaimed the political order of the new European society ... The revolution of 1648 was the victory of the seventeenth century over the sixteenth century; the revolution of 1789 was the victory of the eighteenth century over the seventeenth. These revolutions reflected the needs of the world at that time rather than the needs of those parts of the world where they occurred, that is England and France.

There has been nothing of all this in the Prussian March revolution.[45]

The first article in this pamphlet was a piece by Karl Kautsky on 'Revolution, Old and New'.[46] It set 1905 at the heart of a wider process, whose significance and whose violence [*Gewalt*] made it comparable in scale to 1649 and 1789. He briefly emphasised a few points of similarity between the 'old' revolutions and the 'new' one of 1905, and in particular the struggle against absolutism. The 1871 Commune was negatively referenced as the revolt of one isolated city, which had been overthrown after just a few weeks;[47] Kautsky counterposed this to the breadth of the movement now spreading across Russia. Differences were also highlighted: if the 1905 Revolution marked the beginning of a cycle as important as that which had started in 1789, the Russian events were distinguished by their social content, with the emergence of the proletariat. Moreover, today the once-revolutionary 'petty bourgeoisie' of 'London and Paris' was no more; this was now a 'reactionary' class in the present Russian context.

He devoted greater attention the peasant question, of which he had made himself a specialist within SPD ranks.[48] He highlighted the autonomous role of the peasants as a force, but also the prospect of this leading to failure as it had in 1848 – which he thus again mentioned as a negative example. Yet the peasantry could also pave the way to 'triumph', as in 1789. 'In this regard', he explained, 'the French and Russian revolutions will be alike'.[49] Whatever that may be, the revolution's actions seemed to mark an irreversible shift. Such optimism was also apparent in Kautsky's approach to the international situation. He argued

45 Karl Marx in the *Neue Rheinische Zeitung*, no. 169, 15 December 1848: *MECW*, Vol. 8, p. 161. This citation from Marx was also reproduced in the *Leipziger Volkszeitung* article marking New Year 1906: 'Neujahr', *Leipziger Volkszeitung*, 30 December 1905, p. 1.

46 Kautsky, K., 'Alte und Neue Revolution', *1649–1789–1905*, pp. 3–5. It is notable that a translation of this text immediately appeared in *Le Socialiste* of 9–16 December 1905, which defined this as an article on 'the most important and most urgent of all subjects'.

47 Kautsky, K., 'Alte und Neue Revolution', *1649–1789–1905*, p. 3.

48 Kautsky was author of a volume on the agrarian question, which was considered the standard work on this subject among the social-democracy of the time: Kautsky 1899b.

49 Kautsky, K., 'Alte und Neue Revolution', *1649–1789–1905*, p. 4.

that international relations were now very different from what they had been in the era of the French Revolution, given the emergence of new class struggles and the power of the proletariat. From this he concluded that 'we should not expect a coalition of European powers against the Revolution, like in 1793'.[50] He was confident that the power of the workers' movement would prevent any foreign intervention – much unlike in the eighteenth century, when the monarchies of Europe did not have to deal with any similar domestic counterweight. Mehring had already expressed this same idea in an article for *Die Neue Zeit* a few months previously, when he dismissed any danger that the monarchies would join forces like they had at Pillnitz in August 1791.[51]

The final words of Kautsky's article expressed his unshakeable faith in the advance of socialism. Despite its call for the 'dictatorship of the proletariat', his contribution made no reference to the practical consequences of the revolutionary violence that had been deployed in the 1789–99 period. While his interpretation may seem naïve on certain points, this text also has to be seen in its proper context: published in December 1905, it was probably written no later than the latter part of November. It was thus written just a month after Russia had seen a vast wave of strikes, in which the Russian social-democrats had played an important role, and the Tsar had accepted a manifesto that granted several fundamental freedoms. These events made it possible to believe that the Revolution would continue to a favourable conclusion; the fall of Tsarism looked imminent. We find similar tones in Hugo Schulz's article.[52] His piece offered an overview of the specific dimensions of the English Revolution, in particular through its focus on the struggles of the 'common people' and the role of the Levellers. In this regard, his article echoed Eduard Bernstein's study. Despite certain similarities with the English Revolution, he considered it unimaginable that the revolutionary process that was now underway would lead to a dictatorship. Schulz thought it possible to 'prophesise' that the authoritarian forms that had arisen under Cromwell or Napoleon had now been transcended by history.[53]

It was Franz Mehring who wrote the article dedicated to the French Revolution.[54] Following a Marxist interpretative schema in which he had become a specialist, Mehring emphasised the bourgeois aspects of the Revolution, before

---

50   Kautsky, K., 'Alte und Neue Revolution', *1649–1789–1905*, p. 5.

51   Mehring, F., 'Reflexe der russischen Revolution', *Die Neue Zeit*, 1905, in Stern 1961, Vol. 1, p. 389.

52   Schulz, H., 'Schicksalsmomente der englischen Revolution', *1649–1789–1905*, pp. 5–7.

53   Schulz, H., 'Schicksalsmomente der englischen Revolution', *1649–1789–1905*, p. 7.

54   Mehring, F., 'Die französische Revolution', *1649–1789–1905*, pp. 7–10.

reviewing the major role that the peasantry had played in summer 1789. He noted how useful the Terror had been for defending the Revolution in 1793–4; this had been the only way to save France. But reading Mehring's portrayal of the revolutionaries of 1793–4 – first Marat, and then Danton and Robespierre – we also see how he disapproved of Terror being used as a contemporary means of political action. He did, without doubt, hail Marat, Danton and, indeed, Robespierre as great revolutionary figures;[55] he nonetheless concluded his article with an explicit call not to imitate the means of the bourgeois revolution:

> Revolutions in the manner of the French Revolution are now impossible ... Indeed, [the working class] has now learned that its liberation will not demand recourse to this unreliable dimension of violent actions, which the bourgeoisie used for its own emancipation.[56]

Having reached its 'historical maturity',[57] the proletariat had to turn not to 'the blade of the guillotine' but to 'more peaceful means of expropriation'.[58] In this perspective, the ongoing Russian Revolution would distinguish itself through its different means of seizing and exercising power.[59]

Rosa Luxemburg wrote the article directly devoted to the latest developments in the Russian Revolution.[60] She, too, briefly revisited the history of revolutions in France, from 1789 to the emergence of the Third Republic. The cycle that 1789 had begun was to close with 1905. Her analysis of the French Revolution stood at a distance from Mehring's, given her praise for the Montagnard episode: in her reading, 'the brief domination of the party of the Montagne, which corresponded to the peak of the revolution, was the proletariat's first arrival on the scene'.[61] The time had come for a new type of revolution, with a proletariat that would achieve 'class consciousness' thanks to social democracy. In this new social revolution, the transition to the new society would be realised by the 'dictatorship of the proletariat'. This social

---

55   Mehring, F., 'Die französische Revolution', *1649–1789–1905*, pp. 9–10.
56   Mehring, F., 'Die französische Revolution', *1649–1789–1905*, p. 10.
57   Literally, 'majority'.
58   Ibid.
59   Mehring, who died in 1919, would from the 1950s be hallowed in the German Democratic Republic as a true 'founding father'. However, this particular text was never republished, either in Stern's anthology upon the fiftieth anniversary of the 1905 Revolution – which was otherwise very complete – or in his *Gesammelte Schriften*. Here, there was no place for his argument that violence was an outdated method.
60   Luxemburg, R., 'Die russische Revolution', *1649–1789–1905*, pp. 13–15.
61   Luxemburg, R., 'Die russische Revolution', *1649–1789–1905*, p. 12.

revolution was particularly discussed via the mediation of the 'mass strike'; and here Luxemburg brought matters back to the most burning political questions of the day, for the German union leadership would vigorously resist such a perspective.[62] In this pamphlet, she was the only contributor who went so far in addressing the political conflicts of the present; she was also the only one who explicitly stated that parliamentary strength would not alone be sufficient, for 'with the Russian Revolution, the bourgeoisie's sixty-year period of tranquil parliamentary rule has come to an end'.[63] Nonetheless, she did not elaborate any further on the concrete forms of authority (or the effective means of achieving them) that were to substitute for parliaments ...

In short, reading some of these reflections written in the 'heat of the moment' in 1905, we see how useful the analogy with 1789 was to understanding the present. But beyond this comparison between historical revolutions and present-day political realities, the articles in *1649–1789–1905* also contained important historical overviews. This demonstrated the concern to communicate a knowledge of past revolutionary processes to the social-democratic readership. Indeed, alongside these articles the pamphlet reproduced extracts from books, which were often themselves accompanied by illustrations. Such was the case of a passage from Karl Kautsky's *Die Klassengegensätze von 1789* concerning the *sans-culottes*.[64] This was a quite long extract from a chapter which described the decisive role these latter had played in most of the revolutionary *journées*, and moreover explained the contradictions between the popular movement and the revolutionary government. The extract was reproduced as it had originally appeared, along with a short note to explain the meaning of the word '*sans-culottes*'. The fact that this extract made Kautsky's book the pamphlet's sole reference to the history of the French Revolution itself demonstrates the authority that he enjoyed on this matter. We could also add that he was the only contributor to have two texts in this pamphlet, not to mention a quotation from *Die Klassengegensäze* which followed Mehring's article on the French Revolution. Finally, it is also worth noting that this latter appeared next to a quotation from Marx's *Eighteenth Brumaire*, which mocked the revolutionaries of 1848 for their slavish imitation of the revolutionaries of 1793 ...

---

62   As David, a member of the right wing of the party, put it at the Jena Congress of 17–23 September 1905, 'What may be fit and proper over there could be totally wrong over here, and it is pure folly to draw a conclusion on what tactics we need from the Russian situation'. Cited by Weill 1986, p. 444.

63   Luxemburg, R., 'Die russische Revolution', *1649–1789–1905*, p. 15.

64   Kautsky, K., 'Die Sans-culotten der französischen Revolution', *1649–1789–1905*, pp. 11–12.

Considering this pamphlet's large print run, we can imagine that it allowed Kautsky's short textbook – or at least one extract from it, as well as knowledge of its existence – to reach the attention of a wider audience. This was especially true given that his book had not been reissued since 1889. We should also add that inserts appearing in *Vorwärts* in May 1905 'Recommend[ed] the writings of Karl Kautsky';[65] it highlighted a brief selection of his writings, notably including *Die Klassengegensätze von 1789*. Between the illustrations, the extract from Kautsky's book and the several articles devoted to the 'Great Revolution' or in which it played a prominent role, there can be no doubt that what the editors wanted to offer militants was a pamphlet recalling the heroic deeds of the French Revolution – a revolution whose importance was only surpassed by the Russian Revolution in the present. This was a manual, a 'Need-to-Know Guide' to the French Revolution, for a mass audience. The themes that it addressed (the importance of the *groupes populaires*, the social-democrats' relationship with violence and revolutionary terror) were the same ones that had already been elaborated during the 1889 centenary and its aftermath. Finally, it is worth noting that the success of *1649–1789–1905* extended beyond the German-speaking countries alone. Not only was Karl Kautsky's article translated into French, but the whole pamphlet was republished in Russian. This well illustrated the impact that the German social-democrats' analyses had on Eastern Europe.

Alongside Kautsky, Wilhelm Blos – author of a 'people's history' published at the moment of the 1889 centenary – here again played a role in the transmission of revolutionary history. In the pages of *Leipziger Volkszeitung* we find that over the course of 1905 he gave public lectures on Robespierre.[66] In October 1905 several highly visible inserts promoted his works, including his volume on the French Revolution ('Time to get good books at good prices').[67] The advertisement for his book on the French Revolution appeared not long before the publicity for *1649–1789–1905*. Also worth noting is an article by Blos published in the German *Arbeiter-Kalender*. This essentially descriptive piece on the Russian Revolution drew no analogies with the French Revolution, but did attest to this social-democratic leader's popularity.[68]

---

65   *Vorwärts*, 13 May 1905.
66   Schafers 1961, p. 104.
67   *Leipziger Volkszeitung*, 15 October 1905.
68   Blos, W., 'Die russische Revolution', *Illustrierter Neue Welt-Kalender*, 1906, pp. 10–16.

A Return to 1789?

The SPD's central educational school was created in the wake of its Mannheim Congress in 1906. In Chapter Five we shall mount a detailed study of this *Parteischule* and the place that teaching on the French Revolution occupied therein. The Berlin educational school produced yearly reports on its activity from 1898 to 1914,[69] and the 1905 report contains some details on the content of that year's teaching. These documents are, indeed, useful for our study of the immediate impact of the 1905 Russian Revolution: while in 1899–1900 the course on the French Revolution remained one of the most popular, with 89 signing up and 61 attending,[70] from 1899 to 1905 the detailed plans for the Berlin school contained not the slightest explicit reference to the French Revolution – further evidence that it no longer garnered the same attention as it had at the beginning of the 1890s, for reasons we explored in Chapter Three.

It is thus wholly remarkable to see how the French Revolution made its reappearance in this same school from the first trimester of 1905. This without doubt remained limited: the first trimester of 1905 offered a 'History of the New Times, up to the French Revolution', in which the final part was devoted to 'The Age of Enlightenment and the Preparation of the French Revolution'.[71] But this was one important indicator, among others, which suggested a revived interest in 1789 from 1905 onward.

The opening of the First Duma in May 1906 was again a focus of analogies. This time, however, Karl Kautsky was much less optimistic than he had been in the contributions that he had written a few months earlier. If May 1906 and the meeting of a new assembly were evocative of May 1789 and the opening of the Estates-General, the similarities stopped here. In Russia the opening of the new assembly marked the conclusion of the revolutionary process, and Kautsky denounced the grotesque character of a Duma whose calling was accompanied by a series of repressive measures. Analogy was no longer appropriate, here; or, as Marx said of 1848, as compared to the French Revolution this was a 'farce'. The Russian 1789 had not taken place.

Nonetheless, not all hope had died out. The SPD's Mannheim Congress commemorated 'Red Sunday'. Its highly symbolic date drove an analogy with the French Revolution, just like the one that Kautsky had made the previous year, in which 21 January 1793 evoked 21 January 1905. The minutes of this September 1906 congress set these two dates in parallel, in the context of the social-democratic campaign for the extension of voting rights. After referring to the

---

69   *Arbeiter-Bildungsschule Berlin. Bericht über die Tätigkeit, Berlin, 1898–1914.*
70   *Arbeiter-Bildungsschule Berlin. Bericht über die Tätigkeit, Berlin, 1899–1900*, p. 3.
71   Kautsky, K., 'Die russische Duma', *Die Neue Zeit*, 17 May 1906, pp. 241–5.

many demonstrations in favour of this reform, the report by the party's leadership committee [*Parteivorstand*] evoked the historical link that bound 1793 with 1905:

> On 14 January the leaflet was distributed, in around 6 million copies. The following Sunday was chosen as the date for the assemblies. The fact that this date has a particular importance in the history of revolutions – Louis XVI was put to death in Paris on 21 January 1793, and this was also the day of the St. Petersburg massacres – must have helped to make our rulers particularly nervous. Our leaflets were confiscated entirely by chance.[72]

A few months later, in 1906 the social-democrat Heinrich Cunow published a study devoted to the press during the revolutionary period of 1789 to 1794. This took the form of a series of articles, which appeared in *Die Neue Zeit* from October to December of that same year. Not long afterwards, he combined these articles into a book, just as Kautsky had in 1889; it must, therefore, have been written in early 1906 at the latest.[73] This interest for the revolutionary period of 1789–94 is to be understood in light of the Russian Revolution and its aftermath. But beyond this publication itself, as the social-democratic parties grew substantially in the years following 1905, a whole new mechanism would allow a wider reading and a wider understanding of the history of the French Revolution.

---

72   *Protokoll über die Verhandlungen des Parteitages der Sozialdemokratischen Partei Deutschlands. Mannheim, 23. bis 29. September 1906*, Berlin, 1906, p. 29.

73   Cunow 1908.

PART 2

The Entrenchment of a Reference (1906–17)

∵

The New Conditions of Social-Democratic Production

The period between 1906 and 1914 was marked by the powerful growth of both the Austrian and German social-democratic parties. Jacques Droz notes that the SPD's 'membership more than doubled between 1905 and 1911';[1] by 1912 the party had more than a million members, and 112 seats in the Reichstag. As for Austria, thanks to the 1906 suffrage reform, at the 1907 elections the SDAP secured more than a million votes and had 87 MPs elected; by 1911 it constituted the largest single parliamentary group in the Reichsrat [Imperial Council]. These parties' apparatuses and their means of distributing their propaganda expanded considerable. This was also the moment that the SPD asserted itself at both the national and international levels. The writings of a theorist like Karl Kautsky were a point of reference for numerous socialist and social-democratic currents across Europe.[2] The launching of new press organs and reviews was itself an indicator of the party's dynamism. In Austria, 1907 saw the first publication of *Der Kampf*, a theoretical review equivalent to Germany's *Die Neue Zeit*. It would later become renowned due to its perceived role as one of the main vehicles of 'Austromarxism'.[3]

Party educational structures also expanded considerably. The SPD's Mannheim Congress in 1906 led to the creation of a 'National Education Commission' [*Zentralbildungsausschuss*].[4] Following the German party's example, in 1909 Austria's SDAP created a similar 'Centre for Socialist Education' [*Zentralstelle für das Bildungswesen*]. It would maintain this name until February 1934, and played an important role in providing speakers and materials. This Centre also took the initiative in launching a review, the *Bildungsarbeit*.[5]

These new structures went hand-in-hand with a significant output of printed materials. Their sources were now both better defined and more numerous; the content of the courses, and the short pamphlets or detailed plans that corresponded to them, were published for the benefit of their participants. In parallel to this, there was a proliferation of party libraries. We find evidence of

---

1 Droz (ed.) 1974, p. 66.
2 Blumenberg 1960.
3 On the ambiguities of this term, see Pasteur 2006.
4 The IISG holds a large proportion of these sources: for Austria, see the further materials held at the *Verein für Geschichte der Arbeiterbewegung* (VGA).
5 Pasteur 2000.

this in both the publication of numerous library catalogues and the appearance of *Der Bibliothekar*, a review almost entirely devoted to the workers' libraries in Germany.

In this context, we should pay particular attention to the articulation between the various micro- and macro- scales.[6] Indeed, the greatest force of the social-democratic parties was expressed at several different levels. While we cannot here study the reception of references to the French Revolution in each region where the SPD rallied significant forces, we can get a better understanding of the overall picture by drawing on some telling examples. In this era, a particular measure of the social-democratic parties' power was the extent of their educational apparatuses, which were considered the realisation of the ideal of *Bildung*. The Frankfurt SPD (one of whose leaders Herman Wendel, had a special passion for the history of the French Revolution) and the Berlin educational school will serve as our main examples. Like Heinrich Cunow, Wendel was considered a 'rising star' in the party; the two men's works on the French Revolution, as well as their involvement in educational structures, each contributed to their legitimation. Nonetheless, the emergence of such new actors should not make us lose sight of Karl Kautsky's authority. He would always remain the most authoritative figure, at least up till the early 1910s.

At the chronological level, while the history of the German-speaking social-democrats can hardly be said to have depended on the impact of Russian events alone, we should recognise that after the renewed interest for the French Revolution following the upheavals of 1905, the true rupture came in 1917. The Russian Revolution caused more of a rupture in the perception of the French Revolution than did World War I, for example, given the new analogies that developed along with the emergence of Soviet communism. The historian Horst Dippel highlights the 'impressive number' of books on the French Revolution published in Germany between the end of the nineteenth century and World War I, across all currents of opinion: the condemnation of the French Revolution allowed 'the justification of the Germanic world with its own constitutive principles', while the Revolution itself provided a major source of inspiration for the opponents of the imperial system.[7] The social-democrats counted a great deal, in this context. When we add in the articles and reviews that dealt with this theme, over the period between 1889–1934 we see that this was doubtless the most productive period of writings on the 'Great Revolution'.

---

6   Werner and Zimmermann 2003, p. 23.

7   Dippel 1990, p. 1254.

New Works on the French Revolution

Heinrich Cunow and the French Revolution

The most important work that attested to the renewed interest in the French Revolution after 1905 was Heinrich Cunow's study dedicated to the revolutionary press, *The French Revolutionary Press from 1789 to 1794*. This work published in 1908 was a contribution to the history of the late eighteenth-century clashes between the different classes and parties. It was republished in 1912 under the title *The Parties of the Great Revolution and Their Press*.[1] As well as being the most developed contribution that any pre-1914 social democrat ever wrote on the French Revolution, it was also the object of significant debates. The publication of sources on the revolutionary period (Buonarroti on the Conspiracy of Equals)[2] accompanied by critical apparatuses produced by social-democrats made part of one same general movement more specifically to address certain aspects of the French Revolution. Finally, alongside these studies and translations, the 'Great Revolution' assumed a unique place in theoretical and historical manuals (for instance in Franz Mehring's *History of Germany*).[3]

We should thus identify a dual shift. The social-democratic understanding of the Revolution was deepened through a more specialised or even scholarly history, and at the same time the Revolution was grasped in a wider framework, identified as a major period which the works defining party orthodoxy must necessarily address.

A Study of the Revolutionary Press

An important figure in the Social-Democratic Party, well-known to specialists in the history of the SPD and German workers' movement, Heinrich Cunow is not however particularly well-known for his work on the French Revolution.[4] Historians have more often devoted their attention to Cunow's role on the left wing of the SPD, followed his spectacular about-turn in 1914 – like many social-democrats, he supported the war effort – or indeed the fact that he replaced

---

1 Cunow 1908, republished 1912.
2 Buonarroti 1909.
3 Mehring 1910–11.
4 See biography in Droz 1990, pp. 144–5. There is no mention of his work on the French Revolution.

Karl Kautsky at the head of *Die Neue Zeit* in 1917, on party orders (Kautsky having been removed on account of his participation in the USPD).[5] A member
of *Die Neue Zeit*'s editorial board from 1899, he distinguished himself alongside
Kautsky in the fight against the revisionists, before actively participating in *Vorwärts*, and also taught at the party school from 1907 to 1914. His role during the
Weimar Republic, linked to the university post he reached in 1919, is rather less
well known.[6] Moreover, from the late 1880s onward Cunow published a series of
ethnological works;[7] he had read the academic works on this question, and was
without doubt one of German social democracy's most productive historians.[8]

In the French historiography, we would struggle to find the slightest reference to his work on the 1789–94 period.[9] Conversely, *Die revolutionäre Zeitungsliteratur während der Jahre 1789 bis 1794* does seem to have had a certain echo,
and it was also republished almost immediately, in 1912. A West German anthology includes this work among its classics of German-language historiography
of the Revolution,[10] while in the DDR an important article combined with a biographical essay were devoted to him upon the 1989 bicentenary.[11] An article by
Walter Grab that provided an overview of the German-language historiography,
which was very critical of social-democratic works, highlighted that Cunow's
was by far the most interesting among all of them, and especially as compared
to Kautsky's work.[12] More recently, Cunow and his vision of the Revolution were
the subject of an article appearing in one of the few German-language reviews
dedicated to the history of the workers' movement.[13] It is easy to explain this
sustained attention to Cunow. For in 1908 he put his name to a work of quite
unique importance. This was the first volume on the Revolution by any German social-democratic author that was a real historical study, in the sense that
it was based on significant research into the sources: namely, the revolutionary
press. For the reasons explained above, neither Kautsky or Blos had been able
to accomplish such research.

---

5   A party that split with the SPD in opposition to the war. See the introduction to Part 3,
     p. 225.
6   Studied in Part 3. See Chapter XI, p.230.
7   On his ethnological work, see Ulrich 1987.
8   Florath 2005, p. 496.
9   His work was never translated, and unlike Kautsky his international role was very limited.
10   Grab (ed.) 1975. This work was never republished in Germany. However, it was translated
     in Soviet Russia in 1918, and had a certain echo in the debates in the USSR in the 1920s. See
     Kondratieva 1989, pp. 185–8.
11   Bernd 1987, 1989.
12   Grab 1983, p. 309.
13   Florath 2005.

The basis of this volume was a series of articles published in *Die Neue Zeit* between October and December 1906. Heinrich Cunow's study was much more developed than all the previous contributions on this theme.[14] While it is difficult to trace the exact genesis of this work, there is no doubt as to its chronological context: it was in the wake of the Russian Revolution of 1905 that Cunow wrote his study of the French Revolution. Its first publication in book format came in 1908 with Buchhandlung Vorwärts, a publisher linked to the SPD. Reissued in 1912, the second edition's changed title better reflected Cunow's argument concerning 'political parties' and their 'contradictions'. Two new chapters on 'class contradictions' were also added, without alteration to the greater part of the book.

The very size of this volume, at almost 400 pages, indicated the desire to publish a work that sought to be neither a synthesis nor a militant handbook. To a certain extent it also distanced itself from 'grand narratives', as it turned its attention to shorter-term political and social conflicts. Unlike Kautsky's approach in *Die Klassengegensätze von 1789*, Cunow based his work on research into the texts and the actors in the French Revolution themselves, better to understand its social contradictions. His main sources were the revolutionary press and pamphlets [*Pamphletliteratur*], which he consulted in archives and libraries in both Paris and London.[15] The other sources he used included the *Cahiers de doléances* [Registers of Grievances]. He cited very many extracts from the French revolutionary press: his argument was constantly illustrated by excerpts from papers and speeches from the revolutionary era, thus offering his readers German translations of otherwise little-known documents.

Beyond these sources, Heinrich Cunow used a great deal of other books, demonstrating his extensive knowledge of the historiography: as well as Taine and Mignet we could mention Arthur Kleinschmidt, Émile Levasseur on the working classes, Léonce de Lavergne on France's rural economy, and Léonard Gallois on the journalists and periodicals of the revolutionary period.[16]

A reader of recent historiography, Cunow made repeated reference to Philippe Sagnac;[17] on the peasantry, he cited recent works from the Russian historiography, and especially the studies by Loutchisky that had appeared in French.[18] Such extensive research led his biographer to write that 'more than

14   His articles appeared in instalments in *Die Neue Zeit* between 3 October and 24 December 1906, under the title 'Die französische Presse in den ersten Jahren der grossen Revolution'.
15   Cunow 1912, p. vi.
16   Kleinschmidt 1876; Levasseur 1867; Gallois 1845–6.
17   Sagnac 1899 (cited by Cunow 1912, p. 107).
18   Cunow 1912, p. 123. Loutchisky 1897.

other historiographical texts, the reality of the work that Cunow had accomplished disturbed German professional historiography's own perception of
itself'.[19]

As for Cunow's method, unlike traditional histories his work sought to
explain, within the framework of the materialist conception of history, the
political and social interests of the different groups that made up the Third
Estate. Referring to works like Levasseur's study on the *History of the Working
Classes in France*, he emphasised the wealth of documentation that underpinned them but also their flaws at the level of historical explanation, given
that they were most often limited to a narrative of 'personal rivalries',[20] failing
to grasp that these were themselves 'the products of precise class groupings'.[21]
His foreword noted that there was 'no lack' of political histories of the Revolution, but that one would 'search in vain for an answer to the question of which
layers of the population the different parties represented, and which contradictory political conceptions they led into battle'.[22] Inspired by the 'theory of
the struggle between classes', he explicitly set himself in continuity with Karl
Kautsky: 'I known only one specialist text that takes this same approach: Karl
Kautsky's *Die Klassengegensätze von 1789*'.[23]

Far longer and denser than Kautsky's study, although concentrated on a
shorter period (1789–94), the general structure of Cunow's book nonetheless
resembled that set out by Kautsky, of whom he claimed to be the faithful inher-
itor. Thus after he had provided a panorama of the 'class contradictions' on
the eve of 1789 [*Klassengegensätze*, adopting the title of Kautsky's book], there
were several chapters to deal with the different social groups, and then particular studies on the political 'parties', from the royalists to the Hébertists. One
of Cunow's objectives was to outline a history of the formation of social classes
during the revolutionary process itself, by way of a study of its different actors'
discourse. He accorded an important role to 'intellectuals' [*Intelligentz*] and
more generally the series of figures who assumed the leadership of the revolutionary process. The role of '*déclassé* intellectuals' recurred repeatedly:[24] this
was probably an echo of the conservative history which was then dominant in
Germany, which saw the Revolution as the work of wastrels. Several originalit-
ies are worth underlining in this work, starting with Cunow's treatment of the
counter-revolution and the grievances that it advanced – a question that was

19   Florath 2005, p. 502.
20   Cunow 1912, p. 3.
21   Ibid.
22   Cunow 1912, p. iv.
23   Cunow 1912, p. 2.
24   Cunow 1912, p. 34.

almost totally absent from Kautsky's book.[25] The 'clerical royalist' and 'constitutional aristocratic' press was the focus of a chapter in which Cunow presented
Rivarol, the *Actes des Apôtres*, the *Ami du roi* and the *Mercure de France*. With
the help of numerous excerpts from these publications, Cunow presented their
arguments critical of the revolutionaries. This was not a matter of denunciation
or stigmatisation, but rather of understanding the strategies of the Revolution's
opponents.

   Cunow's narrative was very much articulated around the notion of the
'party' and the variety of revolutionary sensibilities (though he did not really
provide any precise definition of what a 'party' was, during the Revolution).
It mainly emphasised the nuances that divided the different 'parties'. He analysed each revolutionary group: thus the Girondins were the representatives
of 'the commercial middle-bourgeoisie'[26] in search of 'the bourgeois sense of
order'.[27] Some of a party's demands made it possible to understand its *Klassen-
charakter*: for instance, Cunow averred that 'nowhere is a party's class character
better reflected than in its fiscal policy'.[28] His representation of cultural, ideological, religious and political aspects of the Revolution – which were always
considered in close connection with social structures – was far richer than in
Kautsky's work.

   As for Cunow's stance toward the historians he cited, he consistently posi-
tioned himself in opposition to the 'serial historian Taine'[29] [*Geschichtfeuil-
letonist*] and his loathing of the popular movements. Throughout his work,
Cunow was also critical of the German-language historiography, and especially
Heinrich von Sybel.[30] In this regard, it is worth noting the particular attention that he dedicated to the *Ami du peuple*. Counter to the traditional historiography that saw him as a 'bloody savage', the chapter on Marat sought to
re-assert his quality as a figure, through a study of his periodical:

> There is no leading figure of the French Revolution on which the histor-
> ical literature has not formulated a variety of judgments. But on no figure
> do the judgments diverge more than they do for Jean-Paul Marat; no one
> is similarly painted by some as a brutal cynic and by others as the most
> selfless apostle of humanity.[31]

---

25   See, for examle, the analysis of counter-revolutionary currents in Cunow 1912, p. 55.
26   Cunow 1912, p. 202.
27   Cunow 1912, p. 207.
28   Cunow 1912, p. 233.
29   Cunow 1912, p. 79.
30   Cunow 1912, p. 219.
31   Cunow 1912, p. 316.

This portrayal of Marat was consistent with the social-democrats' long tradition of positive evaluations of the revolutionary, dating back to the 1889 centenary. Cunow's sympathies toward the revolutionary groups were also similar to those apparent in previous social-democratic texts. Hébert was the object of particular attention: while Cunow criticised him for his individualism and the 'half-anarchist' [*halb-anarchist*] aspect of his conceptions of politics, the chapter devoted to this figure was one of the longest in the whole book. This was preceded by an elaboration on the 'petty-bourgeoisie' and the significance of the 'proletariat' among the popular layers of Paris. Conversely, there was no reference to Robespierre in any of the chapter headings; Cunow's argument emphasised the 'public disavowal of the Montagne by a considerable part of the people of Paris' at the end of 1793.[32] Moreover, the final chapter on 'Five Years of Party Struggles', added to the 1912 second edition, offered a general overview of class conflicts in which Cunow more sharply asserted his disapproval of the stance taken by Robespierre and his 'clique':

> The heads of the Hébertist leaders – so hated by Robespierre and his clique – fell on 24 March, before the Dantonists drowned in their own blood on 5 April, ... The rule of petty-bourgeois democracy could, perhaps, have lasted longer, had the Parisian ultra-revolutionary Robespierre not broken the radical Jacobins' power to resist, with the guillotine.[33]

Beyond what may, in retrospect, seem historically faithful and pertinent at the methodological level (each group in a 'party' representing a 'class' ...) in Cunow's work we find what was then an unprecedented depth of study of the Revolution's events. His work was, therefore, one of the social-democrats' most important contributions, and for many reasons. It would prompt much further reflection and historical elaboration, further testifying to its impact.

Legitimising a Work

The almost immediate republication of Cunow's study itself reflects its success as a work of history. But what also needs emphasising is the way in which it was legitimised as a work of reference, especially by means of reviews in theoretical journals.

Die Neue Zeit published two texts by Franz Mehring on this subject. The first was a classic review, and the second a reaction to the reception of Cunow's

---

32   Cunow 1912, p. 371.
33   Cunow 1912, pp. 383–4.

study among German historians.[34] In the first text[35] – more an article than
a simple review – Mehring above all praised Cunow's historical-materialist
method, but also paid attention to his work with the sources, for example
with regard to the conflict between the Girondins and Montagnards; the relations between these latter and the popular movement during the Terror; what
they represented in social terms; and so on. Certain questions such as the conflicts between the popular movements and the revolutionary government had
already been addressed by Kautsky; as we have seen, some excerpts on this
theme had been republished in response to the events of 1905.[36] However,
for want of more in-depth historical research Kautsky's arguments had not
prompted any serious discussion, beyond the remarks contained in his correspondence with Engels. Cunow's work was, instead, a case of 'scholarly work
within the party'.[37] Mehring repeatedly criticised the 'legend of the Revolution',[38] which he associated with Mignet, Thiers, Michelet and Louis Blanc.
He levelled a severe indictment against both 'revolutionary' and 'reactionary'
myths, which he put on the same footing.

> [Previous] works of history feature an abundance of legends, of more
> or less vague parameters – be they revolutionary or reactionary, pro-
> Girondin, Dantonist, Robespierrian, Maratist, Hébertist, etc. What we
> [instead] see here are concrete figures ... It goes without saying that
> Cunow steers clear of both revolutionary and reactionary legends ... From
> this class's point of view, the revolutionary legend is just as much to be
> condemned as the reactionary one, or even more so, for it may mislead
> today's class of workers [sic] as to the perspectives and the prior condi-
> tions of their struggle.[39]

The critique of 'revolutionary legends' was above all a critique of previous historians who had defended this or that political camp without analysing the
Revolution's social content. The social-democratic history of the Revolution,
such as Mehring saw it, would not stand in continuity with the historians of

---

34 Mehring, F., 'Bürgerliche Kritik', *Die Neue Zeit*, 1908–9, Vol. 2, pp. 639–40.
35 Mehring, F., 'Eine Geschichte der französischen Revolution', *Die Neue Zeit*, 1908–9, Vol. 1,
    pp. 481–8.
36 And in particular the chapter on the *sans-culottes*. See Chapter Four, p. 111.
37 Mehring, F., 'Eine Geschichte der französischen Revolution', *Die Neue Zeit*, 1908–9, Vol. 1,
    pp. 481–8.
38 Ibid.
39 Mehring, F., 'Eine Geschichte der französischen Revolution', *Die Neue Zeit*, 1908–9, Vol. 1,
    pp. 482–3.

the nineteenth century: historical materialism was an entirely novel method of approaching history. Indeed, he sought to advance this same method in his history of Germany, which was published in this same moment.[40] This article provided Mehring with his opportunity to establish a comparison between the French Revolution and the German situation. If the achievements of the night of 4 August 1789 corresponded to what it took the Prussian state several decades to accomplish between 1807 and 1865, the decisive factor in the first case was the role of the popular movement, which the bourgeoisie used in order to realise its own objectives: in Germany it did so 'from above', without the people. But in each case, the bourgeoisie had 'betrayed' its allies:

> One of the conclusions of Cunow's research richest in lessons is the fact that the bourgeoisie played its treacherous and cowardly double game from the very beginning of the Revolution. It was not as cowardly, but just as treacherous, as the German bourgeoisie was in 1848: and fundamentally, it was playing the same game ... In the case of the German bourgeoisie in 1848, this desire to use the 'energy' of the 'plebs' against the royal troops essentially disappeared. But its betrayal of the victorious proletariat already had its glorious model in the unfolding of the French Revolution.[41]

When Cunow's book was republished with two new chapters as well as a series of corrections, Franz Mehring wrote a brief review in *Die Neue Zeit* to highlight the new edition.[42] This was itself an index of the long-term legitimation of this study. Even in other texts that were not book reviews, in the strict sense, or even articles dedicated to the French Revolution, reference was made to Cunow's book:

> Comrade Cunow's remarkable work, which has just been published, arrives at the right moment to show that even the parliaments of the Revolution, which still tower colossus-like above today's parliaments, had the constant tendency to fall into the basest weakness and dilettanteism, unless there was some pressure from the outside to help them ... With this

---

40   See p. 120.

41   Mehring, F., 'Eine Geschichte der französischen Revolution', *Die Neue Zeit*, 1908–9, Vol. 1, p. 485.

42   Mehring, F., 'Heinrich Cunow, Die Parteien der grossen französischen Revolution und ihre Presse', *Die Neue Zeit*, 1912–13, Vol. 1, pp. 710–11.

passage,[43] Cunow succeeds in clearly demonstrating that the revolutionary processes never had a parliamentary character; rather, they were sustained by political struggles generated by economic antagonisms, whose final expression came in parliamentary debates.[44]

The role that parliaments played in revolutionary processes had to be connected to social and economic forces, or else their role would be posed in exaggerated terms. This was probably an echo of the beliefs of the left wing of the SPD, of which Heinrich Cunow and Franz Mehring were both representatives. Since the 1905 Revolution this left wing had criticised parliamentarism's oversized role within the SPD: this reference to the history of the French Revolution, even in the form of a scholarly work, here made up part of the debates that exercised the party itself.

At the same time, Kautsky republished his 1889 study, which was now renamed *Die Klassengegensätze im Zeitalter der französischen Revolution* ['Class Contradictions in the Time of the French Revolution'].[45] The new title, which better reflected this book's subject matter, was the only change to the thrust of Kautsky's work. Its re-publication should be understood in the context of the renewed interest for the French Revolution that emerged in the wake of the Russian Revolution: it was also recirculated for the sake of making it available to social-democratic educational bodies. The only notable change in this second edition was the new preface which Kautsky added. In the preface there was very little discussion of the French Revolution as such, but it was emphasised that understanding the Revolution was still indispensable to understanding the present:

> While four generations of men will soon have come and gone since the beginning of the Revolution, the consequences of this great event are still playing out today, and it is impossible entirely to grasp the class conflicts of the present if we have not reached an understanding of this upheaval, during which these conflicts broke out for the first time, and unveiled the essence of each of the classes of bourgeois society.[46]

---

43 Cunow's elaborations on 4 August 1789, which he had already signalled in his review.
44 Mehring, F., 'Eine neues Olmütz', *Die Neue Zeit*, 1908–9, Vol. 1, pp. 194–6.
45 Kautsky 1908.
46 Here we base ourselves on the translation (probably by Laura Lafargue) that appeared in *Le Socialiste* on 1 March.

His 1889 argument still appeared as the compulsory point of reference and the only Marxist history of the French Revolution; for Kautsky 'my outline, twenty years ago, of the class conflicts in the era of the Great Revolution has sadly not yet been surpassed or made redundant by any other work'.[47] Just one work today deserved attention: Heinrich Cunow's. Kautsky thus conferred his own legitimacy on Cunow.

Such responses should be compared with the restricted reception of Jean Jaurès's *Histoire socialiste*. This work was evidently buried, indeed in the long term: in 1908–9, neither Kautsky nor Cunow mentioned Jaurès's study. In his introduction on the historiography Cunow mentioned a great number of French historians and authors, but here, again, the absence of reference to Jaurès was remarkable. Walter Grab nonetheless writes that 'one of the historians most influenced by Jaurès was the social-democrat Heinrich Cunow'.[48] It is true that Cunow's work can, in a certain sense, be seen as a German-language *Histoire socialiste*, given that each of these studies were based on considerable work with the sources, indeed with a particular attention to the social and economic causes of the Revolution. From this point of view, the two works did, indeed, make up part of one same whole – one same historiographical moment.[49] How, then, can we explain the total lack of reference to Jaurès? Evidently, Cunow had been aware of the *Histoire socialiste*, at least during the time that he spent in France for his research. But beyond the broad resemblance between these works, their methods differed considerably: the German social-democrat remained faithful to Karl Kautsky, and his materialism stood much closer to the orthodoxy set out by the 'Pope of Marxism', than did Jaurès and his synthesis blending Plutarch, Marx, and Michelet; moreover, this latter's identification with French republican democracy never found a real echo among the German social-democrats, except among a small circle of the 'enlightened'. Without doubt, as a mass party that dominated the International and considered itself the custodian of Marxism, the SPD's pretensions to intellectual superiority also played a role, here.[50]

---

47   Ibid.
48   Grab (ed.) 1975, p. 19.
49   We might also mention, for example (again in 1908) a second, separate edition of Bernstein's work under the title *Sozialismus und Demokratie in der grossen englischen Revolution* (published by Dietz).
50   We should, nonetheless, also highlight the 1913 translation of Jaurès's other great work, *L'Armée nouvelle* (Jaurès 1913) in a context in which military questions had been sharply brought into relief. Our study can hardly overlook such a title, given that it also featured some discussion of the French Revolution. The only major work of Jaurès's to be trans-

Reviewing Books, Criticising the Historiography

Die Neue Zeit's critiques

The book reviews featuring in *Die Neue Zeit* show that the social-democrats were now engaging with academic historiography, in light of their own materialist conception of history. Their intellectual ambitions – as well as the means they now had at had – were incomparable with the situation at the end of the 1880s. Some of their reviews concerned works by French academic historians; these were often short texts, but they were nonetheless telling, given that *Die Neue Zeit* had never previously mentioned even those French-language publications that dealt with the Revolution.[51] One such example was Hermann Wendel's[52] review of a volume of Robespierre's *Discours et rapports* edited by Charles Vellay,[53] who was briefly secretary of the Société des Études Robespierristes created in June 1907.[54] He praised the editors for making these texts available, even as he criticised the pro-Robespierre commentary that accompanied them. Hermann Wendel thus set himself in continuity with two established approaches: firstly, a social-democratic one, which was consistently critical of Robespierre, and secondly, the fight against that German historiography – as in the case of figures such as Heinrich von Sybel – which collapsed socialism and communism into Robespierre's social conceptions.[55]

The reviews of German-language books were more detailed. In 1907 Karl Kautsky wrote a review of John Holland Rose's biography of Napoleon,[56] while Hermann Wendel published an article that addressed a series of works on the

---

lated into German, it was published outside of the SPD's own circles, by Diederichs. This publisher issued books of very different horizons – Max Weber labelled it the 'supermarket of worldviews' – beyond the bounds of social democracy. Rosa Luxemburg reviewed this title in the 9 June 1911 *Leipziger Volkszeitung*.

51   The first such mention that we have identified is the review of a work by Alphonse Aulard: 'Aulard, La société des Jacobins', *Die Neue Zeit*, 1898, Vol. 2, pp. 284–5. This anonymous review was probably written by Karl Kautsky.

52   On the biography of Herman Wendel, see our case study of the Frankfurt SPD, p. 180.

53   Wendel, H., 'Discours et Rapports de Robespierre', *Die Neue Zeit*, 1908–9, Vol. 2, pp. 249–50.

54   On Vellay, see Mazauric 2000, pp. viii–ix.

55   See Heinrich von Sybel's comments on Robespierre, cited in Chapter One, p. 29.

56   Kautsky, K., 'Rezension, Karl John Holland Rose, Napoleon I', *Die Neue Zeit*, 1907, Vol. 1, pp. 610–12. The famous British historian's biography had been translated into German. Kautsky was amused by its conservative tone and also highlighted the mediocre quality of the translation itself. However, he also emphasised that this biography was interesting in certain regards, in particular in terms of its analysis of the economic aspects of Napoleon's conquests.

reforms that had taken place before the Revolution.[57] This latter piece discussed a number of academic historians who had published on this subject, from Eugen Guglia to Adalbert Wahl and Hans Glagau.[58] While Guglia's work was qualified as 'reactionary', and indeed stood far from historical materialism, it did nonetheless speak of the contradictions between different interests.[59] Wendel's article in large part consisted of expounding the arguments that appeared in this book. He especially examined the significance of the Physiocrats on the eve of the Revolution, as well as their 'programme for the state' [*Staatsprogramm*]; Turgot's role, and the question of the liberalisation of trade and wheat prices in 1774; reform efforts like the territorial subsidy; the parliamentary oppositions; and finally the successive failures of Necker and Calonne. This particularly meant an attempt to understand the attitude of the 'feudal classes' and the way in which their 'class interests' clashed on the eve of 1789. In support of his argument, the social-democrat cited Karl Marx's *Theories on Surplus-Value*, which had recently been exhumed by Kautsky;[60] this thus provided an opportunity to compare recent historiography with the intuitions that had appeared in Marx's texts.[61] Also worth mentioning is the review of Tecklenburg's book on *The Development of the Right to Vote in France since 1789*. The review's author criticised this law professor for his apparently very limited understanding of the history of socialism. Despite this, he praised the book for adding to the store of knowledge on the history of the right to vote.

Heinrich Cunow also wrote some reviews. In particular, he wrote a critique of Theodor Bitterauf's 1912 *History of the French Revolution*.[62] Bitterauf was a history professor at the Munich military academy, and Cunow held his work in little esteem: this article was above all an opportunity for the social-democrat to reassert his own arguments as to the decisive role of the 4 August 1789 peasant uprising, which Bitterauf had overlooked. Cunow consistently sought to

---

57   Wendel, H., 'Reformversuche vor der französischen Revolution', *Die Neue Zeit*, 1910, Vol. 2, pp. 140–52.

58   Guglia 1890; Wahl 1905–7, Glagau 1908. The most important of the three was Adalbert Wahl (1871–1957), a historian from Tübingen and author of numerous contributions on the French Revolution. He was one of the most famous representatives of the 'conservative wing' of German historians (Sproll 1992, p. 24).

59   Wendel, H., 'Reformversuche vor der französischen Revolution', *Die Neue Zeit*, 1910, Vol. 2, p. 141.

60   In *MECW*, Vol. 31.

61   Wendel, H., 'Reformversuche vor der französischen Revolution', *Die Neue Zeit*, 1910, Vol. 2, p. 142.

62   Cunow, H., 'Th. Bitterauf, Geschichte der französischen Revolution', *Die Neue Zeit*, 1912, pp. 878–9.

NEW WORKS ON THE FRENCH REVOLUTION   145

present himself as the most expert historian dealing with the questions associated with the French Revolution. His long review of Peter Kropotkin's major
work,[63] whose German edition was published at the same time as his own
Die revolutionären Zeitungsliteratur,[64] shows better still how Cunow sought to
establish his legitimacy.

Heinrich Cunow, Critic of Kropotkin
The publication of the anarchist Peter Kropotkin's *The Great Revolution 1789–93*
represented a significant moment in the historiography of the French Revolution. Kropotkin's study is often cited together with Jean Jaurès's book as one
of the pioneering works on the social history of the Revolution.[65] Born to
the Russian nobility, Kropotkin (1848–1921) deserted his own milieu in order
to throw himself into his efforts to spread anarchist propaganda across all
of Europe. His *Memoirs of a Revolutionary* published in 1902 bore witness to
a career that had taken him from the Russian nobility to life as a political
prisoner. He very early displayed interest in the French Revolution: in 1893
he published a short pamphlet on this subject, as a first outline of his 1909
book.[66] As in the case of Jean Jaurès and Heinrich Cunow's works, the publication of this volume made up part of a general shift toward a kind of history that contemplated social and economic factors and took the activity of
popular layers into proper consideration. For this reason, *La Grande Révolution* was of great interest to the social-democrats, above all given that – unlike
Jaurès's *Histoire socialiste* – it was simultaneously published in several languages, including in German. The translator, Gustav Landauer, was born in
1870, and was close to the *Jungen* movement of anarchists opposed to the
SPD leadership in the early 1890s. His conception of socialism, associated with
free and decentralised communes, took the *sections* of the French Revolution
as its model. Having met Kropotkin in London in 1901, he moved to Berlin
and became a bookseller and translator. His introduction to Kropotkin owed
not to the SPD but to the anarchists; a current that had some influence in
Germany in this period, especially at the level of its intellectual output, even
if this was incomparably lesser than the social-democrats' own. It is worth
noting that despite Kropotkin's support for the *union sacrée* during World
War I, his works – and in particular his history of the Great Revolution –

---

63   Kropotkin 1909.
64   Cunow, H., 'Kropotkins Geschichte der französische Revolution', *Die Neue Zeit*, 1908–9,
      pp. 365–77.
65   Kropotkin 2010.
66   Droz 1990, pp. 293–4.

nonetheless drew praise from Lenin. The latter's respect for Kropotkin allowed Soviet historians to take his work seriously, and this title would be republished on several occasions. Meanwhile, various anarchist currents repeatedly recirculated it in Western countries. Indeed, Kropotkin would have quite a political legacy: he is considered, alongside Bakunin, as one of the most important theorists of anarchism.

While in certain respects Kropotkin stood close to a Marxist analysis, he also elaborated an original history, especially with regard to the question of political representation. He considered state action secondary as compared to popular movements. This was one of his major points of divergence with Heinrich Cunow, as was apparent in this latter's critical review extending across some twelve pages. This piece began with a general panorama of works on the French Revolution: Cunow highlighted their abundance over the last thirty years, thanks to the decisive role of the 'Société d'histoire de la Révolution française' in France.[67] For Cunow, there was no doubt that Kropotkin's work represented an important contribution; and his book was all the more useful for being written in light of the Russian situation.[68] He nonetheless sought to demonstrate that a 'history from below' that idealised the people and its role in the *sections* of Paris was insufficient. For Cunow, 'the mission of meticulous history-writing is not to force research to fit the needs of the illusions and the twists and turns of the political struggle of the moment. This risks ignoring the facts and contradicting the demands of research itself'.[69] In his view, the anarchist historian had barely taken into account the role of political groups other than the ones he sympathised with; and given that he did not discuss France's economic structures in any long-term perspective, the revolutionary process became almost unintelligible. In short, Kropotkin's history fell into the same binary and ideological oppositions as the historians that he purported to be fighting against,[70] especially insofar as the anarchist's writing style seemed to suggest that he was addressing historians more than the people itself. For Cunow, 'despite its easily understandable popular prose, this work is above

---

67 Cunow, H., 'Kropotkins Geschichte der französische Revolution', *Die Neue Zeit*, 1908–9, p. 366.

68 'The importance of the so-called peasant question for Russia has again attracted Russian scholars' and politicians' attention back toward the French peasants' position in the French Revolution'.

69 Cunow, H., 'Kropotkins Geschichte der französische Revolution', *Die Neue Zeit*, 1908–9, p. 371.

70 Cunow, H., 'Kropotkins Geschichte der französische Revolution', *Die Neue Zeit*, 1908–9, p. 366.

all written for politicians and historians, not for the masses'.[71] Indeed, for the social-democrats, the aim of spreading knowledge of the history of the Revolution also implied that the books that dealt with this subject should be readable, even as they maintained a rigorous Marxist analysis. This dual concern, at the foundation of Cunow's critique of Kropotkin, was also apparent in the social-democrats' publishing policy.

Translating and Introducing, from Philippe Buonarroti to Paul Louis

Between 1906 there was a significant focus on translating unpublished works into German. This was itself an expression of the enhancement of the social-democrats' publishing apparatus. For example, Dietz offered two collections, the 'Kleine Bibliothek' (which published small-format books like Kautsky's *Die Klassengegensätze von 1789*), as distinct from the 'Internationale Bibliothek', whose goal was to publish longer, new books.

In 1908, Wihelm Blos, who had long been an important figure in the social-democratic historiography of the French Revolution, translated Philippe Buonarroti's book on Babeuf and the Conspiracy of Equals together with his wife Anna.[72] A major source for understanding Babouvism, to our knowledge this book had never previously been translated into German, even though there was an English edition in 1836.[73] The text was well-known among the German émigrés in Paris in the 1840s, who themselves mixed with some of the 'neo-Babouvists'.[74] But for most, it remained beyond reach. It is worth emphasising the social-democrats' efforts to introduce this work into the German context: in their edition, Buonarroti's own text was preceded by a twenty-page introduction and accompanied by a number of chronological and explanatory notes. This helped to inform readers of certain basic facts, thus allowing them to understand what was sometimes a rather heavy text; the volume also featured a glossary. Taken as a whole, this made up a considerable critical apparatus, which itself revealed the care that was taken in helping those without prior understanding of revolutionary history to read a work that may at first have been difficult for them to access.

---

71   Cunow, H., 'Kropotkins Geschichte der französische Revolution', *Die Neue Zeit*, 1908–9, p. 371.

72   Buonarroti 1909. See Buonarroti 1957 for a French edition; English translation by Mitchell Abidor available at www.marxists.org.

73   Buonarroti, Philippe 1836, *Buonarroti's history of Babeuf's conspiracy for equality: with the author's reflections on the causes & character of the French Revolution, and his estimate of the leading men and events of that epoch*, London.

74   Maillard 1999, pp. 8–10.

Anna and Wilhelm Blos' introduction began with a biography of Buonarroti. It described the path he took during the revolutionary period and his role in the Conspiracy of Equals. Seeking to identify the importance of Babouvism, the Blos cited the passage of Karl Marx's *Communist Manifesto* that mentioned Babeuf directly. They then discussed Babeuf himself, his hatred for Robespierre in 1793–4, and then his reconciliation with him after Thermidor.[75] In passing, they also took the opportunity to criticise Robespierre and his policy toward the Hébertists; while the social-democrats noted that the Babouvists referred positively to Robespierre, they also emphasised their points of division:

> In no sense was the historical Robespierre a friend of 'justice', in the sense of Babeuf's conceptions, but nor, moreover, was he a friend of the abolition of private property ... He looked on socialist agitation with the hatred of a petty-bourgeois; he annihilated Jacques Roux and the Hébertists ... The proletarians understood that Robespierre had already unleashed reaction with the annihilation of the Hébertists.[76]

For the authors, what characterised this pre-history of socialism, which also left traces in the contemporary world, was the desire to regulate politics by decree.[77] But the socialism of the present claimed to have reached a higher stage than the first outlines elaborated by Babeuf. Indeed, they contended that 'in that era there fell to scientific socialism the difficult task of combatting the prejudices born of "the communism of equality", which had soon sunk deep roots'.[78] Their conclusion thus reasserted the SPD's own programme of scientific socialism. As the forerunner of the socialist idea, Babeuf was to be granted his place in history, but the means of action had now changed with the emergence of modern political parties. Once again, Wilhelm Blos clearly distanced himself from anything that might look like an abrupt rupture.

In a review published in *Die Neue Zeit* Hermann Wendel saluted this book's introduction into the German context.[79] He mockingly cited Chancellor Bülow's remarks on Napoleon's 'domination of the Jacobin and communist ter-

---

75   On Babeuf's evolving positions, see the works by Claude Mazauric and in particular his choice of texts and introduction to Babeuf 1988. In German, see Middell and Middell 1988.

76   Buonarroti 1909, pp. 9–11.

77   Buonarroti 1909, p. 13.

78   Buonarroti 1909, p. 14.

79   Wendel, H. 'P. Buonarroti, Babeuf und die Verschwörung für die Gleichheit', *Die Neue Zeit*, 1909–10, Vol. 1, p. 348. On Wendel see below, p. 130.

ror' and noted that far from any kind of communism the Jacobins had protected small peasant property. Wendel presented not the Jacobins but Babeuf as the forerunner of socialism:

> Babeuf's reflections on the arrangement of the new society, on administration, legislation, the education of children and the army are not the only interesting thing. His life's work is also symbolic, not because of his strict Roman virtue, which distinguished his days till the last, but because he, the 'people's tribune',[80] was the first to call on the proletariat to use their own strength to break out of their chains.[81]

Also worth noting is the translation of Paul Lafargue's pamphlet *La langue avant et après la Révolution française* by Kautsky's son in 1912. This work, which was at first translated and published in *Die Neue Zeit*, was then reproduced in a separate edition.[82] The editors wrote a note to introduce the text, emphasising that it had not encountered great popularity in France. It moreover highlighted that this was one of the few texts by Lafargue that had not hitherto been translated into German. This was a kind of tribute to a militant who had committed suicide, together with his wife, the previous year.[83] Notable here, other than Lafargue's own notes, was the considerable amount of notes that the translator himself added in order to provide basic historical explanations and short biographies of the figures mentioned therein. This, again, spoke to the concern to make this text accessible to the widest possible range of people. This was combined with references to more recent social-democratic literature, for example citing Heinrich Cunow in order to provide the reader with more information on Hébert's *Père Duchesne*.[84]

The belated decision to publish this translation – Lafargue's study in fact dated back to 1894 – may seem a rather surprising choice, not least given that

---

80   This notion of a 'people's tribune', explaining to the people what its own objectives should be, can be compared to Marat; social-democratic militants could also identify this with their own role in 'enlightening' the people.

81   Wendel, H. 'P. Buonarroti, Babeuf und die Verschwörung für die Gleichheit', *Die Neue Zeit*, 1909–10, Vol. 1, p. 348.

82   Lafargue 1912. Note also the later edition Lafargue 1988.

83   Lafargue 1912, p. 3.

84   While he criticised Hébert's political conceptions, Lafargue, like Cunow, was particularly interested by his popular manner of speaking. 'Yet, this language, which sought to reach the greatest numbers, reflects the words and expressions that were then commonplace among the popular layers. For Hébert was a writer who effectively turned into their spokesman – but who served as their echo, more than their guide'. Biard 2009, p. 14.

its subject matter was so specific. This was one of the first attempts at a 'political lexicography',[85] which explained how the French language had changed in connection with the revolutionary process, and how its usages evolved in function of the dominant social categories.[86] Most importantly, Lafargue was one of the key leaders of the Guesdist current, and for this reason he maintained privileged relations with Karl Kautsky, after previously having had such a relationship with Friedrich Engels.[87] He was part of *Die Neue Zeit*'s editorial team and one of the German social-democrats' leading interlocutors in France. Even when we look beyond Lafargue's privileged status and stick to the historiography of the French Revolution more specifically, we see that he played an important role in the attempt to promote Kautsky's short book on the Revolution within France itself.[88]

Two works by the French socialist Paul Louis were also translated into German. One was a history of socialism, and the other a history of trade unionism since 1789.[89] Born in 1872, Paul Louis was of Blanquist sensibilities and a former member of the *Parti socialiste de France*, the party opposed to Jaurès and the independents. At the turn of the century, he was part of the tendency opposed to socialist participation in a bourgeois cabinet, and after 1905 he joined the enduring Guesdist sensibility within the SFIO.[90] In his *History of French Socialism* Louis sought to present the proletariat's first socialist demands during its rise in the eighteenth century. As Hermann Wendel's preface highlighted, this volume sought to fill in something of a gap, for no general handbook on the history of French socialism had been available in German up till that point. For Wendel, the translation of this history was an act of solidarity between Frenchmen and Germans.[91] After the first chapter devoted to the emergence of the critique of property during the Enlightenment, a second, thirty-page chapter looked at 'The 1789 Revolution and Babeuf'. As its title indicated, Babeuf here occupied a central position, and indeed was presented as a forerunner of contemporary of socialism: 'The manifesto of the Equals ... remains

---

85   Calvet 1977, p. 9.
86   While Lafargue's study was not much discussed at the time, it became famous worldwide with Joseph Stalin's critique of its arguments in his 1950 work on *Marxism and Problems of Linguistics*: Calvet 1988, pp. 147–96; English translation at www.marxists.org. On language in the revolutionary era, see Biard 2009, a recent study of *Le Père Duchesne*.
87   Derfler 1998.
88   See Chapter Three, pp. 91 et sqq.
89   Louis 1908, 1912.
90   'Paul Louis', in Pennetier (ed.).
91   Louis 1908, 'Vorwort', viii.

in a sense the first of modern socialism's texts'.[92] Louis made no particular
reference to the historiography, apart from a few brief mentions of Michelet
and Aulard, without precise references – this being a highly simplified handbook. Its French edition had first been published in 1901, before Jaurès's *Histoire socialiste* became available. Its vision of the Revolution was very similar
to the social-democrats' own, in terms of both its general characterisation of
the revolutionary process and its critique of certain political groups. 1789 was
presented as the bourgeoisie's revolution and its social and economic aspects
were foregrounded – especially the transfer of property via the sale of the *biens
nationaux*. The Paris Commune's measures were 'far from exclusively the work
of the workers, but the work of the men of the *faubourgs* associated with the
petty bourgeoisie'.[93] Meanwhile, Robespierre's reign was seen as the beginning of the 'counter-revolution', for 'after the execution of the Hébertists, up
till 9 Thermidor the declining Convention consummated the destruction of
radical ideas'.[94] The final part was devoted to a short but positive presentation of the Conspiracy of Equals. Louis like the social-democrats argued that
the Conspiracy could not have succeeded faced with the social conditions of
the time. As for Louis's *History of the Trade-Union Movement in France*, this
work took the highly symbolic starting point of 1789. While this volume did
not feature any chapter directly devoted to the French Revolution, Louis did
highlight the rupture that it produced, for it was this that led to the abolition of
the guilds.[95] Gustav Eckstein's long, ninety-page introduction to the German
edition presented the peculiarities of French trade unionism as compared to
Germany.

Revolutionary Women

Austrian social democracy was notoriously reticent about involving women.[96]
Nonetheless, autonomous movements were organised from an early stage, and
numerous texts were published on this question. The book on women in the
Revolution by Emma Adler – wife of Victor – should be set in this context.[97]
Apart from this work and a *Lichtbilder* (teaching based on slides) which we will
examine below, the Austrians did not produce anything specific on the French

---

92   Louis 1901, p. 2.
93   Louis 1901, p. 37.
94   Louis 1901, p. 38.
95   Particularly the Le Chapelier Law of June 1791.
96   Paul Pasteur notes the exclusion of the only woman delegate to the Hainfeld Congress at
      the turn of 1888–9: Pasteur 2003, p. 54.
97   Adler 1906. See Pasteur 1998.

Revolution in this period. This is a sign of the relative weakness of the 'Austromarxist' historiography, at least on this point, as compared to its German counterpart.

In fact, the initial influence may have arrived from outside Germany. In the 1905 *Maifeier* Clara Zetkin published an article devoted to women's role in the Russian Revolution.[98] Emma Adler's work was essentially based on French-language books like Michelet's,[99] though the two standard social-democratic works (Kautsky's *Die Klassengegensätze von 1789* and Blos's *Die französische Revolution*) were also mentioned. Standing at some distance from a Kautsky-like reading of the French Revolution in terms of 'class', Adler presented the women of the Revolution as 'heroines and victims'.[100] There was a rather disconnected series of biographical portraits, in which she depicted women including Madame Legros, Théroignede Méricourt, Charlotte Corday, Madame Roland, Lucile Desmoulins, Olimpe de Gouge (sic), Rose Lacombe,[101] Madame Tallien, and Sophie de Condorcet. There was no description of the women of the *groupes populaires* during the Revolution. Emma Adler moreover emphasised the use of the guillotine. In this work, we can detect the author's contradictory aspirations, between the 'ideological straitjacket inherited from her bourgeois education' (the concern to be a good wife, and such like), and 'the social-democratic women's aspirations for emancipation' (the concern that women should be equal to men).[102] Adler foregrounded the example of Olimpe (sic) de Gouges, especially for the stance she took against the Terror. The book had a mixed reception in Austria: Adler's husband wrote to her, saying that he considered her book 'arch-reactionary'.[103] What is also true is that any autonomous women's demand might be seen in an even less favourable light now that the Austrian social-democrats had just achieved universal suffrage ... for men.[104] Worth noting in the German press are not only the (short) review in *Die Neue Zeit*,[105] but especially the one by Adelheid Popp (herself a

---

98   Zetkin, C., 'Die Frauen und die russische Revolution', *Maifeier*, 1905, pp. 3–10.

99   Michelet 1855. This work was translated into German in 1913, but not by the social-democrats: see Michelet 1913.

100   Pasteur 1998, p. 460.

101   Claire Lacombe's stage name.

102   Pasteur 1998, p. 461.

103   Adler family archives, VGA, Victor Adler to Emma Adler, 27 December 1905, AA M68/T7.

104   The authorities' concession in 1906 partly owed to the fact that the SDAP had abandoned the demand for votes for women. On Olympe de Gouges, see Blanc 2006.

105   Lerda, O., 'Emma Adler, Die berühmten Frauen der französischen Revolution', *Die Neue Zeit*, 1906, vol. 2, p. 744.

pioneer of the Austrian social-democratic women's movement) that was published in the *Sozialistische Monatshefte*.[106] The important thing, here, is less
the content of this review, which was short and descriptive in character, than
the very fact of its existence: for apart from this, no other book on the French
Revolution by a social-democrat was covered in its pages between 1905 and
1914. As we have seen, the women's question was the object of particular
attention during the revisionism dispute: in this context, the conceptions
expounded in Emma Adler's book were likely to be better received in the
Sozialistische Monatshefte than in other German social-democratic publications.

Lastly worth noting is the translation of Godwin's memoirs of Wollstonecraft, which were issued by a non-social-democratic Austrian publisher. The
translator was Therese Schlesinger, an influential Austrian militant who was
involved in the women's movement and active at the time of the revisionism
crisis. The introduction presented Wollstonecraft as 'the most important forerunner of women's emancipation'.[107]

The French Revolution: the Source of Marxism and German History?

One longstanding idea holds that French politics – seen in light of the 1789
Revolution and its legacy – combined with English economics and German
philosophy to form the sources of Marxism and social democracy.[108] If this
'triarchy' was already in gestation in the 1840s, it gradually assumed canonical
form in the early twentieth century. Kautsky's short 1908 pamphlet known in
French as *The Three Sources of Marx's Thought*[109] sought to establish the doctrine that revolved around this triarchy; it was published on the occasion of the
quarter-century anniversary of Marx's death, and it made up part of a series of
talks that Kautsky gave to SPD militants.

The result of a talk that Kautsky gave in Bremen in 1907, this pamphlet
appeared in the same year as the new editions of *Die Klassengegensätze, Der
Ursprung des Christentums* [*The Origins of Christianity*] and a short biograph-

---

106   Popp, A., 'Emma Adler, Die berühmten Frauen der französischen Revolution', *Sozialistische
      Monatshefte*, 1906, p. 450.
107   Godwin 1912.
108   See preamble, p. 30.
109   Kautsky 1908; we base our translation on the French edition, Kautsky 2000.

ical essay on *Frederick Engels – His Life, His Work and His Writings*.[110] Translated into a large number of languages and reissued on several occasions,[111] this pamphlet sought to provide a simple and clear reading of Marxian and Marxist thought for party cadres. One of its key ideas was the attempt to show the progress that Marx's thought represented for the science of history based on the 'synthesis of German, French and English thought'.[112] Kautsky explained the genesis of French thought in terms of a revolutionary tradition that dated back to 1789. The French Revolution had shown in particular that 'any class struggle is a struggle for political power';[113] he later added that 'the Great Revolution clearly showed the significance that the conquest of state power could have for the liberation of a class'.[114] While there was nothing original in all this, it did set the French Revolution in an overall theoretical framework, and identified it as one of the 'sources' of the social-democrats' Marxism.[115]

As in many articles and pamphlets from this period, 1789 was thus presented as the major historic rupture that marked the turn from one era to another. For example, in a short pamphlet entitled *War or Peace in the Trades Unions?* Otto Bauer spoke of how the Revolution had begun a new era for the nationalities question: 'In Austria-Hungary, in the Russian Empire and in the Balkans, people were still fighting the struggle which, for the Western nations, corresponded to the great period from 1789 to 1870'.[116]

The French Revolution also took up a place within the social-democrats' visions of their own national histories. One case in point was Franz Mehring's *History of Germany Since the Early Middle Ages*. As the title suggests, this was above all a specifically national history,[117] published not long after the series of works on the French Revolution described above. This book was written on the basis of the courses that Mehring gave on German history at the SPD party school; as its subtitle indicated, it was intended to be a textbook for those tak-

---

110 Kautsky, Karl 1908b. English text available at www.marxists.org.
111 Blumenburg 1960, p. 81.
112 Kautsky 2000, p. 18.
113 Ibid.
114 Kautsky 2000, p. 29.
115 Building on George Haupt's analysis of the Marxism of the 1880s, we could identify the years following the 1905 Russian Revolution as a kind of culmination of this party-'Marxism', which would undergo a profound process of recomposition with World War I and the Russian Revolution of 1917.
116 Bauer 1980a, p. 781.
117 Mehring, Franz 1910. In the first years of the DDR this work constituted a basic textbook on German history. In 1947 it was republished in the guise of a 'classic of Marxism-Leninism'.

ing these courses. The friendly thanks to Karl Kautsky in the preface – the only figure to receive such acknowledgement – indicated how important the 'Pope of Marxism's' historical works had been to Franz Mehring as he wrote his own history. In the introduction, Mehring explained his general method and the difficulties involved in explaining the materialist conception of history to an audience of militants:

> I far from share that point of view which holds that the materialist conception of history is impossible for the workers to understand, and that their historical edification must be built on the basis of the biographies of a few great men. But it can be made fundamentally easier for the workers to understand history by explaining the variations in history by way of the figures who were the most remarkable vectors of these variations. Historical materialism is never so disavowed as it is from the perspective of those who either do not want, or are not able, to understand it.[118]

This three-hundred-page textbook reserved very little space for anything other than directly German history. The place that the French Revolution occupied therein was thus all the more exceptional. Indeed, apart from the chapter on the Romans – discussed with reference to the ancient period, and even this in close relationship with the first Germanic peoples – the chapter on the 'Great Revolution' was the only one of the seven that did not concern Germany directly. In quantitative terms, the chapter reserved for the French Revolution was, together with the chapter on the Reformation, the longest, standing at some fifty pages.[119] The end of each chapter featured a short bibliography aimed at the students taking the course. Unsurprisingly, the chapter on the Revolution mentioned the books we have already discussed. The important thing, here, was to understand the consistency of the social-democrats' production, from Blos's 'people's history' to Cunow's more developed approach:

> Sources. Blos's *French Revolution* provides a popular portrayal of the great upheaval of 1789. Kautsky's *Class Contradictions in the Time of the French Revolution* is very useful for understanding how it unfolded. Even more precise is Cunow, who addresses the class struggles of the period in his

---

118   Mehring 1910–11, p. 10.
119   The Reformation and the Peasant War were particular focuses of study, and a key point of reference for the German workers' movement after Engels's famous study on *The Peasant War in Germany* (English version in MECW, Vol. 10).

French Revolutionary Press from 1789 to 1794. He who studies these texts in detail can do without the bourgeois literature on the French Revolution.[120]

As for the chapter's content, the history of the French Revolution allowed for a discussion of everything in the German-speaking countries that had drawn inspiration from this event, and moreover the consequences of the Napoleonic occupation. The Revolution was, most importantly, a great socio-economic rupture in German history; it was the 'bourgeois revolution' whose extension by Napoleon had laid the bases for the abolition of feudalism in Germany. It is worth noting that the first sub-section on 'the French Revolution' – the only one in this book to be entirely devoted to a country other than Germany – was in very large part a synopsis of Kautsky's work. The second sub-section integrated some of the advances that Heinrich Cunow had made in his study, detailing the nature of the social conflicts that lay behind the different political sensibilities. Finally, it is worth noting that Mehring emphasised the profound difference between the social-democrats and the Jacobin and *sans-culotte* revolutionaries. His work thus followed in the same vein as Kautsky's distrust toward 'Jacobin traditions', even as it hailed their historic value.[121]

Otto Bauer's pamphlet on his country's history was the Austrian equivalent of Mehring's book on Germany.[122] Published by the Central Educational Commission, it laid the bases for the party school's teaching of Austrian history. Nonetheless, this volume was far shorter than Mehring's work, and rather more resembled a detailed plan. Nonetheless, the objectives that Bauer set out at the start of his book were similar in nature: the third part addressed 'Austria at the Head of Counter-Revolutionary Europe'. The first few lines explained the 'French Revolution', and in particular the ideas of the Enlightenment and their translation into political life between 1789 and 1792. Even shorter was the part on 'Austria and the French Revolution', which was limited to the measures taken by the enlightened despot Joseph II in 1790 and the war between Austria and France. The only remark that was not simply factual was Bauer's characterisation of Napoleon, presented as 'the heir of the Revolution. He continued the wars against the feudal and absolutist states. The bourgeois legal order which the Revolution had created was introduced in the countries that he subdued.'[123]

---

120   Mehring 1910–11, p. 148.
121   Mehring 1910–11, p. 105.
122   Bauer 1913, with marginal changes from the 1911 first edition. See Bauer 1980a, pp. 889–910.
123   Bauer 1980a, p. 906.

Despite the similarities in their bibliographical references, unlike Mehring's work Bauer did not remark on the French Revolution's own internal processes.[124]

The French Revolution was, then, the only foreign historical event discussed in the national histories written by party leaders. And these two textbooks would constitute the foundations of party cadres' intellectual formation. We shall now turn to presenting this educational mechanism itself.

---

124   It recommended the works of Blos, Kropotkin, Kautsky, and Cunow.

CHAPTER 6

The Social-Democratic Educational Apparatus from 1906 to 1914

Teaching Militants History

Education became increasingly important in the wake of the 1905 Revolution, as the two parties' growth also demanded better-educated cadres.[1] History – and in particular the history of the French Revolution – was a unique focus of courses, classes and talks.

The Berlin Training School

Before we study the *Parteischule* we will again look at the example of the Berlin workers' school, which we already examined in our discussion of the 1889 centenary.[2] As we have already noted, after being absent since 1889 the French Revolution returned to its history programmes from the first semester of 1905. A study of the period from 1906 to 1914 confirms how well-rooted this reference was. Indeed, 1906–7 marked a break with previous years, as the French Revolution assumed a more important place in the school, with a detailed programme that had never previously existed in this form. The history programme for the first trimester of 1906 offered the following course:

The Great Revolution (1789–1799)
- The worldwide historical significance of the French Revolution
- The social and intellectual development of eighteenth-century France
- The outbreak of the Revolution
- The tactics of the crown, the moderates and the radicals
- The unfolding of the Revolution, up till Napoleon's Consulate
- Comparison of the French Revolution with the current Russian Revolution[3]

The sixth point left no doubt that the French Revolution had been restored to the school's programme in response to the Russian Revolution. A year later,

---

1 For a detailed and illustrated overview of the SPD's *Arbeiter-Bildung*, see Ollbrich 1982.
2 For one study on this school, see Heid 2004.
3 *Arbeiter-Bildungsschule Berlin. Bericht über die Tätigkeit*, Berlin, 1906, p. 4.

the school offered the same course in the first trimester of 1907. The French Revolution was a compulsory point of reference, decisive to shedding light on the problems of the present; one could only understand the Russian Revolution if one compared it with the French events of 1789. Moreover, in 1906–7 the only course that was repeated in identical fashion was the one devoted to the French Revolution. This repetition of this course within the space of just a few months is well worth emphasising. Annual reports gave more detailed information on the participants in these programmes. The total numbers signing up for the second trimester of 1906 amounted to only 373 people; it was in the final trimester of 1906 that numbers considerably increased (to 975), and then continued to progress. Sociologically speaking, the report indicates, on the basis of the information collected, that across all the different sessions some 1680 members had given their profession: of these 404 were engineering workers, thus belonging to one of the SPD's main social bases, while all other jobs ranked far behind. The huge majority were men, as was still true of the party as a whole.

As concerned the teaching dedicated to history specifically, the statistics provided for 1906 allow us to summarise the figures for the course dealing with the French Revolution. 107 took part in this course (out of 159 who signed up). This stood in line with average participation levels among many courses, though political economy – at the heart of party education – was well ahead of the others, with 215 participants (out of 314 who signed up). Adding together the different figures (and assuming that those who followed the first course on the French Revolution did not return for its re-running), we reach the figure of 202 participants in this course on the Revolution – that is, similar to the number of militants who took the political economy class. This is a far from minor consideration, especially given that in 1906–7 no other historical event was similarly brought into relief; all the other classes were much more general (from 'contemporary political parties' to 'the birth of Christianity') and were only on the programme once a trimester.

The French Revolution's place, here, was all the more remarkable given that it had been completely absent from the school's courses between 1899 and 1905. In generational terms, most of the militants who followed this course were between 20 and 30 years of age: 95 of the 159 militants who signed up for the class in 1906 were from this age bracket, while only 4 were more than 40 years old. The different age brackets were similarly represented in 1907, when 91 of those who signed up were between 20 and 30 years of age. Someone who was 25 in 1906 would have been a young child in the 1880s and would not have known the publications, talks and other contributions on the Revolution that appeared during the centenary and its aftermath, not least given that the works

published in 1889 had not yet been republished. So it was thanks to the classes
of 1906–7 that a new generation of militants got to know the history of the
French Revolution.

Was the interest for these classes simply a reaction to the Russian Revolution, as these detailed plans would seem to indicate, or was it instead the beginning of a longer-term introduction to the course? A similarly-titled programme
ran from 1907 to 1913, albeit in just one trimester per year. However, we can
also note a course offered in one trimester in 1910–11 that concerned 'the era of
the French Revolution'. This was probably based on Kautsky's book, for its title
exactly corresponded to the subtitle of the new edition organised by Alexander
Conrady, a social-democrat who also gave other history courses over a period of
many years. The French Revolution was also addressed as part of wider themes.
Thus even beyond the sessions specifically addressed to the Revolution, what is
most telling is the fact that it was almost systematically integrated into numerous other history courses. The following table recapitulates the presence of the
Revolution in history courses between 1906 and 1914.

Year (normally three trimesters)	Name of the course concerned	Focus on the French Revolution
1906–7	The French Revolution (held twice)	Total; ended with a comparison with the Russian Revolution
1907–8	Modern Revolutions up till 1789	Conclusion on the build-up to the French Revolution
1908–9	The History of Socialism	Section devoted to socialism in the French Revolution, and in particular Babeuf
1910–11	The Era of the French Revolution	Based on Kautsky's pamphlet
1911–12	None	None
1912–13	None	None
1913–14	The History of Socialism	Communists during the English and French Revolutions

The Central Party School

A party school [*Parteischule*] was created in 1906. It recruited thirty people, who
were left to their own devices for six months in order to prepare the courses.
At first glance, it is difficult to grasp what place teaching on the French Revolution assumed within this programme, given the very broad categories that the

plans indicated: for instance, 'German history' or 'history of socialism'.[4] This latter category became a focus of SPD educational structures in general, including local schools; as the table above shows, from 1908 'the history of socialism' was regularly taught in Berlin. Making use of a variety of sources, we can establish with some accuracy the place that the French Revolution occupied within this programme.[5] The content of this 'history of socialism' course and the place that it occupied have been a matter of debate. Dieter Fricke's list of the classes that were given at the school holds that this course first appeared only in 1909–10,[6] and various conference minutes confirm as much. In one intervention at the Nuremberg Congress in 1908, Rosa Luxemburg – who taught at the party school from 1907 onward – accorded a central place to this history, which, in her view, had been too little-addressed during the first year of the *Parteischule*'s existence.[7] Her correspondence from 1908–9 moreover refers to her reading on the history of revolutions – notably, the French Revolution – with a view to preparing this course on the history of socialism. For example, with regard to Babeuf she consulted the study by Albert Thomas – whose introduction into Germany as part of the revisionism debate we have already discussed – as well as Advielle's work (in French).[8] It seems that Babouvism, as well as the Montagnards, were the subject that most interested Luxemburg. On 19 May 1908 she wrote to her friend Kostja Zetkin, and offered a few well-informed remarks in response to this latter's question as to whether a 'working class' had existed during 'the Great Revolution';[9] perhaps drawing inspiration from Kautsky's handbook, she recommended to Hans Kautsky that he should read Heinrich von Sybel as well as De Tocqueville's *L'Ancien Régime et la Révolution*.[10] Finally, again writing to Kostja Zetkin in the hope that she could entrust him with running this course (he did not ultimately do so), she proposed a detailed course plan including the history of 'socialist ideas during the Great Revolution':[11] the French Revolution was addressed only in terms of the early emergence of 'socialism', and in just one of 24 courses.

---

4   The party congress minutes (*Protokoll*) each year gave information on the content of the *Parteischule* courses. For a partial summary, see Fricke 1987, pp. 694–5.

5   As well as party congress minutes, we have consulted Rosa Luxemburg's correspondence, the many detailed plans and summaries on these courses (for example Eckstein 1910), references in theoretical journals, and, for Austria, *Bildungsarbeit*.

6   Fricke 1987, p. 694.

7   *Protokoll*, 1908, p. 230.

8   Luxemburg 1982, Vol. 2, p. 337. See Advielle 1990.

9   Luxemburg 1982, Vol. 2, p. 341.

10   Luxemburg 1982, Vol. 3, letter of 20 June 1909, p. 37.

11   Letter from 1 October 1909. Cited by Badia 1975, p. 826.

However, ultimately the 'Great Revolution' assumed a more important place
in this programme than Rosa Luxemburg herself intended. We can consult the
final plans still today: the courses were sometimes accompanied by the publication of detailed summaries, which were themselves given to the school's
students. These give us a more detailed idea of the content of the teaching that
was provided. A particular case in point was a detailed plan published in 1910,
entitled *Guide to the Study of Socialism*.[12] Its author was Gustav Eckstein, an
influential militant in the Austrian party who had come to Germany.[13] A doctor in law from the University of Vienna, he had lived for a time in Japan, where
he studied that country's language and civilisation, before becoming a teacher
at the Berlin party school and a member of the *Die Neue Zeit* editorial team
in 1910. He published a study on French trade unionism – which served as an
introduction to the German translation of Paul Louis's work on the history of
the trade-union movement since 1789[14] – as well as several studies on Marxism. Politically speaking, he stood on the left wing of the party, and repeatedly
expressed a fervent internationalism. The French Revolution represented just
over two of the nineteen pages of this plan for the 'History of Socialism' course.
This was the only historical period to occupy such a place, ahead of the English
Revolutions of the seventeenth century, 1848 and the Paris Commune. Taken
as a whole, this programme stretching from Thomas More to the end of the
First International was similar to Luxemburg's own intentions, as expressed in
her letter to Kostja Zetkin. Rather different, however, was the case of the 'Great
Revolution', for it was not only addressed in terms of its 'socialist' aspects. The
period from 1789 to 1799 was divided into two major parts: the first concerned
'the French Revolution' up till the Directory, whereas the shorter second section was entirely devoted to Babeuf. The first part reflected the main themes of
Kautsky's pamphlet, describing the place of each social class on the eve of 1789
before addressing the Revolution itself in line with its chronological development, from 17 June 1789 to the 1795 Constitution. Corresponding to the general
profile of a course that sought to teach the historical development of the socialist idea, it addressed two points in particular detail: namely, the content of the
August 1789 *Declaration of the Rights of Man and the Citizen*, and the 1793 Constitution, whose importance we have repeatedly noted. The second part was
devoted to the life of Babeuf and the content of his doctrine of 'egalitarian communism'. The important place that this plan afforded to the French Revolution

---

12   Eckstein 1910.
13   Apart from *Maitron Autriche*, we can also draw a good deal of information from the obit-
      uary in *Der Kampf*: Adler, F., 'Gustav Eckstein', *Der Kampf*, September 1916, pp. 297–300.
14   See Chapter Five, p. 133.

was also apparent in the list of recommended reading. There were five books on the Revolution, by Cunow, Kautsky, Blos, Buonarroti and Deville (this latter was described as 'out of print' – it had not been republished since 1887). By way of comparison, there were three books on the revolution of 1848 (one by Louis Heritier and two by Karl Marx), and two on the Commune (Marx and Lissagaray).[15]

This plan printed in 1910 would serve for Gustav Eckstein's 1910–11 classes and then all the courses on the 'History of Socialism', taught in particular by Hermann Duncker[16] but also by Heinrich Cunow.

In the years up till 1914, the hours of class time for this course first increased and then stabilised:
- 1909/1910: 56 hours.
- 1910/1911: 74 hours.
- 1912/1913: 80 hours.
- 1913/1914: 72 hours.

This was much shorter than the courses on 'political economy', which from the outset amounted to well over 200 hours. However, the French Revolution was also part of another course devoted to 'German History since the Middle Ages', which from 1912 onward became simply 'German History'. After the first two sessions, this course was taught by Franz Mehring. Here we will not revisit the content of this course, which we already examined above when we mentioned the book which directly resulted from his lectures. We will simply note the importance of the French Revolution as seen, here, through the prism of its influence on the German-speaking countries. And this course, given every year without interruption, varied between 72 and 100 hours. The French Revolution's place in both courses made it the most-studied historical point of reference. If not all the party cadres who went through the school followed all of the history programmes, all of them took at least one of the courses which included a study of the 'Great French Revolution'.

The documents on the Austrian social-democrats' educational programmes are less detailed, but some of the documents gathered in the archives held at the VGA in Vienna do nonetheless allow us to reconstruct their content. One useful example is a manuscript of a report on educational activities, which does not seem to have any printed version.[17] Better still, a central party school

---

15   Lissagaray 1891.
16   A teacher at the *Parteischule*, Duncker would later play an important role in the German Communist Party (KPD). See Chapter Eleven, p. 275.
17   'Bericht der Zentraltelle für das Bildungswesen für das zweite Semester 1909', VGA, Sozialdemokratische Parteistellen, Karton 129, Mappe 809 'Bildungswesen 1898–1918'.

was opened in Bodenbach in 1910, and its first year of programmes were listed in *Bildungsarbeit*.[18] Unlike in the German case, there was no 'history' section. However, a section on 'politics' covering some 27 hours – the longest, along with 'political economy' – proposed a series of courses, one of which was devoted to the French Revolution.[19]

The Importance of Lectures

Travelling Lectures
The Central Educational Commission began its work at the end of 1906; it offered all the local training schools in Germany talks and courses. One document that it published[20] offered the local SPD sections concerned with education talks and conferences by *Wanderlehrer*. These travelling social-democratic educators 'journeyed around the country, and mainly small towns or large outlying villages with a small active community of social-democrats. They offered an overview and then returned to the region for a week or two, depending on the location, giving the same talk one or more times'.[21] The document, dated 18 May 1914, gives us some idea of the place that the French Revolution occupied in the talks that were given in Germany on the eve of World War I. A certain Bernard Rausch gave 'one to three talks' on the 'Great French Revolution', whereas all the other historical periods addressed (including 1848) were limited to just one talk. Another series by Christian Döring offered two talks per revolution on the English Revolution, the Great French Revolution and the German Revolution of 1848. Lastly, it is also worth noting Karl Schröder's talk on 'the history of culture in the era of the French Revolution', although given that it explained the great currents of eighteenth-century thought (the Enlightenment, Sturm und Drang, and so on) only in very general terms, this was more a chronological overview than a real treatment of the revolutionary period.

As for the content of the talks, we know what featured in those given by Bernard Rausch. An education commission document related the contents of six talks devoted to 'The Era of the Great Revolution and the Wars of Lib-

18 *Bildungsarbeit*, September 1910, p. 3.
19 Ibid.
20 *Zentralbildungsausschuss der Sozialdemokratischen Partei Deutschlands, Die wissenschaftliche Wanderkurse für 1914/1915*, Berlin, 1914.
21 Pasteur 2000, p. 17.

eration (1789–1815)'.[22] No date was indicated, but the bibliography mentions books published in 1912–13, so it did come from this same period. This plan was intended to be distributed to those who followed the talks. The six-talk series included three on the French Revolution and three others on the 1813 Wars of Liberation.[23] The first addressed 'The theory of class struggle and the French Revolution' and 'absolutism', reflecting the broad themes of the first parts of Kautsky's pamphlet. The two other talks on the Revolution were centred on events (such as 4 August and 10 August) and mixed portraits of the revolutionaries (from Mirabeau to Marat and Babeuf) with social analyses ('the bourgeois character of the National Constituent Assembly') and a presentation of the struggles between political groups ('the fight between the Girondin and Montagnard parties'). The plan also integrated elements of Heinrich Cunow's work, in simplified form: the two latter talks closely resembled the structure of his book. The bibliography that accompanied the plan very much reflected these choices, for the titles that it chiefly recommended were the ones by Karl Kautsky, Heinrich Cunow, Peter Kropotkin and Franz Mehring. On the eve of the war, Kautsky and Cunow's books served as the basis for courses and talks aimed at an audience of militants who had probably not read these titles.

As for Austria, a 1910 report by the education centre[24] provided a list of the talks and courses offered to the workers' organisations of the different towns and cities. Only one series ('On the History of Revolutions')[25] seems likely to have contained elements on the French Revolution. The available information regarding the local level allow us to complete this very general panorama. We can take the example of a series of classes offered to the social-democrats of Vienna in the last trimester of 1910.[26] The series was mainly political in content: several talks were entirely given over to 'the party programme'. The content of one of the talks, given by Karl Renner,[27] was published in *Bildungsarbeit*.[28]

---

22   *Zentralbildungsausschuss der Sozialdemokratischen Partei Deutschlands, Disposition und Schriftenverzeichnis zu dem Kursus des Genossen Berhard Rausch über: Das Zeitalter der grossen Französischen Revolution und die Befreiungskriege (1789–1815)*.

23   We discuss these latter below in our study of the 1913 centenary: see Chapter Nine, p. 230.

24   'Bericht der Landeszentralstelle für das Bildungswesen für die Zeit vom 1. Juni 1909 bis 30. Juli 1910', VGA, Sozial-demokratische Parteistellen, Karton 129, Mappe 809, 'Bildungswesen 1898–1918'.

25   Ibid.

26   'Unterrichtsprogramm der Wiener Arbeiterorganisationen', *Bildungsarbeit*, 1910–11, p. 10.

27   Karl Renner (1870–1950) was one of the most important leaders of Austrian social democracy, and represented its most moderate wing. He was chancellor during the First and Second Republics. See Haupt and Maitron 1971, pp. 250–5.

28   Renner, K., 'Die demokratischen Forderungen des Parteiprogramms. Disposition zu zwei Programmverträgen', Bildungsarbeit, 1913–14, p. 2.

The introduction made repeated references to the French Revolution, which was portrayed, together with 1848, as the major event that had put an end to *ancien régime* society. No more specific discussion of the Revolution was mentioned, though bibliographical references included Franz Mehring's *Deutsche Geschichte* and Karl Kautsky's *Die Klassengegensätze von 1789*. Only three out of the nineteen talks in this 1910 series were strictly historical in character: there were two on the 'History of Socialism' by Leopold Winarsky, which certainly included some elements on Babeuf,[29] and one by Therese Schlesinger on 'The French Revolution', which likely included discussion on the women's question.[30]

Another report on party education in Vienna in 1911, as well as some of the articles published in *Bildungsarbeit*, allow us to complete this picture.[31] This report similarly covered a series of public talks and courses that were provided for the benefit of party members in Vienna. Here we again see the more limited place that was given to the history of revolutions in the Austrian case: over the many dozens of series offered, only three concerned the history of the English, French and 1848 revolutions. However, a few details in the published plan indicate that the French Revolution was the most studied of the revolutions concerned: while it mentions only one talk for the English Revolution and another one for 1848, the French Revolution was addressed in a succession of talks, on 'The Origins of the Revolution', 'The French Revolution of 1789', 'Babeuf and the Conspiracy of Equals' and 'Napoleon'. As for the public talks, we can refer to the statistics published in *Bildungsarbeit* in 1911–12.[32] With only six talks on the French Revolution and five on Babeuf specifically, less space was dedicated to this period than to 1848 (on which there were 30 talks). The proportions were similar the following year, with seven talks on the Revolution and six on Babeuf, to which we should add a further talk on Napoleon.[33] Lastly, the report for 1913–14 speaks of six talks on the French Revolution and one on 'Schiller and the French Revolution',[34] thus expressing a greater integration of this historical reference into a German-speaking context.

The French Revolution did not, therefore, occupy a central position like it did in Germany, and while some books were recommended, they were almost all

29   On Leopold Winarsky, see pp. 168–9, 178–9.
30   *Bildungsarbeit*, 1911–12, p. 10.
31   'Vortragsverzeichnis der Unterrichtsausschusses der Wiener Arbeiterorganisationen, Wien, Verlag von Robert Danneberg, 1911', VGA, Sozial-demokratische Parteistellen, Karton 129, Mappe 809.
32   'Statistik der Wiener Einzelvorträge (1911/12)', *Bildungsarbeit*, 1912–13, p. 13.
33   'Statistik der Wiener Einzelvorträge (1912/13)', *Bildungsarbeit*, 1913–14, p. 82.
34   'Statistik der Wiener Einzelvorträge (1912/13)', *Bildungsarbeit*, 1913–14, p. 85.

German rather than Austrian. The only originality, here, owed to the handful of talks that were devoted to women and the French Revolution, possibly in connection with the publication of Emma Adler's book. However, it was in Austria that one of the more original documents dedicated to the French Revolution was published.

A Modernised Format: the Lichtbildervorträge[35]

The pre-war period was also characterised by the use of ever more varied forms of educational materials and propaganda. As we have seen, numerous different media like theatre, popular songs, caricatures, and illustrations more generally, could serve as vehicles for the reference to the French Revolution. As the social-democrats pursued a *Bildung* that very much saw culture as a domain with which the party ought to concern itself, historical references were transmitted by various different means. The *Lichtbildervorträge* – talks accompanied by slides – made up part of this same picture.[36]

Talks accompanied by slides seemed to spread shortly before 1914. They would particularly spread as a means of propaganda during World War I. The preponderant subject of this type of talks was more cultural themes, and in particular artistic retrospectives, for which the *Lichtbildervorträge* seem like an ideal format. It also seems to have been particularly appropriate for scientific and anthropological themes. Looking across the different *Lichtbildervorträge* we see that before the 1920s they very seldom dealt with historical subjects. Most important were a few examples of talks that paid homage to great figures of Germanic culture (such as Freiligrath and Schiller). We can get a more detailed idea of these talks from a short handbook published by the SPD educational commission in 1913, straightforwardly titled *Lichtbilder*.[37]

> Given the extraordinary development of the moving image at the 'cinema', slideshows were somewhat left to one side. But since then they have, through great struggle, won back their place, and soon the need for slideshows alongside the moving image will be universally recognised ... We hope that through our endeavour we can stimulate and invigorate proletarian educational activity at this level.[38]

---

35   *Lichtbildervortrag* can be translated as 'talk accompanied by slides'. For the sake of convenience we here stick to the German term.

36   The first projections of slides took place at the Urania educational institute. Urania was supported by the Vienna city administration and part of the imperial aristocracy; after 1919 the social-democrats would place it at their own service.

37   Zentralbildungsausschuss der Sozialdemokratischen Partei Deutschlands 1913.

38   Zentralbildungsausschuss der Sozialdemokratischen Partei Deutschlands 1913, p. 3.

This small handbook also contained a whole series of technical measures and recommendations to make it easier to use this medium. There then followed a list of talks accompanied by slides: the most distant period that featured therein concerned the Wars of Liberation of 1813–15, and in general history was rather under-represented as compared to the natural sciences, geography and art history. The French Revolution was not entirely absent, however. Reading the details of the suggested images, we see that it was included in the 'History of the Development of the Press', prepared by Konrad Haenisch.[39] The greater part of the 43 images, running from the end to the eighteenth century to the final issue of *Der Sozialdemokrat* in 1890, were focused on the history of the revolutionary and workers' movement from 1848 onward. Nonetheless, there were five images depicting the revolutionary press of 1789–92: *Le Point du Jour* (1789), *L'Ami du peuple* (1789), *Le Publiciste parisien* (1789), *Le Journal de Paris* (1790), and *La Gazette nationale* (1792). By way of comparison, there was only one more (a total of six images) on the 1848 Revolution. 1789's role as a precursor to this history was very clear.

This made even more exceptional the 1913 publication of a *Lichtbildervortrag* on the French Revolution. That year, the Austrian party's Central Education Commission published a 'colour *Lichtbildervortrag*' by Leopold Winarsky devoted to the 'great French Revolution'.[40] The attention to the *Lichtbildervorträge* in Austria was the same as that in Germany. A short biography of the social-democrat Winarksy was published in the wake of an exhibition that was dedicated to him.[41] Born in 1873, before World War I he was a member of the SDAP secretariat, in charge of education, and an MP for a Vienna seat. He stood on the left wing of the party and consistently asserted his internationalism, which may in part explain his interest in France one year before war broke out. Both well-known and popular in the Viennese working-class milieu (he was nicknamed 'fescher Poldl', 'smart Leopold'), this bibliophile, great reader and organiser of the Vienna conference of workers' associations [*Arbeiterbildungsvereine*] was the author of a large number of articles on political and historical subjects in both *Der Kampf* and *Arbeiter-Zeitung*. The tributes to Winarsky in the 2 December 1915 issue of *Glühlicher*, in response to his death, reflected his great popularity.[42] The various articles devoted to him represented a significant part of this issue: there was a large portrait of him on the

---

39   Haenisch 1913.
40   Winarsky 1913.
41   Vass and Wolensky 1990; see also the obituary in *Der Kampf*, 'Leopold Winarsky', *Der Kampf*, January 1916, pp. 1–5.
42   *Glühlichter*, 2 December 1915, pp. 1–10.

front page, a far-reaching retrospective of his life, as well as numerous photographs ... One contemporary highlighted Winarsky's interest in the history of
the Revolution with reference to the make-up of his library, emphasising the
significant number of books on this same theme.[43]

Indeed, he published a history of the 1848 Revolution and already in 1895
had given a talk on this same theme to an audience of between 800 and 1,000
workers.[44] His *Lichtbildervortrag* devoted to the 'Great Revolution' was the result of the courses that he gave at the Vienna workers' school [*Arbeiterschule*].[45]
This talk sought to give a general overview of the Revolution;[46] in its first pages
it discussed the final decades of the absolute monarchy and the role of the
Enlightenment (first twenty images). According to Winarsky, the Revolution
began on 28 April 1789 with the revolt of the Réveillon workers; this was a highly
narrative work, centred on the period between 1789 and 1794. While his reading did devote some space to popular action, the heart of his discourse was the
major dates of the Revolution, backed up by the images that represented them.
These events were described in very simple terms, designed to popularise this
history. This was a transcription of what was to be given as a talk, and there
were even pointers as to how to pronounce the most important words: hence
'Gironde: *Schirond*'.[47] A few statements that broke out of the merely narrative stood close to the social-democrats' classic characterisations of this period:
this was a bourgeois Revolution, Robespierre was a 'dictator' and Marat was a
'democrat':

> He was a very advanced democrat in the vanguard of the movement. To
> repeat, he was a democrat, and not a social-democrat, as is often erro-
> neously claimed. Certainly there was no socialist among the leaders of
> France at that time.[48]

The Montagne was 'the party of the popular masses of Paris';[49] its victory after
31 May and 2 June allowed these masses temporarily to rule. The 'state terror' was summarily justified in terms of the needs of the moment, and the

---

43   Brügel, F., 'Die Sozialwissenschaftliche Studienbibliothek bei der Wiener Arbeiterkam-
      mer', *Bildungsarbeit*, October 1925, p. 1.
44   Winarsky 1911.
45   Winarsky 1911, p. 25.
46   Winarsky 1913, p. 2.
47   Winarsky 1913, p. 15.
48   Ibid.
49   Winarsky 1913, p. 17.

achievements of the 1793 Constitution were also foregrounded.[50] Like many social-democratic texts, it also mentioned the repression of the Hébertists by Robespierre.[51] Little more than two pages were devoted to the period between the fall of Robespierre and 18 Brumaire. This period of 'reaction' was presented in very negative terms, as the triumph of the *haute bourgeoisie*. Logically enough, Babeuf was the focus of the concluding part; he was presented as a forerunner, the 'most progressive revolutionary, the only authentic socialist of the whole revolutionary period'.[52] There then followed a brief presentation of Napoleon, whose rule was 'a historical necessity'. The ideas of the Revolution were to be pursued into the present, and the talk ended with a lusty call for the 'building of a world of freedom and equality in a future socialist society'.[53] The talk also emphasised the continuity between the *Marseillaise* and the *Workers' Marseillaise*, a song of very great importance for the workers' movement in the German speaking countries.

This *Lichtbildervortrag* gives a more precise idea of what social-democrats might have been taught before 1914, whether by speech or via the written word. Comparing its content with the educationals at the Berlin school and the *Parteischule*, what is particularly notable is the place that was now occupied by Babeuf; he was systematically presented as the forerunner of socialism, and he took up increasing space in talks and classes.

Beyond this specific element on Babeuf, this talk reflected a now-classic representation of the Revolution based on illustrations. This was comparable to Wilhelm Blos's work and even, to some extent, *Der Wahre Jacob*, as many of the slides were reproductions of cartoons. This talk was a kind of combination of Blos's 'people's history' and elements more reminiscent of Kautsky's approach. The bibliographical essay was revealing in this regard: Blos's work was 'an easy-to-understand written history of the French Revolution, which may usefully be read by all, without the need for prior knowledge'.[54] Cunow, conversely, addressed himself to a specialist readership;[55] as for Kautsky's *Die Klassengegensätze von 1789*, this was presented as 'a short essay ... an excellent attempt to spread clarity on the causes of the French Revolution, aided by the materialist conception of history'.[56] Notably, Kropotkin's work was also recommended

50   Ibid.
51   Winarsky 1913, p. 21.
52   Winarsky 1913, p. 23.
53   Ibid.
54   Ibid.
55   Ibid.
56   Ibid.

as a demonstration of 'the role that the masses played during the revolution-ary struggles'.[57] Mignet and Carlyle's texts were highlighted as portrayals of the events of the Revolution, and two novels were also mentioned; Anatole France's *The Gods are Athirst* and Charles Dickens's *Tale of Two Cities*. As it explained, 'Next, we recommend two novels, a pleasureable read for anyone with a know-ledge of the revolutionary era, which even beyond their artistic quality can offer [such readers] deeper insights into this era than some historical works'.[58]

This recommended reading helped to entrench the reference to the French Revolution. A 1913 report on the *Lichtbildervorträge* offered a short overview of the echo that this new format had encountered.[59] While its success seems to have owed above all to themes that were not directly historical in character (an audience of 1,100 for the series on the origin of human life, and 2,140 for a presentation on China and its peoples), the only historical theme addressed by a *Lichtbildervortäg* was the French Revolution: 300 people attended a talk on this question.

Party Libraries

A study of the sources on party libraries allows us to understand what books appeared on their shelves, and moreover allows some insight into what milit-ants might have read or consulted. Workers' libraries had a long tradition, as old as social-democracy itself; but they took on particular importance follow-ing the creation of a Central Education Commission, charged with centralising the existing book distribution system. These libraries now became a far more structured affair. For example, a book classification system was established for the purposes of standardisation; these measures encountered a certain resist-ance, given that some libraries wished to remain autonomous. A study of the two libraries in Köpenick and Breslau[60] – the first a small structure, and the second a much larger facility – well reflects the diversity of different situations. Also notable is the desire to distinguish between 'instructive' and 'recreational' reading;[61] a concern that we already encountered when we examined the vari-ous writings of Wilhelm Blos and Karl Kautsky.

---

57   Ibid.
58   Ibid.
59   'Lichtbildervorträge', *Bildungsarbeit*, 1912–13, p. 84.
60   Roy-Jacquemart 1979.
61   Roy-Jacquemart 1979, p. 105.

Constituting a Historical Library

The creation of a press organ specifically devoted to party libraries – which was itself presented as an important event[62] – best allows us to understand their importance during this period. Edited by the social-democrat Gustav Henning, *Der Bibliothekar* was an illustration of the great attention that social democracy devoted to access to books, and indeed its will to action on this question.[63] The production of this journal is itself worth studying. As was often the case in the social-democratic press, a great deal of space was occupied by advertisements offering books for sale; for example, the new edition of Kautsky's *Die Klassengegensäzte* in Dietz's 'Kleine Bibliothek' was regularly advertised.[64]

If *Der Bibliothekar* covered a very wide spectrum of books, spanning all domains of knowledge in order to ensure the fullness of the party libraries, what space was there for the French Revolution? The index of the 'history' section for the first year of *Der Bibliothekar* leaves little room for doubt; the three books listed – and thus recommended to the libraries – were all devoted to the French Revolution. From its very first issue, *Der Bibliothekar* sought to emphasise the authority of Heinrich Cunow's study.[65] Citing a passage from Taine that insulted Marat, the review highlighted Cunow's work to counter the legends by using the 'writings, articles and letters' that restored Marat to his proper place – not to criticise him or to martyrise him, but in order to understand him.[66] The article concluded by recommending that libraries avail themselves of a copy of the book. This was, without exception, the constant purpose of the reviews published in *Der Bibliothekar*; they sought to present the qualities of a given book in order to persuade those in charge of libraries to acquire it. *Der Bibliothekar* took the same approach to the anarchist Kropotkin's book on the French Revolution, which had already been discussed in *Die Neue Zeit* (as we discussed at length above). Its tone was more measured than Heinrich Cunow's review of Kropotkin's work in *Die Neue Zeit*, though similar criticisms were advanced in both texts.[67] The review paid tribute to Kropotkin's work for having restored

---

62   See Ryazanov's presentation on this theme in *Die Neue Zeit*, 1908–9, Vol. 2, pp. 125–6; on Austria, see *Der Kampf*, 1907, pp. 191–2. *Der Bibliothekar* was published in Leipzig from 1909 to 1918.

63   *Der Bibliothekar* had a modest print run, for it was above all addressed to those occupied with managing local libraries and those who took a close interest in these questions, such as local party leaders. See *Protokoll* 1907, p. 32.

64   In particular in *Der Bibliothekar*, July 1909, p. 34.

65   Lensch, P., 'Bücherbesprechungen', *Der Bibliothekar*, April 1909, pp. 5–6.

66   Ibid.

67   See above, p. 145.

the popular classes' activity in the Revolution to its proper place, as well as its ability to demonstrate the role of economic forces.[68] However, it sharply distanced itself from the Russian anarchist's discussion of the 'two great tendencies' at work between 1789 and 1793 – a schematic idea that did not give proper account of the complexity of the revolutionary movement. The author nonetheless made clear that despite its flaws, Kropotkin's book ought to have a readership among social-democratic militants.[69] The third work to be reviewed was the Blos' translation of Buonarroti's book. It emphasised the credit due to Babeuf for having heralded a socialist doctrine, even if it was unrealiseable in his own time.[70] The diffidence toward Robespierre that Blos had expressed in his introduction also appeared in this review.

As for Austria, *Bildungsarbeit* – a more generalist publication – was not directly centred on party libraries and also dealt with education more generally. It featured a brief review of the translation of Buonarroti's book on Babeuf and the Conspiracy of Equals.[71] The conclusion praised the quality of the critical apparatus and recommended that libraries acquire a copy of this book, indeed in terms very similar to *Der Bibliothekar*.[72] The second edition of Heinrich Cunow's work on the French Revolution was presented in the same spirit.[73] The review foregrounded the merits of this book, in particular as a 'social history' [*Sozialgeschichte*] of the French Revolution. Again, pedagogical concerns were primary, here; the review emphasised the difficulties a reader without some basic knowledge might find in understanding this work, for 'whoever seeks such a representation [of the history of the Revolution] would do well first to stick to Blos's book and deepen the understanding he draws from this by reading Kropotkin's history of the Revolution and Kautsky's book on class contradictions during the Revolution'.[74]

The Place Occupied by Books on the Revolution

One article appearing across several issues of *Der Bibliothekar* in 1913 offered an overview of a whole series of books, organised according to their theme.[75] One section devoted to the French Revolution included most of the books

---

68   *Der Bibliothekar*, September 1909, p. 52.

69   Ibid.

70   *Der Bibliothekar*, October 1909, p. 75.

71   Winarsky, L., 'Babeuf', *Bildungsarbeit*, 1909–10, p. 7.

72   Ibid.

73   'Heinrich Cunow', *Bildungsarbeit*, 1912–13, p. 56.

74   Ibid.

75   'Zwei Wege', *Der Bibliothekar*, February 1913, p. 549.

that we have mentioned already. A good part of the article consisted of a bibliographical essay on what books each library should offer on certain historical periods. On the eve of the war, this was a structured guide to what social-democrats should read on the French Revolution: as well as Blos's readable and amply-illustrated work, the other title recommended was Kropotkin's history of the Revolution. For a more in-depth understanding, it recommended Cunow's book, whose second edition it also highlighted (albeit under the wrong title). Kautsky's book was mentioned, as was the translation of Buonarroti's work on Babeuf. Lastly, it emphasised the value of reading books outside of a narrowly social-democratic tradition; it thus again mentioned Mignet and Thomas Carlyle, not to forget Taine and Bitterauf's respective biographies of Napoleon, and Linguet's memoirs.[76] Through this bibliography there emerged the idea of proposing a global or at least European history of revolutions and of socialism, in which the French Revolution occupied a decisively important place. The recommendations offered to libraries continued the plan for a 'great history' which the social-democrats had published in 1895. With a few differences of nuance, this same outlook was also apparent in Austrian publications.

An article in the *Bildungsarbeit* reflected the concern to offer a 'global history'. If social-democratic militants often asked 'Which history of the world [*Weltgeschichte*] is the best?',[77] *Bildungsarbeit* responded by publishing a letter by Wilhelm Hausenstein reflecting the differences of choosing one. Noting that there was no appropriate history of the world for workers to turn to,[78] Hausenstein offered some reflections on those works that did exist. He indicated that while there were tomes of undoubtable quality like Von Ranke's, these were too ideologically distant to serve as a basis. He took the example of the French Revolution and the book by Kropotkin; he considered it an excellent work on this subject, but also a vehicle for anarchist conceptions.[79] A few months later *Bildungsarbeit* published a complement to this article, a bibliography of works of *Weltgeschichte*. Again provided by Hausenstein, this text built on the themes to which he had referred in his letter. One section was dedicated to 'the era of the French Revolution and Napoleon'.[80] This first and foremost highlighted

76   Linguet 1886, 2006. These memoirs recounted the daily life of a prisoner in the Bastille at the beginning of the 1780s.
77   'Welche Welgeschichte ist gut?', *Bildungsarbeit*, 1910–11, pp. 25–6.
78   'Welche Welgeschichte ist gut?', *Bildungsarbeit*, 1910–11, p. 26.
79   Ibid.
80   *Bildungsarbeit*, 1910–11, pp. 56–7.

the books by Kautsky and Cunow, and then referred to Kropotkin's book and finally a few other authors, most of whom stood entirely outside the social-democratic tradition but remained incontestable points of reference for the history of the Revolution. To take three examples of Haustenstein's commentary on these works:

> Finally, we like Liebknecht will again gladly choose a work that brilliantly represents the individualist point of view: T. Carlyle's *The French Revolution*.
>
> Taine, *The Origins of Contemporary France*, Leipzig, 1877–1894 ... From this work – which is strongly coloured by reactionary bourgeois tendencies, but nonetheless distinguished – it is worth knowing at least the sections on the (pre-revolutionary) *ancien régime* ...
>
> Meinecke, *The Era of the German Uprising* ... A serious work, certainly not an exhaustive treatment of this question, but which does at least also abstain from any nationalist pride.[81]

Many other sources, and in particular library catalogues, allow us to pinpoint the presence of works devoted to the French Revolution in the social-democratic libraries. The *General Catalogue for the Workers' Libraries*,[82] which was published by the SPD's education commission in 1908, proposed a variety of sets of books for purchase by local party libraries across 'the whole of Germany'. This would allow them to fill any gaps and organise workers' education to the highest possible standards. The ten sets of books the *Catalogue* proposed, ranging in price from 25 to 150 marks, contained a variety of works that sought to reflect the different curriculums proposed by training schools. Since the objective, here, was to cover a large variety of fields, the number of books suggested for a domain like history was rather limited; Kautsky's *Die Klassengegensätze im Zeitalter der französischen Revolution* and Wilhelm Blos's *Die französische Revolution* nonetheless featured in two sets of books. No other historical event occupied such a place, and 1848 and the Paris Commune were represented by only one book each.[83] As for the Austrian party, the *Guide for Workers' Libraries* offered a very detailed bibliography of the books on the shelves of the social-democratic libraries of Austria. This was a rich set of works and extended far beyond contributions by party members alone. One section was devoted to

---

81   Ibid. On Friedrich Meinecke, see Chapter Twelve, p. 277.
82   Bildungsausschuss der sozialdemokratischen Partei Deutschlands 1908.
83   Wilhelm Blos's work on 1848 and Lissagaray's history of the Commune, respectively.

the 'History of Revolutions',[84] and mentioned all the books cited in *Der Bib-liothekar*. Lastly, a 1914 list of books offered by the Vienna workers' education circle featured a similar set of works.[85]

---

84   *Handbuch für Arbeiterbibliothekare*, Vienna, 1914, pp. 109–10.
85   Bücher-Verzeichnis des Arbeiterbildungsverein Wien 1914, Vienna: Verlag des Vereins.

CHAPTER 7

A Powerful Machine

Neither the party educational apparatus nor the social-democratic libraries could have functioned if they had not been backed up by a mighty organisation. The workings of this educational machine cannot be understood in terms of a simple counterposition between the politicians and theorists that formed the party's ruling élite and then the vast mass of grassroots militants. First of all, it is important to differentiate a politician like August Bebel from a theorist like Karl Kautsky, and the MP Wilhelm Blos from a journal editor like the *Die Neue Zeit* director, who held neither a post in the party nor any elected office. Franz Mehring and Heinrich Cunow's works got to grips with historiography and historical sources; their writing on historical questions was very different from that of a figure like Wilhelm Blos, whose works addressed a far broader readership. What they did have in common, however, was the fact that they were well-known figures in the SPD whose works were published and circulated at the national – in some cases, even international – scale. In between prominent leaders like these and the thousands of militants who comprised the base of the social-democratic parties, there existed a whole series of intermediaries – the thousands of cadres whose role included the elaboration of a vulgate that militants would find accessible, either through teaching or simply by writing articles aimed at a wide readership.

'Intermediate Cadres': the Heart of the Party

The Intermediate Cadres' Role in Social Democracy
Paul Pasteur has studied the 'intermediate cadres' in the Austrian social-democratic party; its so-called 'shop stewards' [*Vertrauensmann*], the full-timers, or active militants. For Pasteur 'only their degree of commitment distinguished them from the mass of militants or supporters, with the fact of taking on responsibilities'.[1] An 'essential link in the chain within the party apparatus',[2] these intermediate cadres have left traces of their activity, and in this differ greatly from the wider mass of militants, whose exact thinking or reading pat-

---

1   Pasteur 2003, p. 229.
2   Ibid.

terns are by definition difficult to reconstruct. A study of these intermediate cadres allows us to understand the real circulation of history in the ranks of a party most of whose members did not read journals like *Die Neue Zeit* or sophisticated books. The all-encompassing term 'intermediate cadres' may create problems, here, in the sense that only some of them were actually able to write about the French Revolution – or even teach its history. Nonetheless, even at the risk of being rather schematic, it does seem possible to establish a classification of several different levels of cadres, thus allowing us better to understand how a certain number of mediators and 'smugglers' could transmit a historical reference point through SPD ranks. Building on our study of the social-democratic schools, we can discern at least three different levels. The first is that consisting of local figures who sometimes had a certain national profile (but who were hardly comparable to the likes of Karl Kautsky, for example). These were the authors of pamphlets, of detailed guides, of handbooks and even books on specific themes linked to revolutionary history. The second level consists of those social-democrats who were limited to certain tasks, like writing popularising articles in a newspaper or teaching in a training school (and sometimes they travelled around for this purpose, as in the case of the *Wanderlehrer*). They wrote articles in local papers or even in *Die Neue Welt*; however, their contributions were often anonymous and it is very difficult to reconstruct their biographies beyond the lists of articles they published. Such militants were assiduous readers of the daily press and, from time to time, of certain reviews like *Bildungsarbeit* or *Der Bibliothekar*, and contributed to the choice of books in a library or the organisation of a particular training programme or course. Lastly – those whose activity is most difficult to ascertain – were the hundreds of militants who took on modest responsibilities in local structures, and considered themselves the bearers of a knowledge that they could transmit, perhaps having followed a course.[3]

We can detail the first category on the basis of some of the examples that we have encountered already. Leopold Winarsky and Gustav Eckstein both occupied important positions, and looked like national SPD figures. But they had no major works that were discussed at the national scale, and their essential role was to teach in party schools; they were the authors of detailed guides or short handbooks on the history of the French Revolution. Eckstein was a 'smuggler' between Austria and Germany; of Austrian origins, he then worked at the Berlin party school. Other less-known examples may in fact be even more indicative:

---

3 This typology applies to the period between the turn of the century and 1914; such patterns were profoundly reordered after the war, with the place assumed by academics and the social-democratic parties' new relationship with the state apparatus.

for instance Bernhard Rausch, cited above, whose biography is, however, difficult to reconstruct beyond his function in party education apparatuses.

Alexander Conrady's path seems rather easier to put together. To our knowledge, he has never been the subject of any particular study. His itinerary seems more representative of an intermediate cadre than the likes of Winarsky or Eckstein, who were each nationally renowned. Conrady's importance as a figure is demonstrated by the regular references to him in various documents concerning the educational apparatuses. In generational terms, he was a young cadre relative to a figure like Karl Kautsky – indeed, he was born in 1875.[4] He was trained as a historian and, like Cunow, he first took an interest in ethnology; we know that at university he wrote a study on ancient Scottish history.[5] After joining the SPD he worked on activities linked to the conservation of the party archives. Like many of those who taught in the party's educational structures, Conrady had his own specialisation – history. But even within this field he seems to have taken a particular interest in 'bourgeois revolutions', and especially the French Revolution, whose history he taught at the Berlin workers' school.[6] In 1912–13 and 1913–14 he also taught German history and the history of social democracy at the central party school. However, unlike the large majority of teachers, he was one of the few who was never one of the editors of a social-democratic journal or newspaper.[7] He was, therefore, one of the lower-'ranking' figures in the central party school.

Other than educationals, Conrady mainly published textbooks. For example, he was the author of a large general history of the 'great' revolutions before the 1789 French Revolution.[8] Published in the 'Kulturbilder' collection, it responded to the need for a 'global history' [*Weltgeschichte*] to which Haustenstein had referred in *Bildungsarbeit*.[9] After World War I he also wrote a short handbook on the English Revolution.[10] Also worth noting is a collection of documents on the centenary of 1813, to which we shall return.[11] He also made numerous historical contributions to *Die Neue Welt*, confirming his qualities

---

4   Date of death unknown. Kautsky was born in 1854.
5   Conrady, Alexander 1898, *Geschichte der Clanverfassung in den schottischen Hochlanden*, Leipzig: Duncker & Humblot.
6   See table in Chapter Six, p. 160.
7   Olbrich 1982, p. 201.
8   Conrady 1911. This textbook concerned the 'bourgeois revolutions' before the French Revolution.
9   See the glowing review that appeared at the moment of its publication: *Bildungsarbeit*, 1911–12, p. 30.
10   Conrady 1920.
11   See p. 206.

as a populariser (for instance a 1911 piece on a 'Strike in Paris on the Eve of the Great Revolution').[12] After publishing a few other texts at the beginning of the 1920s, including introductions to some of the works of Karl Marx, he headed for Japan in order to study Asiatic civilisation; he taught at the University of Kochi in the 1930s.[13] Over the decades, hundreds of thousands of militants and party members read his writings, and cadres were also trained thanks to his teaching.

A Regional Example: Frankfurt-am-Main

If we want a better understanding of the relations between these intermediate cadres and the local level, we need to make something of a detour into micro-history.[14] Here we will take Frankfurt as our case study, for one local history on the impact of the French Revolution in Germany has been a focus of particular attention.

Frankfurt is closely associated with the figure of Hermann Wendel, a local leader who rapidly achieved national renown. The author of articles for *Die Neue Zeit*, he became a highly influential figure, even into the mid-1930s. Little-known in France, he has been the focus of a certain degree of attention in Germany: particularly notable was a short biography essentially devoted to his Francophilia, which contributed to making him relatively well-known during his own time.[15] Beyond his contributions to *Die Neue Zeit*, the paper to which he contributed most pieces before 1914 was *Volksstimme* ['People's Voice'], a local social-democratic daily published from 1905 onward. He wrote around two hundred articles for *Volksstimme*, many of them on France. He also authored some highly successful pamphlets on the great figures of the German workers' movement, and in particular one on August Bebel that was repeatedly reissued.[16]

Born in Metz in 1884, Wendel was a German greatly influenced by French culture. With a keen eye for international politics, he also wrote a great deal on the nationalities question; in particular on Alsace-Lorraine – his own home region – but also the Balkans. Having become a social-democrat in 1905, he soon demonstrated his interest in the history of socialism with his 1908 trans-

---

12   Conrady, A., 'Ein Pariser Streik am Voraband der grossen Revolution', *Die Neue Welt*, 1911, pp. 92–3.
13   Olbrich 1982, p. 201.
14   On the significance of this local scale, see Revel, Jacques (ed.) 1996.
15   Stübling 1983.
16   Stübling 1983, p. 12.

lation of Paul Louis's study for the social-democratic publisher Dietz.[17] This translator of both French and German intellectual inspiration was a recognised leader of Frankfurt social-democracy, and in 1910 he was elected to the Frankfurt *Stadtparlament* before then becoming a Reichstag MP.

Wendel always displayed great interest in the French Revolution. His memoir, published soon after the Nazis came to power, gave an idea of the influence that the history of the 'Great Revolution' had on his life.[18] It featured descriptions of French towns, rich in historical references:

> In a city that had jealously defended its communal freedoms in the Middle Ages, some began to become conscious that the people of Metz were the heirs to a great democratic tradition. [Such was the case of] whoever himself knew the details of the still-recent era in which the Lorrains of French stock and even the German speakers had irrevocably become convinced Frenchmen, in a political sense, on account of the French Revolution and the glory of Napoleon! [So, too] whoever knew that the Jacobin Club met in the Notre-Dame church, that the Rue de Piques was once full of their names, that the guillotine stood in the Theatre Square – at that time called Equality Square![19]

And later on

> And without wanting or knowing it, we experience History. Here, in striking blue and red, were Louis XVI's *Gardes Françaises*, which passed over to the people on 14 July 1789 and decided the outcome of that great day; here were the soldiers of the First Republic, with their striped trousers and their great drums, whose drumrolls so turned Victoria's head at the battles of Valmy, Jemmapes, and Fleurus; and so, too, Napoleon's *Vielle Garde*, with the great bear-skin helmets of Austerlitz and Waterloo.[20]

Here we will particularly focus on *Volksstimme*, whose editorial team Wendel joined in 1908. It was typical of a local social-democratic paper; it spoke of the workers' situation, it reproduced texts by local leaders and occasionally political or even theoretical texts, for instance short extracts from Karl Marx's *Wage Labour and Capital* and Engels's articles on the situation of the peas-

---

17   Louis, Paul 1908, *Geschichte des Sozialismus in Frankreich*, Stuttgart: Dietz.
18   Wendel 1934.
19   Wendel 1934, pp. 64–5.
20   Wendel 1934, p. 71.

antry. Like much of the local press, this paper also reproduced articles from the Berlin *Vorwärts*. *Volksstimme* had 21,000 subscribers in 1906, 32,000 at the beginning of 1907, and 40,000 in 1912, before reaching 45,000 on the eve of World War I. Every year it celebrated the memory of the German Revolution of 1848: indeed, this occasion was marked by large social-democratic gatherings.[21] The French Revolution of 1789 did not give rise to similar displays, but that does not mean that this reference was missing entirely. *La Marseillaise* was well-known here as elsewhere; the historian Béatrix Bouvier highlights a telling episode in a counter-commemoration of *Sedantag* in 1895, during which the social-democrats sang the French national anthem.[22] Indeed, the many ceremonies in 1895 and 1896 that celebrated the various battles of the Franco-Prussian war of a quarter-century hence had provided an opportunity to spread anti-French discourse.[23]

Particularly interesting, in this context, is Hermann Wendel's book on the history of Frankfurt, which took the French Revolution for its starting point.[24] In 1910, Wendel began to write a history of the workers' movement in Frankfurt; symbolically, it began with the 'Great Revolution', and its final part evoked Bismarck's 'revolution from above'. This history was published by the local party publisher. This was a theoretically ambitious work – not least given its local focus – and sought to be a simple read above all based on economic information. After presenting a panorama of the economic foundations of eighteenth-century Frankfurt and the city's place in the Holy Roman Empire, one twelve-page chapter was devoted to 'the revolutionary upheaval and the end of the imperial city'. In particular, this descriptive chapter reviewed local reactions to the French Revolution, and noted the weak implantation of revolutionary ideas as compared to other German cities.[25] A description of how Frankfurt evolved in tandem with the various wars was followed by an explanation of the significance of the Napoleonic occupation – seen as the continuation of the 'bourgeois revolution'[26] – which also referred to the great importance of the introduction of the *Code civil* and *Code pénal*.[27]

The part devoted to the French Revolution as such was relatively short; even including the part on the Napoleonic occupation it amounted to no more than

21   Wendel 1934, p. 33.
22   Bouvier 1988, vol. 1, p. 157.
23   Hobsbawm and Ranger 2012.
24   Wendel 1910.
25   Wendel 1910, p. 20.
26   Wendel 1910, p. 30.
27   Wendel 1910, p. 38.

forty pages. But the important thing, here, was that the chronological framework of German history coincided with the French Revolution and its continuation by Napoleon; in this sense, Wendel's local history may be compared to Mehring's national history. Indeed, this history of Frankfurt also had a certain echo in this latter's writings: in a 1910 article published in *Die Neue Zeit*, Mehring indicated the existence of two local histories of social-democracy, by Heinrich Laufenberg and Hermann Wendel respectively.[28] Mehring invoked the name of the SPD's chairman August Bebel, who accorded great importance to 'writing local history'. With their abundant 'documentation' [*Quellenmaterial*], these histories enabled an understanding of the 'class contradictions' [*Klassengegensätze*] operating at the local level. The important thing to grasp was the genesis of the proletariat's history; and its first struggles were part of the history of the French Revolution. Again reaffirmed, here, was the concern to transmit history to social-democratic militants and to make it accessible.

Wendel's contribution should, therefore, be directly connected to his engagement in local *Bildungsarbeit*. In 1906, the Frankfurt SPD and the local unions created a Workers' Education Committee [*Arbeiterbildungsausschuss*] whose activities we can track in the pages of *Volksstimme*. Many hundreds of people turned out for the talks organised by the school and numerous outside speakers [*Wanderlehrer*] came to give presentations there – for instance Hermann Duncker, whose talk on 'Capital and Labour' drew around 120 people.[29] Wendel himself gave numerous talks on the history of the French Revolution and the Napoleonic occupation. One issue of *Volksstimme* mentions five talks on 'The Era of the Capitalist Revolution' in November 1908, and also gives bibliographical recommendations.[30] The first and second meetings were dedicated to the Peasant War and the English Revolution, the third to the French Revolution, and the fourth and fifth to the 1848 Revolution and the 'Revolution from above'. In broad terms, the third to fifth talks corresponded to what Wendel outlined in his book. As for the meeting devoted to the French Revolution, the books by Kautsky, Blos, Mignet and Carlyle were particularly highlighted: as in the case of the presentations with slides, here we find a set of bibliographical suggestions that mix social-democratic reference points with classics of the historiography.

---

28 Mehring, F., 'H. Laufenberg, Hamburg und sein Proletariat im achtzehnten Jahrhundert; Wendel, H., Frankfurt am Main vor der grossen Revolution bis zur Revolution von oben (1789–1866)', *Die Neue Zeit*, 1910–11, vol. 3, pp. 757–60.
29 Stübling 1983, p. 30.
30 'Vom Arbeiterbildungsausschuss', *Volksstimme*, 4 November 1908, p. 3.

The references to the French Revolution were not limited to the advertisements of these talks. We see as much from both news pieces and those of a commemorative character. Two examples are particularly telling in this regard. The first is an incidental piece revisiting the trial of the King:

> When in 1792 the National Convention constituted itself as a High Court to conduct the trial of Louis XVI, the result was a condemnation, even though as constitutional monarchists the Girondins would gladly have saved the King; for the people of Paris, the masses, from the galleries of the audience exercised a salutary influence on the radicalism of their representativies, with pitchforks and cudgels.[31]

The other, a commemorative piece, was connected to one of the Social-Democratic Party's traditional gatherings. On 1 May 1909, a long article by Hermann Wendel on the 'Fêtes of the Revolution' covering almost all of three columns across a page of *Volksstimme* celebrated the revolutionary feats of 1789, one hundred and twenty years on. It above all sought to emphasise the link between the 'Great French Revolution' and the Second International's founding congress in 1889.[32] The article reviewed the numerous revolutionary *fêtes*: the social-democrats' commemorative practices joined in the traditions of 1789, and the proletariat had to realise the promise of 'Freedom, Equality and Brotherhood' that could not be fulfilled in the era of its emergence.

Wendel's interest in the history of the period that started in 1789 came from his Francophilia, linked to both his origins and his reaction against the Francophobia dominant in the years leading up to World War I. Taking his distance from the revisionists before 1914, he virulently attacked the government, popularised Karl Liebknecht's anti-militarist slogans,[33] and called for a German Republic in a time when this demand faced increasing opposition.[34] One of his articles for the *Volksstimme* in 1910 ended with 'Long live international social democracy! Long live the German Republic!';[35] it was written in the wake of the great meeting of the European socialist leaders: indeed, Jaurès, Vandervelde, Keir Hardie and Clara Zetkin were all in Frankfurt in September 1910.

---

31   Ibid.
32   Wendel, H. 'Feste der Revolution', *Volksstimme*, 1 May 1909.
33   Liebknecht 1907.
34   On this debate, see Chapter Eight, p. 202.
35   Wendel, H., 'Die Republik', *Volksstimme*, 27 October 1910.

A locally-rooted social democrat and author of many contributions in a regional paper, his work articulated local history with reviews in a national-level publication like *Die Neue Zeit*. Hermann Wendel provides a characteristic example that explains the importance of regional intermediaries within the SPD, including as concerned writing history.

The French Revolution in the Party Daily

The Presence of Revolutionary History
This example from Frankfurt shows that references to the French Revolution were not limited to the books written by social-democratic leaders. Militants regularly encountered a variety of texts emphasising the importance of the 'Great Revolution'. We can find developed texts on this question even in *Vorwärts*. On 7 February 1909, the Berlin social-democratic daily published a long review of Heinrich Cunow's book by Karl Kautsky.[36] This was totally different in status from the review in *Die Neue Zeit*, for it sought to legitimise this book at a wholly different scale. As the SPD became ever better-established, the vast majority of Berlin social-democrats read *Vorwärts*.[37] In 1907, the daily counted 135,000 subscribers in Berlin; in the Reichstag elections that same year, 413,181 Berliners voted for SPD candidates; thus 32.7% of its voters were subscribers.[38] This review was written for tens of thousands of supporters and voters, and all the more so given that the text appeared in the Sunday edition, which was particularly popular on account of the inclusion of the *Die Neue Welt* supplement. We will go on to study this latter's content in greater depth. Such a review was a rare enough case as to be worth underlining. The terms of Kautsky's text were very similar to his 1889 introduction: 'the class struggle' was, indeed, the main explanation of the French Revolution, and it could not be reduced to a simple clash between 'rich and poor'. To think as much would be to risk remaining at the level of a 'vulgar Marxism' or a 'pre-Marxism'. Kautsky mentioned Cunow's work with the sources, but above all showcased his method:

> Yet even for the most serious and impartial historians, the struggles within the far Left of the Convention, between the partisans of Danton, Hébert and Robespierre, remained an enigma. They saw in all this only per-

---

36   Kautsky, K., 'Ein neues Buch über die französische Revolution', *Vorwärts*, 7 February 1909, p. 6.
37   Badia 1975, p. 140.
38   Fricke 1989, p. 546.

sonal quarrels, a will to power, and absurd bloodlust. To my knowledge, Cunow is the first to have clearly and irrefutably presented the opposition between them as the opposition between classes. But he even expresses the other, already previously recognised class oppositions more clearly and accurately than is ordinarily the case.[39]

For the 'pope of Marxism', this book was now the authority on this question. He almost 'officially' enthroned it as such, repeating the argument of his 1908 preface.[40] Since it was published in the party daily, the article could only conclude with a few more directly political arguments: the method Cunow had used to analyse class contradictions was also useful for understanding the contemporary world (for example, in terms of the distinction between market capital and industrial capital) and the SPD should advance a policy that would allow for unity to be built among highly fragmented social categories.[41] The understanding of the French Revolution that Cunow offered was a tool for grasping the contradictions of the contemporary world.

The supplement that came out with *Vorwärts* and the SPD's regional dailies each week, *Die Neue Welt*, provides an excellent indicator of the renewed interest in the history of the French Revolution. This paper, with its very large readership, allows us a more precise idea of what most of the party's members and militants might have read, given that most of them did not have access to books like Cunow's. The large-format *Die Neue Welt* became a rather richer publication from the 1890s onward, but it maintained the same characteristics. On the eve of 1914 its distribution exceeded 650,000 copies – this, in a party now reaching a membership of one million. From 1906 to 1914 it published articles, short stories and even images concerning the French Revolution every year. This was often an echo of party publishing initiatives, but there were also original contributions for *Die Neue Welt*. France's revolutionary inheritance was often celebrated in counterposition to imperial values (in 1908 *Die Neue Welt* reproduced the *Arbeiter-Marseillaise*)[42] but also in opposition to the dominant historiography. A short article 'On School History Courses' recalled an argument made by Wilhelm Liebknecht, emphasising the importance of a continued reference to revolutionary history:

---

39   Kautsky, K., 'Ein neues Buch über die französische Revolution', *Vorwärts*, 7 February 1909, p. 6.
40   See Chapter Six, p. 190.
41   A remark that reflected the SPD's increasing tendency to be more of a 'people's party' [*Volkspartei*] than a 'class party' [*Klassenpartei*]. See the introduction to Part 3.
42   'Arbeiter-Marseillaise', *Die Neue Welt*, 1908. p. 83.

With regard to history teaching in schools, we find the following quotation in Wilhelm Liebknecht's book "Robert Blum": in no other country in the world as in Germany has history teaching been so brutally placed in service of the dominant powers ... And after the history of the French Revolution, it was the history of the movement of 1848 that came out worst, with this historical falsification and this distortion of the truth. That is why it is doubly important to restore the truth to its rightful place.[43]

The themes that were emphasised reflected the concerns encountered in the books that social-democrats had published. The first regarded workers' and peasants' action. One short story portrayed a German peasant in 1848 remembering the acts of his French alter ego in 1789: 'Their stubborn ancestors had once accumulated in the wild. The French peasants did the same during the summer, even as the great catastrophe approached: once the same was also true in France, where, according to legend the Lord lived so happily!'[44]

Social conflicts were a topos of this type of short story: 'Finally a commission heard him, and its speak told the representatives of his conviction that the war of poor against rich had begun in its sharpest form'.[45] Another important feature was a powerful empathy with the situation of the peasants; the text repeatedly brought into relief the repression of which they were the victims.[46] Again present was the idea that despite its limits the French Revolution had marked the beginning of a 'new era'.[47]

A large illustration in the centre of one 1906 issue portrayed the storming of the Bastille, as according to Lévy's painting. This depiction of 1789 was accompanied by a commentary.[48] This largely narrative text evoked the 'heroic' action of the Parisian people on this famous day, as well as the immediately prior context (the dismissal of Necker) and the people laying hold of weaponry. In 1908 it evoked the 'situation of workers in industry at the beginning of the great French Revolution' in very similar style.[49] In 1910 the situation of the peasants was

---

43   'Über den Geschichtsunterricht in der Schule', *Die Neue Welt*, 1910, p. 200.

44   Schweitzer, R., 'Der französische Bauer im Jahre 1789', *Die Neue Welt*, 1910, p. 85.

45   Schweitzer, R., 'Der französische Bauer im Jahre 1789', *Die Neue Welt*, 1910, p. 86.

46   Ibid.

47   Ibid.

48   'Die Bastille', *Die Neue Welt*, 1906, p. 213.

49   'Der Lage Pariser Industriearbeiter zu Beginn der grossen Französischen Revolution', *Die Neue Welt*, 1908, p. 36.

again highlighted by way of an image of the 'peasants in revolt', as portrayed in a painting, together with a short commentary.[50] In 1911, Conrady evoked a 'workers' strike on the eve of the Great Revolution', namely the Réveillon workshop strike in April 1789.[51] Here he discussed the Parisian people of the *faubourgs* Saint-Marcel and Saint-Antoine, their working conditions and the reasons for their revolt, 'a prelude to the Revolution, to the great events of 1789'.[52] Also worth highlighting is an article on the massacres of September 1792,[53] which was published as a riposte to the 'reactionary legends' based on Jourgniac de Saint-Méard's account.[54]

Beyond this veneration of the people, the other dominant theme was the presentation of the different political groups, and indeed portraits of the revolutionaries. One article evoked 'a meeting of the Jacobin club'.[55] Emphasising that few historians had properly appreciated this club's role, this text re-established its proper place during the Revolution, and in particular the antagonism that divided Girondins from Montagnards. This allowed *Die Neue Welt* to counterbalance those histories that were overly centred on the parliament itself. An 1882 engraving by Alfred Loudet that depicted 'Robespierre, Danton and Marat' was reproduced in *Die Neue Welt* accompanied by a text.[56] This latter described Marat's room, the scene of his assassination. But the explanation of the differences between the three men made clear the author's own sympathies – particularly for Marat, whose name recurred repeatedly. After having noted that among 'the conservative and national-liberal historians' Marat appeared as a bloodthirsty figure, another article sought to restore his proper prestige.[57] An article on 'Babeuf's first communist contributions' was published in the same spirit.[58] This text went beyond a simple commemoration of a forerunner of socialism: rather, it sought to present his pre-revolutionary writings and the precociousness of his communist beliefs. The article was based on Advielle's book, which published Babeuf's correspondence

50   'Aufständliche Bauern', *Die Neue Welt*, 1910, p. 77, 80.
51   Conrady, A., 'Ein Pariser Streik am Vorabend der grossen Revolution', *Die Neue Welt*, 1911, pp. 92–3.
52   Conrady, A., 'Ein Pariser Streik am Vorabend der grossen Revolution', *Die Neue Welt*, 1911, p. 93.
53   'Ein Freigesprochener aus den Septembertagen von 1792', *Die Neue Welt*, 1910, p. 199.
54   Jourgniac de Saint-Méard 1897.
55   'Eine Sammlung', *Die Neue Welt*, 1907, p. 64.
56   'Robespierre, Danton, Marat', *Die Neue Welt*, 1907, p. 184.
57   'Eine Anekdote von Paul Marat', *Die Neue Welt*, 1912, p. 288.
58   'Die ersten kommunistischen Auslassungen Babeufs', *Die Neue Welt*, 1910, p. 176.

with Dubois de Fosseux: some extracts from Babeuf's letter were even reproduced in German translation.[59]

Sometimes the contributions were very short, often simple anecdotes. For
example, this extract from a 1910 piece on the trial of Louis XVI gives a good
impression of the paper's tone:

> A famous Englishwoman of the eighteenth century, Mary Wollstonecraft,
> is best-known as one of the pioneers of women's emancipation. A con-
> temporary of the French Revolution, she had not long been staying in
> Paris when Louis XVI died, and in one of her letters we get an interesting
> portrayal of the impression that the transfer of the King from the Temple
> for the interrogation, after the Convention of 26 December 1792, had on
> her.[60]

Another theme, in line with some of the articles published in the 1890s, was
the history of the revolutionary *fêtes*. A 1910 article by Heinrich Schulz on the
'workers' *fêtes*' recalled the long tradition of such events, and in particular the
ones held on May Day.[61] This article was followed by a short piece by I. Stern on
the '*fêtes* of the French Revolution'.[62] Like a 1893 article cited above, this piece
set the May Day celebrations in continuity with French revolutionary history.[63]
It evoked the *Fête de la Fédération* of 14 July 1790, the *Fête de la Raison* of 10
November 1793, and the role of Jacques-Louis David therein. It then recalled
that the only *fête* which France officially commemorated was 14 July ...[64] Thus
the celebrations at the heart of social-democratic practice found their origins
in the *fêtes* of the French Revolution. A value essential to their political identity – internationalism – also came from this same revolutionary culture.[65] An
article based on the biography of the German revolutionary Anacharsis Cloots
sought to show precisely this:

---

59   Another 'conspiracy' was also discussed: 'Ungarische Revolutionäre von 1795', *Die Neue
      Welt*, 1912, p. 408. There were very few references to the Hungarian and central-European
      Jacobins.
60   (No author, title), *Die Neue Welt*, 1910, p. 152.
61   Schulz, H., 'Arbeiterfeste', *Die Neue Welt*, 1910, pp. 137–8.
62   Stern, I., 'Feste der französischen Revolution', *Die Neue Welt*, 1910, pp. 141–2.
63   Ibid.
64   Also worth noting is an article on theatre during the French Revolution, which displayed
      a certain continuity with the themes developed in the 1890s: 'Die Schauspieler und die
      Revolution', *Die Neue Welt*, 1912, pp. 331–4 and 339–41.
65   Demmer, A., 'Internationales aus der grossen Revolution', *Die Neue Welt*, 1912, pp. 131–2.

The traditional point of view, at least in Germany, saw the famous Anacharsis Cloots – the so-called 'Orator of the Human Race' in the time of the French Revolution – as nothing but a fanatic, on account of his ideas on human brotherhood and a worldwide politics.[66]

The article referenced Heinrich Cunow's book, in a further sign of the importance of this work. Criticising the 'bourgeois history-writing' which saw Mirabeau as the 'great *Realpolitiker*' opposed to the 'unrealistic ideologues', the social-democrat championed his fight for peace and brotherhood between all the peoples of Europe. The piece took a similar approach to Desmoulins, seen as an 'enemy of militarism'; Forster and the Mainz Jacobin club were also mentioned.[67] It highlighted a 7 November 1792 address to the Convention of 5,000 English reformers, which called for peace and friendship between peoples ... The war certainly later became a war of foreign conquest, and the trade rivalry with England overdetermined the relations between the two countries. Yet the social-democrats now embraced this first drive for peace and brotherhood, expressed by some of the revolutionaries.[68]

Lastly, it is worth noting that an extract of Heinrich Cunow's book was published in *Die Neue Welt* in 1909, soon after it had come out.[69] It depicted the general conditions of the press in 1789, the social and political differences between the main papers, and emphased the contradictions in early 1790 which undid the dreams of unity that had emerged in 1789. This short extract gave a broad brush-strokes presentation of the social contradictions, and showed how a scholarly work could possibly be used for a wider militant readership; it cited the main popular papers, and especially *l'Ami du peuple* and *le Père Duschesne*. This type of publication afforded the work a wider audience: as in the case of the extract on the *sans-culottes* taken from Kautsky's book *Die Klassengegensätze von 1789*, published in *1649–1789–1905* in early 1906,[70] militants could here read a short text that spread awareness of the author and some of the main aspects of his interpretation of the French Revolution, even if it could not summarise the full richness of his argument. A few years later, another extract by Cunow was published, thus demonstrating the essential place this work had acquired within social democracy.[71]

---

66   Demmer, A., 'Internationales aus der grossen Revolution', *Die Neue Welt*, 1912, p. 131.
67   On Forster's importance to the German-speaking world, see the works of Marita Gilli and especially her critical edition Gilli 2005.
68   Demmer, A., 'Internationales aus der grossen Revolution', *Die Neue Welt*, 1912, p. 133.
69   'Die Pariser Presse am Schlusse des ersten Revolutionsjahres (1789)', *Die Neue Welt*, 1909, p. 280.
70   See Chapter Four, p. 116.
71   Cunow, H., 'Die Forderungen des Pariser Intelligenzproletariats', *Die Neue Welt*, 1913, p. 435.

Of course, these texts and images did not offer the reader a precise and detailed history of the Revolution. But through literary references, pictures or, indeed, short extracts from books, they helped spread awareness of this history among a wider militant readership. Numerous articles emphasised certain episodes or actors in the Revolution. Carrying forth certain ideas and values, these latter heralded and gave historical justification to the social-democrats' own struggles. This type of writing could also be found, to a certain degree, in the *Arbeiter-Notizkalender* [Workers' Calendars].

Commemorating Historical Occasions

As the social-democrats gained influence, the militant's everyday environment became increasingly 'encadred'. The Austrian *Arbeiter-Notizkalender* represent a fine example of this phenomenon: this very small-format social-democratic calendar (in this sense differing from the traditional *Arbeiter-Kalender*) contained not only a calendar and pages for taking down notes, but also illustrations and brief chunks of information on workers' rights, and sometimes supplementary information on the party and some of its most important figures, whether they were still alive (for instance Karl Kautsky or Victor Adler) or had passed into posterity (for example, in 1913 when it marked the anniversary of Karl Marx's death). From time to time they also featured advertisements for the books issued by the party publishing house.

The references to the French Revolution did not appear systematically. However, two examples – one from the start and one from the end of this period – demonstrate the place that revolutionary history could take in this type of medium. In the 1905 edition there appeared not only a short presentation of Bebel, Kautsky and Adler, but also a small box on the final page on the 'French Revolutionary Calendar'. It highlighted the existence of this calendar from 1792 to 1806, the principle of its *décadis*, and the revolutionary equivalents for the usual months. Already the year beforehand, in 1904, the militant could read a translation of Rouget de l'Isle's *Marseillaise* in the *Notizkalender*.

To take another example, the *Arbeiter-Notizkalender* regularly featured short biographies of Kautsky, thus attesting to his popularity in the Austrian party. His biography in the 1901 edition was accompanied by a short bibliography that included his book *Die Klassengegensätze von 1789*. If we stick to the years before World War I, the 1914 almanac offers a particularly telling example. A photograph of Kautsky was combined with a short, three-page biography – slightly different from the one in the 1901 edition – of almost hagiographical tones. It first of all emphasised his role in popularising Marxism. It cited some of his works, but the only books to be mentioned twice were *Thomas More* and *Die Klassengegensätze in* [sic] *Frankreich*. Kautsky's important role in popularising and 'smuggling across' Marx's thought by way of his *Die Klassengegensätze von 1789* was thus referenced in a large-scale publication. Hence while his works were not always directly read, the themes on which he was a figure of reference could become known to a much greater number of readers.

The *Notizkalender für Arbeiter* (in certain years, *Arbeiter-Notizkalender*) published by the Buchhandlung Vorwärts in Germany were generally similar in composition to their Austrian counterparts, and again here the first one was published in 1898. It is worth noting that the first thirty pages were devoted to a historical calendar, with one or more historical dates corresponding to each day. The dates were in very large part recent, for the most part not dating back to before 1840. In 1898 they did not only refer to the history of the workers' movement; for instance, a whole series of dates referred to the passing of new laws. But the French Revolution was also very much present; between 1906 and 1914 the *Notizkalender* noted the following dates:

- 21 January: 1793. Louis XVI is executed. 1893: The Prefect of Police bans the commemoration of the execution.
- 22 February: 1787. Beginning of the Revolution with the meeting of the Assembly of Notables.
- 25 April: 1792. First use of the guillotine.
- 14 July. 1789. Storming of the Bastille.
- 17 July: 1793. Charlotte Corday guillotined.
- 5 October: 1789. The march on Versailles.
- 31 October: 1796.[72] Execution of the Girondins.

Also worth mentioning, in the same spirit, was the German *Historische Kalender*. This historical calendar was a supplement to the daily *Vorwärts*; it very much resembled the *Notizkalender*, including in terms of its typography.[73] It was probably issued to *Vorwärts*'s subscribers as a supplement at the beginning of each year. For each day in the calendar there was a historical date: many of them concerned the recent history of the workers' movement between 1880 and 1906 (essentially, from the time of the anti-socialist laws to the Russian Revolution of 1905). Nonetheless, the history of the French Revolution was also prevalent therein. This table covers the references to the 1789–99 period in the 1907 calendar:

---

72   According to the *Notizkalender für Arbeiter*, Berlin, Buchhandlung Vorwärts, 1906–14. The Girondins were in fact executed in 1793.

73   *Historischer Kalender*, Berlin, Vorwärts, 1907–14.

January	None
February	22 February 1787: 'Assembly of Notables. Beginning of the Revolution'.
March	9 March 1793: 'Danton founds the revolutionary tribunal'.
	22 March 1794: 'Hébert (Père Duchesne) guillotined'
April	5 April 1794: 'Danton guillotined'
May	3 May 1791: 'Polish Constitution'
June	17 June 1789: 'Third Estate proclaims the National Assembly'
July	14 July 'Storming of the Bastille';[a] 28 July, 'Robespierre executed'
August	10 August 1792, 'Storming of the Tuileries', 13 August 1792, 'Louis XVI at Temple'[b]
September	None
October	None
November	6 November 1793: 'Le Duc d'Orléans (Égalité) guillotined'; 8 November 1793, 'Madame Roland guillotined'.
December	None

a   The other event indicated was the 'International Congress' of 1889, thus establishing the link between these two events.
b   The Prison du Temple where Louis XVI was held.

In a calendar whose references focused on the history of the workers' movement, the French Revolution occupied a very distinct place: it was the most frequently mentioned revolution, apart from the very recent Russian Revolution. A comparison with the revolutions of 1848, the 1871 Paris Commune and the Russian Revolution gives the following results:

Revolutionary period	Number of dates cited
French Revolution	12
1848 (in all countries)	6
Paris Commune	3
1905 Russian Revolution	19[a]

a   Not counting the German events of 1905–6, which were very frequently referenced, and did in some cases take their lead from the Russian Revolution (especially the strikes).

Celebrating Forerunners of Socialism

When we looked at the years following the centenary, we examined the papers published each May Day and the annual *Arbeiter-Kalender* workers' almanac. These publications continued to be circulated in this period. In the German case, there were no specific contributions on the French Revolution in the *Arbeiter-Kalender*. In 1906, Wilhelm Blos described the events of the Russian Revolution without making direct allusion to the French Revolution.[74] Nor did the Austrian *Kalender* devote any articles to the 'Great Revolution'. Nonetheless, on closer reading we see that there were regular references to this history, albeit by way of one particular theme, namely the women's question. Two articles written by Therese Schlesinger continued in the same vein as her 1902 pamphlet, already presented within the context of the revisionism debate.[75] The first was a history of 'Women's right to vote'.[76] Schlesinger evoked the women's delegations to the National Assembly as she presented Olympe de Gouges. A series of portraits were reproduced in the middle of the article, including that of Condorcet – a figure traditionally little-present in social-democratic output, except that concerning women's condition specifically. He was cited on account of his role in the 1793 Consitution and his stand in favour of equal rights for all. This, despite the long-term failure of his appeals – for French women still today had to fight for basic rights.[77] Schlesinger also reviewed the life of Mary Wollstonecraft:[78] this portrait fully corresponded to the general spirit of the *Arbeiter-Kalender*, for her biography provided the opportunity to remind readers of the importance of the French Revolution. The article was marked by the social-democratic context: it emphasised the distinction with 'bourgeois women's' demands, and sought to present Wollstonecraft as the forerunner of contemporary struggles: 'But Mary Wollstonecraft's works, and in particular her *Vindication of the Rights of Woman*, exhort us still to maintain an arduous struggle against the prejudices and oppression from which the female gender still suffers, and in particular proletarian woman'.[79]

---

74   Blos, W., 'Die russische Revolution', *Illustrierter Neue-Welt Kalender*, pp. 5–11.

75   See Chapter Three, pp. 77.

76   Schlesinger, T., 'Das Wahlrecht der Frauen', *Österreichischer Arbeiter-Kalender*, 1907, pp. 97–101.

77   Schlesinger, T., 'Das Wahlrecht der Frauen', *Österreichischer Arbeiter-Kalender*, 1907, p. 99.

78   Schlesinger, T., 'Mary Wollstonecraft. Die Pionierin der Frauenemanzipation', *Österreichischer Arbeiter-Kalender*, 1912, pp. 72–6.

79   Schlesinger, T., 'Mary Wollstonecraft. Die Pionierin der Frauenemanzipation', *Österreichischer Arbeiter-Kalender*, 1912, p. 76.

The end of the article highlighted Wollstonecraft's memoirs on Godwin, which had just been published. The revolutionary past should thus be attached to the struggle that social-democratic women were waging in the present. Tellingly, in an intervention at the Mannheim Congress, Clara Zetkin similarly set contemporary struggles in continuity with the revolutionary past:

> Social democracy everywhere today holds to the very forefront of the struggle for the full political emancipation of the female gender. In 1792, Mary Wollstonecraft raised her voice in her famous work, *Vindication of the Rights of Woman* ... In 1793, women's right to vote was demanded both in tracts and in an appeal to the National Constituent Assembly.[80]

To this set of articles on women we could add a piece by Adelheid Popp in the 1911 *Märzfeier* in Austria. While dedicated to the 1848 Revolution, this contribution also contained some elaboration on the French Revolution.[81] Popp cited Wollstonecraft's 1792 writings on the assertion of women's rights and argued that 'the Great French Revolution brought to the forefront a whole series of illustrious female figures, and she transmitted their memory to posterity'.[82]

There were just as few articles directly devoted to the French Revolution in the papers for May Day (the *Arbeiter-Maifeier* and then the *Maifeier* in Germany, and the *Maifestschrift* in Austria). But while there was nothing on this subject in the 1905 Austrian *Maifestschrift*, we can note an emphatic tribute to Babeuf in the 1906 edition. A long article by Sigmund Kaff on 'Babeuf, the people's tribune' reviewed the revolutionary's career and also provided a translation of some extracts from his writings.[83] This piece marked the 110-year anniversary of the action of the members of the Conspiracy of Equals, arrested in May 1796 and executed in May 1797. Explaining Babeuf's biography and his ideas in very simple terms, Kaff's text was an homage to the revolutionary's career. The eleven articles of a proposed decree from 1796 were translated in full. The author paid tribute to a precursor of the 'communist' idea:

> This, then, was the end: the greatest communist of the French Revolution, who was first to recognise and assert, with keen instinct, the need for economic liberation, had died for his beliefs with the courage of

---

80   *Protokoll über die Verhandlungen des Parteitages der Sozialdemokratischen Partei Deutsch-lands, Mannheim, 23. bis 29. September 1906*, Berlin, 1906, p. 413.

81   'Der Frauen Erwachen', *Märzfeier*, 1911, p. 5.

82   Ibid.

83   Kaff, S., 'Babeuf', *Maifestschrift*, 1906, pp. 7–10.

an ancient hero. But this intrepid people's tribune long survived in the memory of the French people.[84]

This article was part of a wider set of texts showing the increasingly specific place that Babeuf now occupied. We might even wonder whether such a tribute in such a widely distributed organ contributed, a few years later, to the translation of Buonarroti's book. As we have seen, this volume brought together several texts from the Conspiracy, including the one translated by Sigmund Kaff, which had not previously been available in German. We could also cite a few other, more incidental texts which also reflect how rooted this point of reference had become, for instance the portrait of Rouget de l'Isle in the 1910 *Maifestschrift*. It was combined with a depiction of a bust of the poet, as well as the score of the *Marseillaise*, whose importance to the German-speaking workers' movement we have already highlighted.[85]

What Militants Might Have Read about the French Revolution

While it is difficult to know what militants could draw from their reading, by cross-comparing different sources we can investigate the knowledge of the sometimes anonymous or little-known 'intermediate cadres'. A significant body of historiography around Roger Chartier has addressed the question of reading; the reality of 'popular cultures' has long been a focus of attention.[86] Faced with the abundance of social-democratic output, many historians have sought to understand what the militants of the pre-1914 SPD might really have read and assimilated. Georges Haupt has outlined interesting perspectives in terms of understanding the reality of 'Marxism' within the SPD.[87] Hans-Joseph Steinberg's fundamental work on this subject based itself on the data provided by *Der Bibliothekar*.[88] One of its main arguments is that books on politics, the workers' movement and economics were little-borrowed, and that the 'Marxism' in the SPD from the 1870s–90s up till World War I was confined to a narrow circle of leaders, without having any real hold on party militants. Taking the example of the central library in Gera, Steinberg highlights the fact that party literature, political economy and theoretical books in general were very little-

---

84   Kaff, S., 'Babeuf', *Maifestschrift*, 1906, p. 8.
85   'Aus dem Leben Rouget de l'Isles, des Dichters der Marseillaise', *Maifestschrift*, 1910, p. 10.
86   See in particular Chartier (ed.) 1986.
87   Haupt 1980, pp. 77–107.
88   Steinberg 1967.

read. For example, in Gera in 1907, 434 readers borrowed 4,138 books, of which 2,841 were literary works, 297 works of history, 254 concerned the natural sciences, 244 were 'classics', and 106 concerned the social sciences, as against 15 works of 'party literature' and 13 of 'union literature'.[89] Steinberg's conclusions are well-known, and have been widely adopted by the historiography:

> If we consider that [these figures] concerned a zealous minority of workers who borrowed books of scientific content from the library, on this basis we can conclude that even this elite of trade unionists and party members was still far from scientific socialism – meaning, fundamentally, from Marxism.[90]

The historian draws the still more radical conclusion 'that most socialist workers were absolutely at a distance from the theory of socialism, and the greater part of the party's scientific literature did not arouse any interest in their ranks'.[91]

The sciences dominated[92] while Marx was very little read; most of the available library catalogues for the pre-World War I period confirm as much.[93] Vernon Lidtke does not discuss this problem at great length, but in his conclusion, he nonetheless provides a quite similar evaluation as he argues that 'the permeation of Marxism was limited largely to the higher levels' of the party.[94]

Numerous historians have criticised Steinberg's interpretation of his sources, especially Andrew Bonnell[95] and Dick Geary.[96] In their view, militants read a certain number of publications a great deal, including daily newspapers. This medium goes almost ignored in Steinberg's study; for instance, he does not refer to the extracts from books that were published in *Die Neue Welt* (the Sunday supplement) and makes very little use of the workers' almanacs. The fact that Steinberg so rarely cites *Vorwärts*, or popularising texts more generally, makes it difficult to accept some of his conclusions, which are thus mainly based on the low numbers of militants reading the works of Marx and Engels. Yet a vulgate very widely read by militants was published across these various different organs. Bringing together both the German and Austrian calendars

---

89   Steinberg 1967, p. 135.
90   Steinberg 1967, p. 138.
91   Steinberg 1967, p. 141.
92   The influence of Darwinism was very clear, here. See Pasteur 2003, pp. 40–51.
93   Steinberg 1967, p. 140.
94   Lidtke 1985, p. 195.
95   Bonnell 2002.
96   Geary 2000.

and the pamphlets in honour of May Day, we have highlighted the in fact regular appearance of historical pieces. Here was a form of historical materialism – certainly, a schematic one – that was read beyond leadership circles alone. It contributed to spreading a reading of the French Revolution, which was often accompanied by illustrations, songs, and such like. As well as these articles, we should mention the popularising pamphlets highlighted by Andrew Bonnell, such as the commentary on the Erfurt Programme. Hundreds of thousands of copies of this abridged version were sold between 1891 and 1914: this was, without doubt, a rudimentary Marxism, but it also provided an interpretation of the world including no lack of historical references. This was, indeed, a form of Marxism received on a very large scale.[97] Moreover, in his study Steinberg does not analyse the space between novels and theoretical literature in the social-democratic libraries.[98] Certain works of history attracted far more attention than Karl Marx's texts, even if they did not achieve the same success as Zola's works. Thus when we look at a set of figures for book-borrowing in a series of German workers' libraries compiled on the eve of World War I, literature clearly stood well ahead of the other categories (228,419), but history came second with 23,715 books borrowed. In percentage terms, literature represented 73.7 percent of the total and history 7.6 percent: this demands that we put the permeation of social-democratic positions among the wider layers of SPD militants into a certain perspective, but also demonstrates a particular interest for history. For instance, when we look more closely at the borrowing figures in SPD libraries, we find that Wilhelm Blos's book on the French Revolution seems to have enjoyed a certain success. The numerous cases of statistics for local libraries published in *Der Bibliothekar* provide interesting data in this regard. In a 1914 report on the Augsburg library,[99] more leisurely reading again dominated, but it is also worth noting the far from negligible importance of the 'social sciences': the works cited included Bebel's *Die Frau und der Sozialismus* and an unspecified work on the 'Deutsche und Französische Revolution' – very probably Blos's book.[100]

Here it is also worth citing Gustav Henning's balance-sheet for the Leipzig workers' library, drawn up even before *Der Bibliothekar* was first published.[101] Here again, while literature was far in front of other categories (32 copies of

---

97   On these questions, see also Stuart 1992. See also Prochasson 2004.
98   By this we mean the texts that were most complex to master, including Marx and Engels's works.
99   'Bibliothekberichte', *Der Bibliothekar*, April 1914, p. 726.
100   Ibid.
101   Hennig 1908.

Zola's books were taken out a total of 2,012 times),[102] we can also see that some historical works were widely read: firstly Corvin's *Der Pfaffenspiegel* (four copies, borrowed 175 times), immediately followed by Blos (three copies, borrowed 131 times); with the exemption of Bebel's *Die Frau und der Sozialismus* (six copies, borrowed 176 times) it was the only historical work, after Corvin's, to have three copies in the categories 'historical works' [*Geschichtswerke*] and 'popular economics, socialism, politics' [*Volkswirtschaft, Sozialismus, Politik*].

The available information for Austria is even less systematic, but it seems that Blos's book was relatively widely circulated. In 1909 *Bildungsarbeit* featured an article on what the workers of Vienna were reading, backed up by statistical information. Based on the number of times books were borrowed from three party libraries in Vienna, it suggests that historical works enjoyed a certain success.[103] After 'leisure reading', wirth 11,089 books borrowed, the second most successful category was history and geography, with 685 books borrowed. This was a modest figure, but still surpassed the category 'Social sciences, socialism' (357 borrowed), even though this latter included the texts of major leaders of the German party like Bebel, and most importantly Kautsky. While geographical works also contributed to this 685 figure, the details show that the history of revolutions was itself relatively popular: Bach's book on the 1848 Revolution in Vienna was borrowed 35 times, Blos's book on 1848 25 times, immediately followed by his book on the French Revolution, borrowed 24 times. By way of comparison, Schiller and Goethe (all works combined) were borrowed over a hundred times, Lassalle 17 times and Marx 42 (again, all works combined).

We should add that the circulation of more developed works like Kautsky's *Die Klassengegensätze von 1789* cannot be understood solely in terms of the number of times they were borrowed from party libraries. If this title was little read directly, extracts were published in pamphlets and it also served as the basis for numerous popularising texts in newspapers as well as the detailed plans for talks on the French Revolution, distributed throughout all social-democratic schools in the German-speaking countries. If *Die Klassengegensätze von 1789* does not feature among the books borrowed from the workers' libraries, its influence has to be understood in a wider context. It is difficult to determine the exact ways in which it was used, but this cannot simply be reduced to the readership numbers for *Die Neue Zeit* and the books that resulted.

---

102   Hennig 1908, p. 6.
103   Neuhaus, R., 'Was liest der Wiener Arbeiter?', *Bildungsarbeit*, 1909–10, p. 46.

Lastly, we should also take into account the particular case of non-social democratic references. In 1906, the Austrian *Glühlichter* devoted an entire page to a new edition of Thomas Carlyle's *History of the French Revolution*,[104] a book that regularly featured in workers' libraries and recommended reading lists. Written in a very simple style, the presentation of this book – accompanied by a short biography of Carlyle – highlighted the great number of illustrations in the new edition, as well as the way in which it was written, for 'the Great French Revolution has found its historian in Thomas Carlyle'.[105] There was no discussion of his interpretation of the history of the Revolution. Moreover, throughout the whole 1906–14 period no other work on the French Revolution was reviewed in this satirical paper. This example demands that we put the spread of a materialist interpretation of the French Revolution into a certain perspective, given the mention of works from other historiographical traditions. As in the case of Mignet, whose name also repeatedly crops up, Carlyle's historical work was circulated in social-democratic networks. Novels are also worth mentioning: Anatole France's *The Gods Are Athirst* was occasionally mentioned, as was Victor Hugo's *Ninety-Three*, which was republished by the Vorwärts publishing house in 1904. These two novels, whose contents we would struggle to compare to social-democratic interpretations, nonetheless contributed to popularising the history of the French Revolution among militants.

If 70% of loans were novels and barely 10% were historical books, what did this really mean? These borrowing figures refer not only to local party cadres but also the thousands of militants who occasionally consulted historical books, indeed in far greater numbers than the works of Marx and Engels. The few thousand loans of Wilhelm Blos's *Die französische Revolution*, one of the most popular works in this domain, should be set within this context. Most importantly, we should see these library books as part of a wider reception, from the many pamphlets that contained references to the French Revolution, to talks on history, or, indeed, the frequent references to the Revolution in the many different organs distributed by the social democrats. While it is difficult to know what was really being read, we can get some idea of what party cadres were thinking and teaching. Again, this means referring to the 'intermediate cadres', some of whom we highlighted above. These were the cadres who wrote articles popularising history or chose specific passages from Cunow to be reproduced in press organs circulated in tens of thousands of copies. The number

---

104   (Unsigned), 'Neues vom Büchermarkte. Eine Geschichte der französischen Revolution', *Glühlichter*, 25 April 1906.
105   (Unsigned), 'Neues vom Büchermarkte. Eine Geschichte der französischen Revolution', *Glühlichter*, 25 April 1906, p. 3.

of history books borrowed was, indeed, limited. Yet as well as being far from negligible compared to other categories, the borrowing of these books also expressed a wider phenomenon. For among cadres and active militants, we can speak of a historical culture in which the French Revolution occupied a leading place. It seems that in this period of growth for the social-democratic parties, the reference to the French Revolution can hardly be limited to something confined to circles of party leaders or a few inaccessible scholarly works. An extensive reading of newspapers and other publications that were widely-read by militants largely confirms this.

The Reference to 1789: Powerful yet Ambiguous

Two Key Debates

A few years before World War I, internal conflicts developed within the German Social-Democratic Party. Alongside the solidly entrenched tradition of references to the 'Great Revolution', the political uses of revolutionary history were particularly apparent in two debates, indeed the most important disputes since the revisionism crisis and the Russian Revolution of 1905. These debates centred on the question of the German Republic and then, in 1913, the ambiguous commemorations of the Wars of Liberation.

The Republican Question

Around 1910, the debate on revolutionary traditions and the problem of advancing the call for a Republic resumed the polemics that had developed at the turn of the century.[1] Around 1900, the critique of France's political traditions had been important to the revision by Bernstein and his supporters. Social-democratic theorists like Kautsky and Mehring did, of course, see the republican question within a specific national framework, but their positions were also linked to the debates in France.[2] Probably influenced by the achievement of socialist unity in France as well as the SFIO's first positive results, Karl Kautsky seems to have altered somewhat his view of the revolutionary traditions carried forth by the French party. In July 1905 he stated that

> Still today, the events of the Great Revolution continue to have an impact. If the proletariat exercises greater power than in Germany with its three million voters, despite the relative weakness of the socialist organisations in France, this outcome owes not to the ministerial tactic, and very little to the democratic forms of the bourgeois Republic, but above all to the revolutionary instinct that has continued to bear effect from Jacobin rule into our own time ... if the French Revolution had not been 'stained' by the 'Terror', then the lower classes in France would have remained

---

1   Bonnell 1996.
2   Schumacher 1994.

immature and impotent, we would not have seen 1848, and the fight for
the emancipation of the French and international proletariat would have
been indefinitely delayed.[3]

While Kautsky clearly distinguished the 'revolutionary instinct' from the Third
Republic, his analysis now recognised the positive role that the inheritance of
the French Revolution had for contemporary politics, in terms almost opposite
to those of 1889. Without doubt, in the intervening period the French socialists had moved from being splintered among multiple currents to merging into
a single, nationally-influential organisation; this owed, among other things, to
the action of Jean Jaurès, whom Kautsky had severely criticised even just a few
months beforehand.[4] For all that, the question of the call for the republic was
the source of numerous disputes in the German party, and led to one of the
most important ruptures in the pre-war SPD, between Rosa Luxemburg and
Karl Kautsky.

At the beginning of the twentieth century, social democracy theoretically
sought the establishment of a German democratic republic. This old demand
dated back to the 1870s – albeit without being written in the party programme –
but had seen its first concrete expression in the 1848 revolution.[5] In his *Critique
of the Erfurt Programme*, originally a letter to Kautsky with recommendations
for the programme, Engels advised that the programme should include reference to the democratic republic, such as had emerged during the 'Great French
Revolution' in 1792. Engels's recommendation was not acted upon, and the
demand for the republic was never included in the Erfurt programme. Social
democracy made a *de facto* accommodation to the monarchical form of state.
At the Amsterdam Congress in 1904, the SPD chairman August Bebel stated that
he was a republican but did not idealise the 'bourgeois republic'. He told the
French, and especially Jean Jaurès, that 'We have institutions that for your bourgeois republic still remain an ideal'.[6] Austrian social democracy had a certain
nostalgia for the 1848-era plans for a greater German republic, but remained the
'prisoner of its loyalty to Austria-Hungary, which it wanted to transform into a
confederal democratic state, with the effect that some of its leaders ... were still

---

3 Kautsky, K., 'Die Folgen des japanischen Sieges und die Sozial-Demokratie', *Die Neue Zeit*,
   1904–5, p. 462.
4 See the series of articles on 'Republik und Sozialdemokratie', 1904–5, examined in Chapter
   Three, p. 99.
5 Marx, K. and Engels, F., Critiques des programmes de Gotha et d'Erfurt, Paris, Éditions
   sociales, 1966 (1891), p. 103.
6 Cited by Georgen 1998, p. 513.

elaborating reform plans even shortly before the collapse of the multinational state'.[7] Despite some timid pro-republican moves, Austrian social democracy rapidly came to conceive of its reforms within the framework of the existing state.

Around 1910, this debate became particularly acute in Germany, with many demonstrations demanding a reform of the electoral system, in particular in Prussia, where the 'three-class' system imposed a severe inequality. It was at this moment that the radical wing of the party around Rosa Luxemburg demanded that the SPD foreground the call for a republic. Strictly following the Erfurt Programme, Kautsky preferred to remain discreet on this terrain in order to avoid any problems with the law. The refusal to publish one of Rosa Luxemburg's articles formalised the break.[8] Only very few historical references appeared in their exchanges: the debate concerned the SPD's means of action and especially the use of the 'mass strike', parliamentarism and the use of illegal slogans.[9]

Conversely, during these same years the social-democratic inheritors of the revisionist current published ever greater numers of articles referring to the French Revolution in the *Sozialistische Monatshefte*.[10] Opposed to any application of the republican slogan, their critiques – in continuity with the ones issued by Bernstein in 1899 – extended to the French traditions that had emerged from 1789.[11] At the end of 1905, Hugo Lindemann connected what he considered the excessive centralisation of the party to the French tradition.[12] A few months later, an article by Olav Kringen entitled 'Monarchy or Republic'[13] continued the debate that had begun at the turn of the century. For instance, he highlighted the example of Norway, which despite its monarchy was 'the most democratic state in Europe',[14] as against a French republican state that was more conservative on certain points, despite the many revolutions. The conclusion was that there was no merit in calling for a republic in Germany,

---

7   Kreissler 1994, p. 113.
8   On the details of this crisis, see Badia 1975, pp. 161–75.
9   Mehring, F., 'Der Kampf gegen die Monarchie', *Die Neue Zeit*, 1909–10, vol. 2, pp. 609–12. This reply especially relied on Marx and German social democracy's traditional positions, without deploying references to the French experience.
10   To our knowledge, there has been no previous study of this set of articles.
11   *Sozialistische Monatshefte* passed over the German social-democrats' works on the French Revolution in silence. We find no review of Cunow's book in its pages. Apart from Emma Adler's book, the only title it greeted was the new edition of Carlyle: Mämy-Lux I., 'Carlyle: Die französische Revolution', *Sozialistische Monatshefte*, 1907, pp. 258–9.
12   Lindemann, H., 'Zentralismus und Föderalismus in der Sozialdemokratie', *Sozialistische Monatshefte*, 1905, p. 769.
13   Kringen, O., 'Monarchie oder Republik?', *Sozialistische Monatshefte*, 1906, pp. 64–8.
14   Kringen, O., 'Monarchie oder Republik?', *Sozialistische Monatshefte*, 1906, p. 64.

as the left wing of the party did. We could cite multiple examples of texts that reasoned in these terms. An article by Ludwig Quessel, one of the most visible theorists of the revolutionist current, offered a summary of this point of view.[15] He highlighted that while Marx and Engels always displayed their republicanism, Lassalle had taken a different position. The overlaps between democracy and republicanism, and monarchy and absolutism, were more complex than many social-democrats proclaimed. The United Kingdom's evolution toward parliamentarism offered an example of a constitutional monarchy transitioning to a parliamentary, or even democratic regime. There was some doubt as to the real advantages of republicanism: the monarch doubtless had a certain prominence, but was that not also true of the President of the Republic? The article ended by challenging the legitimacy of the French model of rupture, instead favouring an 'English-style development':

> As comrade Vollmar explained to the Reichstag, with the consent of the [SPD parliamentary group], we want English-style development, meaning not the violent overthrow of the monarchical state form as in France, but rather an evolution of the constitutional monarchy toward democratic monarchy, such as took place in England.[16]

The critique of the republican model came together with a critique of the French revolutionary tradition. In an article devoted to the training of party cadres, Max Maurenbrecher expressed his wish to break with the phraseology of 1789, in his view overly present in 'political education':

> This is precisely what we need as political education. It is not enough to endlessly repeat the general formulas of the century of the Revolution, now that we have come almost half-a-century on from that.[17]

We could cite many other articles from the *Sozialistische Monatshefte* that called for a break with the schemas of the SPD's *Sozialrevolutionarismus*, founded on regular references to the French Revolution. Thus in the debate on the republic it was the revisionists who most deployed the reference to the French Revolution, within the perspective of criticising the traditions which this reference carried forward. These positions should be linked to their stance on the national question: increasingly favourable to integration within the state

---

15   Quessel, L., 'Sind wir Republikaner?', *Sozialistische Monatshefte*, 1909, pp. 1254–62.
16   Ibid.
17   Maurenbrecher, M., 'Schulung der Funktionäre', *Sozialistische Monatshefte*, 1909, p. 1407.

and agreements with the parties of government, they for instance supported the Reich's colonial policy and distanced themselves from anything that might seem hostile to Germany and German interests.[18]

The Napoleonic Inheritance in Question: the Commemorations of 1913

Numerous works have been written on the inheritance of the Napoleonic occupation in Germany. It had a profound effect in terms of the reactions that it produced, and its foundational link with the French Revolution was particularly marked in the German-speaking countries, including among the German social-democrats.[19] For Karl Kautsky, Napoleon had 'revolutionised Europe'; this form of continuity was repeatedly expressed in line with the few remarks that Marx and Engels had made on this period. Nonetheless, as far as we know, before 1906–7 there were no social-democratic books or pamphlets that addressed the specific problems posed by the consequences of the arrival of Napoleonic troops in Germany. Napoleon was always mentioned, but the French heritage that was studied and celebrated was above all the period between 1789 and 1799, or even 1789 and 1794, with a unique place reserved for Babeuf. In his history of Germany, Franz Mehring was one of the first to study the Napoleonic occupation in the same detail as the French Revolution. Another important book was Kurt Eisner's *End of the Empire*,[20] where he addressed both the introduction of the Napoleonic reforms and the displays of hostility to the French presence. These studies should be understood in terms of a context of sharp debates over the integration of national reference points into social-democratic culture. For example, the question of the place of Schiller particularly mobilised the social-democrats' different positions on Germanic culture: Rosa Luxemburg strongly criticised those intent on uncritically integrating references to national culture.[21] At the other end of the scale were those on the right of the party who called for an appropriation of these same reference points. One interesting example of the link established between the German nation and the French Revolution was an article by Karl Eugen Schmidt devoted to 'Anacharsis Cloots, who spoke for the human race'.[22]

---

18   Fletcher 1988.
19   Engels considered the period from 1808 to 1813 a stage of the bourgeois revolution in Germany.
20   Eisner 1907.
21   Bonnell 2005.
22   Schmidt, K.E., 'Anacharsis Cloots. Der Sprecher des Menschengeschlechts', *Sozialistische Monatshefte*, 1908, pp. 867–75.

published in *Sozialistische Monatshefte*. Countering the notion that the celebrated figures of German history were all of nationalist propensity, the author underlined that 'during the Great Revolution thousands of Germans fought alongside their French comrades'.[23] Karl Eugen Schmidt emphasised Cloots's international aspects: this latter saw the Revolution in terms that far exceeded the borders within which he had been born. Having noted the insults of which he had been victim – and especially his conflict with Robespierre – the article portrayed Cloots as a forerunner of 'internationalism'.[24]

A mass organisation representing a growing part of the German population, beyond its proclaimed internationalism the SPD inserted itself within national problematics, and gradually became the *Volkspartei* ['people's party'] – although it would embrace this denomination only under the Weimar Republic. It could thus hardly remain indifferent to the large-scale commemorations of the Wars of Liberation. The debates that they drove within the SPD ought to be the object of a specific study; these wars also posed other particular problems like the question of the 'revolution from above'.[25] Here we shall focus on how a link was established with the inheritance of the French Revolution.

'In calling for a fight against Napoleon, the national propaganda was effectively trying to awaken such a perception as would allow Germans' commonalities to appear in as many domains of political and cultural life as possible and determine the geographical space of the German ethnic nation'.[26] Even before Germany was ultimately united, Heinrich von Sybel like other German historians made 1813 the foundational date of a national movement that resulted in unification in 1871.[27] The uprising of 1813 was considered one of the first manifestations of the *Sonderweg*: the German nation took form in reaction against the Napoleonic occupation. The historiography has long repeated this central idea: 'In the beginning was Napoleon' ...[28] The German national story, thus constructed, has recently been challenged by a historiography that

---

23   Schmidt, K.E., 'Anacharsis Cloots. Der Sprecher des Menschengeschlechts', *Sozialistische Monatshefte*, 1908, p. 868.

24   Schmidt, K.E., 'Anacharsis Cloots. Der Sprecher des Menschengeschlechts', *Sozialistische Monatshefte*, 1908, p. 875.

25   As far as we know, there is no article presenting a summary of the very many social-democratic publications on this question, or indeed on the specific question of the SPD's commemoration of the *Befreiungkriege*. See Mariot and Rowell 2004.

26   Jeismann 1997, p. 49.

27   Von Sybel 1860.

28   Nipperdey 1985, p. 11.

has advanced more nuanced approaches, demonstrating the different attitudes toward the French occupiers.[29]

March to October 1913 saw the joint celebration of the centenary of the anti-French uprising and twenty-five years of Wilhelm II's reign. Championing the German people's war of liberation, these celebrations sought to legitimise the monarchy in a context in which social democracy constituted a growing and threatening political force. In Hamburg, for example, evoking the unity of the German people made it possible for the authorities to assert themselves against the great influence of the social-democrats, who appeared as factors for division.[30] Wilhelm II also conducted other commemorations in 1913, like the celebration of the victory at Sedan, and tried to appear as a *Volkskaiser*, notwithstanding the in fact very limited place of the people within these ceremonies. 'Because of the archaic nature of much of the ceremony, popular participation remained very limited and its imagery appareared continuously out of place in an age characterized by increasing social and political activism'.[31] This was, nonetheless, one of the first great mass demonstrations before World War I: one of the high points of the commemoration came on 10 March 1913, the centenary of Friedrich-Wilhelm II's *An Mein Volk* appeal, which marked the beginning of the resistance to Napoleon. 18 October 1913, centenary of the Battle of Leipzig, marked the culmination of this whole set of commemorations.

The 'extremes' were excluded from the festivities, including the social-democrats and the pan-German leagues alike. The centenary of the Wars of Liberation was an opportunity for the parties of the Right to mount an intense monarchist propaganda. An official, pro-imperial almanac devoted to commemorating the centenary of 1813 gave an idea of this committed mobilisation.[32] Numerous rallies were organised in order to incite the population to take part in the official commemorations. The conservative press vigorously attacked an SPD accused of being 'a traitor to the fatherland'; the Imperial League against Social Democracy, charged with the struggle against the SPD, presented this latter as the defender of pro-Napoleonic positions. But if it is true that the social-democrats recognised the beneficial role of the Napoleonic occupation, in continuity with a certain tradition, in fact in 1913 their positions were rather more complex.

While excluded from the commemorations, the social-democrats displayed great interest in this anniversary. Their numerous articles, reviews and books

---

29   Aaslestad 2005.
30   Aaslestad 2005, p. 412.
31   Smith 2000, p. 261.
32   *Volkskalender für das Jahr 1913*, Berlin, 1913.

published as the centenary of 1813 approached themselves bore testament to this. Franz Mehring's two volumes, together with Alexander Conrady's work bringing together various sources on this event,[33] constituted the most important contribiutions. In *Die Neue Welt*, Heinrich Laufenberg published a mixed portrait of Napoleon.[34] A few articles in *Der Kampf* took the opportunity to review Austria's counter-revolutionary role during this period.[35]

Two examples of documents issued by educational structures, based on Mehring and Conrady's works, allow us to understand how they interpreted the events of 1813. The first was a set of talks offered by Bernhard Rausch and published by the educational commission. Its very title – 'The era of the Great French Revolution and the Wars of Liberation' – showed how the social-democrats sought to link 1813 to the period that had begun in 1789.[36] Up till that point, the Napoleonic period had only very fleetingly been mentioned in social-democratic lectures and educational materials. This course adopted the same structure as Mehring's book, which was published simultaneously; after three talks on the French Revolution, the three subsequent ones dealt, in turn, with the Coalition Wars and the end of the Holy Roman Empire, the Prussian reforms and finally the resistance to Napoleon and the end of the French Empire. The series ended with a general conclusion on bourgeois revolutions and their place in history.

The second document was a *Lichtbildervortrag* (talk with slides) by the same author, in turn allowing us better to understand the contents of this first document.[37] While the plan was not exactly the same, it was again issued by the educational commission, was also published in 1913 and was again given by Bernard Rausch. The content must, therefore, have differed very little. Rausch first of all emphasised the 'reactionary and Byzantine character of the commemoration of the centenary'[38] and insisted that 'as the real heirs of the fighters for freedom and democracy, we are opposed to it'.[39] The French Revolution was presented in classic terms as a bourgeois revolution that 'achieved more than sixty years

---

33 Mehring 1912, Conrady 1913.

34 Laufenberg, H., 'Napoléon', *Die Neue Welt*, 1913, pp. 342, 363, 387, 410.

35 Bauer, O., 'Geschichte', *Der Kampf*, 1911–12, pp. 334–5; Weber, H., 'Der Sozialismus und der Krieg', *Der Kampf*, 1912–13, pp. 97–106; Strauss, E., 'Zur Hundertjahrfeier der Befreiungskriege', *Der Kampf*, 1912–13, pp. 300–5.

36 Zentralbildungsausschuss der Sozialdemokratischen Partei Deutschlands, *Disposition und Schriftenverzeichnis zu dem Kursus des Genossen Bernhard Rausch über: Das Zeitalter der grossen Französischen Revolution und die Befreiungskriege (1789–1815)*. (6 Vorträge).

37 Rausch 1914.

38 Rausch 1914, p. 2.

39 Ibid.

of Prussian history'.[40] The various wars and coalitions were seen as one same chronological sequence that began in 1792 and ended in 1815. Within this framework, Napoleon was the 'necessary consequence, if the French Revolution was to be defended in a lasting way ... the son and heir of the Revolution'.[41] After mentioning several reforms that had taken place under the Napoleonic occupation, he set these within a general historical progression that brought a new bourgeois order. But the occupation turned from a historical advance into a burden for the German people ('After the reforms, the weight of the French foreign occupation lost its legitimacy'),[42] in turn making it legitimate for 'the people to rise up'.[43] This educational text then described the different wars and reviewed the reforms that had been implemented in Prussia. These latter showed that 'only a complete revolution, and not reforms going only halfway, was capable of preparing the hundred-times deserved end of the regiment of Prussian squires'.[44]

This *Lichtbildervortrag*'s tendency to associate the French Revolution with its Napoleonic extension accorded with the all-encompassing view that Kautsky had taken in 1889. It rather stood against a tendency that had developed in previous years to focus on certain episodes of the revolution. Its other notable aspect – up till that point little-elaborated – was the importance that ought to be attributed to the Wars of Liberation against French control in 1813. Indeed, the social-democrats sought to place the German popular uprising within their own history, and not to leave it up to the imperial authorities to commemorate this experience.

Hermann Wendel's review of Mehring and Conrady's books, appearing in *Die Neue Zeit*, followed in the same spirit as this approach. His arguments repeated the ones he had made in a pamphlet published in this same moment – the result of one of his speeches[45] – and gave account of the attention paid to analysing the events of 1813. In particular, he praised Mehring's 'materialist conception of history',[46] which offered an exhaustive panorama of the Napoleonic wars, and also emphased the quality of the research behind the two social-democrats' works, in Wendel's view far surpassing all the other books hitherto published on this subject.[47] The insurgents of 1813 were placed on the same

---

40   Rausch 1914, p. 3.
41   Rausch 1914, p. 4.
42   Rausch 1914, p. 6.
43   Rausch 1914, p. 7.
44   Ibid.
45   Wendel 1913.
46   Wendel 1913, p. 293.
47   Wendel 1913, p. 292.

level as those who had stormed the Bastille; his text asserted the continuity between social-democracy and 1813: 'However, given that their lies would otherwise appear badly knocked together, these patriots of the 1913 jubilee carefully pass over in silence the fact that social democracy's opinion on the Wars of Liberation on many points coincides with the conceptions of the true patriots of 1813'.[48]

In one pamphlet, Wendel proposed that the commemoration of 1813 be linked with another anniversary, the creation of the ADAV in 1863.[49] The social-democrats thus reconstituted their own national history; as opposed to the authorities, who foregrounded the moment of German unification in 1871, they foregrounded the creation of their party, which while very much in the minority in 1863 had by 1913 become a major political force.[50]

Given that the Napoleonic occupation had quickly transformed into a matter of foreign domination, 1813 was set at the same level as the storming of the Bastille in 1789. Just a few months before August 1914, the social-democrats embraced – in their own way – a national heritage that combined with traditional revolutionary reference points, albeit not without ambiguities.

The Place of a Reference Point in a Germany at War

A few months before World War I, the hopes expressed in the aftermath of the 1905 Russian Revolution seemed to have become more distant. In *1649–1789–1905* Karl Kautsky and Rosa Luxemburg had heralded the beginning of a wave of revolutions comparable to the wake of 1789. At the end of 1913, the revisionist Edmund Fischer could declare that the SPD was now a 'party of reforms' and, citing this pamphlet, deride the revolutionary references of his adversaries within the party:

> Ah, how quickly these hallucinations were destroyed! But we had to demonstrate our vehement opposition to the idea that again, with the collapse of capitalist society, the results would still be good ones.[51]

---

48 Ibid., p. 294.
49 Wendel 1913, p. 3.
50 The social-democrats' approaches to these questions were the focus of a historiography that had particular echoes in the DDR. The fight against French domination was seen – not without controversy – as a moment that expressed democratic feeling. See Dorpalen 1969. On the historiography of 1813, see Schäfer 2001.
51 Fischer, E., 'Revolution und Reform', *Sozialistische Monatshefte*, 1913, p. 1132.

In recent years, there had been some signs of the social-democrats' increasing integration within the state: many had declared themselves ready to defend Germany if it came under attack, like the SPD's Gustav Noske in April 1907 or, indeed, George von Vollmar when he addressed the Bavarian Diet on 24 August 1912. In this context, the centenary of the Wars of Liberation demonstrated the growing place of national reference points, even though the SPD was formally excluded from the commemorations.

Social Democracy and the War

With the unanimous vote for war credits in August 1914[52] and the social-democrats' embrace of their own governments in both Austria and Germany, we could expect the disappearance or indeed a sharp critique of the traditions of the French Revolution, which French propaganda itself mobilised in an anti-German cause.[53] The writer Jean-Richard Bloch could ask whether 'the armies of the Republic will assure the triumph of democracy in Europe and complete the work of '93'.[54] German propaganda did much to highlight the 'ideas of 1789', negatively presented in counterposition to the 'ideas of 1914'. It foregrounded a 'German idea of liberty', a 'cultural individualism' and 'state socialism' supposedly characteristic of German history and culture.[55] To fight against the inheritance of the French Revolution and its ideas was a means of mobilising the German people[56] and an opportunity to reaffirm the *Sonderweg* – a mix of elements of authoritarianism and democracy, and marker of a particular course of development. Bismarck's efforts upon the 1889 centenary, in which he set forth the foundation of the Empire in 1871 as a response to 1789, were adopted anew and driven to the extreme. The 'appeal to culture' signed by numerous scientists and writers like Werner Sombart and Thomas Mann in 1915 played a significant role in terms of the defence of the 'ideas of 1914'; indeed, German intellectuals and scholars were heavily mobilised to support the war effort.

As for the German and Austrian social-democrats, on closer examination we can see a contradictory situation in which the reference to the French Revolution maintained an important place among the two parties' various different sensibilities. Without doubt, from 1914 to 1917 this reference was almost absent from *Die Neue Welt*; unsurprisingly, there was a priority on themes directly

---

52   Rebérioux 1974, pp. 590–1.
53   Demm 1987. See also Von See 2001.
54   Rolland 1952, p. 37, cited by Demm 1987, p. 152. On intellectuals and the war, see Prochasson 1993.
55   Faulenbach 2008, p. 1065.
56   Demm 1987, pp. 156–7.

linked to the contemporary military situation. In 1917, the only topic with any connection to the French Revolution or its extension was the image of a French defeat, the Battle of Waterloo ...[57]

In the party's reviews, however, the picture was rather more complicated. A 'total war', World War I was an opportunity to review the first examples of mass mobilisation for military purposes. For example, in *Der Kampf* Ian Strasser revisited the 'people's war' of 1792 to 1797 which opposed France to the Coalition forces and explained the economic motives behind the Gironde's slogans.[58] Faced with the powerful national sentiments that were being expressed at the beginning of World War I, it was necessary to understand how the war could become a 'people's war' extending beyond generals and elites alone.[59] Nonetheless, apart from a few historical comparisons of this type, most of the texts that referred to 1789 and its consequences sought either to discredit the French Revolution, or else to champion its legacy in opposition to the propaganda of both enemy camps. While we could choose from among a great number of arguments hostile to the inheritance of the Revolution, here we are most interested in highlighting a characteristic example of the about-turn that began in 1914 – the case of Hermann Wendel.

Hermann Wendel and the Discrediting of 1789 as a Model

In 1916, Hermann Wendel published a pamphlet on Alsace-Lorraine in which he criticised the French Socialists for wielding the glorious Jacobin and *sans-culotte* traditions for propaganda purposes.[60] But it was in a series of articles he published in *Die Glocke* ['The Bell'] in April 1917 – dedicated to 'the bourgeois character of the French Revolution'[61] – that the model of 1789 most clearly fell into discredit. Published in Berlin, *Die Glocke* appeared from 1 September 1915 as a 'socialist bi-monthly', and from 1 October 1916 as a weekly. Konrad Haenisch directed the editorial team, which included, among others, Heinrich Cunow.[62] The cohesion of the group who animated this review owed to the fact that many of them were former members of the left wing of the party who had now changed their position and given unconditional support to the government. The left wing of the SPD and those opposed to the war considered *Die Glocke* the

---

57   'Waterloo', *Die Neue Welt*, 1917, p. 324.
58   Strasser, I., 'Aus einem Volkskrieg', *Der Kampf*, 1916, pp. 359–67.
59   Strasser, I., 'Aus einem Volkskrieg', *Der Kampf*, 1916, p. 360.
60   Wendel 1916.
61   Wendel, H., 'Die bürgerliche Charakter der Französischen Revolution', *Die Glocke*, 14 April 1917, pp. 56–63; 21 April 1917, pp. 92–6; 28 April 1917, pp. 121–31.
62   Fricke 1987, Vol. 1, p. 643.

very embodiment of treachery. This is an important context for understanding Wendel's argument. As the title of this series of articles indicated, he sought to demonstrate the profoundly – and uniquely – bourgeois character of the French Revolution of 1789–99. In Wendel's narrative, the Revolution above all represented 'bourgeois domination';[63] after a short reminder of the reforms that had been undertaken before the French Revolution – here building on his 1910 reasoning in *Die Neue Zeit* – he elaborated a set of arguments that insisted on the 'bourgeois' aspects of the Revolution,[64] all of whose actors above all defended the untouchability of private property.[65] This highly repetitive reasoning allowed him to distance himself from the French Revolution and to hint at the superiority of German socialism, reliant on its own traditions. Wendel particularly sought to minimise the uniqueness of the measures taken by the Convention in 1792–3:

> Even when it was dominated by petty-bourgeois democracy, the Convention remained loyal to this same property-fanaticism, and never did the third revolutionary parliament think any differently to the first two on this question of principle ... In reality, even the bloodiest exponents of Terror were, with all their foresight, just as troubled by the blinkers of property as were the most overfed capitalists.[66]

Wendel particularly took against Robespierre:

> All this Terror was but a means in the service of the petty bourgeoisie, and finally the cohort of spirits of the immortal soul and the higher essence – with which Robespierre surpassed the heights of ridicule – proved to be nothing other than a petty-bourgeois spectre. Incapable of going beyond the world of appearances, Robespierre wrapped himself in a mystical fog ... This petty-bourgeois idyll did suppose a certain equalisation of property, but what the Jacobins aspired to was not some future revolutionary

63   Wendel, H., 'Die bürgerliche Charakter der Französischen Revolution', *Die Glocke*, 14 April 1917, p. 56.
64   Wendel, H., 'Die bürgerliche Charakter der Französischen Revolution', *Die Glocke*, 14 April 1917, p. 59.
65   Wendel, H., 'Die bürgerliche Charakter der Französischen Revolution', *Die Glocke*, 14 April 1917, p. 60.
66   Wendel, H., 'Die bürgerliche Charakter der Französischen Revolution', *Die Glocke*, 28 April 1917, pp. 124–5.

objective that would in turn herald further developments, but rather a reactionary stiffening of the past.[67]

The very brief reference to Babeuf at the end of this series did not threaten to imbalance the general course of Wendel's argument: it appeared almost impossible to lay claim to the inheritance of 1789, and still less to 1913. Given the context of the war, these arguments are worthy of attention, especially given that they were hardly isolated. In Austria, we find this general hostility to the revolutionary model in such a work as a pamphlet by Karl Renner. An article by Norbert Leser – a specialist in Austromarxism, studying Karl Renner in the 1970s – highlighted the specificity of his critiques, which saw Marxism as 'an idealisation of certain historical phenomena, among which the French Revolution occupied a particularly lofty place thanks to reasoning-by-analogy'.[68] In this vein, he cited an extract from a collection of Karl Renner's articles on the war:

> Nothing is more dangerous than pandering to the proletariat with faith in the decrees of the French Revolution and the promise that socialism will bring the marvel of a total creation: If only that were so! And if only it had been like that! When the proletariat has the economy in its hands alone, the phantom of authority will have disappeared and this will mark the beginning of a work of administration. Certainly, it will be freed of all the binds of private interest, will be able to produce more rapidly and efficiently, and will be able to accelerate social development considerably. But there will be no miracle.[69]

A number of German social-democrats would greatly develop this negative analogy with the French Revolution in the immediate aftermath of the Russian Bolsheviks' seizure of power in November 1917. But while these approaches were predominant, they were not totally hegemonic.

The Austrians and Germans Who Sided with the Revolution

The left wing of the party was initially a very small minority, whose positions would only become clear at the end of 1914. It virulently rejected support for the

---

67   Wendel, H., 'Die bürgerliche Charakter der Französischen Revolution', *Die Glocke*, 28 April 1917, pp. 125–6.
68   Leser 1977, p. 22.
69   Renner, K., *Marxismus, Krieg und Internationale*, cited by Leser 1977, p. 22.

war effort.[70] In Austria, the 'social-patriots' around Karl Renner were opposed by the 'internationalists', notably including Friedrich Adler. Son of Victor Adler, this latter is well-known for shooting the Austrian Minister-President Count Stürgkh on 21 October 1916, an act that earned him the admiration of the younger social-democrats.[71] He organised a 'Karl Marx' circle, which brought together militants opposed to the war. In 1918 a collection of texts was published in tribute to him,[72] including his most important articles published since 1914. Here, we see that he deployed references to 1789 in positive terms, as he sought to combat the prevalent propaganda. In the October 1914 *Sozialdemokratische Korrespondenz* he invoked the role of 'Karl Kautsky, our teacher' and his status as a theorist and propagator of Marxism, and highlighted his work popularising the history of 'the Great French Revolution'.[73] A few months later, in a manifesto on 3 December 1914 Friedrich Adler repudiated the SPD's policy of support for the Empire. In 'Social Democracy in France and the War' he dissociated the real heritage of the French Revolution from what war propaganda had turned it into,[74] before he virulently denounced the French Socialists' use of an analogy between 1789 and 1914.[75] Two years leader, Adler sought to pick up the flame of 1789 dropped by the German and Austrian social-democrats; for 'the bourgeoisie has definitively broken with the traditions of 1789, but they survived in the proletariat at least up till the beginning of this war'.[76]

However, Adler's most developed article in opposition to the 'ideas of 1914' was published in *Der Kampf* in July 1916, a few months before the assassination of the Minister-President.[77] This was presented as a reply to various books, especially Rudolf Kjellen's *Die Ideen von 1914*.[78] Indeed, this latter declared that 'the world war is a struggle between 1789 and 1914'.[79] Friedrich Adler cited at some length a number of authors for whom Germany embod-

---

70   The most famous expression of this was Karl Liebknecht's refusal to vote for fresh war credits in the Reichstag in December 1914.
71   Ardelt 1984.
72   Adler 1918.
73   Cited in Adler 1918, p. 5.
74   Adler, F., 'Die Sozialdemokratie in Frankreich und der Krieg', *Der Kampf*, February 1915, cited in Adler 1918, p. 21.
75   Adler 1918, p. 27.
76   Adler, F., 'Kriegziele', *Der Kampf*, 1916, p. 82.
77   Adler, F. 'Die Ideen von 1789 und die Ideen von 1914', *Der Kampf*, 1916, pp. 239–49.
78   Kjellen 1915.
79   Adler, F. 'Die Ideen von 1789 und die Ideen von 1914', *Der Kampf*, 1916, p. 239.

ied 'the ideas of 1914', in a form of 'national socialism ... a German revolution of 1914'.[80] If the French Revolution allowed 'the bourgeoisie to dominate',[81] for Friedrich Adler it was also, in its time, a 'fight for democracy' – a fight that the proletariat had pursued by raising the question of the right to vote.[82]

Some German texts also bore comparisons with such conceptions. Alsace-Lorraine was both at the heart of the war and, for most, a point of discord between French socialists and German social-democrats. *Die Neue Zeit* published an article in response to a new edition of various texts by Heinrich von Treitschke and Heinrich von Sybel regarding Germany's 'historic rights' to Alsace-Lorraine, as well as a pamphlet by Hermann Wendel mentioned above.[83] This article's author Ernst Ludwig sought to take a stand against those who presented Alsace and Lorraine as if they naturally belonged to Germany. To this end, he turned back to the history of the revolutionary period and particularly challenged the German propaganda.[84] He recalled Strasbourg's situation during the French Revolution, which in various ways depended on Germany and struggles that were national as well as social in character.[85] He mentioned Cloots and Forster, before describing Eulogius Schneider's role at some length.[86] The Germans were not organised in the same clubs as the French, and in Von Treitschke's view this demonstrated the hostility to the French character of the Revolution. Conversely, the social-democrat cited Schneider and his attempts to transcend national antagonisms:

> The Germans who actively joined the Revolution were led to this action not because it was a Revolution of the French, but because they believed that the movement that these latter had initiated would lead to the emancipation of humanity, realising their dream of freedom and dignity for the human race.[87]

---

80   Adler, F. 'Die Ideen von 1789 und die Ideen von 1914', *Der Kampf*, 1916, p. 240.

81   Adler, F. 'Die Ideen von 1789 und die Ideen von 1914', *Der Kampf*, 1916, p. 243.

82   Adler, F. 'Die Ideen von 1789 und die Ideen von 1914', *Der Kampf*, 1916, p. 244. He then cited the sixth article of the 1793 Constitution.

83   Ernst, L., 'Das Elsass während der französischen Revolution', *Die Neue Zeit*, 1917, vol. 1, pp. 11–21. The article was published in the October 1916 issue.

84   On the integration of Alsace-Lorraine into France during the Revolution, see Wartelle 1989.

85   Ernst, L., 'Das Elsass während der französischen Revolution', *Die Neue Zeit*, 1917, vol. 1, p. 18.

86   See Gilli 1989.

87   Ernst, L., 'Das Elsass während der französischen Revolution', *Die Neue Zeit*, 1917, vol. 1, p. 21.

He then evoked the battles that Schneider had fought, in particular for the emancipation of the Jews. A rapid history proceeding up till 1870 led to a critique of those social-democrats, like Hermann Wendel, who sought to aggravate the tensions between Frenchmen and Germans over this subject. Despite the difficult historical conditions, the article concluded with an appeal for unity:

> In its struggle for liberation, it [the proletariat] can find an example in the Revolution in Alsace: for in the living struggle the revolutionary milieux in the two countries – whether German Alsatians or French – each adopted the objective that history had fixed for them, without consideration for their cultural differences.[88]

This article, appearing at the height of the war, without doubt remained an isolated case. It nonetheless anticipated a message of reconciliation between France and Germany, based on historical examples from the period of the French Revolution, which part of the SPD would develop further under the Weimar Republic.

The Picture on the Eve of the 1917 Russian Revolution

1906 was marked by the retreat of the Russian Revolution; by the end of that year, the enthusiasm of the social-democrats who had seen it as the beginning of a new 'Great Revolution' was no longer in order. It was time to draw a balance-sheet. Kautsky concluded from this experience that the epoch of bourgeois revolutions was now over:

> The age of bourgeois revolutions – which is to say the age of the revolutions in which the bourgeoisie constitutes the driving force – is now complete, including in Russia. Even in this case, the proletariat no longer constitutes a means and a tool for the bourgeoisie, as was the case in the bourgeois revolutions, but an autonomous class with autonomous revolutionary objectives.[89]

The fact that bourgeois revolutions now belonged to the past allowed them more easily to become the object of classification and historical study. Logically

---

88   Ernst, L., 'Das Elsass während der französischen Revolution', *Die Neue Zeit*, 1917, vol. 1, pp. 69–70.

89   Kautsky, K., 'Triebkräfte und aussichten der russischen revolution', *Die Neue Zeit*, 1906–7, vol. 2, p. 331.

enough, there had been numerous contributions focusing on the most important of these revolutions. Numerous book reviews, books and articles published
in theoretical reviews as well as in the more widely-read papers indicate how
well anchored this reference now was. While the previous years had seen the
teaching of the French Revolution play a diminished role in party education, it
returned in force from 1905 onward, in the wake of the Russian Revolution. If
in many circles in Germany the French Revolution was no longer such a major
point of discussion as it had been in the nineteenth century, this point of reference was still present within the social-democratic context and underwent
unprecedented developments.

The social-democratic parties were now far more powerful than they had
been during the period of the centenary. This era was marked by the peak
of a certain kind of Marxism that combined an increasingly reformist practice with a phraseology in which the horizon of socialism was maintained. It
was thought within a theoretical framework founded on three sources, one of
which – French politics – drew its origins from the tradition of 1789. The French
Revolution – the bourgeois revolution *par excellence*, which had given rise to
the modern world – was also the Revolution that had provided the proletariat with the models of great revolutionary figures and even militant practices.
Lastly, it was very much a moment of national history, given the influence that it
had exerted in Germany. As part of his training, each social-democratic cadre
would have at least taken a course in which the Revolution was mentioned.
Many of them had read one or more books on this subject, available in party
libraries.

As well as being a now solidly-anchored tradition, the French Revolution
remained an object of controversy. It was a particular target for the revisionists: they called for an openly reformist *Reformpartei*, which should abandon
the revolutionary phraseology that came from the inheritance of 1789. During
the war, this legacy was largely discredited, as contrasted with the 'ideas of 1914'.
But the more internationalist wing of social democracy defended it against the
various protagonists' propaganda.

When we compare the German and Austrian cases, we see that the reference
to the French Revolution was mainly anchored in this former context. In 1914,
the Austrian sources clearly indicate that – with the exception of Emma Adler –
all the books published were German works. Nonetheless, this picture is more
complex than it may seem at first glance: for example, the first talk with slides
on the French Revolution took place in Austria. Moreover, there were a whole
series of links between the German and Austrian domains, which were very
visible in the choice of works on the French Revolution read in Austria. Some
figures like Karl Kautsky or, at a different level, Gustav Eckstein, were a pivot

between the two countries. These cases attest to a complex shared history, in which the German position was very much dominant – Kautsky and Eckstein were both Austrians who moved to Germany – although not exclusively so. Austrian social democracy evolved in a country which – need we mention – was not similarly marked by the experience of the French Revolution and Napoleonic occupation. It was also far less central to the Second International. As a party at the centre of European socialism, the SPD had to have a reading of the great historical events: the same demand did not apply to the social-democrats in the Austro-Hungarian empire. This context in fact posed the Austrian party other specific problems, the most important of which was the nationalities question: in the debates on this theme we find no important references to the French Revolution, whether in *Der Kampf* or in Otto Bauer's renowned work.[90]

One expression of the change that had taken place as compared to the 1889– 95 period was the variety of books on the French Revolution. Translations demonstrated the concern to introduce sources from the era of the Revolution as well as French textbooks able to enlighten a social-democratic readership on the history of the Revolution. These sometimes-selective translations reflected the social-democrats' differences with Jaurès, insofar as they privileged Guesdist accounts. This symbolised the effect that political debates had on historiographical choices. The extent of the critical apparatuses that accompanied these works was telling of a social-democratic approach that sought to make these books accessible to a wider public.

The books published by the social-democrats were part of a historiographical moment that extended beyond the German-speaking countries alone. Cunow like Jaurès and Kropotkin explored the documentation of the revolutionary era and wrote a social and economic history of the Revolution. Each of the three had a unique vision of the revolutionary process: Cunow distinguished himself with his strict application of historical materialism, thus placing him at some distance from Jaurès's history and Kropotkin's anti-parliamentarism. The publication of Cunow's *Die revolutionäre Zeitungsliteratur*, the most developed social-democratic work on this period, can also be interpreted – even beyond Cunow's own intentions – as the result of two combined conjunctural factors. It responded to the need to publish a work at the same level as Jaurès's – as demonstrated by Kautsky's insistent efforts to legitimise Cunow's study after its publication – as well as the impact of the Russian Revolution, which drove the use of this analogy at all levels of the party. For their part, the book reviews in *Die Neue Zeit* displayed the concern

---

90   Bauer 2000.

for a more scholarly history that paid particular attention to the examination of the sources and the critique of existing academic works, even while also remaining part of the struggles in the present. Unlike in the French case, where Jaurès managed to secure the creation of a parliamentary commission to study sources from the revolutionary era, this stage in the social-democratic historiography remained limited to the party and its own networks. However, the power of these networks was incomparably greater than French socialism's own.

Lastly, it is worth highlighting the way in which the main figures of the Revolution were criticised or else granted legitimacy. Since 1887 and the translations by Gabriel Deville there had existed a certain interest for Babeuf. But on the eve of 1914 Babouvism was much better known than it had been at the end of the nineteeth century. Particularly important was the translation of Buonarotti's book, which should be understood in terms of its role in enriching the social-democratic educationals regarding this period. Babeuf here himself became the object of particular interest, whether as an extension of the French Revolution or as an important stage in the 'History of socialism'.[91] A forerunner of the ideas carried forth by social democracy, Babeuf was not, however, a political model: care was made to set his means of action at a distance, emphasising that the SPD represented a higher form of organisation.

The other figure who was particularly exalted was Jean-Paul Marat, who had very early seen the class antagonisms at work in the Revolution. He had done so by way of his paper *l'Ami du people*, which was presented as an effective means of propaganda. As we have emphasised, the party newspaper was very important to social-democratic militants, and their identification with Marat on this point in part explains the preference for him specifically. As against the dominant historiography, which saw him as a bloodthirsty madman, Marat was, together with Babeuf, the most widely-popularised figure. Marat died in July 1793, and the fact that he did not live through the period between September 1793 and June 1794 – marked by the Terror, of which the social-democrats were very critical – aided his positive presentation. Indeed, there was a striking continuity in the hostility to the 'Terror' and Robespierre in particular. The low number of works on the Incorruptible, as well as a black legend about him which was particularly developed in Germany, helped to shape the social-democrats' enduring negative image of Robespierre. In their view, he embodied

---

91   As far as we know, Buonarroti's book was not issued by the French socialists in this period, as the last French edition dated back to 1869. It was not again published in France until 1957, with Georges Lefebvre's edition for Éditions Sociales.

the Terror and revolutionary violence – political forms of the bourgeois revolution that they virulently rejected. Such hostility to Robespierre, as contrasted to left-wing historiography in France, was, indeed, notable: by way of example, the creation of the Société des Études Robespierristes in 1907 found no echo among the social-democrats.

In 1914, the reference to the French Revolution was sufficiently well-anchored that it could be mobilised, in contrasting ways, up till 1917. Yet while these mentions of the revolutionary past had their importance, they remained relatively isolated and were incomparably lesser than the blooming references of previous years. It was again revolution in Russia that would now change the terms of the reference to 1789 and especially 1793, indeed in a deep and lasting way. This change came amidst a context of simmering revolution, which would also affect both Germany and Austria in 1918–19.

PART 3

Reinterpretations and New Approaches, 1917–34

∴

The Social Democracies' New Course

The years from 1917 to the early 1920s were a period in which the social-democratic parties experienced structural changes. The Russian Revolution and its consequences – including the Bolsheviks' seizure of power on 7 November 1917 – were inscribed in a wider context of political and social upheavals that would also affect Germany and Austria.

The largely spontaneous German Revolution of 1918–19 was the result of powerful aspirations for peace. The Republic was proclaimed on 9 November 1918, and indeed twice. Firstly, by Philipp Scheidemann (who declared 'the German Republic') and then by Karl Liebknecht (who proclaimed 'the German Socialist Republic') in response to this. A dual-power situation took hold with the emergence of workers' councils (*Räte*) and the parallel election of a Constituent Assembly. In February 1919 the Social Democrat Friedrich Ebert became President of the Republic, a position in which he would remain until 1925, while another SPD member, Philipp Scheidemann, secured the role of Chancellor. The army's rapid elimination of the Spartakists at the beginning of 1919 – supported by the SPD – was a decisive stage in the fragmentation of the German workers' movement into a variety of currents. The SPD's role over the course of these events has been the object of numerous studies: as a whole, 'far from associating itself with the revolutionary movement, social democracy did everything it could to channel and restrain it'.[1]

Losing half of its votes at the 1920 elections, the Social-Democratic Party supported each of the governments that followed, before finding itself in opposition from 1923 onward, returning to power in 1928, and again being pushed out as a presidential régime took hold in 1930. Between 1923 and 1928 it also took part in the Prussian state government. Under the Weimar Republic the SPD was a party with a mass of elected representatives at the local and regional levels. At its 1921 Görlitz Congress it distanced itself from the orthodoxy of the Erfurt Programme, asserting its identity as a 'Party of the entire people' (*Volkspartei*) and situating itself beyond Marxism, even if this latter did remain a major source of inspiration.[2] Despite these profound changes the party continued to be a genu-

---

1   Droz (ed.) 1977, Vol. IV, p. 200. On the German Revolution, see the introductory bibliography in Broué 2005, a recent English translation. For its context in the history of the Weimar Republic, see Winkler 1984. On the relations between the workers' councils and the central authorities see Dobson 2001.
2   Winkler 1982.

ine 'state within a state', with its one million members,[3] 203 dailies and web of associations like no other party in Germany had.[4] It would remain the strongest party until the 1932 Reichstag elections. However, given the extreme parcellisation of the country's political forces its electoral scores were relatively low after 1920: it reached a height of 26 percent in 1924, and hit a low of 20 percent at the end of 1932.[5]

The revolutionary wave also reached Austria. January 1918 was marked by numerous strikes as well as the election of workers' councils.[6] The Austro-Hungarian Empire fell apart in the wake of the 3 November 1918 armistice, and the proclamation of the Republic of Austria followed on 12 November. From February 1919 to autumn 1920 a coalition including the Social Democrats took over the government, with the party's Karl Renner as chancellor, while the Social Democrat Karl Seitz was also temporary head of state up till 1920. In parallel to this, there also persisted a workers' council movement in which the social-democratic Left around Friedrich Adler was an influential force. Foreign Minister Otto Bauer resigned when Austria's re-attachment to Germany became an impossibility. Indeed, one of the great problems posed was the question of the new state's national identity. Otto Bauer was one of the firmest partisans of *Anschluss* after 1918,[7] and not until 1933 would the Social-Democratic Party strike the demand for Austria's right to re-attach itself to Germany out of its statutes.[8] Felix Kreissler notes that 'from 1918 to 1938 this country's history ... was dominated by this important question: are Austrians Germans or Austrians?'[9] As in Germany, up till 1934 the party remained a front-rank political force, as its governance of 'Red Vienna' strongly symbolised. In 1926 it adopted a new programme, the so-called Linz Programme, which maintained a reference to orthodoxy and 'the dictatorship of the proletariat'.[10] Although kept out of government it topped the poll in the 1930 elections: it was banned by Chancellor Dollfuss in February 1934.

---

3   It had 1,180,208 members in 1920, and in 1925 still had some 806,269.

4   Droz (ed.) 1977, p. 215.

5   Möller 2005, p. 119.

6   Hautmann 1987.

7   On 7 June 1919 he said 'Unviable and able to count only on ourselves, our possibility of little-by-little picking ourselves up again relies on being part of a larger structure: that is why we seek unity with the great German motherland, which we were separated from by force just a half-century ago because of Prussia's aspirations to hegemony': cited in Kreissler 1971, pp. 101–2.

8   Kreissler 1971, p. 14.

9   Kreissler 1971, p. 17.

10   Pasteur 2003, pp. 74–86.

We should understand the radicalism of the German and Austrian 'revolu-tions' in relative terms; these were above all political revolutions and did not deeply challenge the existing power relations in society. The pre-1914 German élites largely remained in place, and in Austria – as Felix Kreissler notes – 'whereas there were numerous uprisings in Germany calling for the Republic, even at its most advanced moments the Austrian revolution remained cross-bred with dynastic loyalty'.[11]

In Germany in 1917, even before the split between the Communists and the Social-Democrats, an Independent Social-Democratic Party (USPD)[12] formed bringing together the opponents of the war. The SPD suffered major losses from this split, which was also of considerable consequence for its relations with intellectuals: Karl Kautsky was deposed from his *Die Neue Zeit* editorial role because of his USPD membership, and replaced by Heinrich Cunow. Thus the man whom the 'Pope of Marxism' had named the greatest specialist of the 'Great Revolution' came to substitute for his teacher at the head of European socialism's most prestigious review.

The German Left underwent profound recomposition processes during the upheavals that marked the early days of the Weimar Republic between 1919 and 1923. The independents (USPD), the SPD and the communists of the KPD[13] – and from 1922 just the last two, after what remained of the USPD rejoined the SPD – fought for hegemony over a workers' movement that would remain largely under Social-Democratic influence up till the end of the 1920s. Despite the German Social Democracy's role in putting an end to the Revolution of 1918–19 it had no intention of renouncing its Marxist reference points and it claimed to be the natural representative of the world of labour. Georges Haupt emphasises how the SPD sought to defend its political tradition from Com-munist competition at the end of the 1920s, 'since the historical legitimacy provided by tradition was indispensable to the two rival Internationals, as they each sought to make themselves recognised as the only organised expression of the international workers' movement'.[14] In this context, historiography was an essential component of the ideological conflict between the different currents. If the history of the workers' movement was the primary object of polemic, the

---

11   Kreissler 1994, p. 113.
12   *Unabhängige Sozialdemokratische Partei Deutschlands.*
13   *Kommunistische Partei Deutschlands.*
14   We should also note the Austrians' attempt to create a 'Two-and-a-Half International' after the Revolution, as they sought a third way between Soviet communism and the Germano-phone Social-Democracy integrated into the state. See the introduction and the selection of texts (in French) appearing in Bourdet 1968.

revolutionary traditions dating from 1789 to 1918 also marked dividing lines. Violently hostile to the Social Democrats, the German Communists – many of whom had been members of the SPD until 1917 – sought to appropriate the history of August Bebel's party, and particularly that of its pre-1914 left wing.

The configuration of Austria's left-wing forces differed from the German case: the Communist Party (KPÖ)[15] remained very weak throughout this period, and never bore such influence as might have challenged the Social-Democratic Party. This latter party 'rallied almost the entire working class in its ranks' in June 1919,[16] and it was not identified with 'counter-revolution' as much as the SPD was for its role in 1918, even though it, too, had very much wished to restore order. Nor did it repudiate the Russian Revolution – a factor in the disaggregation of Austro-Hungary[17] – and the USSR in the manner of its German counterpart.

One of the breaks that had now been consummated with the pre-war scenario was the fact that republics had now come into existence in both Germany and Austria. This effectively wiped out a whole series of pre-1914 political demands, while for example in 1919 women obtained the right to vote. Similarly, the Social Democrats' perception was influenced by their integration into the state after 1918 and the difficult conditions that the Treaty of Versailles imposed on Germany. The war had profoundly challenged the idea of internationalism that had been imaginable up until 1914, and in the thirtieth year of the Second International's foundation it was shattered by the Russian Revolution. All these changes also altered the way in which these parties made reference to the French Revolution, whose exemplary role necessarily had to be critically examined in light of the Soviet model. Indeed, the influence of the Soviet example and of the KPD in Germany constituted a competitor model that went beyond the simple critique of the parliamentary republic. Moreover, the years up to the mid-1920s saw the emergence of strong tendencies against adhering to the rules of mere 'bourgeois democracy', as we can see in both the Communists' activities and in those of more leftist splits such as the KAPD.[18] In a more general sense, the revolutionary upheavals and then the state of economic chaos had major repercussions on social democrats' thinking. In many situations we can see the presence of analogies with the French Revolution. One particularly-

---

15   *Kommunistische Parti Österreichs.*

16   Kreissler 1971, p. 93.

17   Kreissler 1971, p. 32.

18   *Kommunistische Arbeiterpartei Deutschlands.* Founded in 1920, it rejected all participation in elections.

discussed historical episode was the Terror of 1793–4, responding to an analogy that the Bolsheviks had themselves already made.

At all events, the historiography of the French Revolution now underwent significant changes.[19] Indeed, Social Democracy now disposed of links with academic institutions, although they were still limited. One history professor, Hedwig Hintze, published reviews and articles on the history and historiography of the French Revolution in the Social-Democratic journal *Die Gesellschaft* ('Society', which followed on from *Die Neue Zeit*). Contacts were also established with the bigger papers: the Social-Democrat Hermann Wendel was by now a journalist for the *Frankfurter Zeitung*, in parallel to his pursuit of his work as a historian of the French Revolution. Taken together, this all implied a major redefinition of how history was written, with new elaborations now standing at some remove from the pre-war Social Democrats' historical materialism. As such, this historiography had little to do with the 1889 volumes that had served as a reference point up until 1914; yet it also combined with interpretations that did build on pre-war SPD works, whose importance should not be minimised.

---

19   Sproll 1992; Friedemann 1989.

The Power of Analogies, in the Face of New Revolutions: 1917–23

The Russian Revolution, and Reinterpreting 1789

Tamara Kondratieva has shown the great influence of analogies between the two great French and Russian Revolutions in the Soviet historiographical and political debates of 1917–18. In the course of the historian's study, she further-more brilliantly brings into relief how these same analogies recurred also in the German-speaking world.[1] Here our intention is to present some such examples. Some of the notes that Kurt Eisner – president of the ephemeral Bavarian Republic of 1919 – wrote on the articles of French historian Albert Mathiez demonstrate the growing interest in the question of the Terror in the wake of the Russian Revolution.[2] But it was through the controversy between Karl Kaut-sky and the Bolshevik leaders that the analogies between 1793 and 1917 began to proliferate. This first of all owed to the Soviet leaders, who took the French Revolution – omnipresent in their references – as a primary example from his-tory.[3] For Lenin and the Bolsheviks, the Russian Revolution had brought the rule of a new social class, doing for the proletariat what the French Revolution had done for the bourgeoisie. Indeed, the proletariat's 'Great October Revolu-tion' was officially designated as such in the USSR by way of analogy with the 'Great French Revolution'.[4]

Certainly, Karl Kautsky's writings no longer had the standing and influence that they had enjoyed before 1914. Kautsky had been at the heart of a Second International whose unity was now shattered by the emergence of Soviet com-munism, and for the social democrats of 1919 he had in a certain sense become too orthodox (and at this point he was still in the USPD) even as the Com-munists saw him as symbolising the abhorred figure of the 'renegade'. After a

---

1   Kondratieva 1989, p. 304.
2   Archives Kurt Eisner NY 4060 (Bundesarchiv, Berlin). A few notes on Albert Mathiez's art-icles from 1917–18 and on his *Études Robespierristes*, whose two volumes were published by Armand Colin in Paris in these same two years.
3   As well as Kondratieva's work, see Narotchnitski (ed.) 1989.
4   On Lenin and the French Revolution, see the summary and the references in Mazauric 2009, pp. 28–30.

brief spell in the under-secretariat of Foreign Affairs, during which he wrote a book on the causes of World War I,[5] he would not again play a political role of any decisive importance. That is not to say that his influence was negligible: indeed, we can see as much from his numerous contributions published in SPD organs up till the 1930s, principally concerning the elaboration of its programme. It was thus that he took part in the preparation of the 1925 Heidelberg Programme, which restored Marxist references to a prominent position. His work as an analyst of Soviet realities was widely recognised. Moreover – signalling the interest for his *oeuvre* during the early days of the Weimar Republic – many of his writings were now re-published, including his 'classic' work on the French Revolution, *Die Klassengegensätze im Zeitalter der Französische Revolution*.[6] This book reappeared at least three times, as did Wilhelm Blos's book on this same subject.[7] Their high print-runs – running into the tens of thousands of copies – demonstrated the continuity in the party publisher Dietz's output.[8] Indeed, we could interpret these re-editions as a mark of the renewed interest in the history of revolutions in the wake of 1918–19; Eduard Bernstein's history of the English Revolution was also republished in 1919 and 1922.[9]

There are countless references to the French Revolution in Karl Kautsky's books and articles on Soviet Russia. Just as he had done in 1905 Kautsky immediately wrote a history of the 1917 Revolution, looking back to the revolutionary processes of the past in order to understand the present period. He elaborated these analogies in three works: namely (in chronological order) *The Dictatorship of the Proletariat*; *Terrorism and Communism*; and, two years later, *From Democracy to State-Slavery*. The first of these books was published in Austria, and the two subsequent ones in Germany. Kautsky himself remained in this latter country up till 1924, when he moved to Vienna, before emigrating to Amsterdam after the 1938 *Anschluss*. It was there that he died a few months later.

---

5   Kautsky 1919.
6   Kautsky 1919b (republished in 1920 and 1923).
7   Blos 1920 (republished in 1921, 1922, and 1923).
8   Information is available on the print-runs of some of the books Dietz published in the Weimar period. Blos's book was printed three times (more than 40,000 copies), while there were some 30,000 copies of Kautsky's volume. See Schwarz 1973, pp. 43, 83.
9   Bernstein 1922.

Karl Kautsky's Books

The first of Kautsky's books, published in 1918,[10] is best-known for being cited in a work contradicting it, with his unwavering condemnation of Bolshevism earning a famous riposte in Lenin's *The Proletarian Revolution and the Renegade Kautsky*.[11] Accusing Kautsky of defending the parliamentary system and 'bourgeois democracy' against the *soviets*, this work argued that he had passed to the ranks of the counter-revolution. His *Dictatorship of the Proletariat* had defined two possible paths to socialism, 'the two methods of democracy and dictatorship'.[12] Kautsky explained that 'Socialism is for us inseparably connected with democracy':[13] it was necessary to defend parliamentary democracy and the rights and freedoms it guaranteed the workers' movement, as against any single-partyist conception. The Bolsheviks maintaining their position by force had thereby identified themselves with the idea of a revolution led by minorities. But without a majority party leading the masses there was the risk of a repeat of the tragic experiences of June 1848 and March 1871, here taken as counter-examples. Moreover, 'Socialism postulates special historical conditions'[14] whereas soviet power was being exercised in a backward country where the social and economic conditions for socialism had not been met. This reasoning was already common knowledge, having been formulated long before the Russian Revolution and adopted by most European social-democrats – indeed, including in Russia itself, principally by the Mensheviks. However, *The Dictatorship of the Proletariat* was one of the first books systematically to expound this point of view after 7 November 1917.

The 1789 Revolution repeatedly served as a basis for understanding the contemporary Russian situation. Kautsky noted that extreme centralisation risked leading to a Bonapartist regime like the one that came about after 18 Brumaire of Year VIII, although he did not specify this point any further.[15] Given Russia's situation, as compared to that of Western countries, he concluded:

> In no case need we anticipate that in Western Europe the course of the
> great French Revolution will be repeated. If present-day Russia exhibits

---

10   Kautsky 1918. English text from the *Marxists Internet Archive*.
11   A book produced and distributed in hundreds of thousands of copies by the world Communist movement.
12   Kautsky 1918.
13   Ibid.
14   Ibid.
15   Ibid.

so much likeness to the France of 1793, that only shows how near it stands to the stage of bourgeois revolution.[16]

The Russian Revolution could not go any further than a revolution like 1789: and the measures that the Bolsheviks had themselves taken proved it. The decree on land, which handed over ownership to the peasants, established private property in the countryside, a measure characteristic of a bourgeois revolution;[17] for this reason 'The Revolution has only achieved in Russia what it effected in France in 1789 and what its aftermath achieved in Germany'.[18] The coming social revolution led by the proletariat and the party representing it would have to differentiate itself from the terroristic methods used in 1793. Kautsky adopted arguments that had already been elaborated before 1914 by Social Democrats hostile to all revolutionary violence – a question now being tested in practice.

Nonetheless, this work's few references to the French Revolution were only limited compared to those appearing in Kautsky's subsequent book. Indeed, while *Terrorism and Communism*[19] was written in the 'heat of the moment' in 1919 and presented as a mainly political text, it nonetheless mobilised a longer-term historical knowledge and set out to analyse the first measures the Bolsheviks had taken in light of past revolutions. Published in Germany, this text had a very major echo at the time: it in turn provoked a response by one of Soviet Russia's leaders, Leon Trotsky, who wrote a book of the same name subtitled 'A Reply to Karl Kautsky', in which he defended the necessity of the terroristic measures that the Soviet government had taken.[20]

In the preface, Kautsky emphasised that his goal was 'to draw a parallel between the Commune and the Soviet Republic', with the Bolsheviks inscribing their efforts in the wake of the revolutions from 1789 to 1871.[21] He thus undertook to turn back to the first Paris Commune of 1792–4 and analyse the French revolutionary Terror. The first chapters offered a classic interpretation of the French Revolution, for example by adopting formulas similar to those of his 1889 book regarding the role the 'proletarians' played in 1792–4.[22] As Kautsky

---

16   Ibid.
17   One of the Soviet government's first acts was the promulgation of two decrees, one on peace and one on land. This latter gave the land to the peasants. Ferro 1977, p. 101.
18   Kautsky 1918.
19   Kautsky 1919c. English text from the *Marxists Internet Archive*.
20   Trotsky 2017. It was published in German in 1920 by Hoym in Hamburg.
21   Kautsky 1919c.
22   'Thus it was the proletariat, the great mass of the population of Paris, which formed

made clear in his preface, he feared he might give rise to misunderstandings if the reader did not know the broad terms of the revolutionary process of 1789–94.

His study of the relations between town and country mobilised a series of analogies between the French and Russian Revolutions, as he built on his previous remarks. But most importantly, in a chapter devoted to 'The Tradition of the Terror' he insisted on the sterility of the Russian revolutionaries' imitation of the past. He deployed numerous citations from Marx and Engels: in 1848 Marx had been critical of imitating 1793, and according to Kautsky in 1871 he had expressed 'a definite repudiation of terrorism ... regarded as a feature of the revolution of the "higher classes", as compared with the proletarian revolution'.[23]

Kautsky's reasoning could be summarised as follows: the nineteenth century had seen a progressive 'softening of mores'; violence in politics was characteristic of bourgeois repression and historically outmoded; and the proletariat did not itself have to adopt this type of method. He explained that the Terror of 1793 was a consequence of the 'bloody legislation' that monarchy had imposed on the people:[24] now, in 1919, this could be nothing other than an unjustifiable archaism. Kautsky nonetheless took care to distinguish the 'excesses, to which a brutalised people ... allowed itself to give way' – which the social-democrat condemned – to 'those excesses, which are the result of a pre-considered system of training, and which are introduced into the State system, in the form of carefully-planned legislation, by those in power, in order to grind down elements, which seemed to those rulers to be dangerous'.[25] Kautsky employed a highly pejorative vocabulary in his characterisation of popular violence, for example describing the September 1792 massacres in terms of 'thirst for blood and cruelty', 'horrors', and 'a very intoxication for blood': 'they literally bathed with delirious delight in blood'.[26] He thus particularly stigmatised movements that were not controlled by political organs. His condemnation did not extend to the Montagnards, the 'conscious leaders'[27] who tried to canalise these movements. The distinction that he made here sometimes also echoed the practice of the Social-Democratic Party, which had opposed the workers' council move-

---

the great driving power in the Revolution. Their desperate inconsiderateness made them masters of Paris, made Paris the ruler of France, and let France triumph over Europe': ibid.

23   Ibid.
24   Ibid.
25   Ibid.
26   Ibid.
27   Ibid.

ment in 1918–19 and the excesses outside of its control.[28] Kautsky reproached the Bolsheviks for lacking this capacity to channel popular violence and for reproducing the excesses of the French Revolution.[29]

For him, the revolutionary tribunals set up in Soviet Russia symbolised the Bolsheviks' caricature of the French counter-example; indeed, this was a worthless resurgence of 1793 in a time when such means were no longer necessary. The political organisation of the proletariat in social democracy had marked a historic advance; it was superior to revolutionary *coups de force*, and made it possible to make violent excesses a matter of the past. Thus organisation and progressive education (the term *Bildung* occurs repeatedly, here)[30] took the upper hand over spontaneous popular violence. Referring to how the SPD had given structure to the German proletariat since the 1890s, Kautsky argued

> Socialism for the proletariat schooled in Marxist thought thus ceased to be something that could at once be introduced and realised everywhere – and under any conditions ... [a]ccording to this conception, Socialism could not be introduced by means of a coup d'état. It was to be the result of a long historical process.

For certain, World War I had rolled back this process, bringing about a resurgence in 'the proletariat in its most primitive form' and its 'blind passion'.[31] Kautsky moreover indicated that the 1914 war was part of a process dating back to the French Revolution: weren't the general arming of the population and the *levée en masse* products of the end of the eighteenth century?[32]

In his denunciation of the Bolsheviks' adventurism, Kautsky's critique converged with all those in Russia who did not want to 'jump' stages on the path to socialism. His originality, here, stemmed from the way in which he articulated this condemnation with a systematic delegitimation of the methods of the French Revolution, which the actors in the Russian Revolution had instead exalted. Nonetheless, Kautsky did not cast opprobrium on the 'Great Revolution' of 1789–94 as such; what he criticised was the mechanical application of methods from another era to a historically novel situation.

---

28   Moreover, Bernstein explicitly made the analogy between the popular violence in the French Revolution and the workers' councils. See above, p. [insert page number].

29   Kautsky 1919c.

30   Ibid. Kautsky also speaks of the 'educated proletariat' in Germany (Kautsky 1919c, German edition, p. 99).

31   Ibid.

32   Ibid.

Already in 1919 Kautsky had posed the question of the Soviet Thermidor and the end of the revolutionary process – a question which would go on to animate historians' and politicians' debates in the USSR, with all the risks that invoking this kind of analogy entailed.[33] For Kautsky, 'Lenin's government is threatened by another 9th Thermidor, but it may come about in some other way', and he went on to argue that 'The final result is quite predictable. It need not be a 9th Thermidor, but I fear it will not be far removed from that'.[34] But only once the regime was stabilised in the late 1920s did Kautsky really return to this subject.[35]

1789–1917

It is difficult to evaluate how exactly these two books were received at a time when the Social-Democratic Party was in the middle of its reorganisation process, Germany was in the grip of great economic and social difficulties, and Kautsky had not yet returned to SPD membership. These books' content should be compared to other pieces in the social-democratic press devoted to the Russian Revolution. This analogy appeared regularly in a great number of articles critical of Bolshevism; Kautsky himself employed it in different contexts, for example in his review of a book by Otto Bauer appearing in *Der Kampf*.[36] Kautsky differed from Otto Bauer's view that while the Bolsheviks' form of organisation should not be applied to the Germanic countries it did correspond to a country like Russia. For Kautsky, 'like the Paris Commune, the Soviet Republic seems to me a phenomenon that will not be historically reproduced'.[37] Beside these analogies there remained the classic characterisation of the French Revolution as a bourgeois revolution. Contrary to later historiographical projections, here there were no Marxist communists and 'anti-Marxist' social democrats. For Bauer and Kautsky's generation – whatever their political trajectories – the corpus of reference was still one largely based on the writings of the pre-1914 Social-Democratic tradition. For instance, this enduring influence was very clear in their characterisation of the bourgeois revolution and the social alliances that it supposed.[38] Even when we look at the heirs

---

33   Kondratieva 1989, pp. 145–71.
34   Kautsky 1919c.
35   See Chapter Twelve, p. [insert page number].
36   'Ein Schrift über den Bolchevismus', *Der Kampf*, 1920, pp. 260–5. A review of Bauer's *Bolschewismus oder Sozialdemokratie?*, published by the Wiener Volksbuchhandlung in Vienna in 1920.
37   'Ein Schrift über den Bolchevismus', *Der Kampf*, 1920, p. 262.
38   For example in Bauer 1976, p. 144.

to the party's revisionist wing, it was the comparison with 1789 that came to Ludwig Quessel's mind at the end of 1917.[39] Moreover, if the 1793–4 period was discredited by way of analogy with the Bolsheviks, the 1789 Revolution was not criticised as such. One example of this effort to separate the two can be found in this same publication. *Sozialistische Monatshefte* did not hesitate in evaluating the inheritance of 1789 positively:

> There was a 4 August in history that demonstrated the will to brother-hood, a date on which the privileged abandoned their privileges in order to live and work with others like Equals. This was the night of 4 August 1789. Alongside many other absurd professorial theories during this world war, we have had the spirit of 1914 presented to us as if it had conquered the spirit of 1789. Five years later, this *conqueror* now lies on the ground. Gaining new forces, what had seemed *conquered* now stands up again after a hundred and thirty years. These ideas have still not been realised; and they can only be realised by socialism, to which the future belongs.[40]

1789 was sharply distinguished from 1793. In the Austrian paper appearing on 1 May 1918 (*Maifestschrift*), Karl Leuthner put his name to a short (and part-censored) contribution with the evocative title '1789–1917'.[41] He was a member of the right wing of the party, and one of the most fervent partisans of Austria's re-attachment to Germany.[42] A member of the *Arbeiter-Zeitung* editorial staff since 1895, responsible for foreign affairs, he had a good knowledge of Europe and thus also of Russia – indeed, *Arbeiter-Zeitung* had devoted major coverage to the 1905 Revolution. In this article Leuthner set out a few basic points of comparison: in both cases a 'tyranny' had been overturned by popular action, and the Russian people crying out for bread in March 1917 resembled the Parisian people of 1789. More telling was the comparison he established between the Bolsheviks and Robespierre – between 1793 and 1918:

> The Terror triumphed, the dictatorship of the St. Petersburg proletariat triumphed ... but domination by Robespierre and his Committee of Pub-lic Safety and domination by Lenin and his Commissars of the People make for domination by a minority, which is incapable of recognising the

---

39   'Realitäten der kontinentaleuropäischen Politik', *Sozialistische Monatshefte*, 1918, p. 12.
40   H. Peus, 'Der 4. August', *Sozialistische Monatshefte*, 1919, pp. 690–1.
41   '1789–1917', *Maifestschrift*, 1918, pp. 8–15.
42   Haupt and Maitron 1971, p. 190.

democratic principle. Just as Robespierre held the Convention under Terror – threatening it with his popular insurrections – Lenin's Red Guards
broke up the Constituent Assembly.[43]

This article, appearing in a very widely distributed periodical, thus condemned
Lenin's use of Terror by analogy with Robespierre. Contrary to Kautsky's reasoning, which dissociated the proceedings of the Committee of Public Safety
from the excesses that took place, Leuthner's condemnation extended also to
the revolutionary government of 1793. In more general terms, he was certain
that the 'terrorist' episode of the 'Great Revolution' was discredited by analogy
with the contemporary events in Russia.

Germany and Austria in Light of 1789 ... and 1793

The German Revolution of 1918 also encouraged a look back to other revolutionary processes. If we are to understand the context in which the reference to
the French Revolution was mobilised, we ought to note the publication of a very
large number of pamphlets hostile to the communist and social-democratic
Left. Negative analogies with the French Revolution were very widespread in
these texts, and that earlier Revolution's inheritance held responsible for the
anarchy to which Germany had now fallen victim. One of the most renowned
such texts – a book by German general Julius Hoppenstedt – assimilated the
Spartakist terror to the *sans-culottes* of 1793.[44] For his part, the [medical] doctor Hans von Hentig published two biographies on Fouché and Robespierre. If
he considered the former a still-acceptable figure, his portrait of the latter was
very hostile, and indeed inscribed in the German historiographical tradition.[45]

'Against the Terror!'

Throughout late 1918, the Social-Democratic *Vorwärts* incessantly attacked 'the
Terror', 'putschism' and 'dictatorship', using these terms to refer to the SPD's
Spartakist adversaries. Between November 1918 and February 1919 the paper
published ever more articles hostile to Bolshevism, the Russian Revolution and

---

43   '1789–1917', *Maifestschrift*, 1918, p. 13.
44   Hoppenstedt 1919.
45   Von Hentig 1919, 1924. Another conservative text is analysed in Voss 1991.

THE POWER OF ANALOGIES, IN THE FACE OF NEW REVOLUTIONS: 1917-23   239

the communists, held responsible for the disorder in Germany. On 27 December 1918 *Vorwärts* bore the headline 'Against the Terror'. This denunciation of terror was consistently accompanied by analogies with the French Revolution. On 19 January 1919 an article by Alfred Nossig, 'Collectivism or Communism', written shortly after the crushing of the Spartakists, reviewed these latters' modes of political action and criticised their imitation of the methods of the 'Great Revolution':

> You have heard that the Great French Revolution confiscated émigrés' assets and worked with the guillotine: at that time, they could not imagine a true revolution any differently. You forget that the men in power during the Great Revolution lived a century ago, in another stage of human development.[46]

As for the Austrian case, we also find such analogies in the *Arbeiter-Zeitung*. For example, the 10 December 1918 article on 'The Class War' compared the present situation to the various revolutions from 1793 to 1871.[47] On 30 November 1918 the main article on its front page was a piece by Karl Kautsky regarding the Constituent Assembly. He called for the alliance and unity of the different factions of the workers' movement. Here, the French Revolution symbolised division – a vestige of the past – as opposed to the need for a great unified party:

> The collaboration of the two factions is certainly not ideal, but it is the only thing that can permit the existence of a social government in the given conditions. Any attempt to overthrow the government born of this compromise would mean opposing one part of the proletariat to the other, rendering it incapable of fighting, and ensuring the victory of the counter-revolution, just as the fights among Hébert, Danton and Robespierre in 1794 sealed the Montagnards' defeat and brought bourgeois domination.[48]

We should read this social-democratic hostility to the Terror not only as part of an old tradition of opposition to revolutionary violence, but also as a response to the arguments of the left wing of the USPD, and the Spartakists after them. Indeed, during the revolutionary processes of 1918–19 references to the French

---

46   'Kollektivismus oder Kommunismus?', *Vorwärts*, 19 January 1919, p. 2.
47   'Der Klassenkrieg', *Arbeiter-Zeitung*, 10 December 1918.
48   'Die Konstituierende Nationversammlung', *Arbeiter-Zeitung*, 30 November 1918.

Revolution – even if not decisively important ones – also appeared in the writings of Karl Liebknecht and Rosa Luxemburg.[49] Each of these figures from pre-1914 Social Democracy were members of the USPD from its creation and then founders of the KPD at the end of December 1918, before their assassination a few days later. In numerous articles, Luxemburg defended the historic role of the Terror and praised the Jacobins' deeds[50] – and this despite her critique of the Russian Revolution (which, we should remember, was not published during her lifetime but only a few years after her death).[51] Upon the Bolsheviks' seizure of power on 7 November 1917 Karl Liebknecht wrote to his wife that the revolutionary process underway in Russia presented 'unlimited possibilities – much greater than the Great French Revolution'.[52] Luxemburg also mobilised an analogy with this same period: 'after four years of struggle, the seizure of power by the Jacobins proved to be the only means of saving the conquests of the revolution, of achieving a republic, of smashing feudalism, of organizing a revolutionary defense against inner as well as outer foes, of suppressing the conspiracies of counter-revolution and spreading the revolutionary wave from France to all Europe'.[53] The Bolsheviks were 'the historic heirs of the English Levellers and the French Jacobins'.[54] Conversely, in October 1918 she saw the governing Social Democrats as the imitators of Lafayette, ready to open fire against the people.[55] And in the Spartakist paper *Die Rote Fahne* Luxemburg defended the value of the Jacobins' deeds, in their own time.[56] On this point, she may seem not to stand very far from Kautsky, for whom the Terror had played a historically important role. But her analogy had the inverse objective: namely, to argue that whatever the criticisms that could be levelled against the Bolsheviks, they were just as elevated figures as the Jacobins of 1793:

> Kautsky and his Russian co-religionists who wanted to see the Russian Revolution keep the 'bourgeois character' of its first phase, are an exact counterpart of those German and English liberals of the preceding century who distinguished between the two well-known periods of the Great

49   Laschitza 1989.
50   Laschitza 1989, p. 223.
51   Written in prison, the text was not published until 1922.
52   Liebknecht 1974, Vol. IX, p. 371.
53   Luxemburg 1918.
54   Ibid.
55   'Die kleinen Lafayette', *Spartakus*, October 1918.
56   Luxemburg 1974, p. 411.

French Revolution: the 'good' revolution of the first Girondin phase and the 'bad' one after the Jacobin uprising. The Liberal shallowness of this conception of history, to be sure, doesn't care to understand that, without the uprising of the 'immoderate' Jacobins, even the first, timid and half-hearted achievements of the Girondin phase would soon have been buried under the ruins of the revolution, and that the real alternative to Jacobin dictatorship – as the iron course of historical development posed the question in 1793 – was not 'moderate' democracy, but ... restoration of the Bourbons! The 'golden mean' cannot be maintained in any revolution. The law of its nature demands a quick decision.

The Analogies Flourish

The Terror was not the only example driving analogies: from the economic situation to political reforms, the prompts to re-explore the history of the French Revolution only multiplied.

At the beginning of 1919 a *Deutscher Revolutions-Almanach für das Jahr 1919* was published,[57] seeking to relate the events of November 1918. Like the May Day newspapers, this was an almanac intended to be published each year in homage to the German Revolution.[58] The first issue began with a series of portraits of the 'fathers of the German Revolution' (Engels, Marx, Lassalle, Wilhelm Liebknecht, Bebel). After this there followed an emphatic homage to Friedrich Ebert, 'founder and leader of the German free state'.[59] If it is difficult to date the texts appearing in this almanac with any precision, Bernstein's piece was signed February 1919 – that is, after the crushing of the Spartakist revolt. The almanac features a range of views: after the homage to Ebert, who had been a decisive actor in the elimination of the Spartakists, a text by Emil Barth called for the union of the three parties – the independent and majority Social Democrats and the Communists.[60] The publication of a short presentation of Marx and the Commune by Franz Mehring – who died in January 1919, after becoming a Spartakist – further demonstrated the plurality of viewpoints. Moreover, this collection was published by a large – and not social-democratic – publisher, Hoffman und Campe.

---

57   Deutscher Revolutions-Almanach 1919.
58   As far as we know, only two issues were published.
59   Deutscher Revolutions-Almanach 1919, pp. 53, 67.
60   Deutscher Revolutions-Almanach 1919, p. 20.

Most of the articles compared the contemporary revolutionary process with earlier ones. Karl Kautsky reiterated his stand against violence ('The worst inheritance [of the bourgeois revolutions] is this cult of violence')[61] and drew an equivalence between Noske and the Spartakists. Bernstein's article was entitled '1789/94–1848–1918/19' and adopted the same reasoning.[62] Some of his comparisons with 1789 recalled those he had established in 1905, emphasising the similarity between Russia's agrarian structures and those of *ancien régime* France.[63] But the originality of this piece owed to the fact that he inscribed his argument in a historical account of his own earlier positions. Indeed, Bernstein established a lineage between his late-nineteenth-century analyses and contemporary events, noting that his historical remarks published in his 1899 book – notably those concerning Blanquism and the traditions of 1793 – had been proven correct by the Bolsheviks' and the Spartakists' toxic methods.

As well as these articles the almanac contained numerous illustrations, including Social-Democratic propaganda posters. The French Revolution was repeatedly mentioned. An analogy already encountered in 1905 – the reproduction of a Russian cartoon representing Nicholas II finding Louis XVI and Marie Antoinette guillotined[64] – was followed by other negative representations consistent with the articles cited above. A counter-revolutionary almanac of 1794 displayed 'French corpulence'[65] and another illustration from 1799 was emblazoned with the heads of the executed members of the National Assembly ... Nonetheless, other images set the inheritance of 1789 in a positive light, tellingly even invoking a German national history: it reproduced several pages from a 1793 almanac published in Göttingen, and later on a Mainz liberty tree from the 1794 edition of this same Göttingen almanac.[66] To this we could also compare the satirical paper *Der Wahre Jacob*: if this latter made few references to the French Revolution as such, it frequently featured Marianne and thus the watchwords of 1789 in association with the nascent Weimar Republic. In March 1919 a Marianne was accompanied by the following text:

> Have confidence in the word, which once taught you
> That the old party must still be honoured

---

61   Deutscher Revolutions-Almanach 1919. His article, 'Aussichten der Revolution', appears on pp. 26–31.
62   Deutscher Revolutions-Almanach 1919, pp. 34–8.
63   Deutscher Revolutions-Almanach 1919, p. 38.
64   Deutscher Revolutions-Almanach 1919, p. 47.
65   Deutscher Revolutions-Almanach 1919, p. 66.
66   Deutscher Revolutions-Almanach 1919, p. 150.

And that *Liberté, Égalité, Fraternité*
Is at each moment our banner[67]

At the beginning of the 1920s political instability reigned. In Germany, the March 1920 Kapp Putsch was foiled by a general strike;[68] the years 1920 to 1924 saw the succession of no fewer than seven governments.[69] In Austria, the coalition came to an end on 11 June 1920 and the Social Democrats were excluded from the affairs of state.[70] The economic and social situation in which Germany and Austria found themselves revealed the difficult conditions in which they came out of the war. At the end of 1919 Austria was ravaged by inflation, and there was a threat of famine.[71] A powerful inflationary process was also developing in Germany, prolonging the wartime inflation and culminating in the events of 1922–3.[72] The difficulties that the nascent republics had to deal with drove the publication of a number of economic-history pieces in *Die Neue Zeit* and *Der Kampf*. Several of these articles looked back to the history of the French Revolution.

Writing in *Die Neue Zeit* Hans Brikmann compared the situation of the German proletariat in the wake of World War I with that of the French people in 1789–94. Setting his analysis in a Marxist-inspired perspective, he argued that the upheavals involved in a revolutionary process brought poverty for the people.[73] This largely descriptive article reviewed the urban hunger riots of 1788–9 (taking the example of the workers of the Réveillon manufactory) as well as those in the countryside (the Great Fear) and other events like the women's march on Versailles in October 1789. Although the author had no original interpretation, he explained the political measures that had been put into effect, for example the Paris city government's actions in creating the *ateliers de charité*.[74] This was evidently an echo of the political solutions then being sought by a young German Republic similarly faced with a situation of poverty. In the same spirit, in a period of powerful inflation the fight for maximum price limits also attracted attention. If the article held back from providing any con-

---

67   *Der Wahre Jacob*, 15 March 1919, p. 3.
68   Könnemann 2002.
69   Möller 2005, p. 172.
70   Pasteur 2008a.
71   Kreissler 1971, p. 115.
72   Möller 2005, p. 162.
73   'Lebensmittelnöte und Hungerrevolution in der französischen Revolution', *Die Neue Zeit*, 1919, Vol. I, pp. 229–35, 257–61.
74   [Public workshops designed to provide employment to the poor].

crete solution to the problems that Germany now encountered, it nonetheless insisted that the new authorities had to take a lead from history in fulfilling the tasks now incumbent upon them:

> Even if the social situation has changed since then, the history of the French Revolution shows how important the problem of food supply is to revolutionary periods. Each revolutionary government must consider ensuring the supply of provisions to the popular masses the foremost and most important of its duties.[75]

At a historiographical level, the article marked a break with pre-war reference points: although it was based on Cunow and Kropotkin's judgments, the first book it cited was Jean Jaurès's history, 'sadly not yet translated into German'.[76] This was the first sign of a consideration of the French socialist's *oeuvre* – a subject to which we will have cause to return.[77]

Two articles by Karl Grünberg[78] in *Der Kampf* devoted to past financial crises adopted this same perspective, seeking to understand the slump that was now taking place and respond with political solutions:[79]

> Thus there is some use in recalling some examples of financial crisis in more distant times, as well as the manner in which they were resolved. I have chosen two that took place at almost the same time: the 1811 silver agio crisis in Austria and the *assignats* crisis in France. They each offer lessons for the present.[80]

What effective impact could political measures have in a situation of economic crisis? The main example to which Grünberg here drew focus was the sale of the clergy's assets and the issuing of *assignats* – the object of an article of Kautsky's

75   'Lebensmittelnöte und Hungerrevolution in der französischen Revolution', *Die Neue Zeit*, 1919, Vol. I, p. 261.
76   'Lebensmittelnöte und Hungerrevolution in der französischen Revolution', *Die Neue Zeit*, 1919, Vol. I, pp. 229–30.
77   See Chapter XII, p. 292.
78   A historian of socialism, Karl Grünberg (1861–1940) was an important figure at the University of Vienna. He moved to the University of Frankfurt in 1924, where he created an Institute of Social Research, at the origin of the famous Frankfurt School. See the biography in Haupt and Maitron 1971, pp. 116–18.
79   'Finanzkrisen in der Vergangenheit', *Der Kampf*, 1920, pp. 1–8 and 50–60.
80   'Finanzkrisen in der Vergangenheit', *Der Kampf*, 1920, p. 2.

appearing in a quite different context in 1883.[81] Showing that the solutions of the revolutionaries of 1789 were themselves linked to the experience and analysis of the past, Grünberg made a long detour through the history of the eighteenth century and the factors behind the financial crisis at the end of the *ancien régime*, turning back to the collapse of the Law system before ultimately arriving at the sale of national assets on 2 November 1789. Grünberg admired this measure, simultaneously both the solution to an economic problem and 'nonetheless a political act: breaking the former state's power of domination once and for all'.[82] Having referred to the resistance coming from the clergy and the political measures that were put into effect, Grünberg explained the problems posed by devaluing paper-money, up to and including the implementation of 'territorial mandates' in 1795. By way of analogy with his own present situation he explained the reasons why issuing paper money could bring major devaluation, and concluded with the lessons of that period:

> The Revolution had stabilised its power. Its essential content could not again be put in doubt. The historical role of the *assignats* was over. They disappeared. Metal reassumed its predominant role[83]

Other subjects also provided prompts to looking back to the French Revolution. In the run-up to the calling of the Constituent Assembly, votes for women were still under discussion. In late 1918 Adelheid Popp published an article calling for universal suffrage: indeed, 'the great era ha[d] begun where even women's voice must also be heard. The hour of liberty and equality must strike also for them'.[84] She turned back to history in order to support her argument, establishing a comparison with the French Revolution:

> the old Austria has ceased to be. Women, too, must draw the necessary conclusions from this ... It is a fact that over a hundred years ago not only did women demand equal rights, but men also supported this same demand. Already in the era of the French Revolution there was an association called the *Société fraternelle des patriotes des deux sexes pour la défense de la constitution.*[85]

---

81   See p. [insert page] of our preamble. *Assignats* were a theme widely addressed in the German historiography of the Weimar period, and particularly by left-liberals. See Sproll 1992, p. 234.
82   'Finanzkrisen in der Vergangenheit', *Der Kampf*, 1920, p. 54.
83   'Finanzkrisen in der Vergangenheit', *Der Kampf*, 1920, p. 60.
84   'Die Frau im neuen Staat', *Der Kampf*, 1918, p. 732.
85   'Die Frau im neuen Staat', *Der Kampf*, 1918, p. 729.

Other articles mobilised historical reference points in the context of the reforms proposed and debated in the Constituent Assembly of 1919. The fact that Heinrich Cunow was at the head of *Die Neue Zeit* certainly encouraged the multiple references to the French Revolution now appearing in a great number of articles: indeed, one of his own contributions dealt with the content of the first French constitution and its intellectual influences.[86] Above all, the question of school reforms regularly recurred in *Die Neue Zeit* in the early 1920s. Having taken part in the affairs of state, Social Democracy posed itself the problem of how to apply pedagogical conceptions that had previously remained limited to its own networks and sphere of influence. Heinrich Cunow wrote numerous articles, including on school reforms, echoing the problems posed during the early days of the Weimar Republic. Two of them looked back to the experience of the French Revolution:[87]

> The revolution in our political life also sets the school in front of new educational tasks ... In no sense is it only characteristic of today's revolution to place an emphasis on new ideals for education and training and the attempt to realise them by school reforms.[88]

Here, Heinrich Cunow built on the examples that had already been present in his book *Die revolutionäre Zeitungsliteratur*. Underlining the very small number of readers of papers like *le Père Duchesne* and *l'Ami du Peuple* during the French Revolution, he noted the role of 'intellectuals' who read the papers aloud to the people. His article then explained the different revolutionary measures of 1793–4 concerning schooling and the university, as well as the oppositions they aroused. For example, Cunow outlined the Condorcet project, building from the elementary school to the national academy via the *lycée*.[89] The article was intended as a historical review of the different measures taken, from the conflicts between Girondins and Montagnards – revealing the deep differences between them, also with regard to schooling – to the measures taken by the Thermidorian Convention, the Directory and then Napoleon. The piece was designed less to provide directly applicable solutions than to give a historical account offering additional considerations to the debate.

---

86   'Der Einfluss des Rousseauischen "Gesellschaftsvertrages" auf die französische National-versammlung 1789 bis 1791', *Die Neue Zeit*, 1919, Vol. 1, pp. 370–6, pp. 389–95.

87   'Schulreformen der Französischen Revolution', *Die Neue Zeit*, 1919–20, Vol. 1, pp. 341–7 and 358–64.

88   'Schulreformen der Französischen Revolution', *Die Neue Zeit*, 1919–20, Vol. 1, p. 342.

89   'Schulreformen der Französischen Revolution', *Die Neue Zeit*, 1919–20, Vol. 1, p. 345.

Two Books on the French Revolution

The end of 1919 and the early 1920s saw the appearance of numerous books favourable to the French Revolution. They do not seem to have had any great echo within Social-Democratic ranks themselves, and did not arouse much discussion in terms of reviews. However, while the information on the authors is very limited, these writings – largely inspired by social-democratic interpretations – nonetheless indicated the revival of interest in the French Revolution in the wake of the revolutions of 1918–19. The difficult general conditions – including the delay in the reorganisation of social democracy, which did not really take place until the economic recovery beginning in 1924 – probably contributed to making these books little-accessible and poorly distributed. Apart from the brief references to their existence by historians Walter Markov and Walter Grab, they seem to have made very little mark on posterity.[90]

Friedrich Muckle's book appeared in two volumes: the first was essentially devoted to the most radical ideas of the Age of Lights (the origins of communism, critiques of property, and so on) and the second to the unfolding of the French Revolution and its consequences.[91] The author, born in 1883, played a role in Kurt Eisner's Bavarian Council Republic,[92] serving as the Bavarians' representative to the central authorities (*Bevollmächtiger*); he has also been cited as a doctor and *Privat-Dozent* at the University of Heidelberg from 1910 onward.[93] He adopted Heinrich Cunow's criteria for explaining the characteristics of the different political groups, including for example his lengthy elaborations on Marat: the only footnote tells us that the documents he uses come from Cunow's *Die revolutionäre Zeitungsliteratur Frankreichs*. Walter Markov terms him a 'critical Robespierrian';[94] lacking any bibliography or references apart from Cunow, and written in a narrative style, his argument was loosely inspired by a materialist perspective. He repeatedly defined the French Revolution as a 'bourgeois revolution'.[95] The contradictions between the government and the popular movement in both towns and countryside – evoked without particular originality – brought into relief the role of the Parisian *petit peuple*, notably the *Enragés* group. ('Without the masses' contribution the French

---

90   Grab 1983, p. 310; Markov 1974, p. 63.
91   Muckle 1921.
92   Grau 2001, p. 389.
93   Sproll 1992, pp. 31, 100.
94   In fact, he saw Robespierre as a 'fanatic': Muckle 1921, p. 131.
95   Muckle 1921, p. 11.

Revolution would never have become this great fire'.)[96] His interest in the conflict between the government and the fringes of the popular movement perhaps had to do with the problems encountered by the Bavarian Republic, which the author had represented to the central authorities, and which had been rapidly isolated. The conclusion returned to the possible analogies with contemporary revolutions, indicating the author's sympathies for the process then underway in Russia.[97]

Sharing a political experience in common with Friedrich Muckle, Gustav Landauer is however much better-known. People's Commissar of Culture and Education in the ephemeral Bavarian Republic of April 1919, he was arrested after its collapse and then assassinated the following month. Anarchist in tendency, he had translated Kropotkin's *The Great French Revolution* before World War I. Soon before he was murdered he published *Letters from the French Revolution*[98] – a book outside the boundaries of social-democracy, but worth mentioning here given that it was reviewed in *Die Neue Zeit*.[99] As the title indicates, this was in no sense a new history of the French Revolution, but rather a selection of letters from the main actors in the Revolution, of whatever sensibility, from Louis XVI to Robespierre and from Camille Desmoulins to Charlotte Corday.[100] This work thus offered a translation of hundreds of pages of source materials, collected in three categories: letters from deputies involved in the Revolution, letters from various correspondents, and finally letters from soldiers. The book was centred on these actors' individual convictions and echoed Landauer's own political beliefs – which stood some distance from any orthodox reading. For example, he considered Mirabeau the most legitimate representative of the French Revolution. The final lines of Landauer's preface contextualised the discovery of these documents in the troubled period that Germany was itself now going through: 'May a precise knowledge of the spirit and the tragedy of the Revolution come to our aid in the grave period awaiting us'.[101]

---

96   Muckle 1921, pp. 46, 103.
97   Muckle 1921, pp. 184–5.
98   Landauer 1919.
99   Hahnewald, K. 'G. Landauer, Briefe aus der Französischen Revolution', *Die Neue Zeit*, 1919, vol. 2, pp. 169–70.
100   Landauer 1919, p. xi (in the preface).
101   Landauer 1919, p. xxxii.

Drawing the Balance-Sheet of the Revolutionary Sequence: Eduard Bernstein and Karl Kautsky

While the majority of the USPD – of which both Bernstein and Kautsky were founding members – decided to join the KPD, these two theorists distanced themselves from this decision and instead returned to the SPD. By 1921 it was time to draw a balance-sheet of the revolutionary sequence.

In the final part of his controversy with the Bolshevik leaders Kautsky made a real case against the Soviet régime,[102] claiming that it was responsible for all the problems that Russia was then going through. Writing in August 1921, at a moment when the New Economic Policy had just been launched in Russia, Kautsky's reactions particularly concerned the growing repression on the political level, as marked by the suppression of faction rights within the Russian party. He situated his argument in continuity with *Terrorism and Communism*, in which – he recalled – he had compared the Bolsheviks' acts with the Terror of 1793. Three questions were posed: the foundations of a true democracy, the meaning of dictatorship, and lastly the relation between socialism and 'forced labour'. A good part of his argument could be summarised as a long denunciation of the communists' anti-democratic 'putschism'. His analysis was punctuated by analogies similar to those appearing in *Terrorism and Communism*, this time underlining German specificities:

> But in Germany a workers' dictatorship did not and could never see the light of day. In France in 1792 war followed the Revolution that had broken out three years previously … The war exhausted and divided the proletariat in Germany. In France in 1792 the peasants were divided, half of them won to the Revolution and the rest to reaction. In Germany in 1918 they had excellent organisation and were all reactionaries.[103]

Kautsky's long elaboration on the 'dictatorship of conspirators' began with a historical look back to the Terror: while he consistently criticised its application in the Russia of 1917, he justified it in the 1793 case, even considering it a first case of the rule of the 'lower classes', in that 'for the first time in world history the proletarian or near-proletarian lower classes ruled a great modern state'.[104] Conversely, he criticised Babeuf's Conspiracy of Equals, presenting it

---

102   Kautsky 1921. Never translated into English.
103   Kautsky 1921, p. 51.
104   Kautsky 1921, p. 52.

as a forebear of the Bolsheviks.[105] Through his critique of Babeuf, he accused an entire revolutionary tradition of representing the wellspring of contemporary Soviet policies.

Bernstein, for some decades a critic of these traditions, expanded on Kautsky's remarks in his own *The German Revolution*.[106] Written in 1921, Bernstein's intention in this book was to draw a balance-sheet of the years since 1917 in Germany. For him, there had been no need for a revolutionary rupture in a developed country like Germany, and the search for compromise over a parliamentary democracy demanded that Social Democracy forge alliances with other political forces. The heart of his work was its rejection of the perpetuation of a council republic, which would have led to civil war in Germany. As against the Soviet insistence on the fusion of legislative and executive powers, he elaborated a social-democratic argument for the separation of powers. As in Kautsky, this implied a return to the foundational French revolutionary experience. Referring to December 1918's first congress of workers' and soldiers' councils, he compared the political conflicts between the government's supporters and the militants who wanted power delegated to the councils to the opposition between the Paris Commune and the revolutionary government during the 'Great Revolution'. ('The conflict ... recalls the violent struggles that repeatedly played out in France between the Paris Commune and the central government'.) Similarly, the pro-Spartakist police prefect Eichhorn's dissent[107] against the central authorities offered a cue to looking back to the Hébertists' fate:

> The role of police prefect for the capital is far too important a role for a government to leave it in the hands of a figure from a party working for the violent overthrow of that same government – and this, during a revolutionary period. We know what happened to the Hébertists during the French Revolution when they seriously took a stance against Robespierre's central government.[108]

Beyond these analogies, this book was essentially composed of a detailed study of the revolutionary events, ending with an elaboration on the role of the Spar-

---

105   Kautsky 1921, p. 53.
106   Bernstein 1998.
107   Emil Eichhorn was Berlin police prefect after 9 November 1918. His removal on 4 January 1919 provoked a Spartakist insurrection. He was subsequently a KPD MP, from 1920 until his death in 1925. See Droz 1990, p. 167.
108   Bernstein 1998, p. 186.

takists, considered 'Blanquist revolutionaries'.[109] Again Bernstein set this characterisation in continuity with his earlier writings:

> The Bolshevik doctrine is certainly Marxist in its rhetoric, but in its essence it is Blanquist. The Blanquist conception is the same one this author described already in his 1899 text.[110]

In Kautsky's last work from this period he published a pamphlet explaining the new Social-Democratic programme – as in the wake of the 1891 Erfurt Congress – entitled *The Proletarian Revolution and its Programme*.[111] 1922 was a moment of reintegration, with the remnants of the USPD fusing with the SPD after the previous year's Görlitz Congress, and Karl Kautsky thus set out to inscribe his argument within the context of a rediscovered unity. The programme that he advanced claimed to be an alternative to the Bolsheviks' programme and more particularly that of the German communists, although another of its declared objectives was to re-unite the different currents of the workers' movement. A text of many hundreds of pages, this was less a propaganda piece than a dense work with multiple historical references. In the foreword to the 1925 French edition – the book was very quickly translated and published by Églantine in Brussels – Kautsky again referred to the centrality of the French Revolution in understanding the processes that were now underway:

> So my book does not apply to Germany alone, but also on the one hand to France – where the traditions of the Great Revolution, regarded as the 'Revolution *par excellence*' are particularly strong – and, on the other hand, the countries of eastern Europe, especially Russia, which are still at the stage of bourgeois revolution, even if the revolution there is carried out by socialists and with socialist phraseology.[112]

A section of one chapter was almost exclusively devoted to the 'Great Revolution'.[113] Kautsky turned back to the balance of class forces during the French Revolution, picking up on certain previously-elaborated analyses. More originally, he reviewed the Russian historiography of the French Revolution and set

---

109   Bernstein 1998, p. 47.
110   Bernstein 1998, p. 50.
111   Kautsky 1922. English text from the *Marxists Internet Archives*.
112   Kautsky 1925, p. 1.
113   In the English edition, 'The Middle-Class Revolution'.

out a few remarks on Kropotkin's book, noting that whereas 'In his History of the Great French Revolution, Kropotkin would have us believe that greater political wisdom was to be found among the revolutionary masses than in the parliaments', 'the real state of affairs' was quite different.[114]

Starting out from from this critique, Kautsky elaborated a whole reflection on the separation and unity of executive and legislative powers, echoing the debates in Soviet Russia. He began with the Communards' 1871 demand for the unity of executive and legislative powers – a demand adopted by Karl Marx – before detailing the historical circumstances that could justify such a fusion. Again, the French Revolution served him as an example. Indeed, according to Kautsky, in 1793 such a combination of powers had allowed the salvation of the Revolution;[115] but the concentration of powers also presented risks, and from this he arrived at the conclusion that henceforth any assembly uniting executive and legislative powers would automatically repress all opposition.[116] The unity of the two had been tolerable – because it was necessary – in the context of the bourgeois revolution, but it could not happen again:

> For the period of transition from capitalism to socialism we most urgently require peace both at home and abroad. Not in the sense of a reconciliation of classes, but in the sense that they will fight out their differences with the agencies of democracy, and not of force. Under these conditions, however, there would not be the slightest reason for combining the executive with the legislative power, and there would be many cogent reasons against it.[117]

A further echo of his constant interrogation of the consequences of 1917 came in the following lines. If formally speaking these words described 1799, they should be understood as a first characterisation of the Soviet régime as 'Bonapartist', as he would further specify a few years later when he sketched out a definition of Stalinism:[118]

> The Middle Class Revolution ended in counter-revolution, the instrument of which is usually military dictatorship ... At this stage democracy is not yet firmly rooted, while the civil war and the foreign wars which are a fre-

---

114   Kautsky 1922.
115   Ibid.
116   Ibid.
117   Ibid.
118   See Chapter Twelve, p. 292.

quent incident of the revolutionary period result in the creation of a new, strictly disciplined army which takes the place of the old and now dissolved army of absolutism ... Thus the revolution ends in what is termed Bonapartism or Caesarism.[119]

Most of the Kautsky texts that we have cited here were repeatedly re-published and reviewed in Germany but also in France.[120] In this regard, we ought to note how the 'anti-totalitarian' school took inspiration from reading Kautsky. In a recent work which we have already cited, Matthias Lemke analyses Kautsky's arguments at some length, especially those from *Terrorism and Communism*.[121] For Lemke, even Lenin's writings from the beginning of the twentieth century were already gestating Soviet 'totalitarianism'. The German historian bases part of his elaborations on Kautsky's analogy between Bolshevism and Jacobinism, while situating himself in the lineage of François Furet, whose mantle he claims. Indeed, in his *The Passing of an Illusion* Furet compares Kautsky's critique of the Terror with that provided by Benjamin Constant.[122] According to Furet, both were similarly shocked by the contrast between the 'softening of mores' in their respective centuries and the unleashing of violence during the revolutions of 1793 and 1917. This reading was founded on Kautsky's writings condemning the Russian Revolution, Bolshevism and the revolutionary violence that accompanied it in 1917; a reasoning so repetitive as to leave no room for debate. Yet in fact the social-democrat theorist Kautsky always considered and presented the Terror as a historical necessity in the conditions of the France of the time; what could be condemned was the Bolsheviks' repetition of this experience, using violent means inherited from the bourgeois revolution. Moreover, Kautsky made skilful use of Marx and his *Eighteenth Brumaire*, which mocked the revolutionaries of 1848 and their sterile imitation of 1793. Kautsky distinguished the means used by the Terror of 1793 – justified, within the context of the bourgeois revolution – from what he considered the Bolsheviks' absurd imitation of these methods in 1917. Besides, what posed a problem for Kautsky in 1793 and 1917 was less the revolutionary government of the Convention than the popular excesses: indeed, he hailed Robespierre and the Montagnards for having tried to rein in the excesses of the Terror, unlike

---

119   Ibid.
120   Note the Social-Democratic publisher Dietz's re-issuing of *Terrorismus und Kommunismus* in 1925.
121   Lemke 2008, pp. 258–96.
122   Furet 1999, p. 82.

the Bolsheviks. In a short 1918 pamphlet *Democracy or Dictatorship?*[123] Kautsky conveyed the 'great historic significance'[124] of the Terror, which ought to be understood as the 'offspring of the war'.[125] One last point differentiating Kautsky from François Furet's theses is his appreciation of France's revolutionary traditions. Furet challenges the entire revolutionary culture emanating from 1793, a culture authorising the emergence of Bolshevism and affording a justification for its means of action.[126] Yet if the Kautsky of 1889 had expressed strong reservations over the usefulness of laying claim to Jacobin traditions, in 1906–7 he revised his position. This was a stance that he would reiterate in 1920, holding that the political culture emanating from 1793 had made an effective contribution to the development of socialism in France in his own time:

> The régime of Terror of 1793 made a significant contribution to raising the level of consciousness of the proletarians of all countries, but above all – naturally – of the French, and it thus also strengthened them in the class struggle.[127]

---

123   Kautsky 1918b. There is no English translation.
124   Kautsky 1918b, p. 37.
125   Ibid.
126   Furet 1999, p. 236.
127   'Ein Schrift über den Bolschevismus', *Der Kampf*, 1920, p. 264.

Continuities and New Approaches in the Mid-1920s

German Social Democracy reorganised its forces in the early 1920s, particularly after 1924 in the context of an improving economic situation. The historian Horst Möller has counterposed the 'years of crisis' of 1920–4 to the 'five better years' of 1924–9.[1] The Social-Democrat Alfred Moeglich declared in the *Sozialistische Monatshefte* that 'the old Social Democracy is no more'.[2] Certainly the Social-Democrats had changed a lot, but even so we should not overlook the forceful continued presence of major pre-1914 actors.

The Pre-war Generation, and a Lasting Reference Point

Numerous influential personalities from the pre-war social-democratic parties continued their trajectory within the SPD. As such, there was no *tabula rasa* of the party's pre-war inheritance, as indicated by Karl Kautsky's major presence in the debates with the Bolshevik leaders. But the one-time 'pope' of the International was gradually marginalised, an old and respected theorist of now much-reduced standing and influence. However, the fact that it was Heinrich Cunow who took over from Kautsky in running *Die Neue Zeit* – a role he would maintain until this publication's disappearance – says a lot about the link between the two epochs, at least up till the mid-1920s. This pair are two exemplary cases – and not the only ones – showing the forms of continuity in the social-democratic historiography of the French Revolution.

Kautsky and Cunow's Paths
The publication of a *Festschrift* in Vienna in honour of Kautsky's seventieth birthday, as he returned to his country of origin (*Karl Kautsky. The Thinker and Fighter*)[3] spoke to the enduring influence of the 'pope of Marxism'. In most of its articles, the dominant theme was Kautsky's great international role prior to 1914; as for the period following 1917, it above all highlighted his works as a critic of the USSR. Two contributions reviewed what Kautsky had added to the historiography of the French Revolution.

---

1 Möller 2005, p. 119.
2 'Die Neue Sozialdemokratie und das neue Programm', *Sozialistische Monatshefte*, 1919, p. 455.
3 Published by Vienna's Verlag der Wiener Buchhandlung in 1924.

In one article on 'Karl Kautsky as a Marxist Historian' Otto Jensen emphasised the great variety of Kautsky's centres of interest as well as his analytical method, a critique of 'historical legends'[4] that allowed the German Social-Democrats to understand the reality of the historical events caricatured by the dominant historiography. He took as an example *Die Klassengegensätze im Zeitalter der Französischen Revolution*, which he held up as a work of reference at the origin of a specific tradition of studies later pursued by Heinrich Cunow. Jensen set the texts regarding the controversies with the Bolsheviks in continuity with Kautsky's historical works, for his 'study of the dynamic of the 1789 French Revolution allowed him a lively but economically-grounded critique of the tactics of the Bolsheviks, who wanted to take the bourgeois revolution in Russia as a prototype for proletarian revolutions'.[5]

A second piece by Alexandre Bracke dealt with the 'pope of Marxism''s relations with the French socialists, and in a sense represented a belated defence of Kautsky, deployed in support of Guesdism. As far as we know this text was not published in French. Taking the role that Guesde and his current – of which Bracke was one of the most renowned exponents – had played before 1905,[6] the article cited some of the works that had contributed 'to enlightening the French socialists about France',[7] noting that ' "*Die Klassengegensätze von 1789*" must be ranked very highly ... Even where this text was not cited it exercised a *post facto* influence on every historical presentation of the Revolution existent in France. We can say without exaggeration that after it was published the history of the great revolutions had to be written differently'.[8] The other work by Kautsky he cited on this subject was the series of articles on the French Republic appearing in *Die Neue Zeit* in 1904, refuting Jaures's conception of the Republic and its historical interpretation. Bracke referred to the great significance of these texts and the Guesdists' use of them in *Le Socialisme*, seeking to give the French a class analysis of what the French Republic then represented – a principally bourgeois political regime.[9] As against Jaurès, he defended a tradition of Marxist analysis of the Republic and the French Revolution.[10] Bracke still enjoyed very great authority in the SFIO: an MP for the Seine region since

4   *Festschrift* 1924, p. 65.
5   *Festschrift* 1924, p. 68.
6   Alexandre Bracke was secretary of the Guesdist *Parti Socialiste de France* between 1902 and 1905.
7   *Festschrift* 1924, p. 104.
8   Ibid.
9   Ibid.
10   Ibid.

1912, and one of the great parliamentary and congress orators, he represented the historic tradition of French socialism. It was probably the contemporary French context that led him to reaffirm Karl Kautsky's historic role and association with Guesdism, with the 1924 discussion of SFIO's support for the *Cartel des gauches*[11] prompting the Left of the party – Guesde's heirs – to remobilise their old reference points. Indeed, the Left looked on the party's support for the government with some hostility.[12] The attack on Jean Jaurès could thus be considered an attempt positively to re-appraise Kautsky's orthodoxy as against Jaurès's own *Histoire socialiste de la Révolution française*, which Albert Mathiez had just republished in France.[13]

In the year this homage appeared Kautsky was regularly publishing articles in the Austrian press, at the same time as maintaining his relations with the German party. With the political situation having stabilised, one of his lines of inquiry regarded the possibility of a counter-revolutionary process developing, given that 'each revolution and each counter-revolution has its own particular conditions'.[14] Having evoked the defeats of 1848 and 1871 his analysis turned to the German Revolution of 1918. For Kautsky, since this was a proletarian revolution – the synonym of historical progress – its methods differed from those of the bourgeois revolution, and the radicalisation leading to counter-revolution ought not take place.[15] Indeed, Kautsky's view of the risks of counter-revolution remained highly optimistic. Until a very late point he would remain convinced of the conquests represented by the strength of the Social-Democratic Party and its capacity to maintain control of the working-class masses, and barely even considered possible the triumph of other political forces:

> The German Revolution found a proletariat that had formed the greatest proletarian party in the world during less than half a century of intense economic and political struggles: it had the best union organisations, the strongest press and the richest educational institutions.[16]

---

11   [The alliance between the Socialists (SFIO) and the Radicals, which stood jointly (and victoriously) in the 1924 French parliamentary elections and provided the basis for a series of governments up until 1926].

12   See Judt 1976.

13   Jaures 1922–4.

14   'Die Aussichten der Gegenrevolution in Deutschland', *Der Kampf*, 1924, p. 1.

15   'Die Aussichten der Gegenrevolution in Deutschland', *Der Kampf*, 1924, p. 3.

16   'Die Aussichten der Gegenrevolution in Deutschland', *Der Kampf*, 1924, p. 7.

If there was to be a confrontation, it would not be the same as in the 1789–99 period. For the strength of these organisations would make it possible to derail any attempt at counter-revolution, or at the very least limit the effects of reaction ...[17]

We have already underlined Heinrich Cunow's role at the head of *Die Neue Zeit* at the moment of the events of 1917–19. His interest in the Revolution continued up until the magazine's last issues in 1924, as attested by its publication of numerous book reviews on this subject, for example a piece on the title by Georges Bourgin – a French socialist, author of several works and curator at the national archives.[18] Most importantly, in parallel to his work for *Die Neue Zeit* Heinrich Cunow also occupied other intellectual posts. The echo of his articles and books was incomparable with that of the pre-war Kautsky, above all at the international level. Nonetheless, numerous manuals sought to identify him as one of the party's main theorists. In this context it is worth noting his new university post as 'professor of political economy at Berlin University' (*Professor für Staatswissenschaften*) from 1919 onward.[19] Cunow's exact status as an *ausserordentlicher Professor* (extraordinary professor) at Humboldt University meant that he was not a chair. A university employee, he did not occupy the higher grade of *Ordinarius Professor* (OP) and was not part of the university's *Kollegium*.[20] Like other party members including Rudolf Hilferding – the economist and future director of the theoretical review *Die Gesellschaft* – he was appointed by government decision.

Heinrich Cunow published a book collecting the university lectures he gave in 1919–20, *The Marxist Theory of History, Society and the State*.[21] After the split with the Communists this textbook 'of general economic history' was the SPD's main theoretical reference manual, and it saw five further editions up till 1930. Recognising the 'grave crisis' in the postwar period following the fragmentation of the old SPD, the book

> set itself the task of drawing out the different sociological precepts of Marx's writings and organising them in their logical context. Finally, hav-

---

17   'Die Aussichten der Gegenrevolution in Deutschland', *Der Kampf*, 1924, p. 10.
18   Bourgin 1922. The unsigned review 'Bourgin, Die französische Revolution' appeared in *Die Neue Zeit*, 1922, p. 430.
19   Droz 1990, p. 145.
20   These considerations are based on the information appearing in a biography of Werner Sombart that provides certain indications on university careers in Germany. See Lenger 1994.
21   Cunow 1920.

ing broken these down into a certain number of fundamental ideas, it will use them to arrive at a systematic presentation of the doctrine of history, society and the state in Marx.[22]

In what was more a course – a didactic presentation – than an original contribution, Cunow sought to provide an overview of the ideas that had contributed to the formation of Marx's concepts. In continuity with the social-democrats' elaborations during the 1914–18 Great War, Cunow criticised Marx's perspective of the abolition of the state, instead attributing the state a major role in the organisation of socialism – and in particular in defining a new law favourable to the working class, allowing the progressive transition to socialism.[23] This work well exemplified the SPD under the Weimar Republic, which while revising its doctrine did not – as the Communists' alleged – intend to 'renounce' it, but rather to situate it in continuity with the pre-1914 period.

This book above all dealt with the theory of history, though it nonetheless presented certain concepts in some detail. Cunow expounded the concept of the 'class struggle' in relation to the French Revolution, within the context of a chapter on Rousseau and the influence of his ideas.[24] Having explained Rousseau's 'general will' and its expression in the French Revolution, Cunow proposed to analyse the revolution in terms of 'the ideas of class struggle',[25] starting from the same terms employed by the actors of that epoch. He considered Marat the precursor to the 'conception of the class struggle'.[26] Through his paper *l'Ami du peuple* Marat had been one of the first figures to become conscious of the primacy of social antagonisms.[27] Finally, in a chapter-section on the Revolution's influence on the materialist conception of history[28] Cunow presented a brief summary of all the historical literature following the Revolution, and of the Revolution's influence on historians. He cited Mignet and

---

22   Cunow 1920, p. 3.
23   Herrera 2003, pp. 83–6.
24   See the chapter 'Rousseaus Sozialphilosophie und ihr Einfluss auf die Staatstheoretik der französische Revolution', in Cunow 1920, pp. 125–55.
25   A chapter-section is devoted to 'Klassenkampfideen': Cunow 1920, pp. 142–5.
26   The chapter-section is entitled 'Jean-Paul Marats Klassenkampfauffassung': Cunow 1920, pp. 145–8.
27   Cunow 1920, p. 148. Cunow had already researched *l'Ami du Peuple* for his 1908 book republished in 1912. Noteworthy in the 1920 edition of his textbook was the whole page devoted to promoting his book on the French Revolution, demonstrating the link that he sought to establish with his pre-war output.
28   Cunow 1920, pp. 155–7.

Barnave as having established a correspondence between economic interests and political conflicts. The *Arbeiter-Bildung*, the new periodical for militants' education, termed Cunow's book a manual of reference:

> The conception of the class struggle, founded on economics and the ideas behind political struggles, is illustrated by the events of the great French Revolution and expressed by Marat in the immediate context of day-to-day events.[29]

The French Revolution was far from absent from this volume. It even constituted a key historical example, important to understanding the genesis of certain concepts. Nonetheless, this manual did not consider the Revolution a source of Marxism, and it here occupied a much more secondary place than it did in Kautsky's 1908 *Historische Leistung*,[30] published once in 1919 and once again in 1933. As Cunow established a new theory of the state *a posteriori* justifying the SPD's participation in government, following the crushing of the Spartakists he was no longer able to set the Revolution at the same historic heights. After all, this was a Revolution some of whose episodes recalled by analogy the upheavals in contemporary Germany, which the SPD had sought to put an end to.

A few years later Cunow published a short illustrated work popularising the history of the French Revolution.[31] This was one of the very few specific contributions on this subject that the Social Democracy published during the Weimar period, and indeed the only one published by Dietz between 1919 and 1933 apart from its reissuing of pre-1914 works. This shows how in the 1920s the Social-Democrats were publishing and writing a lot less on the 'Great Revolution', at least via the party's own publishing house. Lacking major theoretical elaboration, this text was a striking example of the change in how the history of the French Revolution was written. This 85-page book was a short essay designed for the wider public, with a small number of illustrations and without notes or a bibliography. Cunow offered the reader a veritable tour of the geography of Paris during the French Revolution, going on a circuit of the city's cafés in order to present the main actors of the Revolution as well as some of its political

29   Schmidt, 'Ein neues Buch über den historischen Materialismus', *Arbeiter-Bildung*, January 1922, pp. 15–17. *Arbeiter-Bildung* was edited by the party's education commission, and offered a presentation of this commission's activities. It appeared on an irregular basis from 1920 to 1924.
30   See Chapter Five, p. 133.
31   Cunow 1925.

debates. This was a fresh opportunity to evoke the main revolutionary periodicals – a subject that the author had studied in detail, although on this occasion
he presented them only very summarily. Writing this text Cunow drew closer
to a work like Wilhelm Blos's, describing the different sites of sociability, the
individuals who crossed paths therein, and so on. However, while in his book
Blos referred to his application of the materialist conception of history, this was
not the case with Cunow's essay: indeed, we find only very few references in
this text that could suggest such an interpretation. While repeatedly referring
to 'class contradictions'[32] Cunow did not systematically relate political conflicts to social groups, as he had in his pre-World War I *oeuvre*. This was a much
reduced version of his pre-1914 work, shorn of its doctrinal aspects and written
in a lighter style.[33] As one biographical essay on Cunow emphasises, this book
did indeed have a certain echo.[34]

National History and Revolutionary History

Thus by the mid-1920s the French Revolution was no longer the object of such
great Social-Democratic attention. After all, the only book published by Dietz
on this subject was a very modest volume incomparable to the ambitious array
of publications in 1906–14.

Nonetheless, it is worth mentioning the French Revolution's place in the
context of Germany's national history. Of course, here, too, the context had
profoundly changed. Before 1914 the International had sought to be an – essentially European – deployment rallying the various nationally-based socialist
and social-democratic parties around common values, over and above all their
various debates and antagonisms. Even if the SPD's own relation to the nation
already featured certain ambiguities regarding the Wilhelmine monarchy, it did
also suggest a model for the International, and the Marxism it sought to promote was in part founded on foreign reference points including the French
Revolution. By now ambitions for unification – or at least a certain form of
unification – had disappeared. As the historian Serge Wolikow notes, in his
introduction to an important work devoted to the idea of internationalism in
the international workers' movements,

> The First World War profoundly shook up the very foundations of the
> problem. Powerless to ward off the war, working-class internationalism

---

32   Cunow 1925, p. 29.
33   He regularly explained the vocabulary of the time, from 'agioteurs' (Cunow 1925, p. 42) to
      'Muscadins' and 'Fréluquets' (p. 59).
34   Florath 1987, p. 145.

fragmented during the conflict, thus sealing the disunity of the proletarians inserted in national networks whose political and ideological pregnancy had now appeared in all its force. In the interwar period the Labour and Socialist International, which claimed the heritage of the Second International, would give up on any specific project of its own, instead identifying with the establishment of embryonic international institutions.[35]

The weakening of internationalism could not but have important effects on Social Democrats' historical reference points. A recent study has demonstrated that even before 1914 the problem of integrating major national figures into the Social Democrats' cultural references had been a question at the heart of these parties' political debates.[36] After 1920, the Austrian party's Linz Programme expressed the Social Democrats' wish 'to appropriate "German culture" and advances in the most varied domains, in order to integrate them into a proletarian substrate'.[37] This is particularly notable in a programme renowned for its maintenance of orthodoxy; indeed, this was a programme that referred to the 'dictatorship of the proletariat' and itself had an echo in the more marked return of Marxist reference points in the SPD's 1925 Heidelberg Programme.

In continuity with articles published during the war, Alsace-Lorraine and the Left Bank of the Rhine were the object of particular attention. The most important publication at the beginning of the 1920s was a book by the Social-Democrat Alexander Conrady, whom we have already mentioned on account of his role in the party's educational structures. A documented and rather voluminous work, Conrady's book studied in detail the history of the Left Bank of the Rhine in 'the French era', and should be seen in the context of the tense Franco-German relations of the early 1920s.[38] France's annexationist ambitions regarding the Left Bank of the Rhine and its 1923–5 occupation of the Ruhr were accompanied by a whole array of historiography deployed in order to justify annexation. Conversely, in Germany there appeared numerous works hostile to French occupation. School textbooks were particularly mobilised on this subject,[39] taking up a position in continuity with a historiography hostile to all revolutionary movements. Indeed, it was easy enough to establish a link between the occupation of the 1920s and the arrival of French troops on these

---

35   Wolikow and Cordillot 1993, p. 12.
36   Bonnell 2005.
37   Pasteur 2003, p. 24.
38   Conrady 1922.
39   Sproll 1992, p. 217.

same territories during the Revolution. This era saw a number of scenarios out-lined for this region, including that of a *Land* with privileged economic and political relations with France, or even the possibility of an autonomous Rhine state.[40]

In substance, while Conrady's work was not totally 'anti-French' it did rather tend to minimise the impact of the French Revolution, and as the historian Marita Gilli has put it, to 'present the Mainz revolutionaries as utopian enthu-siasts and doubtful types who we should not dwell on for too long'.[41] Published by Dietz, the book seems to have had a very meagre impact: we can find neither reviews nor re-editions, and probably only very few copies were distributed.

Publishing and Education: between Continuities and Innovations

If Heinrich Cunow represented a form of continuity, writing on the French Revolution no longer seems to have been a major question. How did this relate to the 'traditional' publishing and education structures which remained in place, for the most part, up till 1933?

The New Means of Education

Integration into the state offered new opportunities for Social Democracy. Between 1918 and 1922 the SPD culture minister Haenisch created people's uni-versities (*Volkshochschulen*) but most would fall victim to the economic crisis.[42] New collaborations also emerged between communal administrations and the SPD's local organisations. However, these innovations should not lead us to forget the continuities with the era of the Reich. In terms of schooling, des-pite the republication of several works like those by Karl Kautsky and Wil-helm Blos, Social-Democratic interpretations did not break through into sec-ondary schools or into widely-distributed history textbooks. Heinz Sproll, who has mounted a detailed study of the content of different levels of school text-books in the Weimar Republic, notes that Marxist-inspired interpretations of the French Revolution found 'no way into schools, lesson plans or historical works'.[43] Nonetheless, in terms of the SPD's internal education apparatus and publishing houses the Party now placed a priority on reorganising its struc-tures, as a report to its 1919 congress makes clear.[44] This reordering was all

---

40   Bariéty 1977.
41   Gilli 1990, p. 60.
42   On the details of this education see Olbrich 1977.
43   Sproll 1992, p. 238.
44   *Protokoll über die Verhandlungen des Parteitages der Sozialdemokratischen Partei Deutsch-lands, Weimar, 10. bis 15. Juni 1919*, Berlin, 1919, p. 26.

the more necessary given that the SPD had now lost many former educational
cadres who had graduated from the party-school. Before 1914 these latter had
often been close to the Left of the party, and many major such figures had
now passed to the KPD, including Hermann Duncker, Otto Rühle and Clara
Zetkin. In 1922 the SPD created a 'Central Educational Commission for Socialist
Educational Work' (*Reichbildungsausschuss für sozialistische Arbeiterbildung*)
integrated into the wider mechanism of an 'Association for Socialist Culture'
(*Sozialisten Kulturbund*) bringing together all of Social Democracy's cultural
organisations. *Arbeiter-Bildung* was the periodical reporting on its activities in
the early 1920s. Understanding its inner workings can be complicated, given
that a number of publications disappeared between 1922 and 1924 on account
of the crisis; it is easier to track the situation in Austria, where the *Bildungsarbeit* continued appearing up till 1934.

The congress records of the German party in the 1920s also contain information on the educational commission. The place of history and in particular
of revolutionary history seems to have been reduced,[45] and in the absence of
any specific teaching dedicated to the French Revolution it is impossible to tell
what place was reserved for this history with the same accuracy as for the 1906–
14 period.[46] At a more general level, the historian Danièle Ruthmann remarks
that an 'orientation toward the problems of the present moment was manifest' in 1920s SPD educational activity.[47] She mentions an interesting account
by Erich Winkler comparing the content of party education in the 1920s to that
of the pre-war years. Indeed, Weimar's new legislative programme demanded
increased education in this domain, in an era in which the SPD had become a
ruling party integrated into the state:

> In political economy, the practical political economy of modern times
> replaced theoretical political economy (as according to Marx). History
> was limited to contemporary political history. Subjects such as public and
> administrative law and questions relating to labour legislation and eco-
> nomic law now occupied an ever more important role.[48]

---

45 One of the French Revolution's rare appearances came in one 1924 *Lichtbildervortrag*: see
    Sozialdemokratischer Parteitag, Protokoll. Berlin, 11. bis 14. Juni 1924, Berlin, 1924, p. 24.
46 The greater endurance of local structures allows for a more detailed view of the late 1920s
    picture, for example in the case of the Berlin school. See Chapter Twelve, p. 292.
47 Ruthmann 1982, p. 26.
48 Winkler 1926, cited in Olbrich 1977, p. 156.

There are no particular articles in *Arbeiter-Bildung* devoted to the French Revolution or how its history should be taught, and there is also nothing on this theme in the synopses of transcribed lectures, except for fleeting allusions. Nonetheless, the 'history of socialism' still was taught, and the balances of the pre-war years persisted even despite far-reaching changes: the French Revolution still had a place in the 'great history' of socialism, even if a limited one. A pamphlet by Erwin Marquardt[49] published by the SPD educational commission in 1922 provides a detailed outline of the course devoted to the history of socialism. This manual was meant to serve as the basis for the different courses delivered on this subject across Germany, and formally speaking it closely resembled the plan Gustav Eckstein had drawn up in 1910.[50] Conversely, we should also note the considerable changes of substance. Certainly, there were still emphatic references to Marx and many formulations remained similar to what had been elaborated before 1914:[51] the course began with Antiquity and the Middle Ages and then proceeded by way of Thomas More before arriving at the 'modern era', without particularly elaborating the history of revolutions. It only mentioned revolutions in the part devoted to the Middle Ages, for the purposes of underlining the progressive abolition of feudalism. The French Revolution had lost its singular and exemplary role: it was only mentioned as part of a wider ensemble.[52] Finally, the part devoted to 'our socialist theoreticians' mentioned a number of socialist forerunners including Jean Meslier, Charles Fourier, Cabet and others, whereas there was no trace of Babeuf, marking a sharp contrast with the pre-war period. Nonetheless, the bibliography did still refer to Blos and Kautsky's books, which as we have mentioned had each been re-published in 1919.[53] Yet the French Revolution had largely lost its central role in party education.

Workers' Calendars and Libraries

Apart from a few years, there was also a continued publication and distribution of workers' calendars (*Notizkalender*). In 1918 the *Arbeiter-Notiz-Kalender* paid homage to Karl Marx upon the hundredth anniversary of his death.[54] It was now shorn of its historical sections: unlike the pre-war series, it no longer featured systematic references to past revolutions. The following year the his-

---

49   Marquardt 1922.
50   See Chapter Six, p. 158.
51   Marquardt 1922, pp. 3–4.
52   Marquardt 1922, p. 6.
53   Marquardt 1922, p. 15.
54   *Arbeiter-Notiz-Kalender*, published by the Buchhandlung Vorwärts Paul Singer in 1918–23.

torical calendar reappeared in a different form, with each date immediately followed by a historical reference: 21 January, Louis XVI; 5 April, Danton guillotined; 2 June 1793, the fall of the Girondins; 22 September 1792, the onset of the First Republic; and so on. This was an exceptional case, with this kind of references not appearing from the following year onward. However, in 1922 a box for each month featured recommended reading, with many socialist classics figuring among the titles. So in March we find Wilhelm Blos's *Die Französische Revolution*, in June Cunow's book on the revolutionary press, and at the end of the year a near-complete bibliography for Kautsky, notably including *Die Klassengegensätze*. In 1923 no historical dates or bibliography featured, but 'anniversaries' in certain months recalled a few mainly national dates like 9 and 12 November, corresponding to the declaration of the German and Austrian republics respectively. The only date evoking the French revolution was 5 April 1794, 'Danton guillotined'.[55] The *Notizkalender*'s format often changed, with historical references appearing much more irregularly.

We find the same balance in the Austrian *Arbeiternotizkalender*. There were few notable historical dates but between 1919 and 1924 an annotated bibliography 'What is socialism?' presented the indispensable books in various different domains. The pamphlets popularising the 'classics' occupied a significant place therein, with the bibliography citing almost all of Karl Kautsky's works. As regards the French Revolution, 'we find the best presentation of the social situation in France at the moment when the French Revolution broke out in Karl Kautsky's book *Die Klassengegensätze im Zeitalter der französischen Revolution*'.[56] Also mentioned were the books by Wilhelm Blos, Heinrich Cunow, Peter Kropotkin and the Social Democrats' edition of Buonarroti: a certain heritage from the pre-war period thus endured.

Another difficulty echoed in the 1921 Congress was the postwar reorganisation of the workers' libraries. At issue was how to unify the libraries and their nomenclature even though some of them were reluctant to come into the bosom of the party.[57] Party congresses across several years discussed this question. In 1930 there were still 1,600 workers' libraries (*Arbeiterbibliotheken*). This ongoing focus was marked in 1918 by the resumed publication of *Der Bibliothekar*. For example, in July 1918 we can find a review of the second edition

55   It is impossible to draw any conclusions from this example alone; nonetheless, the few leaders still interested in the French Revolution at the end of the 1920s largely proved 'Dantonist' interpreters of the Revolution. See Chapter Eleven, p. 275.

56   *Arbeiternotizkalender*, Vienna, 1923, p. 36.

57   *Protokoll*, Görlitz, 18. bis 24. September 1921, Berlin, 1921, p. 27.

of Theodor Biterrauf's book on the French Revolution;[58] it recommended 'classic' works including Blos and Cunow's books. Noteworthy was the praise for Jean Jaurès's *Histoire socialiste ...*, one of the first signs of a gradually increasing consideration of Jaurès's work, with the reviewer also regretting the lack of a translation. The review *Bücherwarte* was launched after the crisis, replacing *Der Bibliothekar*, which had disappeared in 1918.

The Competing Revolutionary Periods and Their Evaluation

The American and Soviet Cases

The changes we have noted in party education are also visible in the articles published in Social-Democratic reviews and press organs. Nonetheless the weakening of internationalism and the reference to the 1789 Revolution translated not only into a simple withdrawal into national reference points, but also a greater consideration of other revolutionary processes – whether positively or negatively perceived. The 1920s saw the emergence of an interest in the American Revolution, which had been almost non-existent prior to 1914. This evidently reflected the new political conjuncture and the US economic intervention through both 1924's Dawes Plan, bringing an influx of American capital, and then the 1929–30 Young Plan to deal with the crisis. In the pages of *Die Gesellschaft* Hermann Wendel studied the role of George Washington, a subject also regularly addressed in *Vorwärts*.[59] Beyond the American Revolution's economic causes, more specifically political factors were also explored: Heinz Sproll notes that during the extended constitutional debates that followed the 1919 calling of the Constituent Assembly, the liberals put forward the examples of the 1791 French and 1787 US constitutions, as they sought past models for the Weimar order.[60] In this context the United States constituted a new model, and indeed there was a certain fascination for this country among the Social Democrats: its democracy, justice system, and fight against alcohol – also at the heart of the measures taken by 'Red Vienna' – exercised a strong power of attraction. Many travelled to the USA in the late 1920s and came back convinced of the superiority of American democracy. One of those to return enthused by

58   *Der Bibliothekar*, July–August 1918, p. 1147.
59   For example, on the 200th anniversary of George Washington's birth, T. Schulz 'Der erste Präsident von USA Zum 200. Geburtstag von Georges Washington', *Vorwärts*, 21 February 1932, p. 3. See also H. Wendel 'Georges Washington. Zu seinem zweihundersten Geburtstag', *Die Gesellschaft*, 1932, pp. 223–32.
60   Sproll 1992, pp. 228–9.

the United States was the Vienna city government's senator for health Julius Tandler, a major agent of the social reforms in the Austrian capital.[61]

Before 1914, the idea of revolution – whether it was repudiated, appreciated or debated – remained largely abstract and, in the absence of recent victorious revolutionary processes, was logically orientated toward past history. After the Russian Revolution of 1917 and the German and Austrian events of 1918–19 Social Democracy defended the now-established republican régimes – the product of compromises with other political forces – and very sharply opposed Soviet socialism. This latter example showed that a Revolution purporting to continue the 'Great French Revolution' could result in reaction or at least a political régime far from what the social democrats themselves conceived. We can get a measure of this distaste for communism ten years after the Russian Revolution: in 1927 *Sozialistische Monatshefte* described the Soviet régime as reactionary and opened up its columns to Alexander Kerensky, the former head of the 1917 Provisional Government overthrown by the Bolsheviks.[62] The same year, the 1927 Austrian *Arbeiter-Kalender* looked back to 1905, emphasising the very different conditions of 1793 and 1917 which rendered the methods of the Terror unjustifiable in the present day.[63] While there was an article on the Russian Revolution, it was criticised as a means of delegitimising part of the inheritance of the French Revolution via the systematic critique of the Soviet régime.

Faced with the Communists

Indeed, in Germany the Weimar model was little compatible with a Revolution whose 1793–4 phase was so positively evaluated by the Social Democrats' Communist adversaries. As in 1919, the Social Democrats' readings of the French Revolution should be understood in the mirror of the readings produced by the Communists – a force with a far from negligible political influence in Germany, especially at the end of the 1920s. Heinrich Cunow himself provided evidence of this in 1920. Before 1914[64] all the discussions on Marxism had taken place within a single united party, and however big the differences were they had to be expounded and debated in the hope of winning

---

61   Tandler provided an assessment of ten years of Prohibition in the United States in the *Arbeiter-Zeitung* of 17 January 1930, in which he also reviewed his own visit. On Tandler, see Pasteur 1994, pp. 497–626.

62   A. Kerensky, 'Das Jubiläum der Reaktion', *Sozialistische Monatshefte*, 1927, pp. 871–3.

63   S. Kunst 'Zehn Jahre russicher Revolution', *Österreichischer Arbeiter-Kalender*, 1927, pp. 5–16.

64   Cunow 1920, p. 2.

majority approval. The fragmentation of the workers' movement into multiple distinct parties and currents now made this type of configuration difficult.

Nonetheless, no matter how violent the invective between Social Democrats and Communists during the Weimar period, this could not erase their common matrix resulting from the reference points elaborated before 1914, including with regard to the French Revolution. Despite their complex inheritances, the Communist movement and the various different currents of the German Left almost all had ex-SPDers in their ranks, and their intellectual formation was largely dependent on this previous affiliation. Here we will expand upon three telling examples: namely, the Communists of the KPD as well as Otto Rühle and Max Beer, two former Social-Democrats who had each known the SPD from within, left it and written 'great histories'.

We could highlight Paul Adler among the Communists who wrote articles on the French Revolution. For example, on 5 October 1921 he had a piece published in the KPD organ *Die Rote Fahne* regarding the emergence of socialism during the Revolution, and defending the role that Robespierre played therein.[65] Adler made a more developed contribution in a piece published in a major volume retracing the whole history of ideas of 'freedom'.[66] This was a heterogeneous ensemble, its authors notably including Alexander Conrady and other Social-Democrats like Paul Kampffmeyer and Friedrich Muckle. A long introduction situated the whole work in the lineage of Marx, Bebel and Jaurès, here referenced on account of his fight for peace. The chapter devoted to the French Revolution edited by Adler featured regular comparisons with Germany, showing a pedagogical concern properly to present the specificities of this history to a non-specialist reader.[67] An explanation of the French Revolution in social terms was accompanied by a German-language version of the *Marseillaise* and an *hors-texte* plate by Gustave Doré. Basing himself on Louis Blanc as he evaluated the Montagnards and their 1793 constitutional project, the author presented Robespierre and the Jacobins' efforts sympathetically, linking 1793 with 1917.[68]

---

65 P. Adler 'Sozialistische Probleme der grossen französichen Revolution', *Die Rote Fahne*, 5 October 1921, p. 2. Communist propaganda placed particular value on Robespierre, who was represented in the *Arbeiter-Kalender für das Jahr 1925*, Hamburg, 1925 (published by the KPD).

66 Jezower (ed.) 1921.

67 Jezower (ed.) 1921, p. 104.

68 Jezower (ed.) 1921, p. 105.

However, with the KPD not publishing any major volume on the French Revolution in the early 1920s, we principally find eulogies to Marat, Robespierre, and Babeuf by way of references in the Communist press.[69] It is well-known that Bolshevisation and then the 'class against class' strategy beginning in 1928 demanded that the French Communists interpret the French Revolution as simply 'bourgeois'. Indeed, up till the mid-1930s this contributed to reducing this revolution's exemplary role for the PCF, in favour of the example of 1917 in Russia.[70] However, the KPD's situation was rather different given that 1789 was not associated with state power and did not constitute an 'official' national reference point. If there was any comparable example for the consequences of the 'class against class' strategy for German national history, it was that regarding the figure of Martin Luther.[71] The German Communists were thus 'freer' to evaluate the 1789–94 period positively, as evidenced by the Communist publisher Neuer Deutscher Verlag's ('New German Publishing') mid-1920s publication of a collection on the 'Orators of the Revolution', with great revolutionaries' speeches and introductory pieces on their respective histories. The French revolutionary orators published were Robespierre, Saint-Just, Fouquier-Tinville, Marat and Danton.[72] The first volume in the collection was devoted to Robespierre, who while appearing as a 'bourgeois' leader also represented the most highly praised phase of the Revolution, with 'the fall of Robespierre' held to 'signif[y] the victory of the bourgeoisie's counter-revolution over the proletariat'.[73] Following Lenin it evoked the 'revolutionary democratic Jacobin dictatorship', a form of rule that heralded future struggles even despite its bourgeois character.[74]

From Robespierre to Babeuf, the KPD here stood far from the Social-Democratic reference points of the same era; but whereas the SPD had never or only marginally shown any appreciation for Robespierre, it had long built up its positive evaluation of Babeuf, particularly by way of the party's educational apparatuses of 1905–14. Indeed, the way in which the history of the French Revolution was taught in KPD party-schools (the *Marxistischen Arbeiterschule*, known as the 'MASCH') attests to this heritage. The first part of a course dedicated to the 'History of the international workers' movement' accorded a specific place to the 'Great French Revolution'. One text provides a detailed plan for this

---

69   Kinner 1989, pp. 229–57.
70   Wolikow 2002, pp. 239–44.
71   Kinner 1989, p. 249.
72   Robespierre 1925, Saint-Just 1925, Fouquier-Tinville 1925, Marat 1926, Danton 1926.
73   Robespierre 1925, p. 12.
74   Robespierre 1925, p. 25.

course and a substantial summary of its content, together with a complement-ary bibliography.[75] Its authors included Hermann Duncker, a major figure of German communism who like certain others had his first training in the SPD and a certain experience as a Social-Democratic educator, having been *Wan-derlehrer* in the Berlin *Arbeiter-Bildungsschule*. There were clear continuities between what the Berlin SPD school had been able to teach before 1914 and the education that the Communists now offered: a quick introduction encouraged an understanding of the Revolution in its social and economic context, and particularly drew attention to the period of 'petit-bourgeois' rule in 1793–94.[76] Here the Revolution was characterised in terms clearly comparable to those of Kautsky and Cunow's pre-1914 works. This was also reflected in the curriculum, which presented the role of the various different social forces before explaining the unfolding of the Revolution itself and finally concluding with the 'lessons of the Revolution'. Nonetheless, this conclusion was characteristic of the Com-munist vulgate of the era, as it took care to elevate 1917 to the same standing as the French Revolution of 1789.[77] There could, however, only be a limited com-parison between the two revolutionary processes: the French Revolution had remained mainly 'bourgeois' and had been unable to go beyond this stage. If Robespierre had played an appreciable historical function, he remained restric-ted to the role of a leader of the petit bourgeoisie. Conversely, Babeuf was particularly positively evaluated, with his Conspiracy presented as 'the apogee of the class struggle in the history of the Revolution'.[78] The biography at the end of the course confirmed this general perspective: the two first books were the ones by Wilhelm Blos (1922 edition) and Karl Kautsky (1920 edition). Then came Kropotkin's book, a few excerpts from Marx (including *The Holy Fam-ily*) and then two titles referred to as 'bourgeois' but nonetheless useful: the German edition of Alphonse Aulard's *Histoire politique de la Révolution fran-çaise* (edited by Hedwig Hintze),[79] and the 1922 translation of Georges Bourgin's book on the French Revolution.

Thus in the absence of a specifically Communist historiography, the Marxist reference points for the 'Great Revolution' were still the re-editions of works by pre-1914 German Social Democrats. This may seem surprising given the Com-munists' hatred for the 'renegade Kautsky' and the positions this latter had taken with regard to the Bolshevik Revolution. But the 'orthodox' Kautsky's

---

75   Duncker (et al.) 1930.
76   Duncker (et al.) 1930, p. 1.
77   Duncker (et al.) 1930, p. 29.
78   Ibid.
79   On Hedwig Hintze see Chapter Eleven, p. 275.

pre-1914 writings were considered with great respect, with the Russian social-democrats-become-communists having heavily drawn on his writings for their own doctrine. These bibliographical choices moreover had some relation with what was now happening in the USSR: indeed, we can see the structure of this German course as echoing the re-publication of works of Kautsky's in the Soviet Union up till the mid-1920s.[80] As Tamara Kondratieva has observed, up till 1926–7 Soviet historiography largely retraced the same lines as German Social-Democratic historiography: the basic works cited were Kautsky, Blos and Cunow's books, which were quite simply the only Marxist works on this theme available in Russian.[81]

Two further examples – this time, by dissident communists – attest to the perennial influence of the pre-war vulgate. Born in 1874,[82] Otto Rühle joined the SPD in 1896. After being a member of the editorial staff of numerous papers he became – like Hermann Duncker – an SPD *Wanderlehrer* from 1907 to 1913, as well as a deputy in the Prussian Landtag before his election to the Reichstag. An opponent of World War I, he was among the founders of the KPD, but stood on ultra-Left positions hostile to all electoral participation. A founder of the KAPD, he was very rapidly excluded. Becoming detached from any political affiliation, opposed to parties and unions and close to council communism, he wrote numerous political and historical contributions. Now very distant from the SPD, at the end of the 1920s he wrote a vast, three-book work on the history of revolutions, *The Revolutions in Europe*,[83] which had a certain echo. The second volume, devoted to France from 1789 to 1871, mainly focused on the period from 1789 to 1899.[84] With an abundance of illustrations, the book was very much premised on the individual psychology of the Revolution's main actors, but certain of its characterisations showed its derivation from a Marxist analytical framework. From the first page he emphasised that the Revolution was 'capitalist' in character and the work of the 'bourgeois class'. Indeed, he very repeatedly reasserted the bourgeois character of the Revolution up to the end of this study.[85] His initial explanations of the contradictions of the absolute monarchy were a more developed elaboration of the preliminary remarks in Karl

---

80 We have found the following editions of his book on the French Revolution: 1918 (Moscow), 1919 (Moscow) and 1923 (Kharkov) (according to the RGASPI library in Moscow).
81 Kondratieva 1989, p. 185.
82 Groschopp 1994, pp. 406–7.
83 Indeed, Hermann Duncker held certain aspects of this work in great esteem. See Groschopp 1994, p. 406.
84 Covering pp. 1 to 212 out of this volume's 336 pages.
85 Rühle 1927, Vol. 2, p. 206. The Revolution meant 'all for the bourgeois' (p. 78) and 'nothing for the workers' (Ibid.).

Kautsky's book. His presentation of the different social forces ('the bourgeoisie') was also based on a similar structure. As for the unfolding of the Revolution itself, his attention to the political clubs, their conflicts and social forces followed on from the main themes in Heinrich Cunow's *Die Parteien*.[86] Finally Otto Rühle positively evaluated the efforts of the Hébertists[87] and presented Babeuf – in classic fashion – as the precursor to the socialist movement. Part of his explanations and analysis thus adopted a number of elements from Social-Democratic works.[88] Together with this inheritance Otto Rühle elaborated at some length on the personalities of the actors involved and their role, in order to inform an understanding of the revolutionary process. Before the war he had published *The Proletarian Child*,[89] which greatly influenced Social-Democratic pedagogues and was also one of the first books – along with the works of Wilhelm Reich – to set Marxism in relation with psychoanalysis. This book was part of a more general craze for explaining social phenomena in psychological terms.[90] We should understand his negative assessments of Marat, Robespierre and other revolutionary figures in this context.[91]

For his part, Max Beer took up the 1890s project of a general history of socialism. This was a personal – and this time successfully completed – endeavour, a *General History of Socialism and Social Struggles* first published in a series of tomes between 1921 and 1923.[92] The whole text was reproduced in a single volume by a Communist publisher in 1932 together with supplements by Hermann Duncker on the history of the KPD and Communist International.[93] It is worth briefly mentioning Beer's trajectory, for the purposes of understanding the fate of his book.[94] Born in 1864, he soon moved to Berlin (in 1889) and joined the SPD. He was *Vorwärts*'s London correspondent from 1901 to 1911, and in 1913 wrote a *History of British Socialism*.[95] He joined the German Communist

---

86   Cunow 1912.
87   See Chapter Five, p. 5.
88   In terms of its bibliography, as well as referencing Aulard's political history Beer mentioned the Social-Democratic classics, while also presenting Kropotkin as one of his main sources. Also worth noting is the presence of Hans von Hentig's book, which was very hostile to Robespierre.
89   Rühle 1911.
90   In one text Paul Mattick, one of the KAPD's major theorists, aptly emphasised the influence of psychology among the 1920s German ultra-Left. See Mattick 1920.
91   Rühle 1927, Vol. 2, p. 122.
92   Beer 1921–3.
93   Beer 1932. We will cite from this version; the English edition translated by H.J. Stenning has considerable omissions.
94   Barck 1945, p. 56.
95   Beer 1913 (English edition – Beer 1920).

Party in 1919 but soon returned to the SPD, which he left again in 1923. It was during this latter spell in the SPD that he wrote his *General History of Socialism and Social Struggles*. In 1927 he moved to Moscow, where he took charge of the English and American section of the Marx-Engels Institute's library, before returning to Germany and Frankfurt's Institut für Sozialforschung. His *History* had a wide distribution running to some tens of thousands of copies. He knew French and wrote numerous contributions on Jean Jaurès.[96]

The fourth part of his *History* was devoted to the period 1750–1860: as with this work as a whole, this was a history not of the Revolution itself but of the way in which socialist and communist ideas had cut through this era. Marat and *l'Ami du peuple* were set in the foreground, whereas Robespierre was presented as having broken the development of advanced ideas, even if 'unconsciously'.[97] He placed particular value on Roux and Hébert's role as precursors of socialism; still, the central question was the matter of alliances between the government and the popular movement, reflecting the author's interrogation of the problem of social and political conflicts in a revolutionary process.[98] There were a few considerations on 'L'Ange' taken from Jaurès, while one chapter was devoted to Babeuf. Here again, the bibliography very clearly reflected the presence of the Social-Democratic reference points Cunow, Kautsky, and Blos and his editions of Buonarroti and Kropotkin. Also worth noting is a more developed part on the French Revolution's influence in Germany, situating it as a major event also in the latter country's national history: the bibliography also featured Franz Mehring's *Deutsche Geschichte*, itself the product of the SPD's pre-1914 party school. The specific chapter on Babeuf also resembled what had been taught in that school twenty years previously.

Pursuing very different projects for writing the history of the French Revolution, these three 'communist' examples – with all their varied results – each expressed forms of continuity with these men's former party. They had all belonged to the SPD and all continued to write books or education programmes including the French Revolution that were based on the pre-1914 Social-Democratic vulgate. This vulgate thus had a considerable posterity among the political currents breaking from the SPD – from orthodox Communism to Otto Rühle's 'ultra-Left' eclecticism – even after it had fallen out of repute in the party that had instigated it.

---

96   Particularly Beer 1918. See also Haupt 1969.
97   Beer 1932, p. 393.
98   Beer 1932, pp. 394–5.

New Readings of the French Revolution

The mid-1920s saw the emergence of a series of new Social-Democratic publications and periodicals. Not only did the SPD now establish links with academics, but party members like Hermann Wendel also began publishing books and articles on the French Revolution outside of the usual networks. Adding to this picture were changes in how history was written, inscribing the reference to the French Revolution in a very different register to that of the previous decade.

The Academic Milieu: the Example of Hedwig Hintze

Beyond the few Social-Democrats with university posts such as Heinrich Cunow at the University of Berlin, certain academics expressed liberal or even social-democratic views. Apart from the 'pure products' of the SPD like Cunow, there also developed a movement among figures hitherto external to the party's history but sympathetic to its cause. In 1928 Gustav Stresemann, Foreign Minister of a coalition government including the SPD, gave impulse to a policy of rapprochement with France via his French alter ego Aristide Briand. The values of 1789 constituted a rallying point for those who supported French-German friendship. The years 1928 to 1930 corresponded to the apogee of liberal and social-democratic writing on the European question: indeed, numerous intellectuals supported this French-German rapprochement policy, considering it an essential element of the European identity now being constructed.[1]

Moreover, we can see that in these years scholarly debates on the French Revolution in SPD organs became increasingly autonomous and further-removed from activist perspectives, at the same time as history itself became less important within the party's traditional structures. Walter Markov has noted that as the echoes of the revolutionary tumult drifted further into the past historians could devote themselves to more 'tranquil' research on the Revolution.[2] This development should be connected to a more general trend: indeed, here we should also mention the French situation, even though it was

---

1 Chabot 2005.
2 'Once the revolutionary situation had passed ... Jacobinism and the Terror were reduced – by the grace of God – to the purely academic level, no longer troubling people's minds. It was possible to devote oneself to tranquil research': Markov 1974, p. 62.

clearly different from what was happening in Germany. Writing on the times of Georges Lefebvre and the 1937 creation of the Institut d'Histoire de la Révolution française, Alice Gérard notes that 'in becoming professional, in cutting the ties that had hitherto connected the political history of the Revolution and political journalism, this more scholarly history [lost] its audience'.[3]

Nonetheless, the fact that some academics drew closer to social democracy remained a marginal development compared to the wider tendencies in German academia, which very largely remained conservative throughout the Weimar period. Here there was nothing comparable to the influence an academic like Albert Mathiez had in France (and we will return to the question of his exchanges with German historians) or the later case of Georges Lefebvre. After the First World War 'in the period of the Weimar Republic, the conservative or nationalist-minded majority of German historians was far from any idea of a radical and democratic transformation of the state and social order'.[4] Again we can mention the historian Walter Markov's own testimony, since the first courses that he followed on the French Revolution dated from this same era:

> As for me ... I still have the vivid memory of someone who was there. I was a student and I followed Brandenburg's courses on the French Revolution in Leipzig, Ziekursch's ones in Cologne and Oncken[5] and Hedwig Hintze's ones in Berlin ... While in his courses Brandenburg expanded upon the lines traced out by Sybel and Seignobos, while continuing to give a Rankean primacy to *Aussenpolitik* [foreign policy], Oncken acquainted German students with the controversy between Aulard and Mathiez while rejecting this latter's petit-bourgeois radicalism as 'excessive'.[6]

It is worth noting that this phenomenon was even more accentuated in Austria's universities, given the dominance of a strong anti-republican sentiment. Felix Kreissler described the atmosphere of hostility toward the Social Democrats in Austrian academia:

> Both the professorial corps and the student guilds were of a profoundly retrograde, romantic, pan-Germanist mould, and anything but republican ... the students did not limit themselves to the 'arms of the spirit' but mounted daily physical attacks against Jewish, Social-Democratic or

3 Gerard 1970, p. 87.
4 Grab 1983, p. 315.
5 Wilhelm Oncken was an exponent of traditional, conservative Prussian historiography.
6 Markov 1974, pp. 62–3.

even simply liberal students. In this they fully enjoyed the support of the academic authorities from rectors to deans, professors and assistants.[7]

The situation in Germany was more contradictory. Heinz Sproll's study[8] distinguishes between three sensibilities in Germany's universities during the Weimar Republic. The first, conservative sensibility was embodied by Adalbert Wahl at Tübingen University. The second was the liberal current around Friedrich Meinecke, who though not having writing a specific book on the French Revolution did include the reforms under the French occupation as part of the continuity of Prussian history.[9] A 'rational republican' (*Vernunftrepublikaner*), Meinecke favoured a parliamentary democracy balanced by extensive presidential powers, and wanted a large party stretching from the right wing of social democracy to the more moderate nationalists. He particularly elaborated his conceptions in his 1924 work *The Idea of Raison d'État in the New History*.[10] One of the most renowned exponents of 'historism',[11] he defended the unique character of great national units as against the abstractions of the Enlightenment, and wanted to maintain certain forms of the old Germany by democratising them from above, through the state. The third current ran from left-wing liberals to intellectuals close to the Social-Democrats.

A Singular Trajectory

The historian Hedwig Hintze was a telling example of this third current. Rather, she was an exceptional case insofar as she was an academic historian – often presented as a left-wing liberal – who drew close to the Social Democracy without ever to our knowledge formally becoming a member. Her many articles and reviews published in *Die Gesellschaft* and *Sozialistische Monatshefte* evidence her political proximity to the SPD.[12] Born in 1884, this historian of some renown in the German-speaking world[13] owed her formation entirely to the

---

7   Kreissler 1994, p. 123.
8   Sproll 1992, p. 24.
9   On these aspects, consult the Institut d'Histoire de la Révolution française website, which features a set of notes on a 1926 course by Friedrich Meinecke: http://ihrf.univ-paris1.fr/spip.php?article99.
10   Meinecke 1924.
11   Escudier 2006.
12   H. Hintze, 'Staatseinheit und Föderalismus in Frankreich', *Sozialistische Monatshefte*, 1927, pp. 364–71.
13   There is a Hedwig Hintze-Institut in Bremen.

university, unlike a great number of Social-Democratic cadres.[14] Coming from a Munich Jewish family and married to the historian Otto Hintze in 1912, she pursued her studies at Berlin University, in 1919 attending Friedrich Meinecke's course on 'The era of the French Revolution and the war of liberation'. In the 1920s she took an interest in the genesis of the French state, and in particular the question of centralisation. In 1923 she authored a *Dissertation* on 'The problem of federalism at the beginning of the French Revolution',[15] which notably earned the appreciation of Friedrich Meinecke; in 1924 she achieved her doctorate *summa cum laude*. The same year she published an introduction to the translation of Alphonse Aulard's *Political History of the French Revolution*, which she annotated for the German reader.[16] Aulard's work enjoyed a major reception in Germany in the guise of a 'recent new title'.[17] In her introduction Hintze evoked the idea of the 'United States of Europe', praising the French revolutionary inheritance as something that the Germans ought to appropriate for the contemporary era.[18] The idea was to combat militarism – be it French or German – by way of the ideal of 1789.

In this Hedwig Hintze joined a trend with a certain echo in the German Left of that time. Indeed, from the mid-1920s there was a certain elaboration of the idea of the 'United States of Europe': for example in 1924 the socialist Edo Fimmen, leader of the International Federation of Trade Unions and a leading pacifist figure, published a book in Jena entitled *The United States of Europe or Europe*.[19] As against the 'international of Capital', Edo Fimmen advocated that trade union forces internationally rally around the common slogan of the 'Workers' United States of Europe' – much resembling what the Third (Communist) International itself called for. Numerous endeavours sought to concretise this slogan. Among these we could cite Alfred Nossig's July 1926 initiative, organising meetings in the capitals of Europe in order to create a 'Federation for European Entente' on the preparatory basis of an international committee. After a first meeting in London on 1 July 1926, Nossig organised a second meeting in Paris on 12 July chaired by the former French premier Paul Painlevé. The participants included figures from numerous European countries and the most varied political parties, including the French historian Alphonse

---

14   For a bibliography of this historian, little-known in France, see Deppe and Dickmann 1997. See in particular Schöck-Quinteros's piece 'Hedwig Hintze 1884–1942. Ein biographischer Abriss' on pp. 9–10. For one of the first studies on Hintze, see Schleier 1975, pp. 272–302.
15   Schleier 1975, p. 276.
16   Aulard 1924.
17   Markov 1977, p. 64.
18   In her introduction to Aulard 1924, p. xiii.
19   Fimmen 1924. For a biography of the author see Bushack 2002.

Aulard. This committee decided to call a 'Conference for European Entente', to be held in Geneva on 2 September that same year. For the most part composed of French and German participants, and chaired by the former French minister Émile Borel, the Conference decided to constitute Nossig's planned Federation.[20] Echoing these initiatives, in a 1926 piece for the *Frankfurter Zeitung* Hedwig Hintze looked back to the publication of Aulard's *Political History* ..., linking her work as a historianto her engagement in support of the Weimar Republic:

> in the era of our young German Republic's continued struggle to establish itself, I think that it was a national responsibility, in the best sense of the word, to present to my compatriots a celebrated model of republican and democratic struggle and its success.[21]

The same year that this piece was published, in 1926, Hedwig Hintze became a contributor to the reviews section of the prestigious *Historische Zeitschrift*, at that time edited by Friedrich Meinecke.[22] Her role up till 1933 was essentially limited to reviewing works on the French Revolution, including those written by Albert Mathiez. While these reviews were often very short, they nonetheless showed that the German historian was informed about recent developments in French historiography on the Revolution.

Passing her *Habilitation* in 1929 with her study on *The Unity of the State and Federalism in Ancien Régime France and During the Revolution*, it was this work that made her name, as she became the second woman in German history to pass the *Habilitation*.[23] Lecturing as a *Privatdozentin* at Berlin University from this date onward, she did not occupy any important university post: the *Privatdozent* had no chair and was not paid by the university, but only by the students attending the course.

Her first lecture, concerning 'bourgeois and socialist' historians – which we will study later in the present volume – was published in the German Social Democrats' theoretical review *Die Gesellschaft*.[24] The list of her courses from 1929 and 1933 shows the clear predominance of the French Revolution:

---

20   As well as Chabot 2005 see Lorrain 1999.
21   H. Hintze 'Geist von Locarno und historische Kritik', *Frankfurter Zeitung*, 14 February 1926.
22   On the history of this publication see Gall 2009. The journal was directed by Heinrich von Sybel (1859–95) Heinrich von Treitschke (1895–6) and then Friedrich Meinecke (1896–1935).
23   Schöck-Quinteros 1997, p. 10.
24   Hintze 1929.

'Overview of French constitutional history in the Middle Ages and the
modern era (1929). Introduction to the study of the sources of the French
Revolution (1929–30). History of French socialism (1930). Debates on the
history of the French Revolution (1931). Overview of German and French
constitutional history (1931–2). History of the French Revolution' (1932–
3).[25]

Hedwig Hintze lost her job after the Nazis came to power in 1933, and headed
to Parisian exile. She then moved to the Netherlands, after briefly returning
to Germany. In 1942, faced with certain deportation, she preferred to kill herself.

Studying Federalism[26]

Our concern here is not to present all the points raised by Hintze's book, or
even to mount a detailed study of its reception. After all, this was a principally
academic work distributed outside of Social-Democratic networks and only
partially devoted to the French Revolution. Nonetheless, it is worth presenting its essential ideas: situated in the context of her own epoch, they show
the importance of the late 1920s debate on 'federalism'[27] cutting through all
political currents. Indeed, this work reviewed the questions of 'federalism'
and centralisation, 'state unity' [*Staatseinheit*], and decentralisation and its
different declinations under the *ancien régime* and then during the French
Revolution: for example, it was from this perspective that it studied Necker and
Calonne's pre-revolutionary projects. Hintze repeatedly mentioned Proudhon's
ideas, and her sympathies clearly lay with the Girondins (as against Sieyès, held
among other things to be the bearer of a 'fanaticism for unification').[28] For her,
their failure marked the end of a certain idea of federalism. This learned work
studied everything that could be interpreted as 'decentralisation' measures: the
law creating the *départements* (and the disappearance of the old provinces)
together with numerous citations and translations of parliamentary speeches;
the degree to which the *communes* were autonomous during the revolutionary

---

25   *Vorlesungsverzeichnisse der Friedrich-Wilhelms-Universität zu Berlin*, 1929–33.
26   Hintze 1928.
27   On the meaning of Federation (*Bund*) and the debates on what this term signified, see
       Koselleck 1997, pp. 121–135.
28   Hintze 1928, p. 3.

process; and political currents' different perceptions of centralisation and the form of the republic.[29] Hintze took a position in a lineage we can compare to Tocqueville's study of the continuity of the statethrough the *ancien régime* and the Revolution:[30] she elaborated the history of the federal idea as incarnated in the succession of political forms appearing throughout France's history. Logically enough, in the course of her argument she evoked 'the Montagne' and its 'dictatorial role'.[31] However, while in her conclusion she attacked 'centralisation' and 'dictatorship', she did not cast her opprobrium on the whole of the Montagnards' efforts, noting that in difficult historical circumstances they had shown a certain effectiveness.[32]

Such arguments can only be understood within a political context in which the partisans of strengthened centralisation and presidential power were becoming increasingly important. Across the course of the 1920s critiques of the 'régime of the parties' [*Parteienstaat*] proliferated: the parliamentary system became the target of a 'conservative revolution', one of whose most renowned exponents was the jurist Carl Schmitt.[33] The idea of reforming the Constitution and strengthening the powers of the President of the Republic – at that time elected by universal suffrage – was widely debated. The *Bund zur Erneuerung des Reiches* ['League for the Renovation of the Reich'] founded by Wilhelm Cuno in 1928 advocated the strengthening of the president's powers and the greater centralisation of powers.[34] Numerous reforms were proposed in this context, and the Weimar Republic sharply developed toward an ever-more presidential régime. The political crisis was soon doubled by the heavy impact of the 1929 world economic crisis, which hit Germany particularly hard. The conflict between different authorities in any case went back to the origins of the Republic itself, when it had been necessary to delimit the powers of the National Assembly as distinct from those of the *Länder*. Hostile to the 'unitarists', the Prussian Justice Minister had declared:

If the revolution had begun from a central point ... that met with a unitarist German sentiment, it would have been possible to get from that to a

---

29   Hintze 1928, pp. 270–1.
30   It is worth noting that Tocqueville was well-known in Germany: Kautsky had used him as a reference point as early as 1889.
31   Hintze 1928, p. 322.
32   Hintze 1928, p. 471.
33   On the debates of this era see Beaud 2002, pp. 125–49.
34   Baechler 2007, p. 295.

centralised Germany. But the Revolution began as a series of local revolutions, and we have to do nothing more than bring together what took form
by itself.[35]

Indeed, there were regular conflicts between the Republic and the *Länder*, for
example in Saxony and Thuringia where in 1923 a ruling coalition of Communists and Social Democrats was broken up by the central authorities. The
historian Albert Mathiez aptly – if bluntly – emphasised that Hedwig Hintze's
book should be understood in this context. His critical review appearing in
the *Annales historiques de la Révolution Française* moreover gives an interesting idea of how French historiography perceived this debate.[36] Indeed, while
recognising this book's 'valuable qualities' and its great erudition Mathiez
sought to refute its essential argument. Noting the 'very determinate and very
current political goals' to which this work corresponded – namely, the debate
on federalism in Germany – Mathiez considered the term 'federalism' as itself
being anachronistic, a contemporary and specifically German reality grafted
onto France's past. Hintze was researching realities that had nothing to do with
her understanding of them, 'blinded by her partiality to find federalism where
not even its shadow existed'.[37] On account of her own convictions the author
had totally overestimated the role of 'federalism' in the 1793 debates, where
it had been of only 'subsidiary' importance. Colouring the French historian's
whole review was his reproach that Hintze was favourable to Aulard and hostile
to the Montagnards. Mathiez showed himself to be strongly critical of those like
Hintze who advocated French-German rapprochement on the basis of a federal
structure inspired by the Girondins of the French Revolution, as he wryly criticised 'a hymn to the future United States of Europe'.[38] Conversely, the 21 April
1929 edition of the SPD daily *Vorwärts* gave a positive account of Hintze's book,
attesting to her links with that party.[39]

In discussing these debates it is worth dwelling on Hintze's historiographical interests. At the end of her book Hintze recognised what she owed to
Jaurès's authority, citing his *Armée nouvelle*;[40] it was also from him that she

---

35   Möller 2005, p. 134.
36   Mathiez 1928.
37   Mathiez 1928, p. 583.
38   Mathiez 1928, p. 577.
39   'Hedwig Hintze', *Vorwärts*, 21 April 1929, p. 8. Also note the critical review by the 'ultra-
      leftist' Karl Korsch, highlighted by Haupt 1980, p. 30. See Korsch 1996, pp. 406–7.
40   Hintze 1928, p. 486.

took 'the class struggle' as a factor of historical explanation. Her Chapter Fifteen on the battles at the Convention de *l'Histoire socialiste de la Révolution française* would be very widely used for understanding the motivations of the various different political groups. This was important insofar as it effectively meant the first real introduction of Jaurès in Germany. However, the historian very little interrogated – if at all – Jaurès position regarding Robespierre or how far the link between the Republic and socialism was specific to him.

It was above all in Hintze's significant article on the historiography of the French Revolution, published in the SPD review *Die Gesellschaft*, that Jaurès occupied a major role.[41] This historiographical study on Taine, Aulard, Jaurès and Mathiez, taken from her *Habilitation* on 'bourgeois and socialist' historians, began with a general historiographical recap, mentioning the most renowned examples (Quinet, Michelet, Tocqueville). For her, Taine was an important historiographical milestone despite his very marked political bearings.[42] She sought to challenge the simplistic idea – often present in the French historiography – that Aulard's 'democratic' interpretation had taken over from Taine's conservative reading. The historian reviewed the numerous critical pieces on Taine (including Gabriel Monod's 9 July 1904 contribution to the *Revue bleue*),[43] highlighting Mathiez's early hostility toward this representative of the 'ferocious spirit of the property-owner'[44] as well as Aulard's famous hostility in declaring that 'to understand [Taine] you'd have to love him'.[45] According to Hintze, Aulard's work was marked by a certain naivety, assimilating the Revolution to 'the people' without noting the preponderant role that the bourgeoisie had occupied therein.[46] Moreover, she did not think that Aulard had good cause to reproach Taine's impartiality, given his Dantonist fervour. Despite the merits of his *Political History ...* 'what is most missing in Aulard's work is that he does not delve into the economic and social conditions of the events of the Revolution'.[47] This comment served as the bridge to 'the new and major advances of the historiography of the Revolution, which owes above all to the genial élan and inspiring example of Jean Jaurès'.[48] Hintze provided several bio-

---

41   Hintze 1929.
42   Hintze 1929, p. 74.
43   See in particular Aulard 1907.
44   Hintze 1929, p. 76 (she cites this in French).
45   Hintze 1929, p. 77 (she cites this in French).
46   Hintze 1929, p. 80.
47   Ibid.
48   Hintze 1929, p. 81.

graphical considerations on the French socialist, describing the conditions in which his *Histoire socialiste* ... was produced; his desire for a synthesis between Michelet and Marx; and finally the relations between Jaurès and Aulard, including how the former's book was received in the latter's review *La Révolution française*.[49]

These were so many elements lacking any great historiographical originality. But what they did do was present Jaurès and the context of his academic reception to an audience of SPD cadres and intellectuals that was all the more unaware of Jaurès's historical conceptions given his very weak prior reception in Germany. Translating from the French, Hintze cited numerous extracts from the general introduction to Jaurès's *Histoire Socialiste* ..., which as we have seen contained an exposition of his method. As compared to the abstract 'people' appearing in Michelet and Aulard's works, Jaurès had opened up new perspectives: indeed, 'helped by his book we can now understand the composition of the different layers of the people in the different phases of the French Revolution'.[50] Nonetheless, again here she only brought into relief Jaurès the historian, barely referring to his role in the socialist movement and the Second International. She did not mention either the Social-Democratic critiques of Jaurès between 1900 and 1904 or Eduard Bernstein's favourable response. There was no reference to Karl Kautsky – even though he so esteemed Taine's work that he used it as the documentary basis for *Die Klassengegensätze von 1789* – or to Heinrich Cunow.

Having shown that under Jaurès's influence Aulard had been compelled to take economic interpretations into account, Hintze turned from Jaurès to Mathiez, via this latter's 1922–4 re-publication of the *Histoire socialiste* ...[51] In this same spirit she provided a series of pieces of factual information on Mathiez, from the creation of the Société des Études Robespierristes to the birth of the *Annales Historiques de la Révolution française*, as well as a summary of his main works published thus far. As against Aulard, Mathiez was presented as a 'fanatical partisan of Robespierre';[52] Hintze explained his arguments in defence of *l'Incorruptible*, again making extensive use of translated quotations. While criticising the French historian's excessive Robespierrism, she recognised his great qualities and his immense contribution to the understanding of the revolutionary process, in particular as concerned the conflict between

---

49   Aulard 1902.
50   Hintze 1929, p. 81.
51   Jaurès 1922–4.
52   Hintze 1929, p. 90.

Girondins and Montagnards.[53] The article ended with a very long quotation from Jaurès exalting what the Revolution had accomplished.

Hintze in fact stood far from the intellectual profile of a figure like Karl Kautsky.[54] An academic, she wrote for *Die Gesellschaft* and only published in the 'big' reviews, without participating in the elaboration of the Social-Democratic vulgate. However, while her conception of history remained at a distance from the pre-war Marxist orthodoxy as embodied by the writings of Kautsky and Cunow, Hedwig Hintze did not reject all interpretations resulting from the pre-1914 socialist and social-democratic production, and she studied Mathiez's works attentively. If in the overwhelmingly conservative environment of the German university even Aulard's book was perceived as a 'recent new title',[55] this sense of novelty applied still further to Mathiez and – even more so – Jaurès's work. Hintze thus occupied a unique position in Germany, allowing her to help introduce both Aulard and Mathiez. Her testimonial upon the death of Albert Mathiez for the *Annales historiques de la Révolution française* attests to the meetings between the two historians and their good relations.[56] Noting that she had above all been in contact with Alphonse Aulard in the context of the translation of his *Histoire politique*, she commented that it was she herself who had first brought Mathiez to Germany through her reviews in the *Historische Zeitschrift* and above all with her first lecture on the French historiography, published in *Die Gesellschaft*. She referred to several stays in Paris in 1929–30 which had allowed her to attend his courses. According to this piece, Mathiez had offered his 'Thanks to you, Madame' for having introduced his works to Germany via the *Historische Zeitschrift*.[57]

A New History Writing

Hermann Wendel's approaches in a sense set him halfway between the pre-1914 Social-Democratic tradition – of which he had been one of the most eminent representatives – and these new conceptions standing at some distance from

---

53 For example, she noted that there was no German translation of *La réaction thermidorienne*, while it did exist in English, Russian and Norwegian.

54 This did not stop there being certain links between them, as demonstrated by her requests for Kautsky's help.

55 Markov 1977, p. 64.

56 Hintze 1932.

57 In return Mathiez had an article of Hedwig Hintze's translated into French: Hintze 1932b. Here she presented Goethe's evolving positions on the French Revolution, notably at the moment of the trial of Louis XVI.

the party-members' vulgate. Already renowned before the war, he became a major figure in the Social Democracy: a historian whose pieces on revolutionary history had a major echo.

Hermann Wendel in *Die Gesellschaft* and *Vorwärts*

Hermann Wendel was one of the regular contributors to *Die Gesellschaft*, principally writing on historical questions. Like Heinrich Cunow he illustrates a form of continuity with the pre-war period: from his reviews for *Die Gesellschaft* to his 1930 biography of Danton, he showed a continued interest in the French Revolution.[58] A major figure in Frankfurt Social Democracy prior to 1914, in 1922 he became a journalist at the *Frankfurter Zeiting*, a liberal paper that opened up its columns to the German Left. As in the case of the university, this type of collaboration would have been unthinkable a decade previously. Under the Weimar Republic he was a recognised Social-Democratic intellectual and probably one of those in the SPD who best knew France, its history and its political life.

In continuity with pre-1914 approaches he took an interest in the emergence of the first workers' struggles during the bourgeois revolutions: hence his combined review of two books, one by Grace M. Jaffé on the workers' movement in Paris between 1789 and 1791 – one of the first syntheses on this subject[59] – and Max Quarck's work on the 'first German workers' movement'.[60] While Jaurès and Kropotkin had each addressed this subject, here Wendel emphasised that these studies mobilised a more substantial set of sources. Referencing the question of the Le Chapelier law – which, he noted, Marx had termed the 'bourgeois' law *par excellence* – he set the French Revolution back within the habitual conceptual framework holding that 'at its origins it represented the triumph of the bourgeoisie which, once the battle was won, tried to exploit its victory'.[61]

Reading *Vorwärts*, for which Wendel was a regular contributor, we see that references to the 'Great Revolution' had not totally disappeared from its pages. Without doubt, on 14 July 1929 it did more to commemorate the anniversary of the Second International than the birth of the French Revolution. It only pointed to a few of the episodes of 1789, though it did also establish a connection with 1929, in accordance with the Social-Democratic press's ritualistic formulas:

58   Hermann 1930.
59   Jaffé 1924.
60   Die Gesellschaft, 1925, pp. 280–3.
61   *Die Gesellschaft*, 1925, p. 281.

In 1789 the people broke open the dungeons of royal power, in the first revolutionary uprising to secure the rights of man and the citizen anywhere on the European continent ...

In 1889 the proletariat woke up, becoming conscious of its strength ...

In 1929 the socialist youth of all countries sends its representatives to Vienna.

Our ancestors conquered the Bastille in one of those fits of despair characteristic of the downtrodden. Our fathers founded unions and parties which opposed the bourgeois world with the ordered strength of the organised working class. Our youth, the fighters of tomorrow, are the ambassadors of the future, of the will for renewal in millions of hope-filled hearts: the future is ours![62]

Hermann Wendel pursued his interest in the Revolution in a wholly different context. On 15 July 1929 he published a major commemorative piece, 'The storming of the Bastille 1789–14 July 1929'.[63] 14 July was the 'springtime of humanity'.[64] Wendel cited a few of the big names of German culture like Klopstock and Goethe ('This time and place marked a new era in world history').[65] Emphasising that in its time the Revolution had been above all bourgeois, he also insisted that its importance went beyond that:

That is why the working class, aspiring to socialism through democracy, has rightly picked up the sublime principles of 1789, why *Liberté Égalité Fraternité* is also their motto, and why their fight is nonetheless fought for the ideal for which the men of 14 July gave their lives.[66]

This was followed by a reminder of the foundation of the Second International and of the numerous Bastilles that still had to be stormed. This article should be compared to another piece by the same author appearing less than a month later, on 10 August 1929, upon the tenth anniversary of the Weimar Constitution.[67] Wendel marked this anniversary by emphasising the inheritance of the Revolution and its worldwide significance. For him, this ought to be compared to the lack of 'brilliance' in the commemoration of the Weimar Republic:

---

62   Ibid.
63   'Der Bastillesturm 1789–14. Juli 1929', *Vorwärts*, 15 July 1929, p. 4.
64   Ibid.
65   Ibid.
66   Ibid.
67   Wendel, H., '1919–1929 10 Jahre Weimarer Verfassung', *Vorwärts*, 10 August 1929, p. 5.

If the French national day of 14 July refers to an event of worldwide importance, the storming of the Bastille, which continues to inspire the masses' imagination, the national day of the German Republic, 11 August, apparently lacks any outward brilliance; it is almost a routine matter, for what distinguishes it from the other 364 days of the year is the issue of the official gazette that set the Weimar Republic in operation.[68]

The next day, in the supplement to the 11 August issue, an article by Wendel presented the great dates from 1789 to 1919 worthy of commemoration ... In all these articles there was no mention of anything but 1789 – or, to be precise, 1789 and 1792. There was no mention of the Terror, the 1793 Constitution or Babeuf, but only of the beginning of the Revolution. It is worth comparing these choices – concentrating on the 'moderate' episodes of the revolutionary process – with the Danton biography that Wendel published a few months after these articles.

Danton as Seen by Wendel

Wendel in fact published two books in the early 1930s, one devoted to Danton and the other to portraits of great figures in France's history.[69] Henceforth Wendel no longer published within the Social-Democratic apparatus but with the major literary publisher Ernst Rowohlt Verlag.[70] As compared to his history of Frankfurt written twenty years earlier, these two books demonstrated a transition from a history of economic and social structures to a history more centred on revolutionary events and the role played by great figures. Wendel's biography of Danton, a highly narrative and almost novelised historical work without notes,[71] was designed for a wide audience: it related in detail the unfolding of the Revolution, including its best-known events. It provided a handsome portrayal of the final conflict with Robespierre. Nonetheless, the bibliography pointed to numerous academic references, including the works of Aulard and Mathiez, which had not been cited as such in the text itself.

---

68   Ibid.
69   Wendel 1930 (English edition: 1936), 1932.
70   Gieselbusch et al. 2008.
71   'Desmoulins ..., Barère, Robespierre, Couthon ... none of them knew the other; none of them knew Danton. And yet Danton was destined to meet all of them on his road through life, and some of them on his way to the grave'. Wendel 1936, p. 27.

Although he concentrated his attention on leading personalities, some of Wendel's formulas and analyses demonstrated this work's ancestry in a Social-Democratic lineage that considered the revolutionary process as a bourgeois revolution. 'Yet a single walk through the streets sufficed to show how the new class, the bourgeoisie, was elbowing its way ahead'.[72] Numerous examples show the place of economic and social history therein; the Revolution was incarnated by the 'revolutionary bourgeoisie', and indeed the presence of Kautsky, Kropotkin and Jaurès[73] in the bibliography at the end of this volume ought to be set in this same analytical framework. Nonetheless, this approach – and this type of formulation – had little presence in this volume, and only marginally affected to the style of a biography aimed at the wider public and centred on a positive evaluation of Danton's activity. Indeed, while Wendel's book was not hagiographical it did present Danton in a very favourable light. There was an abundance of positive formulations, as Wendel spoke of Danton's 'sense of realities',[74] 'evident moderation',[75] 'Danton's fierce energy ... an elixir of life for millions'[76] and his being 'guided by an almost infallible instinct as to what was possible and necessary'.[77] The formulations should be compared to what he said of the other Montagnards, including on the subject of Marat and the massacres of September 1792: he referred to the 'September massacres' as 'the realization of Marat's dreams',[78] the better to clear Danton's name.[79] As for Robespierre: 'the urge to destroy whoever threatened to hinder the progress of the Revolution swept aside every inhibition of this cold calculator'.[80] The rivalry between the two revolutionaries was the object of the final part of the book, with Wendel particularly stigmatising a Robespierre whom he presented as a dictator arrogating all powers to himself.[81] Danton, conversely, had conserved a privileged connection with the people, as against the Hébertists and the Enragés with their excessive demands.[82] He was the

---

72   Wendel 1936, p. 17.
73   His allusion to Barnave – seen as a precursor of socio-economic analyses of the French Revolution – is directly taken from Jaurès.
74   Wendel 1936, p. 58.
75   Wendel 1936, p. ix.
76   Wendel 1936, p. 151.
77   Wendel 1936, p. 179.
78   Wendel 1936, p. 138.
79   Wendel 1936, p. 189.
80   Wendel 1936, p. 184.
81   Wendel 1936.
82   'Jacques-René Hébert edited *Le Père Duchesne*, whose dirty language, vulgar tone and infamous accusations all the other papers paled in comparison with': Wendel 1936, p. 383.

man of synthesis ('Danton was called on to reconcile adversaries and dam the holes in the revolutionary front').[83]

Wendel's other book dealt with personalities from across French history, and not just from the French Revolution.[84] Moreover, those chosen were far from canonical, as he selected an eclectic set of figures in order to draw in the reader: Marie-Antoinette, Louise Contat,[85] Mathilde Bonaparte, Marc-Guillaume Vadier[86] and Bertrand Barère. The variety of other figures included stretched from Joan of Arc to Louise Michel and from Jules Verne to Alexandre Dumas. These were short portraits written in journalistic style: Wendel wanted to bring to life the major moments of French history for his readers, by way of singular personal biographies. Worth noting are the two portraits of Alphonse Aulard[87] and Jean Jaures:[88] the first was presented as the model historian, a champion of scholarship immersed in the archives. Jean Jaurès was also referenced on account of the creation of the economic and social history commission that was founded upon his instigation. The *Histoire socialiste de la Révolution française* was presented as characteristic of his *oeuvre*, mixing materialism and idealism just as his politics stood between reform and revolution.[89] Finally – corresponding to Wendel's own ideals – Jaurès's convictions were portrayed as the 'precursors to an authentic European peace'.[90]

Hermann Wendel's two books were each reviewed by Hedwig Hintze for the SPD journal *Die Gesellschaft*, indicating the existence of an intellectual space where there was real interest in the French Revolution. Hintze briefly retraced the historiography regarding Danton, who had long been identified with Büchner's play before he became a major battleground among historians – hence the great difficulty in establishing his history. She formulated certain criticisms, emphasising Mathiez's great role in adding several elements to the 'charges' against Danton,[91] emphasing that 'even if the proceedings on the Danton affair

---

83 Pierre Caron's preface to the French edition aptly indicates the author's leanings. Noting that Wendel was a member of the *Société d'histoire de la Révolution française* – of which Caron himself was president – he recalled 'the highly-appreciated articles from the Frankfurt Gazette'. Wendel perhaps gave in too much to his 'imaginative intuition' (Wendel 1930b, p. 5) and thus his arguments against Robespierre were too 'harsh' (p. 6).
84 Wendel 1932.
85 An actress of Beaumarchais's, resolutely hostile to the Revolution.
86 President of the Committee of General Security in 1793.
87 Wendel 1932, pp. 201–6.
88 Wendel 1932, pp. 219–23.
89 Wendel 1932, p. 221.
90 Wendel 1932, p. 222.
91 Hintze 1932b, p. 459. She alluded to Mathiez's premature death on 26 February 1932.

are not yet closed, I do not think the moment for an essentially positive bio-graphy is well-chosen, given the difficult state of the controversy'.[92]

This Danton biography without doubt marked an ever-weaker expression of militant history and of the application of historical materialism. This change should be seen in relative terms, insofar as this type of presentation had been widespread in Social-Democratic publications already in the 1880s: the work-ers' almanacs had always had this type of presentations of major figures. Non-etheless, if the negative evaluation of Robespierre and the Terror corresponded to pre-war concerns, now the activity of popular groups like the *sans-culottes* was either criticised or relegated to the background. Here we are very far from the vulgate that saw Hébert as the first socialist, or from any positive appreci-ation of Marat.

Although the Social-Democratic journalist Wendel and the historian Hintze expounded differing points of view and used almost opposite methods, we can nonetheless draw a certain comparison between them. After all, each was the bearer of a significant interest in the Revolution, and in each case this was also linked to a Francophilia that should be considered in connection to their active support for the policy of Franco-German rapprochement. Their positive evalu-ation of the French Revolution implied a reading that excluded its more radical and 'centralising'[93] aspects. Yet however far they stood from the old Social-Democratic vulgate, their references remained inspired by Marxist approaches including Jaurès's conceptions, which now had their first real introduction in Germany.

---

92   Ibid.
93   Such conceptions, long-commonplace across the historiography, have been sharply chal-lenged by recent works. See Biard (ed.) 2008.

Analogies and Controversies: the French Revolution, 1927–34

At the beginning of the 1930s, the critique of the French Revolution and its legacy, which had remained a constant among conservative historians during the Weimar Republic, assumed renewed relevance with the rise of Nazism. 1930 saw the publication of Nazi ideologue Alfred Rosenberg's work *The Myth of the Twentieth Century*. Widely circulated under the Third Reich, this book held the French revolutionary inheritance responsible for all the ills of the past century. He would reassert the main arguments of this book in his famous speech at the Palais Bourbon on 14 July 1940, after the German troops' arrival in Paris.[1]

While perspectives on the French Revolution had changed considerably, it remained an object of polemic that was discussed far beyond expert circles alone. In parallel to the scholarly and academic output, analogies continued to be made with the present-day political situation. For contemporary observers, the repression in Austria in summer 1927 was evocative of July 1791 in France. The consolidation of Soviet power, the growing influence of the KPD and the rise of National Socialism provided an increasing number of reasons to revisit the French Revolution, and especially the 'Terror'. Thus, in parallel to the near-disappearance of specific lessons on the French Revolution in party schools, and its reduced place in the social-democratic publishing machine, a reference to the 'Great Revolution' persisted, as an echo of contemporary events.

A Reduced Place in Educationals and Publications

The New Periodicals

The change in writing on the French Revolution, and the reduced place it now occupied, was apparent across the numerous social-democratic cultural reviews in the late 1920s. One study has shown how social democracy attempted to promote a new culture in this era, especially through the publication of

---

1 Rosenberg 1930: see also his speech 'Das Ende der französischen Revolution', *Völkischer Beobachter*, 14 July 1940, best known in France by way of its refutation by the Communist philosopher Georges Politzer: see Politzer 1947.

a variety of reviews.[2] Among the various important sources, three major publications particularly testify to this commitment during the Weimar Republic, continuing the prewar *Bildung* in a different context. These were *Die Bücherwarte* ['Library Attendant'], *Der Bücherkreis* ['The Book Circle'] and *Kulturwille* ['Will to Culture'].

The book clubs of all political tendencies developed in the mid-1920s. The social-democrats' *Bücherkreis* emerged in 1924.[3] The social-democratic militants who subscribed received not only a book but also the *Bücherkreis* review, sent to members for free.[4] The books published by this club covered a great number of fields, reflecting the different types of titles that social-democratic workers best appreciated: popular science, travel stories, the history of socialism and, most importantly, a very great number of novels,[5] including historical novels. The average print-run for the books stood at 24,000 copies, and the consumption of these works functioned as a closed circuit within social-democratic networks.[6] None of the titles in the book club were histories of the French Revolution as such; the only one that related to this theme was Friedrich Kircheisen's *Die Bastille*.[7] The author was a non-SPD historian, renowned for his works on Napoleon, who favoured French-German rapprochement;[8] this book was a history not of the most famous episode in the Revolution – the storming of the Bastille – but of the prison itself, from its origins until its destruction in 1789. Its second part brought together texts from prisoners of the time, such as Constantin de Renneville and Latude. Rich in illustrations and lacking in notes or precise historical references, the history of the prison was made up of anecdotes from the time as well as individual biographies. This stood very far from any kind of Marxist vulgate, instead bearing closer comparison to the other works circulated by the club, principally meaning novels.

The *Bücherkreis* was also an illustrated cultural review: history seems to have taken a more limited place, and, indeed, over the years historical references played an ever less important role. Short historical articles in 1924 evoked

---

2   Ruthmann 1982.
3   The review bearing the same name as the club was published from 1924 to 1933. It was a monthly up till 1928, when it became a quarterly.
4   Ruthmann 1982, pp. 102–12.
5   Ruthmann 1982, pp. 234–8.
6   Ruthmann 1982, p. 111.
7   Kircheisen 1927.
8   Dunan, M., 'Nécrologie. La vie et l' oeuvre de Kircheisen', *Revues d'études napoléoniennes*, 1933, pp. 317–20.

the Peasant War in Germany, and a few lines from Rousseau and Schiller also appeared in its pages.[9] 1925 saw an homage to Lassalle[10] and a piece on art in the ancient world which noted how the ancient democracy had inspired the revolutionaries of 1789.[11] The only article to mention 1789 in 1929 was devoted to the 'German lyric poetry of the nineteenth and twentieth centuries'.[12]

Bücherwarte was published from 1926 to 1928 and then, after a brief interruption, from 1929 to 1933. It was the monthly organ of the educational commission and so, too, from 1929, of the Zentralstelle für das Arbeiterbüchereiwesen [Central Workers' Libraries Commission]. As of 1926 the review had a print-run of 3,000, and was addressed to the cadres responsible for party education and organising the libraries. Its sizeable bibliographic section, including a great number of book reviews, pursued the work of *Der Bibliothekar*. History occupied a notably weak place, reflecting the lack of publications in this field. One November 1926 issue nonetheless offered a bibliography of the history of revolutions;[13] an introduction emphasised that the bourgeois revolutions were still a contemporary question in the East, and proletarian revolutions were on their way in the West, thus making it necessary to revisit past history. Karl Kautsky, Wilhelm Blos and Heinrich Cunow's books on the French Revolution were listed among the 'best works of Marxist historical literature'.[14] Aulard's work, translated by Hedwig Hintze in 1924, was mentioned as a source on the details of political history. The following year, a review of a book on the French Revolution and the Napoleonic period by Georges Bourgin specified some of the titles that militants may have read;[15] the review did not mention Kautsky and Cunow's books, which were probably assumed to be little-accessible to the wider militant readership. In subsequent years, short reviews highlighted a few recent publications on this subject;[16] the one given greatest pride of place was Hermann Wendel's book on Danton. This was the only major publication on

---

9   *Bücherkreis*, February 1924, pp. 6–7.
10   *Bücherkreis*, July 1925.
11   *Bücherkreis*, August 1925, p. 17.
12   Offenburg, K. 'Deutsche Lyrik des 19. und 20. Jahrhunderts', *Bücherkreis*, October–November 1929, p. 147.
13   Jenssen, O., 'Geschichte der Revolutionen', *Bücherwarte*, 1926, pp. 321–9.
14   Jenssen, O., 'Geschichte der Revolutionen', *Bücherwarte*, 1926, p. 323.
15   Marquardt, E., 'G. Bourgin, Die französische Revolution-Napoleon und seine Zeit', *Bücherwarte*, 1927, p. 239.
16   See, for example, Schröder, K., 'O. Rühle, Die Revolutionen Europas', *Bücherwarte*, 1928, p. 333; Hieber, H., 'Kircheisen Die Bastille', *Bücherwarte*, 1928, p. 355; Friede, W., 'Ehrenburg, Die Verschwörung der Gleichen', *Bücherwarte*, 1929, p. 70.

this theme in this period,[17] and its readable prose allowed for a proper understanding of the revolutionary process and its various protagonists.

Lastly, in the *Kulturwille* (monthly organ of the Leipzig Workers' Educational Institute/ *Arbeiterbildungsinstitut* between 1924 and 1931) cultural subjects again predominated. The visual arts were very much present, as was contemporary literature. This was not a strictly social-democratic review, with communists also participating. It reported on workers' cultural and sporting activities, the 'culture week' programme organised by the SPD, and occasionally published educational guides.[18] Historical subjects had a rather limited place in this publication, but an attentive reading shows that there were several references to the French Revolution. We can cite a few telling examples of this. In February 1924, the review announced a new series of talks with slides, including one on the French Revolution,[19] while in January 1925 an article on the social-democratic women's movement included a reference to the historical importance of the 'Great Revolution'.[20] A history of the *Marseillaise* provided an opportunity to revisit the connection that bound the German workers' movement to this revolutionary song;[21] a few months later, a historical text marking May Day returned to the origins of this annual jubilee and evoked the numerous social-democratic fêtes.[22] Yet unlike in the articles published in *Die Neue Welt* before 1914, these fêtes were not set in the tradition of the French Revolution.

Photographs and themes from the news were omnipresent in *Volk und Zeit*, the new Sunday supplement for the social-democratic dailies after *Die Neue Welt* ceased publication in 1919. Its coverage of travel and leisure, shows and advertising left little space for forays into history. The short historical pieces of the pre-war years were now almost absent, with the exception of the occasional tributes reserved for figures from Germany's past.[23] There were some brief references to the French Revolution: on 27 April 1930, the commemor-

---

17   Friedjung, L., 'H. Wendel, Danton', 1931, p. 67.

18   The same ones as *Sozialistische Bildung*; a subject to which we will return.

19   'Lichtbildvorträge', *Kulturwille*, February 1924, p. 11. This was probably a reproduction of the Vienna *Lichtbildernvortrag* of 1913, for the archives that we have consulted do not feature any other examples.

20   Wurm, M., 'Bürgerliche und proletarische Frauenbewegung', *Kulturwille*, January 1925, pp. 2–3.

21   Brügel, F. 'Die deutsche Marseillaise', *Kulturwille*, February 1929, pp. 46–8.

22   *Kulturwille*, May 1925.

23   'Lassalle', *Volk und Zeit*, 12 April 1925, p. 2; there were frequent tributes to Marx, Engels, Liebknecht and Bebel or national figures like Beethoven.

ation of May Day was the occasion for a rapid reminder of the centenary of the Revolution at the moment of the Second International's founding congress. But this organ featured no specific piece on the French Revolution across several years.

The workers' calendars (*Arbeiter-Notizkalender*), which the SPD had hitherto published almost without interruption since 1889, now ceased publication. From 1926 they were replaced by a *Taschenbuch der Arbeit* ['Labour Pocket-Book'].[24] Contemporary events occupied a predominant place, while most pages were reserved for an organisational map of the SPD and a list of addresses that would be useful for a social-democratic militant. We can, without doubt, note a certain interest in history: in 1926 it featured a rich chronology that spread across over twenty pages.[25] However, it was essentially devoted to the party's history since its origins in the 1840s.[26] The chronology in the 1928 edition only went so far back as 1900.

A Secondary Point of Reference in Educationals

The late 1920s and early 1930s saw a confirmation of the general fall in historical education and revolutionary history in particular. The reduced number of hours devoted to the 'Great Revolution' in the Berlin school founded by Wilhelm Liebknecht in 1891 – where before 1914 it had been among the most widely-taught historical events – leaves no room for doubt on this score.[27] A detailed plan is available for the 1928–9 course on 'Introductions to Marxism':[28] it featured nothing specific on the history of revolutions, or still less on the French Revolution. The same was true of the 'history of socialism', from which revolutionary history was now absent.[29] Occasionally there was a point on the era of the French Revolution, for instance in a course on cultural history since the Middle Ages.[30] Lastly, on the few occasions on which the 'history of revolutions' was presented,[31] the detailed course plan shows that the French Revolution made up part of a wider whole, as in the case of Erwin Marquardt's 1922 plan:

---

24   *Taschenbuch der Arbeit*, 1926 and 1928.
25   *Taschenbuch der Arbeit*, 1926, pp. 52–75.
26   Ibid.
27   *Arbeitsplan für das Lehrjahr der Arbeiter-Bildungsschule*, Berlin, 1928–9, 1930–31; the archives do not include any *Arbeitsplan* for previous years.
28   *Arbeiterbildungsschule*, 1928–9, pp. 16–17.
29   *Arbeiterbildungsschule*, 1928–9, p. 21.
30   *Arbeiterbildungsschule*, 1928–9, p. 20.
31   Ibid.

The fundamental questions of the nature of revolutions.

Antiquity: the Greeks and the era of the Roman civil war.

Middle Ages: the lack of a real revolution – pseudo-revolutions.

Modern times: Sixteenth century. The German Revolution; the Peasants' War. Seventeenth century. The English Revolution: the triumph of parliamentarism.

The French Revolution: the 'Great Revolution'. 1815 to 1848.

The revolutions of World War I.[32]

The plan for 1930–1 corresponds to the fortieth year of the school's activity. It is also the last similarly detailed document we have for the SPD before Hitler came to power. A short historical introduction sought to situate the schools' activity in continuity with its founder Wilhelm Liebknecht's intentions. This time, none of the educational programme was devoted to the history of revolutions. The main themes addressed were contemporary political questions, in line with what we already saw when we looked at the mid-1920s. The only look back to the past concerned the history of the SPD itself, and its origins dating back to the 1840s. Forerunners of socialism like Babeuf had now disappeared. Conversely, the extensive presence of meetings on 'Bolshevism and fascism' – of unknown content – was a new addition. This should be understood in terms of the political situation of the time, which saw violent clashes between the KPD and SPD.[33] Across all the educational plans for 1930–1 we find only very brief mentions of the French Revolution, for instance in an educational entitled 'The workers of Germany, in struggle for democracy and economic and political power',[34] whose first sentence indicates that a new Europe had taken form after the 'Great French Revolution'.[35] But nowhere was the French experience of 1789 to 1799 itself the object of specific attention. One last, essential point is that the French Revolution no longer appeared in connection with the 'history of the German party' or anything regarding German history in general. Thus, the manner in which German history was expounded in 1930 strongly contrasted with the situation in 1910, when the Revolution had occupied a major role in Franz Mehring's textbook.

Sozialistische Bildung review, which featured regular balance-sheets of SPD educational work in Germany, offers us some idea of what was being taught

---

32   *Arbeiterbildungsschule*, 1928–9, p. 25.

33   In the late 1920s issues of *Der Wahre Jacob*, the two main threats seem to be Nazism and communism.

34   *Arbeiterbildungsschule*, 1930, p. 19.

35   Ibid.

in structures other than the Berlin school.[36] The overall balance was similar. Educationals highly centred on present-day themes (and especially the characterisation of Bolshevism and fascism) only sporadically referred to the 'Great Revolution'. In 1929, the detailed plan for a talk on 'Democracy and Republic' featured a brief examination of the *Declaration of the Rights of Man and the Citizen*.[37] A 1932 talk on 'the crisis of the state' also referred to the 1789 declaration, though no further details are available.[38]

The material tasks that occupied full-timers, together with the competition with the Communists and the Nazis, pushed historical references onto an only secondary level of importance. The school for party full-timers between 1930 and 1932 did not devote any time to history.[39] Nonetheless, in Bremen in 1930 Christian Döring gave an educational on 'The history of bourgeois revolutions'. That same year, Döring provided a more general breakdown of the courses that had been given,[40] based on the statistics provided by local party schools between 1924 and 1930. His figures also showed the place occupied by revolutionary history:

> Economic history and political economy: 83 courses
> The economic consequences of the war and the global economy: 55 courses
> Socialism (its nature and history): 53 courses
> The history of bourgeois revolutions: 15 courses
> Roman history: 1 course[41]

The contents of this history of bourgeois revolutions must have varied between the different local schools, but they probably stood close to what was set out in the blueprint for the Berlin school, such as we saw above. The lack of history

36   *Sozialistische Bildung*, Monthly Organ of the National Commission for Socialist Workers' Education [*Monatsschrift des Reichsausschusses für sozialistische Bildungsarbeit*] was published from 1929 to 1933. It took over the reins from *Arbeiter-Bildung*, which had appeared on an irregular basis from 1926 to 1928.
37   Mierendorff, C., 'Demokratie und Republik', *Sozialistische Bildung*, 1929, p. 202.
38   'Die Staatskrise und der Kampf um den Staat', *Sozialistische Bildung*, 1932, pp. 236–9.
39   'Funktionärschulung', *Sozialistische Bildung*, 1930, pp. 153–5; 'Zentrale Funktionärschulung', *Sozialistische Bildung*, 1931, pp. 144–7; 'Unsere wissenschaftlichen Wanderkurse. Vorschläge für die Bezirke', *Sozialistische Bildung*, 1932, p. 123.
40   Döring, C., 'Sechs Jahre Wanderkurse', *Sozialistische Bildung*, 1930, pp. 372–6. A summary of a certain amount of regional data in 1931 gave less precise figures than had the previous year's study, but the results were similar.
41   Döring, C., 'Sechs Jahre Wanderkurse', *Sozialistische Bildung*, 1930, p. 372.

teaching did produce a reaction: following the publication of these figures, several contributions discussed what place history should play in the educationals for new party cadres. In an article on the themes addressed by courses and talks, August Siemen reaffirmed the importance of history classes for understanding the usefulness of the materialist conception of history, even as he also recognised the problems that transmitting this understanding posed.[42] The following year, Otto Jenssen – author of a *Festschrift* article in defence of Kautsky, examined above – echoed these same questions.[43] He wrote what can only be described as a plea in defence of the need to teach history, precisely for the sake of understanding the modern world.[44] He argued that history should remain in the forefront of *Bildungsarbeit*, for the 'ignorance in the historical domain is particularly great among those generations who followed history classes during World War I'.[45] He returned to the specific problem posed by teaching the history of the French Revolutions, and the difficulties in communicating its importance:

> One may object that the history of the French Revolution and the decades that followed are no longer of political interest for us today, since after the World War and the revolution in central Europe and Russia, the era of the early nineteenth century no longer has so much effect. This is only partly true. The French Revolution was the classic continental-European bourgeois revolution. The particularities of its successes should be understood by comparison with the French events; only on the basis of these latter can we study certain principles of the bourgeois revolution which were reawakened in very recent times, in China and even in the Russian Revolution.[46]

While these contributions were not enough to shift the general balance, they did express a reaction against the reduction of history teaching, which came from militants who were attached to the transmission of revolutionary points of reference.

---

42   *Sozialistische Bildung*, 1930, p. 147.
43   See the article on Karl Kautsky, p. 255.
44   Jenssen, O., 'Geschichte als Mittel politischer Bildungsarbeit', *Sozialistische Bildung*, pp. 110–14.
45   Jenssen, O., 'Geschichte als Mittel politischer Bildungsarbeit', *Sozialistische Bildung*, p. 110.
46   Jenssen, O., 'Geschichte als Mittel politischer Bildungsarbeit', *Sozialistische Bildung*, pp. 110–11.

We find a similar balance in Heinrich Cunow's *General Economic History*. Issued by the SPD publishing house Dietz between 1926 and 1931, this book was particularly directed at party training schools.[47] Cunow's work was intended as a social-democratic economic history textbook, building on the textbook that he had published in 1920 on Marx's concepts. Its general blueprint was an overview of economic history since the age of primitive communities. The fourth volume, published in 1931, concerned 'The Development of the Capitalist Economy in Germany, England and the United States of America'.[48] France's history occupied little space compared to not only German history but also that of England and the United States. The French Revolution was presented in a short chapter on 'The Agrarian Laws of the French Revolution and its Aftermath'.[49] Cunow mentioned numerous episodes (the events of 4 August, the sale of the *biens nationaux*, the various laws concerning feudal rights up till 10 June 1793), within the perspective of an explanation of the particularity of small property-holding in France.[50] The ten final pages of the following chapter were devoted to the development of French industry and also evoked the Revolution, the first workers' strikes and the Le Chapelier law. The author explained the specificities of France's industrial development, just like its agrarian structures, on the basis of the events of the Revolution.

A 1928 report by the Austrian party's education commission indicated that here, too, history's place had been reduced.[51] None of the various sections in the report was devoted to history: 'Socialism', 'The workers' movement' and the other categories included afforded only very little space to historical events. At the very most, we might imagine that the section dedicated to socialism, which featured a talk on 'the forerunners of socialism', may have included some discussion of Babeuf. In a 'chronological table', calling for the commemoration of 'dates to be remembered', only two of the many dates cited concerned the 140-year anniversary of 1789. 17 May of that year was given as the date of the meeting of the three orders, and 4 August for the proclamation of the Declaration of the Rights of Man: there were just two dates from the French Revolution ... and both of them were errors.

A 1929 report nonetheless suggested that the history of the 'French revolutions' was sporadically taught, likely covering a cycle running from 1789 to

---

47   Cunow 1926–31.
48   Cunow 1926–31, vol. 4.
49   Cunow 1926–31, vol. 4, pp. 219–40.
50   Cunow 1926–31, vol. 4, p. 234.
51   Zentralstelle für das Bildungswesen der Sozialdemokratischen Arbeiterpartei-Vortragsabteilung, *Vorträge und Kurse*, September 1928.

1871.[52] In this same spirit, a complete course guide included a section on 'the development of society since early capitalism':

The birth of capitalism and the proletariat
The oppression of the peasants and the Reformation
Economics, society and politics in the age of absolutism
The revolt of the bourgeoisie and its fight for power
The French revolutions
The Revolution of 1848
World war and revolution[53]

In 1929 a pamphlet was published entitled *Talks and Courses*. This directory offered a more detailed overview. It proposed a lecture series on 'the history of revolutions' in nine talks, including three on 'The Great French Revolution'.[54] 'The History of Socialism' proposed a series of talks, including one on 'class contradictions' during the French Revolution.[55] Here, as in the German case, the French Revolution was present but as part of a series of talks on revolutionary history.

Equally worth noting are *Bildungsarbeit*'s occasional mentions of the 1913 talk with slides devoted to the French Revolution, even if it is difficult really to quantify its use. In 1931, this 1913 *Lichtbilder* was still being advertised in a general guide to this format, published by the central educational commission.[56] But among the many synopses of talks published in the *Bildungsarbeit* between 1919 and 1934, none was devoted to the French Revolution. This reference was thus much less present than it had once been, even if it is certainly possible to find it recurring occasionally, for example in a tribute to Karl Kautsky,[57] or in a general presentation of the history of counter-revolution and its

---

52   *Die Tätigkeit der Zentralstelle für das Bildungswesen (Arbeiterbildungszentrale) im Jahre 1929*, Sonderabdruck aus der 'Bildungsarbeit', 1930.

53   *Die Tätigkeit der Zentralstelle für das Bildungswesen (Arbeiterbildungszentrale) im Jahre 1929*, Sonderabdruck aus der 'Bildungsarbeit', 1930., p. 7.

54   *Die Tätigkeit der Zentralstelle für das Bildungswesen (Arbeiterbildungszentrale) im Jahre 1929*, Sonderabdruck aus der 'Bildungsarbeit', 1930, p. 8.

55   *Die Tätigkeit der Zentralstelle für das Bildungswesen (Arbeiterbildungszentrale) im Jahre 1929*, Sonderabdruck aus der 'Bildungsarbeit', 1930, p. 15.

56   Zentralstelle für das Bildungswesen der Sozialdemokratischen Arbeiterpartei, *Lichtbilder Filme und Schmalfilme. Ein Verzeichnis*, 1932, p. 14.

57   'Karl Kautsky', *Bildungsarbeit*, 1929, pp. 137–9. It mentioned *Die Klassengegensätze von 1789.*

contemporary expressions:[58] here, the author looked back to the French émigré
organisations in 1789 in order to shed light on the situation of the extreme-right
paramilitary gangs. Similarly, the social-democratic women's movement maintained a strong tie to the 'Great Revolution', in this sense building on Emma
Adler's interests. In 1924 *Frauentag* published extracts from her 1906 work on
women and the French Revolution,[59] and in a 1926 pamphlet tracing the history of women's rights,[60] Adolf Schärf devoted part of his explanation to a
presentation of Olympe de Gouges's declaration of the rights of woman and
the difficulties the women's clubs ran into between 1789 and 1794.

A 'Cold Shower' for Workers' Education

Nonetheless, these few mentions of the French Revolution were hardly comparable to the structured educationals of the pre-war period. An inquiry published in the *Bildungsarbeit* offered some insight into the problems encountered at the level of educating militants ('A cold shower for worker-educa-
tors').[61] It offered an eloquent demonstration of the limited references to the
French Revolution, as it asked 'where have we got to, with our comrades'
knowledge?'[62] The article published the results of a survey among several
Vienna workers' circles who had followed educationals.[63] A series of general
knowledge questions were posed, corresponding to various courses. 144 people
responded, most of them workers. The respondents spanned the different generations, with a good part of them aged between 20 and 30. The overall results
gave around 45% correct answers, 30% wrong answers, and 20% 'not entirely
wrong';[64] the remainder, around 5 percent, did not answer at all. One of the
questions concerned the French Revolution, and it was by far the one that drew
the most wrong answers. The responses were summarised as follows:

> The second question was 'When did the French Revolution happen?' Out
> of 144 comrades, only 17 answered correctly – 12% – while a few gave
> an answer that was not entirely wrong, 62% gave a wrong answer and
> 10% said that they did not know. We might highlight the following wrong
> answers: in the seventeenth century, 1719, 1768, 1769, 1766 and 1772, 1770,

58   'Die Gegenrevolution. Ihre Formen und Spielarten', *Bildungsarbeit*, 1932, pp. 75–9.
59   *Frauentag*, 1924, p. 4.
60   Schärf 1926, p. 7. The author was later president of Austria, from 1957 to 1965.
61   Ehrlich, O., 'Kalte Dusche für Arbeiterbildner', *Bildungsarbeit*, 1931, pp. 70–3.
62   Ehrlich, O., 'Kalte Dusche für Arbeiterbildner', *Bildungsarbeit*, 1931, p. 70.
63   Ibid.
64   Ibid.

1780, 1762 and 1763, 1809, from 1820 to 1850, 1836, 1838, 1839, 1848, 1886, around 1860, 1863, 1868, 1869, 1870, 1874, 1876, 1878, or even as late as 1885.[65]

By way of example, this result could be compared to the one for the question 'Who is Karl Kautsky': 70 percent gave a correct answer, and he was most often described as a 'leader of the Austrian workers' movement'.[66] It is difficult to draw broader conclusions from this, given the lack of any comparable survey for previous decades. Nonetheless, we can draw a link – if not a mechanical connection – between the results of this inquiry and the weak presence of the French Revolution in party educationals from the early 1920s onward, not least given that this was indeed a survey among militants who followed party educationals and thus knew some of the fundamentals of the Social-Democratic Party.

From the 'Bloody July' of 1927 to the USSR in 1930: the Play of Analogies

Bloody July, from the Champ-de-Mars to Schattendorf

It was the political tension of the early 1930s that created the conditions for analyses of the Terror to 'come back in force'. Yet already a few years earlier, the events of 1927, which confronted political forces that would clash on a higher scale in 1934, had raised an analogy with the French Revolution.

On 15 July 1927 there was a major demonstration in Vienna protesting the acquittal of the Schattendorf murderers. Schattendorf was a small town where far-Right paramilitaries had murdered a social-democratic worker-militant and a six year-old child in January 1927. The 15 July protest saw violent clashes with the police, and it ended when these latter opened fire on the demonstrators, upon the orders of the chancellor and police prefect.[67] There were more than 80 victims and almost 300 wounded, in what became known as 'Bloody July'. During these clashes the social-democratic leadership was overwhelmed and a two-day general strike was unleashed. Two weeks later, Karl Kautsky published an article in the *Arbeiter-Zeitung* dedicated to the 'bloody July' ... of 1791, which was published in *Vorwärts* in Germany the following

---

65   Ehrlich, O., 'Kalte Dusche für Arbeiterbildner', *Bildungsarbeit*, 1931, p. 72.
66   Ibid.
67   Pasteur 2008b.

day.[68] He compared the Austrian insurrection with the shootings at the Champ-de-Mars, an essential date in the 'Great French Revolution'. This was an interesting expression of continuity, for in his first courses directed at workers Lassalle had presented 17 July 1791 as the first stage in the history of the division between bourgeoisie and proletariat.

Kautsky suggested that looking back to the past would aid an understanding of the contemporary situation, even while he also noted the particularities of each era (the actors, back then, had been the 'toiling masses' and not yet the 'proletarians' of 1927). A considerable part of the article recalled the basic historical facts of the history of the Revolution: 14 July 1789, the gradual decline in the King's popularity and then the emergence of a republican current. The events of 17 July 1791 allowed a return to the former meaning of the red flag, which had recently been used to indicate martial law. One year after this bloody clash, the King was overthrown. Did Kautsky suggest the possibility of a victory similar to that of the 'toiling masses' of 1791–2 because he wanted to reassure social-democratic militants? It does not seem that he believed that history was simply repeating itself:

> Without doubt, events of this kind leave traces, terrible traces in the soul of the population affected. Yet the consequences of the bloodbath of 1927 will not necessarily be the same as in 1791. In that era, the massacres of September of the following year were the consequence of 17 July, massacres perpetrated by precisely those who had been most affected by the massacre at the Champ-de-Mars. In that era, the petty-bourgeois and proletarian terror of 1792–3 followed the bourgeois terror of 1791.[69]

Kautsky continued with the reasoning that he had elaborated over many years: the power of social-democratic organisation would make it possible to avoid the traps of the era of the French Revolution:

> The masses of 1791 were completely unorganised and politically ignorant. They believed all kinds of rumours, could be permeated by all kinds of illusions, and the simple fact of being together reinforced their fears ... Things changed over the following decades, especially since the toiling masses now had the possibility of organising, of having their own press,

---

68   Kautsky, K., 'Ein blutiger Julitag in der grossen Revolution', *Arbeiter-Zeitung*, 31 July 1927, pp. 3–4. Abridged version in *Vorwärts*, Berlin, 1 August 1927. Here we cite from the *Arbeiter-Zeitung* version.
69   Ibid.

of acquiring culture not only in the schools but also through political and trade-union practice, in strikes, in following parliamentary and municipal activities, and so on.[70]

While he recognised that it was mistaken to believe in a 'softening of class contradictions' before 1914, and that these contradictions had been aggravated by World War I, any new 'blood bath' would be prejudicial to the proletariat. In a context of great hostility to the Soviet regime, the French Revolution now in fact served almost as a foil.

Criticising the USSR through Analogies

Kautsky's 1930 work *Bolshevism at a Deadlock*[71] analysed the 'great turning point' that marked the beginning of the collectivisation in the Soviet countryside. Here Kautsky sought to denounce the Bolshevik Party's agrarian policy, on the basis of the information available to him. His critique proceeded through a whole series of formal analogies with 1789, which built on the remarks he had made in his works between 1918 and 1921. For him, the real achievement of 1917, like 1789, was the land given to the peasants.

Two years later, in a work of several hundred pages called *War and Democracy*,[72] Kautsky explored the whole of human history through the prism of the connection between war and politics. This was the first volume of what would remain an unfinished work. One major chapter was dedicated to the 'Great French Revolution'.[73] It was based on a reading of the recent historiography (Aulard, Hintze, Mathiez, Wendel). Logically enough, it emphasised the importance of the conditions in which France had entered the war in 1792 and detailed the conditions in which the new military structures took form.[74] His theoretical framework for explaining the French Revolution remained unchanged. More originally, having read Mathiez,[75] Kautsky compared the English and French revolutionary processes[76] and highlighted the fact that the Girondins and Montagnards were largely part of the same social class, unlike in previous works like 1919's *Terrorism and Communism* where he had seen differences between them.[77] Kautsky's thinking built on his earlier writings,

---

70   Ibid.
71   Kautsky 1931.
72   Kautsky 1932.
73   Kautsky 1932, pp. 159–247.
74   Kautsky 1932, pp. 178–87.
75   Kautsky 1932, p. 196. He cited from Mathiez 1927, vol. 2, p. 69.
76   Kautsky 1932, p. 237.
77   Kautsky 1932, p. 201.

especially with regard to the analogy with the Russian Revolution. While Terror had been justifiable in 1793 as the offspring of the war, the Russian Revolution maintained a permanent state of war to the detriment of democratic structures. Kautsky emphasised the profound link between war and 'dictatorship', even though the Montagnards were mostly hostile to it. His conclusion was critical of the French revolutionary tradition that he had celebrated even in 1920,[78] and contrasted it to what the Socialist International had built:

> On the contrary, the French Revolution, which has to this day deeply influenced French thought and phraseology among all social classes, including the workers, has left behind a particular predilection for the methods of war in both domestic and foreign policy. During the second half of the nineteenth century this tendency was countered by the Socialist International.[79]

At the same time, the reading coming from Otto Bauer and part of the Austrian social-democrats differed from Kautsky's. These 'Austromarxists' are often presented as originators of the elaboration of a third way between Soviet socialism and German social democracy, whose impact transcended their own national borders.[80] While he underlined some of the undeniable Soviet successes, Bauer was nonetheless comparable Kautsky in terms of his criticisms of the methods used during the Russian Revolution. At the 1932 social-democratic congress he declared that:

> This does not mean that the proletariat will everywhere copy the Russian methods. These methods, which are based on Russia's structures and historical experience, cannot be slavishly imitated in other countries. We have learned from history. While the French Jacobins used an iron dictatorship to sweep aside French feudalism and secure the victory of a new legal order in France, the liberals and democrats in other countries did not imitate the French dictatorship. In no other country in the world did they roll out the guillotine. But the French Jacobins opened up a breach that was decisive to putting an end to the feudal world, and even using different methods the other countries could henceforth overcome feudalism.[81]

---

78   See Chapter Ten, p. 255.
79   Kautsky 1932, p. 247.
80   Bourdet 1968.
81   'Parteitag', 1932, cited in Bauer 1980, vol. 5, p. 662.

Such arguments recurred frequently. We can similarly note a talk Otto Bauer gave on the Soviet Five-Year Plan in Vienna during this same period:

> Each people must find its own path. What was France like after the victory of the bourgeois Revolution? It imposed the rights of man, and the fact that they had been imposed in France gave strength to the bourgeois revolution across Europe. But did the other countries simply copy France? No. France gave the signal, making the decisive breakthrough for the other countries.[82]

The Entangled Debate around Robespierre

The final controversy over the French Revolution, which took place at the moment of the banning of the social-democrats in 1933–4, concerned the figure of Robespierre.

'Albert Mathier's Final Work': the Critique of Hermann Wendel

While in this study it is not our concern to review the French historiography as such, or to provide any detailed presentation of the German reception of Albert Mathiez's work we nonetheless need to make a detour by way of the reception of Hermann Wendel's work in France. Just as the social-democrats defined their positions through the debate with Jaurès in 1902–5, the debate on Robespierre in *Die Gesellschaft* and *Der Kampf* in 1933–4 can only be understood if we take the French context into account.

The 'Robespierrian' historian came to German for a talk at Leipzig University on 14 November 1930. We only have very little information on his stay. Walter Markov wrote a short piece on this subject for a conference on Mathiez.[83] The only indications appeared in the moderate daily *Leipziger Neueste Nachrichten* ['Latest News from Leipzig'], which carried an announcement of Mathiez's French-language talk on 'Robespierre, History and Legend'. Without further indicators it is difficult to know how well-attended this talk was, though as Markov notes it probably sparked some debate, given the unpopularity of Robespierre among German historians, well beyond the 'reactionaries' alone. As he returned to that country, Albert Mathiez would surely have been convinced that reaction was going to triumph in Germany ...

---

82   Bauer 1980, vol. 6, p. 550.
83   Markov 1977.

Albert Mathiez's sudden death in February 1932 provided Hermann Wendel his opportunity to revisit the opposition between Robespierre and Danton, which was one of the major subjects of Albert Mathiez's study. His obituary, published by the *Annales historiques de la Révolution Française*, was the translation of an article that had appeared in a German daily on 12 March 1932.[84] From this piece we learn that Mathiez had sent Hermann a book with the following dedication: 'the rehabilitation of Danton is not only an outrage against the truth, but the index of a dubious politics dangerous to democracy'.[85] Wendel's text was very critical of Mathiez,[86] and spoke of his 'fanatical brutality with regard to Danton'.[87] Nonetheless, Mathiez's break with the Soviet historians allowed Wendel to find points of convergence between them: 'for having so intrepidly stood up against this argument, against the terroristic system and the suppression of all freedom of opinion in Russia, [Mathiez] was struck by a great excommunication by the patented Soviet historians who had initially fêted him as one of the most brilliant scribes on the history of the French Revolution'.[88] Indeed, while he had soon quit the Section Française de l'Internationale Communiste in 1921–2, Mathiez had nonetheless long preserved good relations with a number of Soviet historians. Across almost a decade, book reviews, exhibitions and even cultural displays on the reception of the French Revolution in the USSR were constantly mentioned in *Annales historiques de la Révolution française*. 'The young Soviet historians of the French Revolution were admirers of Albert Mathiez. Faced with their proliferation of studies, he suggested to French historians that they ought to learn Russian'.[89] In 1931 there came an abrupt about-turn: a letter signed by numerous Soviet historians expressed unconditional defence of the USSR and sharply criticised the French historian. The pretext for this critique was the *Annales'* 1929 publication of an art-

---

84   It was first published in the liberal Frankfurt daily *Das Tage-Buch*, founded in the early 1920s with the aid of Ernst Rowohlt, the publisher of Hermann Wendel's books. Wendel, H., 'Albert Mathiez vu par un "dantoniste" allemand par Hermann Wendel', *Annales historiques de la Révolution française*, 1932, pp. 235–9. Another, similar obituary was published in the *Frankfurter Zeitung* on 19 April.

85   Wendel, H., 'Albert Mathiez vu par un "dantoniste" allemand par Hermann Wendel', *Annales historiques de la Révolution française*, 1932, p. 236.

86   'That is how even the shadows of those who ... felled others' heads still recruit faithful new disciples among our contemporaries'. Ibid.

87   Wendel, H., 'Albert Mathiez vu par un "dantoniste" allemand par Hermann Wendel', *Annales historiques de la Révolution française*, 1932, p. 237.

88   Wendel, H., 'Albert Mathiez vu par un "dantoniste" allemand par Hermann Wendel', *Annales historiques de la Révolution française*, 1932, p. 239.

89   Broué 2004, pp. 244–5.

icle by Kazan historian Buchemakin on 9 Thermidor 1799.[90] For the authors
of the letter addressed to Mathiez, this article was an incorrect characterisation of Thermidor, and they considered it unacceptable that Mathiez – who in
his introduction to this article wrote cutting remarks on the Marxist dogmatism dominant in the USSR – had reductively attached Buchemakin's errors to
Soviet historians in general. More broadly, this break should be interpreted as
a rejection of the theses advanced in Albert Mathiez's own 1929 work on *The
Thermidorean Reaction* and, in general, the quasi-prohibition against mentioning the Thermidor in analogy with the present situation.[91] The Soviets' letter
was published in the *Annales* in French under the title 'Things as Seen from
Soviet Russia',[92] shortly before his death. Mathiez issued a response backed by
French historians like Pierre Renouvin, which after mounting a severe charge-
sheet against the Soviet regime and its treatment of historical scholarship,
demanded the release of Eugene Tarle, a Soviet historian who had just been
arrested. These difficult relations brought a sharp worsening of Mathiez's relations with the French Communists: the obituary published in the Communists'
l'Humanité showed how deep the break had become.[93] Such committed acts,
which Wendel knew about, in part explain why the social-democratic journalist
maintained a certain sympathy for Mathiez, and indeed expressed it publicly.

Wendel's fervour for Danton nonetheless stood opposite to the French historian's defence of Robespierre's work. Particularly telling, in this regard, is a
little-known historiographical episode. When he was writing his obituary of
Albert Mathiez, Wendel was probably unaware that Mathiez's last struggle in
his defence of Robespierre was a plan for a critical article on Wendel's own biography of Danton. Mathiez's assistant Henri Calvet published the preparatory
notes for this book review in the *Annales historiques de la Révolution française* a
few months after the historian's death.[94] It is worth commenting that Mathiez
could have written such a review at any point since the book was published in
German in 1930; the fact that he did not do so owed not to linguistic reasons,
but perhaps a lack of time.[95] These notes are worthy of attention because their
publication led Wendel to issue a critique directed at the *Annales* itself, which

90   Bouchemakine, M. 'Le neuf thermidor dans la nouvelle littérature historique', *Annales his-
     toriques de la Révolution française*, 1930, pp. 401–10.
91   Mathiez 1929.
92   Mathiez, A., 'Choses vues de Russie soviétique', *Annales historiques de la Révolution fran-
     çaise*, 1931, pp. 149–58.
93   Fréville, J., 'Nécrologie: Albert Mathiez', *l'Humanité*, 8 March 1932.
94   Calvet, H., 'Le dernier travail d' Albert Mathiez', *Annales historiques de la Révolution fran-
     çaise*, 1932, pp. 343–8.
95   He read German, as his many reviews of books in this language testify.

he pursued in an article for *Die Gesellschaft*. Thus 'Albert Mathiez's final work' was a critique of the social-democrat Hermann Wendel.

Henri Calvet indicated that 'in the last days before his death, Albert Mathiez read Hermann Wendel's work devoted to Danton'.[96] The true review of this book published in the *Annales* was written by Georges Lefebvre, who succeeded Mathiez at the head of this review. It appeared in the subsequent issue of the *Annales* and provided the opportunity for an extensive review of several of the points on Danton that were being discussed in this period, especially his venality. It was made clear that the review had been written before the publication of the transcript of Mathiez's notes. While Lefebvre recognised that this book had some merit, he saw the Danton-admiring social-democrat Wendel as an ... 'epigone of Nietzsche'.[97]

As for Mathiez's – highly fragmentary – notes, they concerned the first 152 pages of the French edition of Wendel's book, corresponding to the first 240 pages of the German edition. For Henri Calvet, who mentioned neither the social-democrat's political engagement nor his long-term interest in the French Revolution, 'They [these notes] sufficed to underline the imperfections of the German journalist's work'.[98] This text compiled a list of Wendel's errors and imprecisions, as well as the two men's disagreements on both Danton and Robespierre. Among its most interesting remarks, it is worth mentioning a note which emphasised that 'while he speaks of the rivalry between Girondins and Montagnards, he sheds no light on the social and economic grievances. He recounts the whole Revolution'.[99] By way of response, Hermann Wendel sent a letter dated 15 August 1932, which was in turn followed by a reply by Henri Calvet.[100] An editors' note, itself proof of the importance of this incident, summed up the discussion and put an end to the debate. Wendel defended the style of his work: 'If Mathiez says "He recounts the whole Revolution", I am proud of that, for my book is not written for experts on the Revolution, but addresses the wider German public, whom I could not assume had any knowledge of the events and the development of the Revolution'.[101] He reaffirmed his admiration

---

96   Calvet, H., 'Le dernier travail d'Albert Mathiez', *Annales historiques de la Révolution française*, 1932, p. 344.

97   Lefebvre, G., 'Sur Danton. À propos de deux livres récents', *Annales historiques de la Révolution française*, 1932, pp. 385–424. The other book addressed was by Barthou.

98   Calvet, H., 'Le dernier travail d'Albert Mathiez', *Annales historiques de la Révolution française*, 1932, p. 347.

99   Calvet, H., 'Le dernier travail d'Albert Mathiez', *Annales historiques de la Révolution française*, 1932, p. 348. Wendel 1930, p. 194.

100 'Correspondance', *Annales historiques de la Révolution française*, 1932, pp. 565–9.

101 'Correspondance', *Annales historiques de la Révolution française*, 1932, p. 565.

of Danton and played down his 'venality', so foregrounded by Mathiez. He again criticised Robespierre, holding that he was not initially interested in the debate between active and passive citizens – as claimed by Jaurès's *Histoire socialiste*, which, Wendel recalled with some malice, had been republished by Mathiez.[102] His missive earned a sharp and 'professional' response from Henri Calvet:

> For me there could be no question of discussing the very foundation of Mr. Wendel's reasoning (?). And with good reason! There is no scholarly apparatus accompanying his book ... One first remark. Mathiez formulates sixty observations; Wendel responds on just seven points. This is rather thin ... even when he is writing for a wider public, which has the right to be informed in a more impartial manner.[103]

Robespierre and Danton in Die Gesellschaft[104]

A few weeks later, pursuing this debate, Hermann Wendel devoted a long article in *Die Gesellschaft* to 'Danton and Robespirre'.[105] Following a biography of Albert Mathiez – except among specialists the historian was probably little known among the social-democrats who read *Die Gesellschaft*[106] – Wendel underlined the French historian's theoretical influences, and especially Jean Jaurès. While Wendel repeatedly cited Mathiez, he sought above all to criticise his work. Signalling Mathiez's brief engagement in Communist ranks, Wendel discussed his writings on Robespierre and Danton, which after his break with his teacher Alphonse Aulard principally involved the rehabilitation of the former and the severe critique of the latter. The context was a proliferation of recent publications on Danton and Robespierre: other than his own book on Danton, Wendel noted the recent publication of the biography by Louis Barthou.[107] While a large part of the article was devoted to specific points of interpretation, for instance Danton's attitude on the massacres of September 1792 or Robespierre's position on the Paris Commune, the political backdrop

---

102   Jaurès 1922–4.

103   'Correspondance', *Annales historiques de la Révolution française*, 1932, pp. 568–9.

104   Wendel, H., 'Danton und Robespierre', *Die Gesellschaft*, 1932, pp. 521–544. Marmorek, S., 'Robespierre und die Nachwelt', *Der Kampf*, 1933, pp. 69–79; Wendel, H., 'St. Robespierre. Eine Entgegnung', *Der Kampf*, 1934, pp. 226–8.

105   Wendel, H., 'Danton und Robespierre', *Die Gesellschaft*, 1932, pp. 521–44.

106   This should doubtless be qualified by reference to Hedwig Hintze's 1929 article on the historiography.

107   A moderate republican MP and then senator, Louis Barthou was a minister on several occasions throughout the 1920s. He was the author of numerous works of history including a highly positive biography of Danton: Barthou 1934.

was also present. He sought to criticise the methods of government during the Terror as well as its supposed inheritors in the contemporary world, all the better to defend Danton and the moderate path he had represented in early 1794.[108] Wendel made use of an 1870 letter from Engels to Marx in order to criticise the Terror:

> In his 4 September 1870 letter Engels was right to explain the Terror not as a popular terror designed to spread fear, but as a terror that was itself a product of fear: 'The Terror of 1793 was in large part pointless cruelty committed by people who were themselves afraid and sought to reassure themselves through such means'.[109]

Wendel did not mention the fact that in other texts Engels had, if not celebrated the Terror, at least recognised it as a legitimate means of action in the context of that period. Be that as it may, this reference displayed Wendel's concern to present himself as loyal to historical materialism. He moreover revisited an advance that came from Mathiez's reasoning, namely the common bourgeois character of both the Montagnards and Girondins, which stood above their political differences. For Wendel, this demonstrated the fundamentally bourgeois character of the Revolution.[110] Rather more delicate was the question of whether any forerunners of socialism had emerged during the Terror. Wendel highlighted a certain tendency to look for forerunners of socialism in the Revolution where, in his view, there were none; in support of his argument he cited Stefan Zweig's novel on Fouché, which saw some of the declarations from 1793 as ancestors of the *Communist Manifesto*.[111] After having emphasised that the measures taken during the Terror were above all the result of the 'demands of war'[112] and not any social objective, Wendel dwelt at length on the meaning of the Ventôse decrees of 1794, which stipulated the confiscation of suspects' assets and their redistribution among the poor.[113] The characterisation of these decrees had, moreover, given rise to a lively debate among Soviet historians in this same period.[114] For the social-

108   Wendel, H., 'Danton und Robespierre', *Die Gesellschaft*, 1932, p. 527.
109   Wendel, H., 'Danton und Robespierre', *Die Gesellschaft*, 1932, p. 534. On Engels's 4 September 1870 letter to Marx, see MECW 44, p. 61.
110   Wendel, H., 'Danton und Robespierre', *Die Gesellschaft*, 1932, p. 537.
111   Zweig 1929, pp. 42–3.
112   Wendel, H., 'Danton und Robespierre', *Die Gesellschaft*, 1932, p. 534.
113   See Françoise Brunel's article on these decrees in Soboul (ed.) 1989, pp. 1081–3.
114   See Kondratieva 1989, p. 204. Wendel also mentioned the judgement of the Soviet historian Friedland (p. 543).

democratic historian, this 'was above all a means of political struggle in the context of civil war, seeking to confront the enemies of the Republic, and nothing else. In fact, just like when Sulla seized the assets of the supporters of Marius or when Cromwell confiscated the property of those opposed to his rule'.[115] Mathiez, conversely, saw this as the beginning of the expropriation of one class by another.[116] For Wendel, this was a 'reactionary utopia'; in his view, the policy being concocted behind this decree was that of a 'primitive democracy' ... he even went so far as to compare it to Nazism, arguing that 'not socialism, but the plan of our Nazi economists takes its place at this same level, seeking to divide each department store into hundreds of little shops for independent grocers'.[117] In this framework, to go beyond the limits of a 'bourgeois revolution' was thus a dangerous utopia; Wendel concluded that Danton's great merit was that he was, indeed, a 'bourgeois' in step with his times.

It is worth noting the echoes that Wendel's text encountered in France: a summary by Georges Lefebvre was published in the *Annales*.[118] The French historian was inclined to think that Wendel was right about the Ventôse decrees:

> He rightly refuses to see them as socialist, and rightly notes that there was a lack of clarity on this point in Mathiez's explanation, which attributed the Ventôse decrees' authors the intention of 'suppressing the [condition of the] proletariat'[119]

Conversely, Lefebvre linked the contemporary socialists' struggles to those waged by the Robespierrians, on this point greatly differing from Wendel's vision.

> Accepting that the Robespierrians could have foreseen big capitalism, they would have done. But the truth is that they wanted to aid the people by using the means that their present situation offered them. They used utopian means? That may be so. But what links them to today's socialists is their intention.[120]

---

115   Wendel, H., 'Danton und Robespierre', *Die Gesellschaft*, 1932, p. 540.

116   He cited Mathiez 1927, vol. 3, pp. 147–9: 'a new revolution'.

117   Wendel, H., 'Danton und Robespierre', *Die Gesellschaft*, 1932, p. 541.

118   Lefebvre, G., 'Notices', *Annales historiques de la Révolution française*, 1933, pp. 273–4.

119   Ibid., p. 273. On the contrasts between Lefebvre and Mathiez, see François Brunel's article in Soboul (ed.) 1989.

120   Lefebvre, G., 'Notices', *Annales historiques de la Révolution française*, 1933, p. 274.

Wendel's text was published in December 1932. From March 1933, all social-democratic publications were banned in Germany, including *Die Gesellschaft*, which ceased publication. The debate on Robespierre would continue a few months further in the pages of Austria's *Der Kampf*, which continued publication in Vienna up till the aftermath of the February 1934 civil war, then in Czechoslovakia and finally in Paris.

Replying to Wendel was a certain Schiller Marmorek. He was born in Vienna in 1880 and died in exile in New York in 1943.[121] At a young age he took an interest in literature, much like his father, who gave him the poet's name. Marmorek pursued his studies at the Sorbonne and from that point onward maintained regular contact with France. A member of the Austrian social-democratic party, he worked on the *Arbeiter-Zeitung* editorial team before taking charge of the evening daily *Das Kleine Blatt* ['The Little Paper'].[122] In his article published in *Der Kampf*, Marmorek set himself up as the defender of Albert Mathiez and, in a certain measure, also Robespierre.[123] While he emphasised the social-democratic historian Wendel's great knowledge of the French Revolution, Marmorek rejected his critique of Robespierre. He started by reconstructing Mathiez's career; here again, the article was not aimed at those expert in the historiography, especially given that to our knowledge *Der Kampf* had never previously published anything on the French historian. He contextualised the defence of Robespierre within the French situation, and recalled the manner in which Danton and the *Indulgents* had been at the heart of the debates constructed under the bourgeois Third Republic:

> The French Republic of 1871, ... led by parties who defended, under different names, the opportunist conception of the world; the high-bourgeois Republic of the *Indulgents*, of the indulgent agents and advocats of capitalism, who, from time to time, railed against the priests in order to capture the people's attention – this Republic needed a distorted history ... That is how Danton became its hero – a man who Hermann Wendel himself designates as "no innocent rascal", the opportunist ever prepared for compromises, the friend of all the inscrutable, wheeler-dealer politicians.[124]

Especially basing himself on Jaurès's work, he defended Albert Mathiez's rehabilitation of Robespierre and in particular his role in the fight against the war:

---

121   Haupt and Maitron 1971, p. 200.
122   *Das Kleine Blatt* (Vienna), 1927–34.
123   Marmorek, S. 'Robespierre und die Nachwelt', *Der Kampf*, 1934, pp. 69–79.
124   Marmorek, S. 'Robespierre und die Nachwelt', *Der Kampf*, 1934, p. 71.

His own book was so new and unprecedented, and he had such good documentary bases, that the following message should have got through: each republican and socialist must revise all his judgements on the French Revolution.[125]

As against Wendel, he saw the Ventôse decrees and, more generally, the outline social policy advanced during the Terror as essential new reforms, from which one should draw inspiration.[126] Lastly, he appealed to the heritage of French socialism, which had always celebrated Robespierre's deeds. This is worth underlining, since such arguments were foreign to the social-democratic tradition. Such a position was not unrelated to the violent clashes now taking place in Austria, which would soon result in a Civil War; this brought the radicalisation of part of the Austrian party's intermediate cadres, who were probably more inclined to this type of inheritance. Such considerations brought a short and sharp riposte by Hermann Wendel, published in the pages of the same review.[127] Ever since his death, Robespierre had had his 'fanatical admirers',[128] who were now rallied behind the name of Albert Mathiez. His reply insisted on the naivety of believing that it would have been possible to go beyond the bourgeois revolution in that era:

> The French Revolution was a truly bourgeois overhaul ... Whoever best served this objective, best served the French Revolution and was the best revolutionary. Who acted in any other way worked against this development and produced a counter-revolutionary effect ... That is why Schiller Marmorek hardens Mathiez's argument according to which Robespierre aimed at a 'new social revolution' in the form of a 'redivision of the land' or an 'agrarian reform'.[129]

An Ongoing Point of Reference

While the history of the French Revolution was now less unique, and less widely taught and circulated, it remained a controversial subject debated in both social-democratic parties' reviews – as these long exchanges on Robespierre

---

125   Marmorek, S. 'Robespierre und die Nachwelt', *Der Kampf*, 1934, p. 72.
126   Marmorek, S. 'Robespierre und die Nachwelt', *Der Kampf*, 1934, p. 76.
127   Wendel, H., 'St Robespierre. Eine Entgegnung', *Der Kampf*, 1934, pp. 226–8.
128   Wendel, H., 'St Robespierre. Eine Entgegnung', *Der Kampf*, 1934, p. 226.
129   Wendel, H., 'St Robespierre. Eine Entgegnung', *Der Kampf*, 1934, p. 227.

proved. Even beyond this debate, while the history of the French Revolution took a lesser place in educationals and in most party organs generally, references to this history continued to be present till the end of this period.

References to Revolutionary History

The 'Great French Revolution' had not disappeared from the horizons of *Vorwärts*'s readers, even after the rather weak commemorations of 1929. It is unsurprising that we find no obituary of Albert Mathiez, given that Robespierrianism was, without exception, foreign to the social-democrats; we might also note another death that certainly contributed to eclipsing Mathiez's, namely the passing of Aristide Briand on 7 March 1932. Nonetheless, in a newspaper in which historical references were becoming rare, this history did occasionally serve to illustrate the contemporary political situation. Thus in one article on 12 February 1932 Hermann Wendel addressed the problem of creating a unitary national language, comparing the present-day demands of the Spanish socialists with the actions of the French revolutionaries between 1789 and 1794.[130] What place should the young Spanish Republic accord to minority languages?[131] The aim was to understand some Spanish socialists' position in favour of a unitary national language: they were fighting against the division among multiple languages, which itself overlapped with political questions: 'Spanish appeared as the language of the revolution, as against Basque which seemed to him to be the language of the counter-revolution'.[132] And 'what is playing out today in Spain has its historical twin in the France of the Great Revolution'.[133] Noting that in 1789 France's multiple regional tongues resembled a real 'tower of Babel', he highlighted the way in which the unification of the French language had represented a means of identification for the revolutionaries. For 'language had a new meaning: it was no longer only a means of understanding one another, but a link which bound the national community together'.[134] Wendel particularly cited the arguments on the French language that Barère had advanced at the Convention on 17 January 1794. This was a revolutionary language; it stood against 'federalism' and 'superstition', which spoke Breton, German, Italian ... Wendel highlighted that these were essentially ideological proclamations, for the regional languages had in fact endured into

130   Wendel, H., 'Revolution und Sprachenfrage. In Spanien heute wie einst in Frankreich', *Vorwärts*, 12 February 1932, p. 4.
131   The Second Spanish Republic was proclaimed on 11 February 1931.
132   Ibid.
133   Ibid.
134   Ibid.

the present. While he himself offered no answer, he underlined the complexity of this debate and warned against the unifying approach advanced by some of the members of the National Convention and perpetuated by the Spanish socialists.[135]

On 1 March 1932, one article presented Marat as a 'man of science'.[136] Known as a revolutionary, pamphleteer, *l'Ami du peuple* journalist and deputy in the Convention, Marat was less famous as a philosopher, physicist and doctor. The article thus reviewed Marat's early years – especially the 1770s, when he practiced medicine in London – as well as his various writings from this era. This was a rather incidental piece, but nonetheless showed that in the early 1930s a reader of the social-democratic daily would still regularly encounter pieces on the main actors in the Revolution. We could cite numerous other examples.[137]

Moreover, when we consult the party library catalogues from the late 1920s and early 1930s, we see the continued presence of pre-1914 works, but also confirmation of the very low numbers of recent contributions on the French Revolution. For Germany the main source is the *Guide to the Workers' Libraries* published in 1928.[138] This was a complete guide for classifying the books in the workers' libraries, down to the most technical details (the reader's card, the form to fill out in a book ...). History was not a theme unto itself, but included in a wider category entitled 'History, biographies, memoirs'. Wilhelm Blos's book on the French Revolution regularly recurred in the examples of classifications. An annex presented the 'basic stock of a workers' library': the section devoted to history featured, for example, the most recent edition of Kautsky's *Die Klassengegensätze* (from 1923) and even Max Beer's *Allgemeine Geschichte*.

There is also a series of catalogues regarding Austria in this same period: in the catalogue for Hietzing, categorised by theme, works on the French Revolution were, as in the educationals, integrated into a wider set of titles on the history of revolutions.[139] The 'classics', for the most part published or re-issued between 1906 and 1923 (Buonarroti, Conrady, Blos, Kropotkin and Kautsky) appeared among a very large number of other references. In the list of 'good books' published by the party educational commission in 1931, the French Revolution made up a sub-section of the 'history of wars and revolutions'; these

---

135   Ibid.

136   Poetzsch, H., 'Marat als Mann der Wissenschaft', *Vorwärts*, 1 March 1932, p. 6.

137   For example, Wendel, H., 'Die Friedhöfe der Schreckenszeit-Wurden Ludwig XVI und Robespierre am gleichen Ort beerdigt?', *Vorwärts*, 14 March 1932, p. 5.

138   *Leitfaden für Arbeiter-Büchereien*, Berlin, Reichausschuss für sozialistische Bildungsarbeit, 1928.

139   *Arbeiterbücherei Hietzing. Bücher-Katalog, Hietzing*, Haustruckerei der Organisation Hietzing.

same works appeared alongside Thomas Carlyle and Georges Bourgin.[140] The same balance was apparent in many district catalogues of 'good books'.[141] In some district libraries, this theme was more notable for its absence: at the library in Rudolfsheim, Vienna, the section devoted to revolutionary history featured almost no reference to the 1789 Revolution ... except the Lassallean Bernhard Becker's old book on the Commune of 1793.[142] We can draw an over-all balance-sheet by basing ourselves on the bibliography established by Karl Kautsky's son Benedikt in 1933, entitled *Do You Want to Become a Marxist?* It compiled most of the books published by both the German and Austrian parties since their origins: the part devoted to the 'Great Revolution' noted all the books published before 1914.[143] Here, the discrepancy with the prewar period appeared with all the greater clarity. For want of statistics as precise as those which *Der Bibliothekar* provided before the war, it is difficult to know if these books were still read. But considering their weak presence in the party schools, their use must have been clearly reduced.

A Return to Jaurès?

A tribute published in *Sozialistische Monatshefte* on the fifteenth anniversary of Jaurès's murder asked, 'When will we have a Jean Jaurès Street in Berlin?'[144] In Austria, a set of buildings and a street did bear the French socialist's name.[145] Beyond these incidental examples, we can see that from the early 1920s onward his *Histoire socialiste* enjoyed a belated but real reception in Germany: tellingly, in their dispute over Robespierre, Schiller Marmorek and Hermann Wendel each sought to legitimise their point of view by drawing on Jaurès's work.

Following Bernstein's efforts to bring this work into the German context at the turn of the century, this was a second introduction of Jaurès's history of the French Revolution. At the end of the 1920s, Hedwig Hintze highlighted the value of his work as an innovative example of social and economic history.

---

140   *Gute Bücher*, Vienna: Verlag der Zentralstelle für das Bildungswesen, 1931.

141   *Die Besten Bücher der Hernalser Arbeiter-Bibliothek. Erste Auswahl*, Vienna: Verlag der Sozialdemokratischen Unterrichtsorganisation Hernals, 1931; *Die Besten Bücher der Land-strasser Arbeiter-Bibliotheken. Erste Auswahl*, Vienna: Verlag der Sozialdemokratischen Unterrichtsorganisation Landstrasse, 1931.

142   *Bücherverzeichnis. Arbeiterbücherei Rudolfsheim*, Vienna: Verlag der Arbeiter-Bücherei, 1931.

143   Kautsky 1933, p. 22.

144   Thurow, H., 'Jean Jaurès: zu seinem 70. Geburtstag', *Sozialistische Monatshefte*, 1929, pp. 671–6.

145   Between 1925 and 1927 a block baptised 'Jean-Jaurès-Hof' was built by Vienna's social-democratic city hall. See Hautmann 1980.

Not long after this, continuing her interest for the French socialist tribune, the historian made plans to write a biography of Jaurès: she reported that Albert Mathiez helped her in this task during her stay in Paris.[146] However, the Nazis' arrival in power, and its consequences, without doubt prevented her from proceeding with this project. Nonetheless, Hintze had published several articles on Jaurès. One of them reviewed his conception of history, especially as seen through the example of his work on the French Revolution.[147] Written in late 1932, this article appeared in early 1933 in one of the last issues of *Archiv für Sozialwissenschaft und Sozialpolitik*, a highly authoritative review founded by Werner Sombart, Max Weber and Edgar Jaffe. Here, we will address this article insofar as it made up part of the social-democrats' debates on the materialist conception of history.

Hintze examined the elements in Jaurès that came from Marxism, as well the other sources of his thinking. She invoked the texts in which Marx had polemicised with Proudhon (*Poverty of Philosophy*) and presented the gestation of historical materialism as far as the collection of Engels's letters published under the title 'On Historical Materialism'[148] and the revisionism debate, before reviewing Jaurès's own arguments. Expressing the weak impact of the 1902 edition of the *Études socialistes* published by the *Sozialistische Monatshefte*, Hintze directly referred to the French Revolution, even as she also mentioned other texts that had appeared in social-democratic reviews. As against those who saw his synthesis as a 'petty-bourgeois method'[149] Hintze sought to reassert Jaurès's full singularity precisely by means of his history of the French Revolution. Speaking of his role in advancing the understanding of the sources, building on Aulard, Hintze repeatedly quoted long extracts from the Introduction to the *Histoire socialiste* in order to explain Jaurès's conception of history. She returned to the problem the French socialist had raised of why there had been no 'German 1789', as well as highlighting his turn-of-the-century dispute with Franz Mehring. These long extracts, which carried little commentary, like the

---

146   Hintze, H., 'Albert Mathiez. Une page de souvenirs', *Annales historiques de la Révolution française*, 1932, p. 483.

147   Hintze, H., 'Jean Jaurès und die materialistische Geschichtstheorie', *Archiv für Sozialwissenschaft und Sozialpolitik*, 1933, pp. 194–218.

148   Marx and Engels 1930–1.

149   Hintze, H., 'Jean Jaurès und die materialistische Geschichtstheorie', *Archiv für Sozialwissenschaft und Sozialpolitik*, 1933, pp. 198. Written in 1932, Hintze's article was probably referring to the Communist Klément's work and in general to those in the Communist current who followed the 'class against strategy' and wanted to transform the Communist Parties by tearing them from their old references, which were considered non-Marxist: Klément 1931.

ones cited in *Die Gesellschaft* served as an introduction. The purpose of the text was to present Jaurès's work. She concluded on the connection between Marx's thought and Jaurès:

> Without the experience of Marxism, Jaurès would very certainly have gloriously continued the line of the French humanist socialists who proclaimed and represented the ideals of justice, peace between peoples and reconciliation between classes; but, through his study of Marx, his socialism obtained the material economic foundation, a stronger note of revolution and class struggle and an energetic tension of contradiction, from which there came the admirable dynamism of his system and his political effectiveness.[150]

Here Jaurès's problematics were set in a precise historiographical framework that was far from comparable to the many polemical texts published between 1900 and 1905. Nonetheless, we can note a certain wider respect for the *Histoire socialiste*, even among those who had rejected it when it was published. Kautsky – one of Jaurès's leading critics in 1905 – critically reappraised a *Histoire socialiste* which he had earlier evaluated in severe terms, at least publicly. In *War and Democracy*, Jaurès's *Histoire socialiste* was one of his sources. Less well-known is that his archives include a draft of a portrait of Jaurès, probably drawn up soon after Hitler seized power.[151] Its short length and the writing style would suggest that this was originally intended as a newspaper article which was, to our knowledge, never published.[152] Among other things, Kautsky revisited his own past appreciation of the *Histoire socialiste*:

> Alongside all this, what particularly impressed me was his incredible capacity for work. He drew my admiration, for example, when he was leading the party and a daily newspaper at the same time as he was finishing a history of the French Revolution, a work of 2,000 pages based on in-depth study ... I awaited this book with great scepticism on account of Jaurès's conception of history, which I did not share. The impression that it made on me when it came out was thus all the more intense. The result was that I had a greater appreciation for the man who produced this powerful work. He here proved himself a great researcher, up to the

---

150   Hintze, H., 'Jean Jaurès und die materialistische Geschichtstheorie', *Archiv für Sozialwissenschaft und Sozialpolitik*, 1933, pp. 218.
151   Translated and presented in full in Ducange 2007b.
152   This text goes unmentioned in Blumenberg 1960.

standards of this fighter and his public acitivities. He was one of those rare publicists who shone as much as a writer as as an orator.[153]

Heritage and Change

The invention of a tradition – a historical reference to which a political organisation refers – closely depends on its particular context. Eric Hobsbawm emphasises that such an invention can also take place 'when old traditions and their institutional carriers and promulgators no longer prove sufficiently adaptable and flexible, or are otherwise eliminated; in short, when there are sufficiently large and rapid changes on the demand or the supply side'.[154] Here the British historian is speaking of a much broader tendency, which must necessarily apply only imperfectly to social democracy alone. Nonetheless, the 'carriers' and 'promulgators' of the history of the French Revolution did, indeed, undergo major upheavals, especially in connection to the social-democratic parties' new position in the wake of the events of 1918–19. Its greatly reduced place in educational structures and the near-absence of specific publications on the French Revolution in this period are evident: no book dedicated to this subject was published, in the pre-1914 sense, throughout the Weimar Republic (which is to say, issued by the party publishing house, recommended in workers' libraries and used as a basis for militants' educationals). References to the 'Great Revolution' nonetheless remained present in numerous social-democratic texts and publications. They can be summarised by way of analogies with the situations that called for them. We can identify three distinct forms.

The first was the most 'classic' case: understanding the present demanded a return to some episode in the Revolution. Several debates or events allowed for a series of analogies, from Adelheid Popp revisiting the history of the Constituent Assembly in order to set her fight for women's right to vote in a historical tradition, to Karl Kautsky comparing July 1791 to July 1927. In this same spirit, in numerous texts the Revolution remained the bourgeois revolution *par excellence*, and in this regard a basis for historical reflection. Nonetheless, it had visibly lost its singular role: 1789 constituted less a model than one democratic revolution among others, in a context in which other alternative models also emerged. One such example was the model offered

---

153   IISG, Karl Kautsky Archiv, A 202, 'Erinnerungen an Jean Jaurès. (1934?)'.
154   Hobsbawm and Ranger 2012, pp. 4–5.

by the United States of America, from which certain social-democratic visit-
ors returned full of enthusiasm, and whose 1787 Constitution was taken as an
example.

The other, concurrent model, at the origin of a proliferation of analogies,
was the 1917 Revolution. The definition of social-democratic policy involved a
recognition of the Soviet model, especially as the Communists gradually gained
influence in Germany. From *Die Gesellschaft* to the *Arbeiter-Kalender*, the rejection of revolutionary violence and the Soviet Terror proceeded by way of analogy with the Terror of 1793. Certainly, the likes of Karl Kautsky and Otto Bauer
showed greater nuance, above all directing their fire at the Bolshevik policy and
dissociating the excesses of the popular terror from the Jacobins who sought to
impose limits on it. But there is no doubt that on a larger scale, the assimilation of the French Revolution to 'terrorism' contributed to discrediting it as a
point of reference. In turn, the German Communists offered an almost opposite reading: albeit not without certain nuances, they embraced the legacy of
the revolutionary Terror. In their educational structures, they built on a vulgate
that the social-democrats had elaborated before 1914 but barely still promoted,
as they themselves sought to offer an overall explanation of the revolutionary
process.

The discrediting of the 'terrorist' episode, by analogy with the Soviet model –
or even, for Wendel, Nazism – should not make us forget that the motto 'Liberté,
Égalité, Fraternité' was still being used in parallel, for example upon the 1929
anniversary of both the Revolution and the Weimar Republic. 1789 and other
'moderate' episodes were sometimes still in good standing, even outside of traditional party circles. From the study of federalism by an academic close to the
SPD like Hedwig Hintze, to Hermann Wendell's Dantonist fervour, these two
approaches – whatever their great differences – shared a common rejection of
the most radical episodes of 1793–4 and a sustained political engagement in
favour of Franco-German friendship, the 'United States of Europe'.

The example of the belated reception of Jean Jaurès is worth mentioning, in
this regard. Without doubt, in the absence of any translation or real circulation
of this work in Germany, the appreciation of Jaurès's study remained limited
to a few intellectuals who were either in or close to the SPD. Yet for that, it
was no less indicative of a paradigm shift. For in the prewar years Jaurès's history had produced much reticence, not least on account of the conception of
republican socialism that it implied. It was first anchored in the academic tradition by way of Albert Mathiez's 1924 French re-edition of the *Histoire socialiste*,
the same year as Hintze introduced Aulard's *Histoire politique* in Germany, and
this probably helped make this new reading possible. Jaurès could all the more
be a reference for Hedwig Hintze or Hermann Wendel insofar as the French

socialist's final struggles had resonance for intellectuals who considered a rapprochement between France and Germany to be vitally important.

The debate around Robespierre, linked to the exchanges with Mathiez, marked the conclusion of this period. The Société des Études Robespierristes founder's often conflictual relations with foreign historians would probably deserve a study of its own.[155] Sticking to German examples, it is worth noting that Mathiez's debate with Hedwig Hintze and then Hermann Wendel took place at the very moment when his relations with his Soviet colleagues were becoming more strained, to the point of total rupture. From Robespierre to the Ventôse decrees and from federalism to the execution of Danton, Mathiez conducted a debate with historians from various countries who – in very different ways – used methodological tools drawn from Marxism, from Hintze's Jaurèsian inspiration to the Soviet orthodoxy that was now being fixed in place. Despite the vigour of the debates, these intellectual exchanges contributed to introducing and spreading awareness of other traditions of the study of the French Revolution. The social-democratic cadres in Germany and Austria reading *Die Gesellschaft* and *Der Kampf* thus became aware of the French historiography and Mathiez's works. A deeper study of these relations in the perspective of *histoire croisée*, which would demand a closer knowledge of other national contexts, would probably show what Mathiez's works owed to his exchanges with foreign colleagues, in the political and historiographical context of the early 1930s.

One last example, a few months after the debate on Robespierre in *Der Kampf*, shows the continued French interest for works by German-speaking authors. It took more than ten years for Kautsky's *Die Klassengegensätze von 1789* to be translated into French. But immediately after its publication, Engels's letter to Kautsky on his book dedicated to the French Revolution – whose historiographical importance we underlined at the beginning of the present volume – was immediately translated and published by the *Annales historiques de la Révolution française*.[156] This critical letter, highlighting the role of the peas-

---

155   James Frigulietti's biography of Albert Mathiez reviews his break with the Soviets but has very little on his relations with German historians. Beyond the most famous case, namely Friedrich Sieburg's book (Sieburg 1935), a detailed study of the various publications would allow much light to be shed on the German historiography.

156   'Lettre d' Engels à Kautsky', *Annales historiques de la Révolution française*, 1934, pp. 361–5. The second version was in its 1935 run, pp. 47–51. It had in fact first been published in Russian in the review 'Marxist Historian' in July–August 1933, thanks to Lukin, a professor at Moscow University. Kautsky published it in German in Prague, where he was now exiled, together with all the correspondence with Engels he had in his possession. Kautsky and Engels 1935.

ants, the *sans-culottes* and more generally the question of the alliance between
the revolutionary government and the popular movement, concerned problems that also resonated with the themes addressed by French historians. Its
rapid translation continued in the same vein as the attention that Mathiez had
always paid to German-language articles and books on the French Revolution.
It drew so many comments from readers that the same journal republished it
the following year,[157] now with a considerable critical apparatus that would
allow a French audience better to understand the stakes of a debate on the
'Great Revolution' among two of the most important figures in the history of
European socialism.

---

157 'The translation was done in full without removing Mr. Lukin's notes from the text; our
     readers must, therefore, have found certain passages difficult to understand. We think
     we are responding to their wishes by presenting this interesting document anew'. 'Lettre
     d'Engels à Kautsky', 1935, p. 47.

Conclusion

Social-democratic movements around Europe claimed the legacy of what was called the 'Great Revolution'; in Austria and above all in Germany they sought better to understand this history in order to shed light on the problems posed in their own time. As they gained strength in their respective countries, they were the first parties in the history of the European Left to write and circulate a developed interpretation of the French Revolution inspired by Marxism. From their book reviews of academic studies to their popular dailies, the history of the 'Great Revolution' gradually took up a place at the heart of social-democratic identity. In the period between Marx's first notes and Jaurès's *Histoire socialiste*, when French socialism was greatly divided and still only raising its head, the social-democrats picked up Marx's project of writing a history of the 'Great Revolution'. For the centenary, Karl Kautsky wrote a handbook based on a series of articles, which sought to grasp the 'class contradictions' during the French Revolution. For his part, Wilhelm Blos wrote a 'people's history' of these events, destined to become one of the most widely read historical works among the pre-1914 social-democrats. Faced with the German-speaking countries' own lack of revolutionary experience, they celebrated the 1789 Revolution, which though considered bourgeois was also the only one that had fulfilled the tasks of its era. It was a bourgeois revolution that had exerted a powerful influence in Germany, especially by way of the Napoleonic occupation; and it also heralded fresh struggles. The social-democrats saw themselves as heirs to the demands of the 'Great Revolution', and regularly expressed as much by way of the foundational link between the centenary of the French Revolution and the creation of the Second International in 1889. In Germany and Austria unlike in France, there was no heritage to pursue, no socialism that could be inscribed within a political regime like the Republic; rather, up till 1914 it was necessary to establish a social-democratic history and fight an authoritarian regime. In the absence of any victorious revolution in their own nations, the social-democrats drew on French points of reference.

From Bebel's speech to Kautsky's study, via the vulgate in the pages of the *Arbeiter-Kalender*, the French Revolution made up part of militants' surroundings. One of the most telling examples was the presence of the 1793 Constitution in the commentary on the Erfurt Programme, a pamphlet distributed in hundreds of thousands of copies. While the historiography of the French Revolution is sometimes addressed in light of the content of historians or theorists' writings alone – texts whose real impact is difficult to measure – the social-democratic example allows us to see how a work seeking to link theoretical imperatives to political practice was considered a tool available to party militants and supporters, such that it could become the basis of the vulgate expounded in newspapers and educational schools. In this sense, the teaching of this history is an important indicator; it was considered in the context of *Bildung*, itself a much-prioritised element of social-democratic organisation at least up till the early 1920s. When we study the variety of sources offered by the social-democratic parties and the way in which historical references appeared therein, we can get a measure of the specificity of this output, even beyond its content. From *Die Neue Zeit*'s theoretical elaboration to the regular presence of revolutionary dates in the workers' calendars, we can reconstruct a whole hierarchy within which 'smugglers' and intermediaries played an essential role.

The Uses and Transmission of History

The study of the production of a vulgate on the history of the 'Great Revolution' shows that it does not constitute a linear project, a dogma, which was defined in some moment and then simply reproduced in various media and structures. Indeed, there is always a tension between the concern to establish an interpretative tradition that can be assimilated by militants, and the transmission of this same history at the scale of several decades, which closely depends on the developments and the debates of the present moment. The production – the writing – of history should itself be seen in the context of the social and political upheavals which traversed this whole period. For example, the Russian Revolution of 1905 marked an important turning point because even beyond all the reflection and analogies which it sparked in that moment, it drove a revived interest for the history of the French Revolution at all levels of the party, including in the party schools. It helped give a stimulus to numerous publications on this theme, the most important and ambitious of which was Heinrich Cunow's *Die revolutionäre Zeitungsliteratur*, whose contents – extracts of which were reproduced in the party press – were a fundamental basis for the 'itinerant professors' in charge of transmitting the history of the French Revolution. We should note that while most of this output was transferred from Germany into Austria, this latter had its own specificities, such as the greater attention in the Austrian context to the women's movement during the French Revolution: Emma Adler published a book on the women of the Revolution while Adelheid Popp regularly referred to the first women's clubs of 1789–94.

Attentive to social and economic structures, the social-democratic historiography regularly revisited the 'terrorist' episode in the Revolution. From the outset, the social-democrats' relationship with the revolutionary model of 1789 and – even more so – 1793 was never unambiguous. Even in 1889, Wilhelm Blos had distanced himself from any kind of radical rupture. In countries where a historiography hostile to the legacy of the French Revolution had dominated for decades, the social-democrats, instead, sought to celebrate this inheritance. But the problem of the use of revolutionary violence demonstrated the tensions running through their analyses. Indeed, from 1889 to 1934 this was one of the clearest continuities: on all but a handful of occasions, Robespierre and Robespierrism appeared in a negative light, in this sense greatly differing from a whole section of the left-wing historiography in France. Greeting Gustav Tridon's work and his rehabilitation of Hébert, in the 1870s Wilhelm Liebknecht began a long tradition of celebrating this latter as a popular tribune, or even a precursor of the workers' movement. The social-democrats laid claim not to the 'over-the-top' aspects of the Hébertists, but their supposed role as spokesmen of the Parisian people. Up till World War I the vulgate would spread a positive image of Hébert and also Marat, described as a visionary with an early understanding of the class struggle ... and who, we could add, had died too early to have had any relation to the state Terror. Again in his case, what was foregrounded was his role as a spokesman of the popular masses, through the connection with his paper *l'Ami du peuple*.

The repeated expressions of hostility to the state Terror – identified with Robespierre personally – should be understood in line with the social-democrats' wider orientations. While repressive measures could be justified as a means of politics in the era of the bourgeois revolutions, they were now unthinkable: a constant of the social-democrats' writings was the superiority of party organisation over disorderly revolutionary violence. The great bourgeois revolution in France must be followed by another, future, superior proletarian revolution, which would stand in continuity with Marx and the German philosophers of the 1840s. From the 1880s this superiority was embodied in the Social-Democratic Party, a united party which contrasted with the fragmentation and weakness of its French Socialist counterparts, who were unworthy of their past. The gradual strengthening and growing rootedness of the social-democratic parties within a context of legality provided the space for such an interpretation.

From the Atlantic to the Urals ...

While it was closely linked to a German-speaking context, we can also situate this social-democratic history in a wider, European movement. The turn of the century saw the birth of the social and economic history of the French Revolution. From France to Russia, from the 'Great Revolution' of 1789 to the failure of the 1905 Russian Revolution, similar questions appeared across Karl Kautsky and Heinrich Cunow's works just like those of Jean Jaurès and Peter Kropotkin. All of them sought to write a social history – particularly of the popular layers – that broke with the dominant political history. Jaurès's echo in Germany and Austria, and perhaps even more so Kropotkin's, spoke to common objectives as well as real differences. Jaurès's rarely-studied engagement with the foreign historiography deserves a specific study. From the first volumes of his *Histoire socialiste*, the German social-democrats debated his conceptions; exchanges with Eduard Bernstein, Franz Mehring and Karl Kautsky compelled Jaurès to add greater definition to his conception of a socialism that pursued the ideals of the French Revolution, while the socialists hostile to him sought to use the German orthodoxy to promote an alternative reading of the Revolution itself. This was an entangled history, and also the history of the refusal to introduce certain theoretical choices: as with most works on the French Revolution in this era, political stakes were closely intertwined with historiographical debates. Yet among other things, what was new here was the international aspect of this engagement.

As for a large part of the European Left, existing political models and interpretations of revolutionary history were challenged by the Russian Revolution of 1917, which took place in the same sequence as the German and Austrian revolutions. There was a proliferation of analogies – and they were negative. The idea that the Bolsheviks constituted a minority of conspirators among an uncontrolled mass seemed to the social-democrats to be a sterile imitation of the Jacobin past, especially since the protagonists themselves laid claim to such a comparison. A rejection of revolutionary violence present already in the 1880s took on its full meaning after 1917 with the appearance of Soviet communism. The question of violence and its structural rejection in the German and Austrian social-democratic movements is still to be examined more closely and would merit a specific study. This latter would necessarily have to pay attention to their reading of the revolutions of the past.

The shattering of internationalism, the difficult postwar relations between France and Germany, and the parties' participation in the business of state – and, at the same time, the emergence of new models like the USA – combined to diminish the place that went to the history of the French Revolution. Party educationals concentrated on more technical aspects of immediate political questions. Heinrich Cunow well illustrates this profound change: his only specific publication on the French Revolution in these years was a short essay on the cafés during the Revolution ... as compared to a 400-page book in the prewar period. In this same era, particularly in the 1920s, new contacts were established with intellectuals and some academics, within the framework of Franco-German rapprochement. It was in this context that the first real discussion on Robespierre took place in the social-democratic reviews, echoing Albert Mathiez's works. This latter's attention for German studies and then the publication, after his sudden death in 1932, of his notes criticising the social-democrat Hermann Wendel's book on Danton, were the origin of an international debate on Robespierre and the Montagnards, in a moment in which fresh attention for academic historiography now allowed Jaurès's interpretation to be introduced into Germany, as against the largely critical reception of two decades previously.

The winding paths of *Die Klassengegensätze von 89*, the first handbook elaborated within the context of the 1880s establishment of a Germanophone Marxism, are themselves testament to these evolutions from the 1880s to the early 1930s. The effectiveness of this paperback volume, which may seem to have been outmoded by the distance of time and the many new pieces of research, should itself be considered as an object of historical inquiry. A study of its international reception before 1914 would probably show that across two decades a great number of socialists and social-democrats in many countries were introduced to the history of the French Revolution by this short textbook. This was, of course, true in Austria, where it served as the basis for one of the first talks with slides, but so, too, in central and eastern Europe, where it was translated into numerous languages corresponding to the Second International's sphere of influence; the several Russian editions in particular indicate a wide readership.[1] It was from the 1920s, when the vulgate based on this pamphlet was no longer in use in the party that had elaborated it, that its posterity became clearest: the communists of the KPD, often leaders who had come from the pre-war SPD, partly themselves adopted it. Kautsky's summary, which had so irritated Engels when it was first published in *Die Neue Zeit*, would spread beyond the boundaries of the German-speaking world and help train the cadres and militants of the international workers' movement. It was republished in the USSR during the first years of the new regime.[2] The first translations of works on the French Revolution in China began after the '4 May 1919 Movement'. In response to the conservatives who had translated Gustav Le Bon's *The Crowd*, there were translations of Kropotkin (in 1930–1) and the books from the social-democratic centenary by Blos (1929) and Kautsky (1930), with which the Chinese Communists educated themselves in the history of the

---

1   Blumenberg 1960, p. 43.
2   Petrograd, 1918; Moscow, 1919; Moscow, 1923; Kharkov, 1923 (RGASPI library, Moscow).

French Revolution.[3] One of the last translations of *Die Klassengegensätze von 1789* took place in Japan in the mid-1950s.[4] In 1939, upon the 150th anniversary of 1789, a French textbook for Soviet schools copied word-for-word some of the passages on the *sans-culottes* and the revolutionary government from Kautsky's book ... without citing the author. The name of this 'renegade' had become unmentionable; yet the theoretical matrix that he had carried forth remained a fundamental reference point, not long before the official interpretation of the French Revolution was established in 1941.

These examples all testify to the international influence of the German social-democrat's textbook among thousands of cadres and militants, including in communist ranks, long beyond the golden age of the Second International. In France itself, where there was an abundance of textbooks and histories of the French Revolution, we still find traces of Kautsky's *La lutte des classes en France en 1789* in the PCF party school in 1936, even though it had not been reissued since 1901.[5] There was no Marxist textbook on the French Revolution, while both the style and the substance of Jaurès's vast fresco were difficult to get to grips with. The social-democratic vulgate thus remained somewhat effective, even beyond its initial readership. Such an example well illustrates how in a certain theoretical and political conjuncture, a foreign historiography can represent a point of reference on a historical event where there is no similar work in the country concerned.

Other continuities remain to be studied. In exile in Paris and then Zürich, Hermann Wendel sought in his own way to celebrate 1789 and its values. In 1936 he published a book on the history of *La Marseillaise* since its origins, mainly in France but also in Germany.[6] If this song was the anthem of the Third Republic, it was also the 'hymn of the freedom of peoples', especially the Germans forced to flee Nazi Germany. As in his final articles in *Die Gesellschaft* where he had spoken of the 'primitive utopia' of the Ventôse decrees, in a German political journal published in Paris called *Tage-Buch* he compared Robespierre's terror to National Socialism.[7] If Wendel celebrated 1789, he rejected a 1793 which in his view corresponded to the terrors of the regimes of the present.

---

3 Information from an (unpublished) talk at a conference on 'La storia della rivoluzione francese' held at Naples University in 2003: YI Gao 'La Révolution française en Chine'.
4 Blumenberg 1960, p. 43.
5 *École élémentaire du Parti communiste français, Cinquième leçon, la France de 1789 à nos jours*, 1936.
6 Wendel 1936.
7 *Das Tage-Buch* 1936, 6 May 1936, p. 550, indicated by Stübling 1983, p. 102.

The Legacy for Germany, and the two Germanies

A close study of the transmission of these references over the long term allows us to understand the link between the social-democratic tradition and the emergence of a renewed study of the French Revolution in the two German states and to a lesser degree in Austria. This historiography particularly focused on studying the Jacobins in the German-speaking countries, in the manner of Walter Grab's studies published in West Germany and Helmut Reinalter in Austria.[8] While none of the pre-1934 social-democratic books were republished, we can find an example like the extracts from Cunow's *Die revolutionäre Zeitungsliteratur* republished in an anthology compiled by Walter Grab, next to some of the most famous historians of the time.[9] As for the DDR, where historians laid claim to their Marxist ancestry, the works by Kautsky and Cunow were sometimes cited, though never republished. Conversely, the reappropriation of Franz Mehring – who from the late 1950s became something of a national hero in the DDR – allowed the reintroduction of his early-twentieth-cenutry texts, as part of a vast endeavour to publish his collected works. A proper understanding of the exaltation of the Spartakist leaders' works in the DDR would demand a close study of the careers of certain 'smugglers' who had earned their spurs in the SPD schools before 1914 before joining the KPD in the 1920s and then finding themselves in positions of responsibility after the collapse of Nazism. Hermann Duncker, a teacher at the SPD and then KPD party school, would up to his death in 1960 occupy important educational functions in the DDR;[10] for his part, the DDR's first president Wilhelm Pieck had himself been an 'itinerant teacher' for the SPD before 1914. Walter Markov, one of the most important historians of the French Revolution, whose work extended across the whole history of the DDR, had been steeped in French revolutionary history during the Weimar Republic.[11] The German historiography's contribution to the knowledge of France's popular movements can also be set in a longer-term picture. The first collection of source documents on the *sans-culottes*, prior to the publication of Albert Soboul's thesis, came out in East Berlin in 1957, in collaboration with Walter Markov.[12] Thus the space of the Franco-German debate between socialists and social-democrats, underway since the beginning of the twentieth century, persisted notwithstanding the very different conditions.

---

8   See especially Grab 1971–8.
9   Grab 1975.
10   Griep, Förster and Siegel 1974.
11   Markow 2009.
12   Soboul and Markow 1957.

The history of the French Revolution has long been influenced by Marxism, or at least engaged in debate with methods and concepts that came from Marxism. The social-democratic work on this subject was a unique moment of this history. It allows us to measure the extent to which the history of the Revolution was elaborated in function of the imperatives weighing down on those who endeavoured to write it. Within an entangled history of the historiography of one of the most controversial events facing historical scholarship, the social-democrats' output deserved to be restored to its proper place.

References

Aaslestad, Katherine 2005, 'Remembering and Forgetting: The Local and the Nation in Hamburg's Commemorations of the Wars of Liberation', *Central European History*, 3: 384–416.

Adler, Emma 1906, *Die berühmten Frauen der französischen Revolution: 1789–1795*, Vienna: C.W. Stern.

Adler, Friedrich 1918, *Die Erneuerung der Internationale. Aufsätze aus der Kriegzeit*, Vienna: Verlag der Wiener Buchhandlung Ignaz Brand.

Advielle, Victor 1990, *Histoire de Gracchus Babeuf et du babouvisme*, 2 vols., Paris, CTHS.

Agulhon, Maurice 1989, *Marianne au pouvoir: L'imagerie et la symbolique républicaines de 1880 à 1914*, Paris, Flammarion.

Angel, Peter 1961, *Edouard Bernstein et l'évolution du socialisme allemand*, Paris: Didier

Ardelt, Rudolf 1984, *Friedrich Adler-Probleme einer Persönlichkeitsentwicklung um die Jahrhundertwende*, Vienna: Österreichischer Bundesverlag.

Assmann, Aleida 1994, *Construction de la mémoire nationale, une brève histoire de l'idée allemande de Bildung*, Paris: Editions de la MSH.

Aubry, Dominique 1988, *Quatre-vingt-treize et les jacobins*, Lyon: Presses universitaires de Lyon.

Aulard, Alphonse 1902, 'Monsieur Jaurès, historien de la Révolution', *La Révolution française*, October: 289–99.

Aulard, Alphonse 1907, *Taine historien de la Révolution française*, Paris: A. Colin.

Aulard, Alphonse 1924, *Politische Geschichte der französischen Revolution*, 2 Vols, Leipzig: Duncker & Humblot.

Babeuf, Gracchus 2009, *Écrits*, Paris: Le Temps des Cerises.

Bach, Maximilian 1898, *Geschichte der Wiener Revolution im Jahre 1848*, Vienna: Ignaz Brand.

Badia, Gilbert 1975, *Rosa Luxemburg. Journaliste, Polémiste, Révolutionnaire*, Paris: Éditions sociales.

Baechler, Christian 2007, *L'Allemagne de Weimar 1919–33*, Paris: Fayard.

Bagger, Wolfgang 1983, *Untersuchungen zur Geschichte des Berliner Arbeiter-Bildungs-Instituts von 1878 und der Arbeiter-Bildungsschule Berlin 1891 bis 1914*, Leipzig: Dissertation.

Barck, Simone 1994, 'Max Beer', in Barck, Simone et al. (ed.), *Lexicon sozialistischer Literatur. Ihre Geschichte in Deutschland bis 1945*, Stuttgart: Verlag J.B. Metzler.

Barck, Simone et al. (eds.) 1994, *Lexicon sozialistischer Literatur. Ihre Geschichte in Deutschland bis 1945*, Stuttgart-Weimar: Verlag J.B. Metzler.

Bariéty, Jacques 1977, *Les relations franco-allemandes après la Première Guerre mondiale*, Paris: Publications de la Sorbonne.

Barnave, Antoine 1971, *Introduction à la Révolution française*, Paris: A. Colin.

Barthou, Louis 1934, *Danton*, Paris: Albin Michel.

Bauer Otto 1913, *Geschichte Österreichs: eine Anleitung zum Studium der österreichischen Geschichte und Politik*, Vienna: Danneberg.

Bauer, Otto 1920, *Bolschewismus oder Sozialdemokratie?*, Vienna: Wiener Volksbuchhandlung.

Bauer, Otto 1976, 'Räte Diktatur oder Demokratie', in *Werkausgabe*, vol. 2, Vienna: Europaverlag.

Bauer, Otto 1980, *Werkausgabe*, Vienna: Europaverlag.

Bauer, Otto 1980a, *Werkausgabe*, Vol. 1, Vienna: Europa Verlag.

Bauer, Otto 1980b, 'Der Balkankrieg und die deusche Weltpolitik', in *Werkausgabe*, Vol. 1, Vienna: Europa Verlag.

Bauer, Otto 2000, *The Question of Nationalities and Social Democracy*, Minneapolis: University of Minnesota Press.

Beaud, O. 2002, 'Légalité et légitimité: la lutte de Carl Schmitt contre la république de Weimar et sa défense d'une "contre-constitution" allemande', in Kervégan, J.-F. (ed.), *Crise et pensée de la crise en droit. Weimar, sa république et ses juristes*, Paris: Éditions de l'ENS.

Bebel, August 1950, *Die Frau und der Sozialismus*, Berlin: Dietz Verlag.

Bebel, August 1970, 'Zum 100. Jahrestag der Französischen Revolution', in *Ausgewählte Reden und Schriften*, East Berlin.

Becker, Bernhard 1875, *Geschichte der revolutionären Pariser Kommune in den Jahren 1789 bis 1794*, Braunschweig: W. Bracke.

Beer, Max 1913, *Geschichte des Sozialismus in England*, Stuttgart: Dietz.

Beer, Max 1918, *Jean Jaurès. Sozialist und Staatsman*, Berlin: Druck und Verlag für Sozialwissenschaft.

Beer, Max 1920, *History of British Socialism*, London: G. Bell and Sons.

Beer, Max 1921–3, *Allgemeine Geschichte des Sozialismus und der sozialen Kämpfe*, Berlin: Verlag für Sozialwissenschaft.

Beer, Max 1932, *Allgemeine Geschichte des Sozialismus und der sozialen Kämpfe*, Berlin, Sozialwissenschaftliche Bibliothek.

Bernstein, Eduard 1895, *Kommunistische und demokratisch-sozialistische Strömungen während der englischen Revolution*, Stuttgart: Dietz.

Bernstein, Eduard 1899, *Die Voraussetzungen des Sozialismus und die Aufgaben der Sozialdemokratie*, Stuttgart: Dietz.

Bernstein, Eduard 1904, *Lassalle und seine Bedeutung für die Arbeiterklasse*, Berlin: Buchhandlung Vorwärts.

Bernstein, Eduard 1922, *Sozialismus und Demokratie in der grossen englischen Revolution*, Berlin: Dietz.

Bernstein, Eduard 1930, *Cromwell and Communism: Socialism and Democracy in the Great English Revolution*, London: George Allen & Unwin.

Bernstein, Eduard 1998, *Die deutsche Revolution von 1918/19, Geschichte der Entstehung und ersten Arbeitsperiode der deutschen Republik*, Bonn: Dietz.

Bernstein, Eduard 2004, *The Preconditions of Socialism*, Cambridge: Cambridge University Press.

Biard, Michel (ed.) 2008, *Les politiques de la Terreur*, Rennes: PUR.

Biard, Michel 2009, *Parlez-vous sans-culotte? Dictionnaire du Père Duchesne 1790–1794*, Paris, Tallandier.

Bildungsausschuss der sozialdemokratischen Partei Deutschlands 1908, *Muster-Kataloge für Arbeiter-Bibliotheken*, Berlin: Buchhandlung Vorwärts.

Blanc, Louis, 1847–67, *Histoire de la Révolution française*, 12 vols., Paris: Langlois et Leclercq.

Blanc, Olivier 2006, 'Femmes en Révolution, l'exemple d'Olympe de Gouges', in Biard, Michel. (ed.), 'Les représentations de l'"homme politique" en France', *Les Cahiers du GRHis*, 17: 53–63.

Blanchard, Pascal (ed.) 2008, *Les guerres de mémoires. La France et son histoire*, Paris: La Découverte.

Blos, Wilhelm 1875, *Die Revolution zu Mainz 1792–1793. Nach Quellen dargestellt*, Nürnberg: Genossenschaftsbuchdrückerei.

Blos, Wilhelm 1888, *Die französische Revolution. Volkstümliche Darstellung der Ereignisse und Zustände in Frankreich von 1789 bis 1804*, Stuttgart: Dietz.

Blos, Wilhelm 1893, *Die Deutsche Revolution: Geschichte der Deutschen Bewegung von 1848 und 1849*, Stuttgart, Dietz

Blos, Wilhelm 1920, *Die französische Revolution. Volkstümliche Darstellung der Ereignisse und Zustände in Frankreich von 1789 bis 1804*, Berlin: Dietz.

Blumenberg, Werner 1960, *Karl Kautskys literarisches Werk*, Amsterdam: Mouton and Co.

Bonnell, Andrew 1996, 'Socialism and Republicanism in imperial Germany', *Australian Journal of Politics and History*, 2: 192–202.

Bonnell, Andrew 2002, 'Did they read Marx? Marx reception and Social Democratic Party members in Imperial Germany, 1890–1914', *The Australian Journal of Politics and History*, 31: 4–15.

Bonnell, Andrew 2005, *The People's Stage in Imperial Germany: Social Democracy and Culture 1890–1914*, London: Tauris Academic Studies.

Bourdet, Yvon 1968, *Otto Bauer et la révolution*, Paris: EDI.

Bourdin, Philippe (ed.) 2008, *La Révolution 1789–1871: écriture d'une histoire immédiate*, Clermont-Ferrand: Presses Universitaires Blaise-Pascal.

Bourgin, Georges 1922, *Die Französische Revolution*, Stuttgart: Perthes.

Bouvier, Béatrix 1982, *Französische Revolution und deutsche Arbeiterbewegung*, Bonn: Dietz.

Bouvier, Béatrix 1988, 'Die Marseillaise in der deutschen Arbeiterbewegung vor 1914', *Internationalism in the labour movement, 1830–1940*, Leiden: Brill.

Bouvier, Béatrix 1992, 'Karl Kautsky als Historiker, Kautsky und diefranzösische Revolution', in Rojahn, Jürgen (ed.)*Marxismus und Demokratie*, Frankfurt: Campus Verlag.

Bouvier, Béatrix 2003, 'The influence of the French Revolution on socialism and the
German socialist movement in the nineteenth century', in Jeremy Jennings (ed.)
Socialism, London: Routledge.

Broué, Pierre 2004, *Communistes contre Staline. Massacre d'une génération*, Paris:
Fayard.

Broué, Pierre 2005, *The German Revolution 1917–1923*, Leiden: Brill.

Buchez, P.-J. and Roux, P. 1834–8, *Histoire parlementaire de la Révolution française*, Paris:
Paulin.

Buonarroti, Philippe 1836, *Buonarroti's history of Babeuf's conspiracy for equality: with
the author's reflections on the causes & character of the French Revolution, and his
estimate of the leading men and events of that epoch*, London.

Buonarroti, Philippe 1909, *Babeuf und die Verschwörung für die Gleichheit, mit dem
durch sie veranlassten Prozess und den Belegstücken*, Stuttgart: Dietz.

Buonarroti, Philippe 1957, *Conspiration pour l'égalité dite de Babeuf*, 2 vols., Paris: Éditions Sociales.

Bürgel, T. 1994, 'Die Neue Welt', in Barck, Simone et al. (eds.), *Lexicon sozialistischer Literatur. Ihre Geschichte in Deutschland bis 1945*, Stuttgart-Weimar: Verlag J.B. Metzler.

Buschak, Willy 2002, *Edo Fimmen: der schöne Traum von Europa und die Globalisierung.
Eine Biografie*, Essen: Klartext.

Calvet, Louis-Jean (ed.) 1977, *Marxisme et linguistique*, Paris: Payot.

Candar, Gilles 1991, 'L'accueil de l'Histoire socialiste de la Révolution française', *Jean
Jaurès, bulletin de la Société d'études jaurésiennes*, July–September, 122: 81–97.

Candar, Gilles 2007, 'Les socialistes français et la Révolution russe de 1905', *Cahiers du
monde russe*, 2–3: 365–8.

Chabot, Jean-Luc 2005, *Aux origines intellectuelles de l'Union européenne: l'idée d'Europe unie de 1919 à 1939*, Grenoble: Presses universitaires de Grenoble.

Charle, Christophe 1996, *Les intellectuels en Europe au XIXe siècle, essai d'histoire com-
parée*, Paris: Seuil

Chartier, Roger (ed.), 1986, *Les usages de l'imprimé (XVe–XIXe siècle)*, Paris: Fayard.

Conrady, Alexander 1911, *Geschichte der Revolutionen vom niederländischen Aufstand bis
zum Vorabend der französischen Revolution*, 2 vols., Berlin: Vorwärts.

Conrady, Alexander 1913, *Völkerschlachten und Klassenkämpfe. Urkundliche Beiträge zur
Jahrhundertfeier gesammelt*, 2 vols, Berlin: Buchhandlung Vorwärts Paul Singer.

Conrady, Alexander 1920, *Werden der Demokratie. Anfänge der Demokratie in England.
Studien zur Geschichte der Levellerbewegung*, Berlin: Vorwärts.

Conrady, Alexander 1922, *Die Rheinlande in der Franzosenzeit (1750 bis 1815)*, Stuttgart:
Dietz.

Cunow, Heinrich 1908, *Die revolutionäre Zeitungsliteratur Frankreichs während der Jah-*

re 1789 bis 1794. Ein Beitrag zur Geschichte der französischen Klassen- und Partei-kämpfe gegen Ende des 18. Jahrhunderts, Berlin: Buchhandlung Vorwärts.

Cunow, Heinrich 1912, *Die Parteien der Grossen Französischen Revolution und ihre Presse*, Berlin, Buchhandlung Vorwärts.

Cunow, Heinrich 1920, *Die marxsche Geschichts- Gesellschafts- und Staats-theorie*, Berlin, Buchhandlung Vorwärts.

Cunow, Heinrich 1925, *Politische Kaffeehäuser. Pariser Silhouetten aus der Grossen Französischen Revolution*, Berlin, Dietz.

Cunow, Heinrich 1926–31, *Allgemeine Wirtschaftsgeschichte: eine Übersicht über die Wirtschaftsentwicklung von der primitiven Sammelwirtschaft bis zum Hochkapitalismus*, Berlin: Dietz.

Dachary de Flers, Marion 1982, *Lagardelle et l'équipe du Mouvement socialiste*. Doctoral thesis at the IEP.

Danton, Georges 1926, *Reden*, Berlin: Neuer Deutscher Verlag.

Day, Richard and Daniel Gaido (eds.) 2009, *Witnesses to Permanent Revolution: The Documentary Record*, Leiden: Brill.

Dayan-Herzbrun, S. 1990, 'Révolution française, révolution en Allemagne: l'enseignement de Ferdinand Lassalle dans les années 1850', in Allard, M. (ed.), *1789 enseigné et imaginé. Regards croisés France-Québec*, Montréal: Éditions Noir sur Blanc.

Demm, E. 1987, 'Les idées de 1789 et les idées de 1914, la Révolution française dans la propagande de guerre allemande', *Annales littéraires de l'Université de Besançon*, 1987: 152–8.

Deppe, B. and Dickmann, E., *Hedwig Hintze (1884–1942). Bibliographie*, Bremen Hedwig Hintze-Institut, 1997

Deutscher Revolutions-Almanach für das Jahr 1919, Berlin: Hoffmann & Campe Verlag, 1919.

Deville, Gabriel 1887, *Gracchus Babeuf und die Verschwörung der Gleichen*, Zurich: Sozialdemokratische Bibliothek.

Deville, Gabriel 1901, *Histoire socialiste. Thermidor et Directoire (1794–1799)*, Paris: J. Rouff.

Dikreiter, Heinrich Georg 1988, *Vom Waisenhaus zur Fabrik, Eine Autobiographie*, Berlin: Buchhandlung Vorwärts.

Dippel, Horst 1990, 'La Révolution française et l'historiographie allemande xixe et xxe siècles', in Vovelle, Michel (ed.), *L'image de la Révolution française*, Vol. II., Oxford: Pergamon Press.

Dobson, Sean 2001, *Authority and Upheaval in Leipzig, 1910–1920: The Story of a Relationship*, New York, Columbia University Press.

Dorpalen, Andreas 1969, 'The German Struggle against Napoleon: The East German View', *The Journal of Modern History*, 4: 485–516

Droz, Jacques (ed.) 1974, *Histoire générale du socialisme. De 1875 à 1918*, Paris: PUF.

Droz, Jacques (ed.) 1977, *Histoire générale du socialisme*, Paris: PUF.

Droz, Jacques 1990, *Dictionnaire biographique du mouvement ouvrier international. Allemagne*, Paris: Éditions ouvrières.

Ducange, Jean-Numa 2007, 'Socialistes français et allemands face à la Révolution de 1905: la force de l'analogie à 1789', in Pigenet, Michel and Pierre Robin (eds.), *Regards sur le syndicalisme révolutionnaire*, Nérac: Éditions d'Albret.

Ducange, Jean-Numa 2007b, 'Un portrait inédit de Jean Jaurès par Karl Kautsky. Introduction, traduction, notes de "Souvenirs sur Jean Jaurès" de K. Kautsky', *Cahiers Jaurès*, 3: 107–13.

Ducange, Jean-Numa 2008, 'Un moment méconnu de l'historiographie: l'introduction et la diffusion en France de l'ouvrage de Karl Kautsky', *Annales historiques de la Révolution française*, 4: 105–30.

Ducange, Jean-Numa (ed.) 2010, *Le Socialisme et la Révolution française*, Paris: Demopolis.

Duncker, Hermann (et al.) 1930, *Geschichte der internationalen Arbeiterbewegung, 'Marxistische Arbeiterschulung'*, Berlin: Verlag für Literatur und Politik.

Eckstein, Gustav 1910, *Leitfaden zum Studium der Geschichte des Sozialismus*, Berlin: Vorwärts.

Eisner, Kurt 1907, *Das Ende des Reichs. Preussen und Deutschland im Zeitalter der grossen Revolution*, Berlin: Vorwärts.

Ek, Sverker 1989, 'Avatars d'un mythe. "La mort de Danton", drame de Georg Büchner et son histoire', *Annales historiques de la Révolution française*, 2: 274–92.

Emig, B. (et al.) 1981, *Literatur für eine neue Wirklichkeit-Bibliographie/Geschichte des Verlages JHW Dietz*, East Berlin: Dietz.

Engels, Friedrich 1964, *Die Rolle der Gewalt in der Geschichte*, East Berlin: Dietz.

Engels, Friedrich 2002, *Werke, Artikel, Entwürf. Oktober 1886 bis Februar 1891. Marx-Engels Gesamtausgabe I. 31. Apparat*, Amsterdam: Akademie-Verlag.

Engels, Friedrich, Ferdinand Lassalle, and Karl Marx, 1902, *Aus dem literarischen Nachlass von Karl Marx, Friedrich Engelsund Ferdinand Lassalle*, 4 vols., Stuttgart: Dietz.

Escudier, Alexandre 2004, 'Épistémologies croisées? L'impossible lecture des théoriciens allemands de l'histoire en France autour de 1900', in Werner, Michael and Bénédicte Zimmermann (eds.) 'De la comparaison à l'histoire croisée', *Le genre humain*, 2004: 139–77.

Escudier, Alexandre 2006, 'Historisme', in Mesure, Sylvie and Patrick Savidan (eds.), *Dictionnaire des sciences humaines*, Paris, PUF.

Espagne, Michel 1999, *Les transferts culturels franco-allemands*, Paris: PUF.

Faulenbach, Bernd 2008, 'Sonderweg, l'exception allemande', in Espagne, Michel et al. (eds.), *Dictionnaire du monde germanique*, Paris: Bayard.

Ferro, Marc 1977, *La Révolution russe*, Paris: Flammarion.

Fimmen, E. 1924, *Vereinigte Staaten Europas oder Europa*, Jena: Thüringer Verlagsanstalt und Drukkerei.

Fletcher, Roger 1988, 'Revisionism and Wilhelmine Imperialism', *Journal of Contemporary History*, 3: 347–66.

Florath, Bernd 1987, 'Heinrich Cunow. Eine biograpisch-historiographische Skizze', *Jahrbuch für Geschichte*, 34: 85–145.

Florath, Bernd 1989, 'Die Klassenkämpfe der Französischen Revolution in Heinrich Cunows Geschichte der Revolutionspresse', in Schmidt, Walter (ed.) *Grosse französische Revolution und revolutionäre Arbeiterbewegung*, East Berlin: Akademie Verlag.

Florath, Bernd 2005, 'Heinrich Cunow oder der Narren Mühsal', *Internationale wissenschaftliche Korrespondenz zur Geschichte der deutschen Arbeiterbewegung*, 2005: 496–507.

Fouquier-Tinville, Antoine Quentin 1925, *Reden*, Berlin, Neuer Deutscher Verlag.

Francois, Étienne (et al.) 1998, *Marianne-Germania: deutsch-französischer Kulturtransfer im europäischen Kontext: 1789–1914*, Leipzig: Leipziger Universitätsverlag.

Fricke, Dieter 1960, 'Der Fall Leo Arons', *Zeitschrift für Geschichtsgewissenschaft*, 1960: 1069–1107.

Fricke, Dieter 1987, *Handbuch zur Geschichten der deutschen Arbeiterbewegung*, 2 vols, East Berlin: Dietz.

Fricke, Dieter (ed.) 1989, *Übersichten der Berliner politischen Polizei über die allgemeine Lage der sozialdemokratischen und anarchistischen Bewegung 1878–1913*, Weimar: Böhlaus Nachfolger

Friedemann, P. 1989, 'Französische Revolution und deutsche sozialistische Arbeiterpresse, 1918–1933', *Tel Aviver Jahrbuch für deutsche Geschichte*, 18: 233–49

Friedrich, C. 1994, 'Kalender der Arbeiterbewegung', in Barck, Simone et al. (eds.), *Lexicon sozialistischer Literatur. Ihre Geschichte in Deutschland bis 1945*, Stuttgart-Weimar: Verlag J.B. Metzler.

Furet, François 1999, *The Passing of An Illusion*, Chicago: University of Chicago Press.

Gall, Lothar 2009, '150 Jahre Historische Zeitschrift', *Historische Zeitschrift*, 1/2009: 1–23.

Gallois, Léonard 1845–6, *Histoire des journaux et des journalistes de la Révolution française (1789–1796)*, Paris: Société de l'industrie fraternelle.

Gardes, Jean-Claude 1981, *Der Wahre Jacob 1890–1914*, German Studies dissertation supervised by Gilbert Badia, Université de Paris VIII.

Gardes, Jean-Claude 1995, 'Le Peuple français est un allié. L'image de la France dans l'organe satirique socialiste *Der Wahre Jacob* (1889–1914)', in Abret, Helga and Michel Grunewald (eds.), *Visions allemandes de la France (1871–1914) – Frankreich aus deutscher Sicht (1871–1914)*, Berne: Peter Lang.

Geary, Dick 2000, 'Beer and Skittles? Workers and Culture in Early Twentieth-Century Germany', *Australian Journal of Politics and History*, 2000: 388–402.

Georgen, M.-L. 1998, *Les relations entre socialistes allemands et français à l'époque de la deuxième Internationale (1889–1914)*, Paris VIII, PhD thesis.

Gérard, Alice 1970, *La Révolution française, mythes et interprétations 1789–1970*, Paris: Flammarion.

Gieselbusch, H. (et al.) 2008, *100 Jahre Rowohlt. Eine illustrierte Chronik*, Hamburg: Rowohlt Verlag.

Gilcher-Holtey, Ingrid 1986, *Das Mandat des Intellektuellen. Karl Kautsky und die Sozialdemokratie*, Berlin: Siedler.

Gilli, Marita 1989, 'Eulogius Schneider' in Soboul, Albert (ed.) *Dictionnaire historique de la Révolution française*, Paris: PUF.

Gilli, Marita 1990, 'L' historiographie allemande du jacobinisme allemand', in *La storia della storiografia europea sulla rivoluzione francese (Relazioni Congresso maggio 1989)*, Rome: Istituto storico italiano per l' età moderna e contemporanea.

Glagau, Hans 1908, *Reformversuche und Sturz des Absolutismus in Frankreich (1774 bis 1788)*, Berlin: Verlag von R. Oldenburg.

Godechot, Jacques 1974, *Un jury pour La Révolution*, Paris: R. Laffont.

Godwin, William 1912, *Erinnerungen an Mary Wollstonecraft*, Halle.

Grab, Walter 1971–8, *Deutsche revolutionäre Demokraten*, Stuttgart: J.B. Metzler.

Grab, Walter (ed.) 1975, *Die Debatte um die Französische Revolution. 35 Beiträge*, Munich: Nymphenburger Verlagshandlung GmbH.

Grab, Walter 1983, 'Französische Revolution und deutsche Geschichtswissenschaft', in Voss, Jürgen (ed.), *Deutschland und die Französische Revolution*, Munich: Artemis.

Grandjonc, Jean and Michael Werner 1983, 'Les émigrations allemandes au 19e siècle (1815–1914)', in *Émigrés français en Allemagne, émigrés allemands en France (1685–1945)*, Paris: Goethe Institut et Ministère des Relations Extérieures.

Grau, Bernhard 2001, Kurt Eisner: 1867–1919. eine Biographie, Munich: Beck.

Grenlich, Hermann 1985, *Die Revolution des Bürgertums und der Befreiungskampf der arbeiten Klasse. Vor hundert Jahren und heute*, Zurich: Verlag der Buchhandlung des Schweiz.

Griep, G., A. Förster and H. Siegel 1974, *Hermann Duncker-Lehrer dreier Generationen*, East Berlin: Dietz.

Groh, Dieter 1989, 'Jaurès und die deutsche Sozialdemokratie', in Brummert, Ulrike (ed.), *Jean Jaurès, Frankreich, Deutschland und die Zweite Internationale am Vorabend des Ersten Weltkrieges*, Tübingen: Gunter Narr Verlag.

Groh, Dieter 1999, *Emanzipation und Integration. Beiträge zur Sozial- und Politikgeschichte der deutschen Arbeiterbewegung und des 2. Reiches*, Konstanz: Univ. Verlag Konstanz.

Groschopp, Horst 1994, 'Otto Rühle', in Barck, S. et al. (eds.), *Lexicon sozialistischer Literatur. Ihre Geschichte in Deutschland bis 1945*, Stuttgart: Verlag J.B. Metzler.

Guglia, Eugen 1890, *Die konservativen Elemente Frankreichs am Vorabend der Revolution*, Gotha: F.A. Perthes.

Guillet, Éric 2006, 'Le refus des simplifications: l' image de l' Allemagne dans trois oeuvres de Jean Jaurès: *Hegel* (1892), *La Guerre franco-allemande* (1908) et *L'Armée nouvelle* (1911)', *Cahiers Jaurès*, 179: 33–80.

Haenisch, Konrad 1913, *Zur Geschichte des Zeitungswesen, Entwurf für einen Vortrag mit 43 Lichtbildern, Berlin*, Berlin: Zentralbildungsausschuss der Sozialdemokratischen Partei Deutschlands. Berlin.

Harald, K. 1989, 'Die Grosse Französische Revolution in den Revisionismusdebatten der Wende vom 19. zum 20. Jahrhundert', in Schmidt, Walter (ed.), *Grosse französische Revolution und revolutionäre Arbeiterbewegung*, East Berlin: Akademie-Verlag.

Hartig, Irmgard 1973, 'Observations sur la querelle entre Jaurès et Mehring', *Annales historiques de la Révolution française*, 1: 112–27.

Haupt, Georges 1969, 'Jaurès vu par les socialistes étrangers: Max Beer', *Bulletin de la Société d'études jaurésiennes*, October–December: 1–8.

Haupt, Georges 1980, *L'historien et le mouvement social*, Paris: Maspero.

Haupt, Georges and Maitron, Jean 1971, *Dictionnaire biographique du mouvement ouvrier international. Autriche*, Paris: Éditions ouvrières.

Haupt, Heinz-Gerhard 2002, '1848 en Allemagne: une perspective comparative', in Mayaud J.-L., *1848. Actes du colloque international du cent cinquantenaire*, Paris: Créaphis.

Hauptmann, Gerhart 1894, *Die Weber. Schauspiel aus den vierziger Jahren Die Weber. Schauspiel aus den vierziger Jahren*, Berlin: Fischer.

Hautmann, Hans and Rudolf 1980, *Die Gemeindebauten des Roten Wien 1919–1934*, Vienna: Schönbrunn-Verlag.

Hautmann, Hans 1987, *Geschichte der Rätebewegung in Österreich 1918–1924*, Vienna: Europa Verlag.

Heid, L. 2004, 'Oskar Cohn und die berliner Arbeiter-Bildungsschule', *IWK*, 1: 22–55.

Heller, Henry 2006., *The Bourgeois Revolution in France 1789–1815*, New York, Berghahn Books.

Hennig, Gustav 1908, *Zehn Jahre Bibliothekarbeit. Geschichte einer Arbeiterbibliothek. Ein Wegweiser für Bibliothekverwaltungen*, Leipzig: Verlag der Leipziger Buchdruckerei Aktiengesellschaft.

Héritier, Louis 1897, *Geschichte der französischen Revolution von 1848 und der zweiten Republik in volksthümlicher Darstellung*, Stuttgart: Dietz.

Hermann, Wendel 1930, *Danton*, Berlin: Ernst Rowohlt Verlag.

Herrera, Carlos Miguel 2003, *Droit et gauche. Pour une identification*, Laval: Presses universitaires de Laval.

Hess, Moses 1841, *Die europäische Triarchie*, Leipzig.

Hintze, Hedwig 1928, *Staatseinheit und Föderalismus in alten Frankreich und in der Revolution*, Berlin: Politische Bücherei.

Hintze, Hedwig 1929, 'Bürgerliche und sozialistische Geschichtsschreiber der französischen Revolution', *Die Gesellschaft*, 1929: 73–95.

Hintze Hedwig 1932, 'Hermann Wendel, Danton', *Die Gesellschaft*, 1932: 458–89.

Hintze, Hedwig 1932a, 'Albert Mathiez. Une page de souvenirs', *Annales historiques de la Révolution française*, 1932: 481–3

Hintze, Hedwig 1932b, 'Goethe et la Révolution française', *Annales historiques de la Révolution française*, 1932: 425–41.

Hobsbawm, Eric and Terence Ranger 2012, *The Invention of Tradition*, Cambridge: Cambridge University Press.

Hoppenstedt, Julius 1919, *Die französische Revolution*, Berlin: Kittel.

INRA (ed.) 1989, *La Révolution française et le monde rural, actes du colloque tenu en Sorbonne les 23, 24 et 25 octobre 1987*, Paris: CTHS.

Ivernel, P. 1987., 'Aux origines du mouvement ouvrier. Le débat théâtral dans la social-démocratie allemande avant la Première Guerre mondiale', *Cahiers théâtre Louvain* (*Travaux de Laboratoire derecherches sur les arts du spectacle du CNRS*), 58–9: 25.

Jaffé, Grace Mary 1924, *Le mouvement ouvrier à Paris pendant la Révolution française 1789–1791*, Paris: PUF.

Janet, Paul 1889, *Centenaire de 1789, Histoire de la Révolution française*, Paris: Librairie Ch. Delagrave.

Jaurès, Jean 1901, *Études socialistes*, Paris: Cahiers de la quinzaine.

Jaurès, Jean 1902, *Aus Theorie und Praxis. Sozialistische Studien*, Berlin: Verlag der Sozialistischen Monatshefte.

Jaurès, Jean 1913, *Die neue Armee*, Jena: Diederichs.

Jaures, Jean 1922–4, *Histoire socialiste de la Révolution française*, Paris: Librairie de 'l'Humanité'.

Jaurès, Jean 1960, *Les origines du socialisme allemand*, Paris: François Maspero.

Jaurès, Jean 1968–72, *Histoire socialiste de la Révolution française*, (reviewed and annotated by Albert Soboul), Paris: Éditions sociales.

Jaurès, Jean 1972, *Histoire socialiste de la Révolution française*, Vol. IV, *La Révolution française et l'Europe*, Paris: Éditions sociales.

Jaurès, Jean 2001, *Œuvres. L'Affaire Dreyfus* (2), vol. 7, Paris: Fayard.

Jeismann, Michael 1997, *La patrie de l'ennemi. La notion d'ennemi national et la representation de la nation en Allemagne et en France de 1792 à 1918*, Paris: CNRS éditions.

Jezower, Ignaz (ed.) 1921, *Die Befreiung der Menschheit. Freiheitsideen in Vergangenheit und Gegenwart, Deutsches Verlagshaus Bong and Co*, Berlin: Bong & Co.

Jourgniac de Saint Meard, François 1897, *Les Massacres de septembre. Mon agonie de trente-huit heures*, Paris: H. Gautier.

Jousse, Emmanuel 2007, *Réviser le marxisme? d'Édouard Bernstein à Albert Thomas, 1894–1914*, Paris: L'Harmattan.

Jousse, Emmanuel 2009, 'Jean Jaurès et le révisionnisme de Bernstein: logiques d'une méprise', *Cahiers Jaurès*, April–June, 192: 13–49.

Judt, Tony 1976, *La reconstruction du Parti Socialiste 1921–1926*, Paris: Presses de la FNSP.

Julia, D. 1989, 'Lakanal', in Soboul, Alfred (ed.), *Dictionnaire historique de la Révolution française*, Paris, PUF.

Kaiser, Joachim-Christoph 1981, *Arbeiterbewegung und organisierte Religionskritik*, Stuttgart: Klett-Cotta.

Karéiew, N. 1879, *Les paysans et la question paysanne en France dans le dernier quart du XVIIIe siècle*, Moscow.

Kautsky, Benedikt 1933, *Willst du Marxist werden?*, Vienna: Verlag der Wiener Volksbuchhandlung.

Kautsky, Karl 1887, *Karl Marx'ökonomische Lehren*, Stuttgart: Dietz.

Kautsky, Karl 1888, *Thomas More und seine Utopie*, Stuttgart: Dietz.

Kautsky, Karl 1889, *Die Klassengegensätze von 1789. Zum 100jährigen Gedenktag der grossen Revolution*, Stuttgart: Dietz, 1889.

Kautsky, Karl 1895, *Die Vorläufer des neueren Sozialismus*, Stuttgart: Dietz.

Kautsky, Karl 1899a, *Bernstein and das sozialdemokratische Programm. Eine Antikritik*, Stuttgart: Dietz

Kautsky, Karl 1899b, *Die Agrarfrage*, Stuttgart: Dietz.

Kautsky, Karl 1901, *La lutte des classes en France en 1789*, Paris: G. Jacques.

Kautsky, Karl 1902, *Die soziale Revolution*, Berlin: Vorwärts.

Kautsky, Karl 1908a, *Die historische Leistung von Karl Marx*, Berlin: Buchhandlung Vorwärts.

Kautsky, Karl 1908b, *Friedrich Engels. Sein Leben, sein Wirken, seine Schriften*, Berlin: Vorwärts.

Kautsky, Karl 1908c, *Die Klassengegensätze im Zeitalter der fransösischen Revolution*, Stuttgart: Dietz.

Kautsky, Karl 1916, *The Social Revolution*, Chicago: Charles H. Kerr & Company.

Kautsky, Karl 1918, *Die Diktatur des Proletariats*, Vienna: Verlag der Wiener Volksbuchhandlung Ignaz Brand.

Kautsky, Karl 1919a, *Wie der Weltkrieg entstand. Dargestellt nach dem Aktenmaterial des deutschen Auswärtigen Amts*, Berlin: Paul Cassirer.

Kautsky, Karl 1919b, *Die Klassengegensätze im Zeitalter der fransösischen Revolution*, Berlin: Dietz.

Kautsky, Karl 1921, *Von der Demokratie zur Staats-Sklaverei. Eine Auseinandersetzung mit Trotzki*, Berlin: Verlag Genossensch. 'Freiheit'.

Kautsky, Karl 1922, *Die proletarische Revolution und ihr Programm*, Stuttgart: Dietz.

Kautsky, Karl 1925, *La Révolution prolétarienne et son programme*, Brussels: L' Eglantine.

Kautsky, Karl 1930, *Das Werden eines Marxisten*, Leipzig: Meiner.

Kautsky, Karl 1931, *Bolshevism at a Deadlock*, London: Allen & Unwin.

Kautsky, Karl 1932, *Krieg und Demokratie*, Berlin: Dietz

Kautsky, Karl 1960, *Erinnerungen und Erörterungen*, The Hague: Mouton and Co.

Kautsky, Karl 2000, *Les Trois sources du marxisme, l'oeuvre historique de Marx*, Paris: Spartacus.

Kautsky, Karl and Bruno Schoenlank 1897, *Grundsätze und Forderungen der Sozialde-mokratie. Erläuterungen zum Erfurter Programm*, Berlin: Vorwärts.

Kautsky, Karl and Friedrich Engels 1935, *Aus der Frühzeit des Marxismus. Briefwechsel*, Prague: Orbis-Verlag.

Kautsky, Karl and Paul Lafargue 1895, *Die beiden ersten grossen Utopisten: Thomas More. Thomas Campanella. Der Jesuitenstaat in Paul Lafargue*, Berlin: Dietz.

Kinner, K. 1989, 'Die Grosse Französische Revolution im Geschichtsdenken der deut-schen und französischen Kommunisten', in Schmidt, Walter (ed.) *Grosse französ-ische Revolution und revolutionäre Arbeiterbewegung: Geschichtsbewusstsein, Gesell-schaftstheorie und revolutionärer Kampf*, East Berlin: Akademie-Verlag.

Kircheisen, Friedrich 1927, *Die Bastille*, Berlin: Verlag "Der Bücherkreis".

Kjellen, Rudolf 1915, *Die Ideen von 1914: eine weltgeschichtliche Perspektive*, Leipzig: Hirzel.

Klatt, G. 1994, 'Scaevola' in Barck, Simone et al. (eds.), *Lexicon sozialistischer Literatur. Ihre Geschichte in Deutschland bis 1945*, Stuttgart-Weimar: Verlag J.B. Metzler.

Kleinschmidt, Arthur 1876, *Die drei Stände in Frankreich vor der Revolution*, Vienna: Har-tleben.

Klément, J. 1931, *Jaurès réformiste*, Paris: Bureau d' édition.

Knilli, Friedrich and Ursula Munchow 1970, *Frühes deutsches Arbeitertheater, 1847–1918. Eine Dokumentation*, East Berlin: Akademie Verlag.

Koch, Ursula (ed.) 1999, *Marianne und Germania in der Karikatur (1550–1999). Eine Interréseaux-Ausstellung*, Munich: Goethe Institut.

Kolpinskaja, A. 1939, *La Révolution française bourgeoise du XVIIIe siècle (1789–1794), recueil historique et littéraire, Edition pédagogique d'Etat du commissariat du peuple de l'instruction publique de la RSFSR*, Moscow

Kondratieva, Tamara 1989, *Bolcheviks et Jacobins: itinéraire des analogies*, Paris: Payot.

Könnemann, Erwin 2002, *Der Kapp-Lüttwitz-Ludendorff-Putsch: Dokumente*, Munich: Olzog.

Korsch, Karl 1996, 'Das Problem Staatseinheit-Föderalismus in der französischen Revo-lution', in *Gesamtausgabe. Krise des Marxismus. Schriften 1928–1935*, vol. 5. Amster-dam: Stichting Beheer IISG.

Koselleck, Reinhart 1997, *L'expérience de l'histoire*, Paris: Gallimard-Le Seuil.

Krause, Horst 1980, *Wilhelm Blos. Zwischen Marxismus und demokratischem Sozialis-mus in Geschichtsschreibung und Politik*, Husum: Matthiesen Verlag.

Kreissler, Felix 1971, *De la Révolution à l'annexion: l'Autriche de 1918 à 1938*, Paris: PUF.

Kreissler, Felix 1993, 'Les avatars de l'idée républicaine en Autriche. Avancées et reculs: 1848, 1867, 1918, 1934 et la suite', in Gilli, Marita (ed.), *L'idée d'Europe, vecteur des aspirations démocratiques: les idéaux républicains depuis 1848*, Besançon: Annales lit-téraires de l'Université de Besançon.

Kropotkin, Peter 1893, *La Grande Révolution*, Paris: 'La Révolte'.

Kropotkin, Peter 1909, *Die Französische Revolution 1789–1793*, 2 vols. Leipzig: Thomas.

Kropotkin, Peter 2010, *Memoirs of a Revolutionist*, New York: Dover.

Lafargue, Paul 1912, *Die französische Sprache vor und nach der Revolution*: Stuttgart, Dietz, 1912.

Lafargue, Paul 1988, *Die französische Sprache vor und nach der Revolution*, Hamburg: Sammlung Junius.

Landauer, Gustav 1919, *Briefe aus der Französischen Revolution*, Frankfurt am Main: Rütten und Loening.

Laponneraye, Albert (ed.) 1840., *Œuvres de Maximilien Robespierre*, 3 Vols. Paris: Chez l'éditeur.

Laschitza, A. 1989, 'Der Platz der Grossen Französischen Revolution im Geschichts- und Revolutionverständnis von Karl Liebknecht und Rosa Luxemburg', in Schmidt, Walter (ed.), *Grosse französische Revolution und revolutionäre Arbeiterbewegung: Geschichtsbewusstsein, Gesellschaftstheorie und revolutionärer Kampf*, East Berlin: Akadamie-Verlag.

Lassalle, Ferdinand 1926, *Nachgelassene Briefe und Schriften*, Vol. 6, Stuttgart: Deutsche Verlags-Anstalt,

Lassalle, Ferdinand 1970, *Reden und Schriften*, Munich: Deutscher Taschenbuch Verlag.

Lefranc, Georges 1977, *Le mouvement socialiste sous la Troisième République*, Paris: Payot.

Lemke, Matthias 2008, *Republikanischer Sozialismus. Positionen von Bernstein, Kautsky, Jaurès und Blum*, Frankfurt am Main: Campus Verlag.

Lenger, Friedrich 1994, *Werner Sombart: 1863–1941: eine Biographie*, Munich: C.H. Beck.

Leser, Norbert 1977, 'Karl Renner et le marxisme', in *Histoire du marxisme contemporain*, vol. 3, Paris: 10/18.

Levasseur, Émile 1867, *Histoire des classes ouvrières en France depuis 1789 jusqu'à nos jours*, 2 vols. Paris: Hachette.

Lidtke, Vernon 1979, 'Lieder der deutschen Arbeiterbewegung 1864–1914', *Geschichte und Gesellschaft*, 5: 54–82.

Lidtke, Vernon 1985, *The Alternative Culture: Socialist Labor in Imperial Germany*, Oxford: Oxford University Press.

Liebknecht, Karl 1907, *Militarismus und Antimilitarismus unter besonderer Berücksichtigung der internationalen Jugendbewegung*, Leipzig: Leipziger Buchdruckerei.

Liebknecht, Karl 1968, *Wissen ist Macht-Macht ist Wissen, und andere bildungspolitisch-pädagogische Äusserungen*, Berlin: Dietz.

Liebknecht, Karl 1974, *Gesammelte Werke*, East Berlin: Dietz.

Liebknecht, Wilhelm 1891, *Was die Sozialdemokraten sind und was sie wollen?* Berlin: Vorwärts, 1891.

Liebknecht, Wilhelm 1988, *Briefwechsel mit deutschen Sozialdemokraten*, Frankfurt am Main: Campus Verlag.

Linguet, Simon-Nicolas-Henri 1886, *Linguets Denkwürdigkeiten über die Bastille*, Leipzig: Reclam.

Linguet, Simon-Nicolas-Henri 2006, *Mémoires sur la Bastille*, Paris, Arléa.

Lissagaray, Prosper-Olivier 1891, *Geschichte der Kommune von 1871*, Stuttgart: Dietz.

Louis, Paul 1901, *Histoire du socialisme français*, Paris: Editions de la Revue Blanche.

Louis, Paul 1908, *Geschichte des Sozialismus in Frankreich*, Stuttgart: Dietz

Louis, Paul 1912, *Geschichte der Gewerkschaftsbewegung in Frankreich (1789 bis 1912)*, Stuttgart: Dietz Verlag International.

Loutchisky, Ivan Vasilievich 1897 *La Petite propriété en France avant la Révolution et de la vente des biens nationaux*, Paris: Honoré Champion.

Luxemburg, Rosa 1899, *Sozialreform oder Revolution?*, Leipzig: Verlag der Leipziger Volkszeitung.

Luxemburg, Rosa 1982, *Gesammelte Briefe*, East Berlin: Dietz.

Maillard, Alain 1999, *La communauté des égaux: le communisme néo-babouviste dans la France des années 1840*, Paris: Kimé.

Mainfroy, Claude 1985, 'Marx et la Révolution française après 1870', *Cahiers d'histoire de l'institut de recherches marxistes*, 21.

Marat, Jean-Paul 1926 (no title), Berlin: Neuer Deutscher Verlag.

Marie, Jean-Jacques 2008, *Le dimanche rouge*, Paris: Larousse.

Mariot, Nicolas and Jay Rowell 2004, 'Une comparaison asymétrique. Visites de souverainetés et construction nationale en France et en Allemagne à la veille de la Première Guerre mondiale', in Werner, Michael and Bénédicte Zimmermann (eds.), 'De la comparaison à l'histoire croisée', *Le genre humain*, 2004.

Markov, Walter 1974, 'La Révolution française vue par les historiens de la République de Weimar', *Revue d'Allemagne et des pays de langue allemande*, 2: 58–66.

Markov, Walter 1977, 'Albert Mathiez à Leipzig', *Annales historiques de la Révolution française*, 2: 64–5.

Markov, Walter 2009, *Wie viele Leben lebt der Mensch: Eine Autobiographie aus dem Nachlass*, Leipzig.

Marquardt, Erwin 1922, *Geschichte des Sozialismus vom Altertum bis zur Neuzeit: eine Kursusdisposition*, Berlin: Zentralbildungsausschuss der Sozialdemokratischen Partei Deutschlands.

Marx, Karl 1964, *Pre-Capitalist Economic Formations*, New York: International Publishers.

Marx, Karl and Friedrich Engels 1930–1, *Über historischen Materialismus*, 2 vols., Berlin: Internationaler Arbeiter-Verlag.

Marx, Karl and Friedrich Engels 1985, *Sur la Révolution française. Écrits de Marx et Engels*, Paris: Editions Sociales.

Mathiez, Albert 1917–18, *Études Robespierristes*, Paris: Armand Colin.

Mathiez, Albert 1927, *La Révolution française*, Paris: A. Colin.

Mathiez, Albert 1928, 'Edwig (sic) Hintze, Staatseinheit und Foedarlismus im alten Frankreich und in der Revolution', *Annales Historiques de la Révolution française*, 1928: 577–88.

Mathiez, Albert 1929, *La réaction thermidorienne*, Paris: A. Colin.

Matthias, E. 1957, 'Kautsky und der Kautskyanismus. Die Funktion der Ideologie in der deutschen Sozialdemokratie vor dem ersten Weltkrieg', *Marxismusstudien*, 151–97.

Mattick, Paul 1970, *Von der Bürgerlichen zur proletarischen Revolution*, Berlin: R. Blankertz.

Mazauric, Claude 1989, 'Babeuf' in Soboul, Alfred (ed.), *Dictionnaire historique de la Révolution française*, Paris: PUF.

Mazauric, Claude 2000, 'Présentation', in Robespierre, Maximilien, *Œuvres*, Vol. I, Paris: Phénix éditions.

Mazauric, Claude 2009, *L'histoire de la Révolution française et la pensée marxiste*, Paris: PUF.

Mehring, Franz 1893, *Die Lessing Legende. Zur Geschichte und Kritik des preussischen Despotismus und der klassischen Literatur*, Stuttgart: Dietz.

Mehring, Franz 1897–8, *Geschichte der deutschen Sozialdemokratie*, Stuttgart: Dietz.

Mehring, Franz 1910–11, *Deutsche Geschichte vom Ausgange des Mittelalters: ein Leitfaden für Lehrende und Lernende*, 2 vols., Berlin: Vorwärts.

Mehring, Franz 1912, *Von Tilsit nach Tauroggen*, Stuttgart: Dietz.

Meinecke, F. 1924, *Die Idee der Staatsräson in der neueren Geschichte*, Berlin: R. Oldenbourg.

Mély, Benoît 2004, *La question de la séparation des Églises et de l'école dans quelques pays européens (Allemagne, France, Grande-Bretagne, Italie)*, *1789–1914*, Lausanne: Page deux.

Michelet, Jules 1855, *Les femmes de la Révolution*, Paris: Delahays

Michelet, Jules 1913, *Die Frauen der Revolution*, Munich: Langen.

Michels, Robert 2009, *Les partis politiques. Essai sur les tendances oligarchiques des démocraties*, Brussels: Éditions de l'Université de Bruxelles.

Middell, M. 1994, 'La réception de l'idée républicaine au 19e siècle: le cas des journaux leipzigois 1848–1849', in Gilli, Marita (ed.), *L'idée d'Europe, vecteur des aspirations démocratiques: les idéaux républicains depuis 1848*, Besançon: Annales littéraires de l'Université de Besançon.

Middell, M. 1999, 'Französische Revolution', in Haug, Wolfgang Fritz, *Historisch-Kritisches Wörterbuch des Marxismus*, vol. 4, Berlin: Argument.

Middell, Katharina and Matthias 1988, *François Noël Babeuf: Märtyrer der Gleichheit. Biografie*, East Berlin: Verlag Neues Leben.

Mignet, François 1825, *Geschichte der französischen Revolution von 1789 bis 1814: Nebst einer chronologischen Uebersicht und einem Steindruck*, Jena: Friedrich Frommann.

Mirow, Jürgen 1981, *Das alte Preussen im deutschen Geschichtsbild seit der Reichsgründung*, Berlin.

Möller, Horst 2005, *La République de Weimar*, Paris: Tallandier.

Morel, Roger 1976, *La collaboration de Franz Mehring à la Neue Zeit (1900–1906)*, Master's dissertation supervised by Jacques Droz, Paris I.

Muckle, Friedrich 1921, *Das Kulturproblem der französische Revolution*, Jena: Kichterstein.

Müller, Peter 1989 'Karl Kautsky und die französische Revolution' in Schmidt, Walter (ed.), *Grosse französische Revolution und revolutionäre Arbeiterbewegung*, East Berlin: Akademie-Verlag.

Narotchnitski, Aleksei (ed.), *La Révolution française et Russie*, Moscow: Progrès.

Nipperdey, Thomas 1985, *Deutsche Geschichte 1800–1866. Bürgerwelt und starker Staat*, Munich: Beck.

Olbrich, Josef 1977, *Arbeiterbildung in der Weimarer Zeit: Konzeption und Praxis*, Braunschweig: Westermann.

Olbrich, Josef 1982, *Arbeiterbildung nach dem Fall des Sozialistengesetzes (1890–1914). Konzeption und Praxis*, Braunschweig: Westermann.

Pasteur, Paul 1994, *Vers l'homme nouveau? Pratiques politiques et culturelles de la social-démocratie autrichienne 1888–1934*, dissertation, Université de Poitiers.

Pasteur, Paul 1998, 'La mise en scène des femmes de la Révolution française par Emma Adler', in Le Bozec, Christine and Eric Wauters, *En hommage à Claude Mazauric. Pour la Révolution française*, Rouen, Publications de l'Université de Rouen.

Pasteur, Paul 2000, 'Le système de formation du Parti social-démocrate en Autriche (1908–1934)', *Cahiers d'histoire. Revue d'histoire critique*, 79:13–28.

Pasteur, Paul 2003, *Pratiques politiques et militantes de la social-démocratie autrichienne 1888–1934*, Paris: Belin.

Pasteur, Paul 2006, 'L'austromarxisme ou une bouée de sauvetage pour une gauche en crise?', *Austriaca*, December, 63: 195–211.

Pasteur, Paul 2008a, 'Entre tradition et instrumentalisation: les coalitions gouvernementales en Autriche', *Revue d'Allemagne et des pays de langue allemande*, 4: 537–51.

Pasteur, Paul 2008b, 'La lente agonie de la démocratie en Autriche du 15 juillet 1927 au 12 février 1934', in Heimberg, Charles (ed.), *Mourir en manifestant*, Geneva: Éditions d'en bas.

Pelinka, Peter and Manfred Scheuch 1989, *100 Jahre Arbeiter-Zeitung*, Vienna: Europa Verlag.

Pennetier, Claude (ed.) n.d., *Dictionnaire biographique du mouvement ouvrier français (Maitron)*, CD-ROM.

Perfahl, Brigitte 1982, *Marx oder Lassalle? Zur ideologischen Position der österreichischen Arbeiterbewegung 1869–1889*, Vienna: Europa Verlag.

Petrasch, Wilhem 2007, *Die Wiener Urania, Von den Wurzeln der Erwachsenenbildung zum lebenslangen Lernen*, Vienna: Böhlau.

Politzer, Georges 1947, *Révolution et contre-révolution au xxe siècle: réponse à "Sang et Or" de M. Rosenberg*, Paris: Éditions sociales.

Pouffary, Marion 2009, '1891, l'affaire Thermidor', *Histoire, économie et sociétés*, 2: 87–108

Prochasson Christophe 1993, *Les intellectuels, le socialisme et la guerre: 1900–1938*, Paris: Seuil.

Prochasson, Christophe 2004, 'L' introduction du marxisme en France', in Candar, Gilles and Jean-Jacques Becker (eds.), *Histoire des gauches en France*, vol. 1: 'L' héritage du xixe siècle', Paris: La Découverte.

Rausch, Bernard 1914, *Die Befreiungskriege*, Berlin: Zentralbildungsausschuss der Sozialdemokratischen Partei Deutschlands (Lichtbilderzentrale).

Rebérioux, Madeleine 1974, 'Le socialisme et la Première guerre mondiale (1914–1918)', in Droz, Jacques (ed.), *Histoire générale du socialisme. De 1875 à 1918*, Paris: PUF.

Rebérioux, Madeleine 1977, 'Jaurès et le marxisme', *Histoire du marxisme contemporain*, Vol. 3, Paris: 10/18.

Revel, Jacques (ed.) 1996, *Jeux d'échelles. La microanalyse à l'expérience*, Paris: EHESS/Gallimard/Seuil.

Robespierre, Maximilien 1925, *Reden*, Berlin: Neuer Deutscher Verlag.

Rolland, Romain 1952, *Journal des années de guerre 1914–1919*, Paris: A. Michel.

Rosenberg, Arthur 1930, *Der Mythus des 20. Jahrhunderts*, Munich: Hoheneichen-Verlag.

Roy-Jacquemart, Marie-Ange 1979, 'Deux bibliothèques ouvrières sous le Deuxième Reich: Köpenick et Breslau. À propos de la politique culturelle de la Social-Démocratie allemande', *Cahiers d'Études Germaniques*, 3: 103–38.

Rühle, Otto 1911, *Das proletarische Kind: eine Monographie*, Munich: Langen.

Rühle, Otto 1927, *Die Revolutionen Europas*, 3 Vols., Dresden: Kaden.

Ruthmann Danièle 1982, *Vers une nouvelle culture social-démocrate: conditions, objectifs et évolution de l'oeuvre éducative réalisée par la social-démocratie allemande sous la République de Weimar de 1924 à 1933*, Frankfurt am Main-Bern: P. Lang.

Sagnac, Philippe 1899, *La Législation civile de la Révolution française, la propriété et la famille (1789–1804)*, Paris: A. Fontemoing.

Saint-Just, Louis-Antoine de 1925, *Reden*, Berlin: Neuer Deutscher Verlag.

Scävola, C.M. 1893, *Die französische Revolution. Episch-dramatische Dichtung in 12 lebenden Bildern*, Berlin: Verlag von Hermann Sumpel.

Schäfer, Kirstin Anne 2001, 'Die Völkerschlacht' in François, É. And H. Schulze (eds.) *Deutsche Erinnerungsorte*, Munich: Beck.

Schafers, Hans-Joachim 1961, *Zur sozialistische Arbeiterbildung in Leipzig 1890 bis 1914*, Leipzig.

Schärf, Adolf 1926, *Die Frau im Spiegel des Rechts*, Vienna: Verlag der Organisation Wien der sozialdemokratischen Partei.

Schelz-Brandenburg, Till (ed.) 2003, *Eduard Bernsteins Briefwechsel mit Karl Kautsky (1895–1905)*, Frankfurt am Main: Campus Verlag.

Schleier, H. 1975, *Die bürgerliche deutsche Geschichtsschreibung der Weimarer Republik*, East Berlin: Akademieverlag.

Schlesinger-Eckstein, Therese 1902, *Am Anfang des Jahrhunderts*, Berlin: Verlag Aufklärung Berlin.

Schmidt, Walter 1989, 'Karl Friedrich Köppen, Friedrich Engels und die Erklärung der historischen Funktion des Terrorismus in der Grossen Französiche Revolution', *Studien zur Geschichte*, 12: 166–87.

Schmidt, Walter 1990, 'Friedrich Engels, das Zentenarium der Grossen Französischen Revolution und die Strategie der revolutionären Arbeiterbewegung', *Jahrbuch für Geschichte*, East Berlin.

Schöck-Quinteros 1997, 'Hedwig Hintze 1884–1942. Ein biographischer Abriss' in Deppe and Dickmann 1997.

Schröder, Walter 1989, '"... dem deutschen Volk zu widmen, damit es lerne ..." Die Revolution von 1789 in den Gefängnisaufzeichnungen Wilhelm Liebknechts', in Schmidt, Walter (ed.), *Grosse französische Revolution und revolutionäre Arbeiterbewegung*, East Berlin: Akademie-Verlag.

Schroth, Hans (ed.) 1977, *Verlag der Wiener Volksbuchhandlung 1894–1934*. Vienna: Europa Verlag.

Schumacher, Alois 1994, 'La social-démocratie et la vision du modèle républicain 1870–1914', in Gilli, Marita (ed.), *L'idée d'Europe, vecteur des aspirations démocratiques: les idéaux républicains depuis 1848*, Besançon: Annales littéraires de l'Université de Besançon.

Schumacher, Alois 2001, *La Social-démocratie allemande et la IIIe République. Le regard de la revue 'Die Neue Zeit'*, Paris: CNRS Editions.

Schwarz, Max 1973, *Seit 1881. Bibliographie des Verlages J.H.W. Dietz Nachf.*, Bonn: Dietz.

Seidel, Jutta 1999, 'Internationale *Maifestschriften* 1890–1914: Überblick und komparativer Versuch', in Küttler, Wolfgang (ed.), *Das lange 19. Jahrhundert. Personen-Ereignisse-Ideen-Umwälzungen. Ernst Engelberg zum 90. Geburstag*, Berlin: Trafo Verlag.

Seiter, Josef 1990, 'Organisatorisches und Technisches in der Herausgabe der Maifestschriften', in Riesenfellner, Stefan (ed.), *Freiheitsbilder: Kunst und Agitation in den Maifestschriften der österreichischen Arbeiterbewegung 1890–1918*, Graz: Leykamp.

Sieburg, Friedrich 1935, *Robespierre*, Frankfurt-am-Main: Societäts-Verlag.

Smith, Helmut Walter 2008, 'When the Sonderweg Debate Left Us', *German Studies Review*, 2008: 225–40.

Smith, Jeffrey R. 2000, 'The Monarchy versus the Nation: The "Festive Year" 1913 in Wilhelmine Germany', *German Studies Review*, 23, 2: 257–74.

Soboul, Alfred (ed.) 1989, *Dictionnaire historique de la Révolution française*, Paris, PUF.

Soboul, Alfred and Walter Markow 1957, *Die Sans-culotten von Paris. Dokumente zur Geschichte der Volksbewegung, 1793–1794*, East Berlin, Akademie Verlag.

Sproll, Heinz 1992, *Französische Revolution und Napoleonische Zeit in der historisch-politischen Kultur der Weimarer Republik: Geschichtswissenschaft und Geschichtsunterricht 1918–1933*, Munich: E. Vögel.

Steinberg Hans-Joseph 1967. *Sozialismus und deutsche Sozialdemokratie. Zur Ideologie der Partei vor dem 1. Weltkrieg*, Hanover: Verlag für Literatur und Zeitgeschehen

Steiner, Gerhard 1961, 'Un utopiste allemand du 18e siècle: Carl Wilhelm Fröhlich', *Annales historiques de la Révolution française*, 166: 449–60.

Stern, Leo 1954–6, *Die Auswirkungen der ersten russischen Revolution von 1905–1907 auf Deutschland*, 2 vols., East Berlin: Rutten & Loening.

Stern, Leo 1961, *Die russische Revolution von 1905–1907 im Spiegel der deutschen Presse*, 5 vols., East Berlin: Rutten & Loening.

Stuart, Robert 1992, *Marxism at Work. Ideology, Class and French Socialism during the Third Republic*, Cambridge: Cambridge University Press.

Stübling, Rainer 1983, *"Vive la France!" Der Sozialdemokrat Hermann Wendel (1884–1936)*, Frankfurt am Main: P. Lang.

Taine, Hippolyte 1877–93, *Die Entstehung des modernen Frankreich*, 3 vols., Leipzig: Günther.

Tchoudinov, A. 2002, 'La Révolution française: de l'historiographie soviétique à l'historiographie russe, "changements de jalons"', *Cahiers du monde russe*, 2–3: 449–450.

Thiers, Adolphe 1826–30, *Geschichte der französischen Revolution*, 4 vols., Leipzig: Basse.

Thomas, Albert 1903, *Le syndicalisme allemand. Résumé historique (1848–1903)*, Paris: G. Bellais.

Tiemann, D. 1989, 'Die Rezeption der Französischen Revolution in der deutschen Arbeiterbewegung: Wilhelm Blos Volkstümliche Darstellung der Ereignisse und Zustände in Frankreich 1789–1804', in Timmermann, H. (ed.) *Die Französische Revolution und Europa 1789–1799*, Saarbrücken-Scheidt: Dadder.

Traverso, Enzo 2005, *Le passé, mode d'emploi*, Paris: La Fabrique.

Trotsky, Leon 1920, *Terrorisme et communisme. L'anti-Kautsky*, Paris: Librairie de l'Humanité.

Trotsky, Leon 2017, *Terrorism and Communism*, London: Verso.

Tudor, Henry (ed.) 1988, *Marxism and Social Democracy, The Revisionist Debate, 1896–1898*, Cambridge, Cambridge University Press

Ulrich, Marietta 1987, *Heinrich Cunow: 1862–1936: sein ethnologisches Werk vor dem Hintergrund der Persönlichkeit, der Zeitgeschichte und der wissenschaftlichen Traditionen*, dissertation, University of Vienna.

Vass, Josef and Madeleine Wolensky 1990, *'Er ist gekommen als ein schwärmerischer Idealist': Leopold Winarsky (1873–1915). Sozialdemokrat und Bücherfreund*, Vienna: Sozialwissenschaftliche Studienbibliothek.

Von Bueltzingsloewen, Isabelle 1992, 'Le centenaire de la Révolution française et l'opinion publique allemande: l'Allemagne face à son histoire', in Bariéty, Jacques (ed.),

1889: Centenaire de la Révolutionfrançaise. Réactions et Représentations politiques en Europe, Bern: Lang.

Von Hentig, Hans 1919, *Fouché*, Tübingen: Mohr.

Von Hentig, Hans 1924, *Robespierre*, Stuttgart: H. Hoffmann.

Von Ranke, Leopold 1875, *Ursprung und Beginn der Revolutionskriege 1791 und 1792*, Leipzig: Duncker und Humblot.

Von Rüden, Peter (ed.) 1979, *Beiträge zur Kulturgeschichte der deutschen Arbeiterbewegung 1848–1918*, Frankfurt am Main: Büchergilde.

Von See, Klaus 2001, *Freiheit und Gemeinschaft. Völkisch-nationales Denken in Deutschland zwischen Französischer Revolution und Erstem Weltkrieg*, Heidelberg: Universitätsverlag Heidelberg.

Von Sybel, Heinrich 1853–79, *Geschichte der Revolutionszeit (1789–1800)*, 5 vols., Düsseldorf.

Von Sybel, Heinrich 1860, *Die Erhebung Europas gegen Napoleon 1.*, Munich: R. Oldenburg.

Voss, Jürgen 1991, 'La Révolution française et la révolution allemande de 1918/1919. Une comparaison établie en 1920', *Francia-Forschungen zur westeuropäischen Geschichte*, 3: 151–4.

Vovelle, Michel 2003, 'Un centenaire qui n'aura pas lieu', *Annales historiques de la Révolution française*, 2: 179–88.

Vovelle, Michel and Christine Peyrard 2002, *Héritages de la Révolution française à la lumière de Jaurès*, Aix-en-Provence: PUP.

Wahl, Adalbert 1905–7, *Vorgeschichte der französischen Revolution*, 2 vols, Tübingen.

Waldenberg, Marek 1980, *Il papa rosso Karl Kautsky*, Rome: Editori Riuniti.

Wartelle, F. 1989, 'Alsace' in Soboul, Albert (ed.) *Dictionnaire historique de la Révolution française*, Paris: PUF.

Weber, Henri 1983, *Socialisme, la voie occidentale*, Paris: PUF.

Weill, Claudie, 1986, 'La Révolution russe de 1905 et le mouvement ouvrier allemand', in Coquin, François-Xavier (ed.), *1905. La première révolution russe*, Paris: Publication de la Sorbonne.

Wendel, Hermann 1910, *Frankfurt am Main vor der grossen Revolution bis zur Revolution von oben 1789–1866*, Frankfurt-am-Main: Buchhandlung Volksstimme.

Wendel, Hermann 1913, *1813: Vortrag, gehalten am 9. März 1913 im Kaufmännischen Vereinshaus zu Frankfurt am Main*, Frankfurt am Main: Buchhandlung Volksstimme.

Wendel, Hermann 1916, *Elsass-Lothringen und die Sozialdemokratie*, Berlin: Buchhandlung Vorwärts.

Wendel, Hermann 1932, *Französische Menschen*, Berlin: Ernst Rowohlt Verlag

Wendel, Hermann 1934, *Jugenderinnerungen eines Metzers*, Strasbourg: Librairie de la Mésange.

Wendel, Hermann 1936, *Die Marseillaise, Biographie einer Hymne*, Zürich: Europa Verlag.

Werner, Michael 1987, 'Rupture et continuité à propos de la réception de la Révolution française en Allemagne pendant le XIXe siècle', *Annales littéraires de l'Université de Besançon*.

Werner, Michael and Bénédicte Zimmermann 2003, 'Penser l'histoire croisée: entre empirie et réflexivité', *Annales. Histoire, sciences sociales*, 1: 7–34.

Winarsky, Leopold 1911, *Die Revolution von 1848*, Vienna.

Winarsky, Leopold 1913, *Die grosse französische Revolution: Vortrag mit 102 farbigen Lichtbildern*, Vienna: Danneberg.

Winkler, E. 1926, *Bildungsfragen der Sozialdemokratie*, Berlin.

Winkler, Heinrich A. 1982, 'Klassenbewegung oder Volkspartei? Zur sozialdemokratischen Programmdebatte 1920–1925', *Geschichte und Gesellschaft*, 1982: 9–54

Winkler, Heinrich A. 1984, *Von der Revolution zur Stabilisierung: Arbeiter und Arbeiterbewegung in der Weimarer Republik 1918 bis 1924*, Berlin: Dietz.

Witz, Albert 1893, *Bilder aus der Grossen Revolution. Epische-dramatische Dichtung in 8 lebenden Bildern*, Berlin: Verlag des Vereins für Volksthümliche Kunst.

Wolikow Serge 2002, 'Les références de la Révolution française dans les mouvements "révolutionnaires" en France au xxe siècle', in Biard, Michel (ed.), *Terminée la Révolution ... IVe Colloque européen de Calais, Bulletin des Amis du Vieux Calais*, 2002: 239–44

Wolikow, Serge and Jean Vigreux (eds.) 2003, *Cultures communistes au XXe siècle: entre guerre et modernité*, Paris: La Dispute.

Wolikow, Serge and Michel Cordillot 1993, *Prolétaires de tous les pays, unissez-vous? Les difficiles chemins de l'internationalisme (1848–1956)*, Dijon; EUD.

Zentralbildungsausschuss der Sozialdemokratischen Partei Deutschlands 1913, *Lichtbilder*, Berlin: Vorwärts.

Zweig, Stefan 1929, *Joseph Fouché*, Leipzig: Insel-Verlag.

Index